THE DOCTRINES OF
AMERICAN FOREIGN POLICY

THE DOCTRINES OF AMERICAN FOREIGN POLICY

Their Meaning, Role, and Future

Cecil V. Crabb, Jr.

Louisiana State University Press

Baton Rouge and London

Designer: Albert Crochet
Typeface: Linotron Sabon
Typesetter: G & S Typesetters, Inc.
Printer: Thomson-Shore, Inc.
Binder: John Dekker & Sons, Inc.

LIBRARY OF CONGRESS CATALOGING IN PUBLICATION DATA

Crabb, Cecil Van Meter, 1924–
    The doctrines of American foreign policy; their
meaning, role, and future.

    Includes index.
    1. United States—Foreign relations. I. Title.
E183.7.C7   327.73   81–20846
ISBN 0–8071–1016–7   AACR2

Contents

Acknowledgments

In limited space, it is not possible to thank and to acknowledge adequately the invaluable assistance of those who have contributed directly and indirectly to this analysis of American diplomatic doctrines. Since I joined the faculty of Louisiana State University and Agricultural and Mechanical College in 1968, the administration of the University has been generous in providing continuing support for my research activities. The bulk of the research for this volume was conducted during a sabbatical leave awarded me by the Graduate School during the academic year 1975–1976. The university's ongoing commitment to faculty research is gratefully acknowledged.

As will become apparent to the reader, my analysis of the principal doctrines of American diplomacy draws extensively from the studies and commentaries of literally hundreds of scholars and analysts who have dealt with various aspects of the American diplomatic record over the past two centuries. It is impossible to acknowledge their contributions individually. Collectively, their findings comprise a rich reservoir of data and ideas from which I have drawn freely in this attempt to evaluate the meaning and significance of doctrines in the diplomatic experience of the United States. Their individual contributions will be highlighted in the documentation accompanying each chapter.

As always, the staff of the Troy H. Middleton Library at LSU was resourceful, indefatigable, and cooperative beyond the call of duty in meeting my research requirements. A special debt of gratitude is owed to the Head of the Business Administration/Government Documents Department, Jimmie H. Hoover, and to the Associate Head, Roberta A. Scull, for their expertise, their unfailing patience, and their ingenuity in responding to my numerous requests for assistance. No author could ask for more cooperation than they have routinely provided me in this and other research endeavors.

As in all my research and writing activities, my wife Harriet contributed indispensable assistance at every stage. Her sharp eye saved me from countless stylistic lapses, and her keen mind convinced me that numerous murky passages in the book needed revision. Her contributions to the study's successful completion were more extensive and essential than she will ever know.

The anonymous reviewers engaged by the LSU Press to evaluate an earlier version of the manuscript also contributed positively to the volume's completion. Their comments were informed, cogent, and nearly always constructive. Every chapter of the revised manuscript reflects their insights, suggestions, and criticisms.

The Director of the LSU Press, Leslie E. Phillabaum; the Executive Editor, Beverly Jarrett; the Managing Editor, Martha Hall; and other members of the staff provided valuable suggestions and guidance during all stages of manuscript preparation and publication. Their contribution is acknowledged with genuine gratitude.

A number of individuals typed and retyped portions of the manuscript. The skill and efficiency of the departmental secretary, Josephine Scurria, is deeply appreciated in this respect. Typing service was also provided by Angel Benton, Linda Cook, Karen Cox, and Angela Dupont.

The contributions of those who made this study possible in no way diminish the accountability of the author for its contents. If any errors of fact or questionable judgments are present in the study, they are solely my own, for which I accept full responsibility.

THE DOCTRINES OF
AMERICAN FOREIGN POLICY

Introduction

This study of the major and minor diplomatic doctrines of the United States stems from awareness of, and fascination with, an intriguing paradox about the political behavior of the American society. In their internal affairs the American people have exhibited a consistent preference for *nondoctrinal approaches* to public policy issues. With rare exceptions, for some two centuries Americans have shunned political movements, parties, and candidates advocating "doctrinal" or ideological solutions to national problems. An outstanding example of this behavior trait was the New Deal—a mélange of social and economic theories and of concrete governmental programs designed by the Roosevelt Administration to deal with the manifold problems created by the Great Depression. Whatever its accomplishments, the New Deal will *not* be remembered because of the philosophical consistency of its ideas or the logical cohesion of its constituent parts. Typically, the New Deal was an exercise in experimentation and *ad hoc* problem solving. For the vast majority of Americans, the only test applied to the New Deal was the traditionally pragmatic one: how well did the Roosevelt Administration's program *work* in meeting the challenges posed by the depression? Even during this period of severe and pervasive economic dislocation and social upheaval, political movements having a high doctrinal or ideological content—such as nazism, communism, and socialism—held very little appeal for the American people.

The American society's eclectic, nondoctrinal political orientation in the domestic sphere is one side of the paradox. The other side is the fact that no nation in modern history has relied so heavily upon "doctrinal" statements and principles in foreign affairs as the United States. Sooner or later, most of the guiding principles actuating American foreign policy have been embodied in a Monroe Doctrine, a Truman Doctrine, a Carter Doctrine, or some comparable doctrinal pronouncement. In some instances (and the Monroe Doctrine serves as the prototype), these foreign policy doctrines have received the veneration normally accorded to constitutional principles or religious dogmas. Not infrequently, the diplomatic doctrine has functioned in much the same way as a religious article of faith: its adherents have sometimes believed that the doctrine's mere invocation and reiteration would accomplish miraculous results!

This is not meant to suggest that the role of doctrines in American foreign policy has been of trivial or secondary importance. To the contrary, many of the landmark developments in American diplomatic history are encompassed by the foreign policy doctrines included in our analysis. Anyone who is well grounded in the issuance and development of these doctrines would possess a reasonably adequate understanding of the evolution of American foreign policy since the early 1800s.

For example, two dominant themes were conspicuous in the Monroe Doctrine. One of these was the "isolationist" principle which shaped American attitudes toward Europe from the founding of the Republic until World War II. Insight into the isolationist outlook is of course necessary for an informed understanding of American diplomacy prior to World War II. It is no less essential for comprehending the various species of "neoisolationist" thought that have appeared in the American society since the war, especially during and after the Vietnam conflict. As the evidence presented in the chapters which follow demonstrates, many of the ideas and expectations associated with the traditional isolationist viewpoint continue to influence public attitudes toward foreign affairs.

Second, a number of the most significant developments in United States policy toward Latin America—particularly as they relate to hemispheric security—involve the Monroe Doctrine. No real comprehension of inter-American relations is possible without reference to the foreign policy declaration of President Monroe in 1823 and its subsequent applications. As every informed student of inter-American relations is aware, for the past generation or so officials in Washington have been reluctant to invoke the Monroe Doctrine publicly. Today, as in the past, the Latin American reaction to "Monroeism" continues to be negative. Yet as the Soviet Union discovered during the Cuban Missile Crisis of 1962, many of the basic principles embodied in the Monroe Doctrine continue to guide the hemispheric policy of the United States. As our discussion in Chapter 1 will indicate, the Soviet Union or any other nation which concludes that the Monroe Doctrine is "obsolete" (as Soviet Premier Nikita Khrushchev once commented) is likely to make a serious miscalculation in dealing with the United States.

Our discussion of the Open Door policy and the Stimson Doctrine (Chapter 2) highlights certain other important dimensions and guiding principles of American foreign relations. The key idea affirmed by the Open Door principle issued at the end of the nineteenth century was that no foreign power should be allowed to dominate China. This principle lay at the heart of American policy toward Asia down to the communization of China in the late 1940s. The concept of the Open Door also directly influenced official and public attitudes toward the country for some twenty years after the Communist victory in the Chinese civil war. According to realpolitik interpretations, America's devotion to the Open Door principle was an implicit commitment by the United States to maintain the balance of power in East Asia. By contrast, the idealist regards Washington's commitment to the Open Door concept as a pledge to defend the cause of national self-determination or political freedom abroad—initially with respect to China, but after issuance of the Truman Doctrine in 1947, on a global basis as well. The Stimson Doctrine of 1932 was a noteworthy application of the historic Open Door concept to the case of Japanese aggression in

Manchuria. Sometimes interpreted as an exercise in futility, the Stimson Doctrine was a forceful affirmation of America's traditional interest in strengthening and gaining national compliance with international law. Japan's attack against the United States at Pearl Harbor in 1941 was in some measure a result of Washington's refusal to recognize (or accord legal legitimacy to) Japanese territorial conquests.

For more than a generation after World War II, many of the most significant developments in American foreign relations revolved around the issuance and later applications of the Truman Doctrine. In a historic speech to Congress early in 1947, President Harry S. Truman publicly committed the United States to a strategy of "containment" of Soviet expansionism. Implementation of the containment strategy required the United States to undertake a variety of programs and activities—from bolstering the defenses of the North Atlantic area, to supplying arms-aid to vulnerable allies and friendly countries, to assisting in the "modernization" of the Third World—designed to counter Soviet hegemonic tendencies. Insight into the rationale, implementation, and consequences of the Truman Doctrine is thus essential in order to comprehend the postwar evolution of American foreign policy. It is indispensable, for example, for understanding the transition in Soviet-American relations from the period of Cold War to the recent era of détente.

Chapter 4 is devoted to an analysis of the Eisenhower Doctrine, marking the emergence of the United States as a Middle Eastern power. Increasingly since the late 1950s, the challenge of preserving stability and peace in the Middle East has become a high-priority concern of American policy-makers. After the evacuation of American forces from Southeast Asia in the early 1970s, the Middle East qualified as the most volatile region in international politics, requiring direct and continuing American diplomatic involvement. Clearer understanding of the issuance and implementation of the Eisenhower Doctrine provides necessary background for assessing this phenomenon, and it calls attention to several problems which continue to hinder the effectiveness of American diplomacy in the region.

President Lyndon B. Johnson was unique among American chief executives: LBJ issued two foreign policy doctrines bearing his name. The first Johnson Doctrine (analyzed in Chapter 5) was a momentous development in America's prolonged involvement in the Vietnam War.

Construed narrowly, the Johnson Doctrine for Southeast Asia merits attention because of its central role in the most frustrating and traumatic military conflict in American history. Viewed more broadly, the doctrine was significant because it serves as a case study of the means by which the United States became militarily and diplomatically "overextended" abroad. Many of the foreign policy challenges facing the Nixon, Ford, Carter, and Reagan administrations can be described as efforts by national policy-makers to discover a defensible middle ground between the kind of American "overcommitment" witnessed in Vietnam and the traditional isolationist approach to foreign policy issues. Informed students of American foreign relations will find the first Johnson Doctrine worthy of attention for another reason: it was an illuminating episode in the recent and continuing struggle between the executive and legislative branches for a dominant role in the foreign policy process. To no inconsiderable extent, the effort made by Congress since the late 1960s to reassert its authority in foreign affairs is explicable by reference to lingering disaffection on Capitol Hill with the Johnson Doctrine for Southeast Asia.

President Johnson's other diplomatic doctrine—issued in connection with a political crisis in the Dominican Republic in 1965—is no less deserving of detailed examination. It was directed at a vexatious and recurrent problem in inter-American relations: revolutionary activities by Communists and their sympathizers in the Western Hemisphere, whose efforts are sometimes actively assisted by foreign powers. Under the mantle of the second Johnson Doctrine, the United States intervened militarily in the Dominican Republic—and as a result, national policy-makers encountered vocal criticism at home and abroad. More objective understanding of the circumstances engendering the doctrine, of its formulation, and of its application not only illuminates an important aspect of inter-American relations. Deeper insight into LBJ's second doctrine also sheds light on the general problem encountered by the United States in successfully applying military force in behalf of diplomatic objectives.

Chapter 7 is devoted to a discussion of the Nixon Doctrine. For a variety of reasons, President Nixon's doctrine occupies a unique place in the annals of American diplomacy. The Nixon Doctrine was of course distinctive in part because of the ultimate fate of its promulgator and the impact of the Watergate crisis upon the conduct and substance of American diplomacy. In addition, the Nixon Doctrine has no peer because it was the most comprehensive foreign policy declaration in the nation's history. The doctrine covered such diverse issues as America's involvement in the Vietnam War, the future of Soviet-American relations, the "thaw" in Sino-American relations, and major changes in the nation's defense strategy.

But perhaps the most significant aspect of the Nixon Doctrine was its effort to redefine the nation's global role in the new period of diplomatic "retrenchment" following America's massive involvement in the Vietnam War. As our discussion makes clear, it cannot be said that President Nixon's diplomatic doctrine satisfactorily or definitively resolved that problem. It can be asserted, however, that the Nixon Doctrine began the process of intensive reexamination of the nature and scope of America's overseas commitments, and that it at least posed many of the questions which must be answered before a new national consensus emerges on that complex question.

The most recent doctrinal pronouncement in American foreign relations was the Carter Doctrine, examined in detail in Chapter 8. Prompted by the Soviet effort to subjugate Afghanistan, and to a lesser degree by the successful revolution against the monarchy in Iran, Carter's policy statement committed the United States to preserve the peace and security of the oil-rich Persian Gulf area. President Carter's diplomatic manifesto merits closer scrutiny for three paramount reasons. First, its issuance marked a dramatic change in the Carter Administration's approach to the Soviet Union, comparable to the policy of "patience and firmness" exhibited by the Truman Doctrine in 1947. Second, the doctrine signified that the United States was prepared to assume a permanent commitment for the defense of the Persian Gulf region, as symbolized by the creation of the Rapid Deployment Force (RDF) established to enforce the Carter Doctrine. Third, after he entered the White House in 1981, Republican President Ronald Reagan repeatedly indicated that his administration was even more staunchly opposed to Communist expansionism in the Middle East and other regions than its predecessor. Just as the Roosevelt Administration maintained the continuity of the Stimson Doctrine directed against Japanese expansionism in China, so too did the Reagan Administration honor the Carter Doctrine and move ahead energetically to acquire the means for its enforcement. Recent as it is—and as qualified as judgments about its future at this stage must be—the Carter Doctrine appears to be emerging as one of the landmark developments in the history of American diplomacy.

To date, no statement of diplomatic principles designated the "Reagan Doctrine" has appeared. Yet, for reasons explained more fully in the concluding chapter of our study, it seems highly probable that Reagan and subsequent chief executives will join the list of presidents Monroe, Truman, Eisenhower, and other national leaders who left diplomatic pronouncements bearing their names. After the experience of over a century and a half, the American penchant for promulgating diplomatic doctrines seems now to have become institutionalized; and for a number of reasons (identified in greater detail in Chapter 9) the habit of embodying diplomatic guidelines in foreign policy doctrines may be more deeply ingrained today than ever before in the American diplomatic tradition.

In the detailed analysis of the individual diplomatic doctrines included in our study, a common format—adapted to the exigencies of particular cases—is employed. At the outset, the reader is familiarized with the essential provisions of the doctrine being discussed. Next, the meaning of the doctrine's key provisions and concepts is explicated. There follows an examination of the external circumstances which elicited the doctrine. Such dimensions of the subject as why the doctrine was promulgated, what its main purposes were, and the mode of its issuance are discussed.

Each chapter also contains a detailed analysis of the formulation of the doctrine in question. In this section, attention is devoted to the dominant forces—the influence of the president, of the State Department and other executive agencies, of Congress, and of public opinion (including interest groups)—upon the doctrine's formulation and implementation.

This is followed by a discussion of the application of the doctrine in question. What were the circumstances inducing the United States to rely upon the doctrine in its relations with other countries? What action did policy-makers take when the doctrine was invoked? What immediate impact did the doctrine have upon the conduct of American foreign relations? In what respects did the meaning of the doctrine change in the light of new conditions overseas? What were the more significant long-range consequences of the doctrine for American diplomacy? What is the doctrine's current status and future?

In the concluding chapter, the leading doctrines of American foreign policy are evaluated collectively, and an effort is made to assess their overall impact upon the conduct of foreign relations by the United States. Several fundamental questions provide the frame of reference for this inquiry. What have been the distinguishing features of those foreign policy pronouncements which are counted among the diplomatic "doctrines" of the United States? What characteristics of America's history and ethos account for its long-standing reliance upon this distinctive diplomatic instrument? What contributions—both positive and negative—have doctrinal pronouncements made to the conduct of foreign affairs by the United States? Finally what future role can doctrines be expected to play in American diplomatic experience, and what forces are likely to be decisive in answering that question?

Since the early nineteenth century, the tendency of the United States to embody the guiding principles of its foreign policy in diplomatic doctrines has been a conspicuous element in the American approach to external affairs. To some commentators, this behavior pattern continues to rank as a cardinal defect of the policy-making process in the United States, illustrating America's long-standing preference for "words, not action" and for dramatic gestures instead of effective deeds in the foreign policy field. To other well informed observers, the principal doctrines of American foreign policy have made noteworthy contributions to the achievement of diplomatic objectives and are a unique American contribution to the art of diplomacy.

Regardless of the verdict the informed student of American diplomatic conduct may reach on such questions, one point seems beyond reasonable doubt. More adequate understanding of the diplomatic behavior of perhaps the most powerful nation in modern history is not possible without insight into this unique, important, and in many ways mystifying, phenomenon.

1 / The Monroe Doctrine: Palladium of American Foreign Policy

I believe in the Monroe Doctrine, in our Constitution and in the laws of God.
                                            —Mary Baker Eddy

The [Monroe] Doctrine is not written in the Constitution, but it is more fundamental than the Constitution itself.
                    —R. Walton Moore (Congressman from Virginia)

In the entire history of the United States since 1823 there has been but one basis of our foreign policy which has been supported by all the people of this country and to which all political parties have consistently adhered, and that is the Monroe Doctrine.   —Sumner Welles

Our analysis of the role of doctrines in American foreign relations begins with what is sometimes referred to as the "immortal message" of President James Monroe, delivered to Congress on December 2, 1823.[1] The Monroe Doctrine serves as an appropriate starting point for our discussion for two reasons. First, it was the earliest set of foreign policy principles to be later identified as a major "doctrine" of American foreign policy.

Second and more significantly, much as it came to be reinterpreted and adapted to new conditions after 1823, the Monroe Doctrine remains in many respects the sheet anchor of American foreign and defense policy. According to several criteria—its venerable position in the annals of American diplomacy, the extent to which it has come to

1. For the text of the Monroe Doctrine, see Monroe's Seventh Annual Message to Congress, in James D. Richardson (ed.), *A Compilation of the Messages and Papers of the Presidents, 1789–1897* (Washington, D.C.: Government Printing Office, 1896), II, 207–20.

be viewed at home and abroad as an integral part of "the American way of life," the degree of overwhelming and consistent public support for the principles associated with it, or the willingness with which successive administrations in Washington have been prepared to defend its principles by reliance upon armed force—the Monroe Doctrine has no peers among the foreign policy pronouncements identified with later presidents. Among the countless tributes paid to it by students of the nation's diplomatic record was the one by its most authoritative interpreter, Dexter Perkins, who called Monroe's message "the most significant of all American state papers." The historian Albert B. Hart said, "No public policy of the United States has ever taken such hold upon the imagination of the American people as the . . . Monroe Doctrine." Charles G. Fenwick called the Monroe Doctrine the "ark of the convenant" of American foreign policy, while Graham H. Stuart described it as "the Holy of Holies" of national diplomacy. So perfectly has the Monroe Doctrine coincided with the American society's ethos and outlook toward other countries that it is sometimes referred to as "the American doctrine." [2]

These descriptions call attention to a salient aspect of the Monroe Doctrine, and perhaps of less well known diplomatic doctrines enunciated by later presidents. The Monroe Doctrine in time came to possess a unique religious-like quality, a kind of mystical connotation, making it tantamount to a religious incantation or nostrum whose invocation per se would ward off forces inimical to national security and independence. For the general public, if not sometimes even for foreign policy officials themselves, *faith in* the Monroe Doctrine often exceeded understanding of its provisions or intentions. Illustrative of this response is the judgment of one commentator about President Grover Cleveland: "Cleveland's concept of the scope and meaning of the Monroe Doctrine was muddy. He regarded it with considerable awe, having seen the magic it could work on public opinion whenever invoked by the Jingoes. To merely utter the phrase seemed a sort of ulti-

2. Samuel F. Bemis, *John Quincy Adams and the Foundations of American Foreign Policy* (New York: Alfred A. Knopf, 1969), 408; Albert B. Hart, *The Monroe Doctrine: An Interpretation* (Boston: Little, Brown, 1916), v; Donald M. Dozer (ed.), *The Monroe Doctrine: Its Modern Significance* (New York: Alfred A. Knopf, 1965), 135; Graham H. Stuart, *Latin America and the United States* (New York: Appleton-Century-Crofts, 1943), 491; Arnold B. Hall, *The Monroe Doctrine and the Great War* (Chicago: A. C. McClung, 1920), 81.

mate weapon to use against Europeans who interfered in American affairs." [3]

Monroe's Principles: Context and Connotations

The New York *Sun* once observed: "The Monroe Doctrine is as elastic as India rubber and as comprehensive as all outdoors." [4] The comment highlights a problem associated with foreign policy doctrines in general; but again, the Monroe Doctrine poses special difficulties in this respect. By definition, a diplomatic doctrine is a statement of general principles. In nearly every case its issuance was precipitated by a foreign crisis or a specific set of circumstances abroad to which the United States was required to respond. Yet policy-makers cannot anticipate the future course of events. They desire maximum flexibility to adapt the principles to new and changing circumstances overseas. With some doctrines examined in our study, policy-makers unquestionably sought deliberately to leave an area of unpredictability regarding America's future course of action.

With respect to the Monroe Doctrine, there is a further problem: differentiating between the principles enunciated in President Monroe's message to Congress in 1823 and those expressed in innumerable applications and reinterpretations of his message in the century and a half which followed. As we shall see, the more important reinterpretations of the Monroe Doctrine took the form of "corollaries" which, according to some interpretations, fundamentally altered the meaning of Monroe's original declaration. Thus the student of American foreign relations must be continually mindful that when he is discussing the Monroe Doctrine, he is referring to President Monroe's speech to Congress in 1823, *plus* the reinterpretations and accretions which have been added since that time. The result is that genuine ambiguity and doubt can exist, even among well informed historians and authorities on American foreign policy, concerning what the Monroe Doctrine has come to mean and its precise role in contemporary American foreign policy.

3. Gerald G. Eggert, *Richard Olney: Evolution of a Statesman* (University Park, Pa.: Pennsylvania State University Press, 1974), 202.
4. Quoted in Alejando Alvarez, *The Monroe Doctrine: Its Importance in the International Life of the States of the New World* (New York: Oxford University Press, 1924), 394.

Insofar as President Monroe's speech may legitimately be viewed as a kind of constitutional document in the field of American foreign policy, there is an additional problem. As with the Constitution of the United States itself, in their interpretations courts routinely refer to the "spirit" of the Constitution, reliance upon which may yield a very different meaning from adherence to the letter of its provisions. Similarly, American diplomatic history is replete with references to the "spirit" of Monroe's message—which in the mid-twentieth century may produce interpretations very different from those existing in the early nineteenth century. Accordingly, it is necessary to examine briefly the language of the Monroe Doctrine; to become familiar with the circumstances surrounding its issuance and the specific problems toward which it was directed; and to gain at least limited insight into how the Monroe Doctrine evolved for some one hundred and fifty years after 1823.

In common with nearly every other diplomatic doctrine in American history, President Monroe's pronouncement was prompted by a perceived foreign policy crisis, involving the security interests of the United States. In view of their central role in the foreign policy of the United States after World War II, it is interesting to note that Russian-American relations were one factor that elicited the Monroe Doctrine. After establishing an extensive fur trade in the American Northwest, in 1799 the czarist government of Imperial Russia formed the Russian-American Company; in time, the company exercised a monopoly over the fur trade, down to fifty-one degrees north latitude in North America. Based on the fur trade, Russian commercial activity grew steadily in the years thereafter. Official and public opinion in the United States became especially apprehensive about Russian intentions after Czar Alexander I's imperial decree of September 4, 1821, prohibiting foreigners (including Americans) from trading in the Russian zone. Many Americans concluded (incorrectly, the evidence indicates) that this order presaged a new Russian expansionist drive into new territories on the American continent. President Monroe and his advisers viewed these Russian activities in the Northwest with growing concern.

The other, and better known, threat to the security of the Western Hemisphere was posed by the creation and possible intervention of the Holy Alliance, formed by the European powers after Napoleon's defeat in 1815. Ostensibly founded to regulate the affairs of post-Napoleonic Europe in accordance with Christian principle, events soon revealed that the Holy Alliance existed primarily to uphold the principles of autocracy and monarchial government. Officials of the Monroe Administration became convinced that another purpose of the Holy Alliance was to reimpose European colonial jurisdiction upon the countries of Latin America, which had won (or were in the process of winning) their independence. President Monroe's doctrine was designed to avert that danger.

In its original form, the Monroe Doctrine consisted of three scattered paragraphs in a lengthy message to Congress by President Monroe. In a statement aimed specifically at the government of Imperial Russia, Monroe enunciated the principle that "the American continents, by the free and independent condition which they have assumed and maintained, are henceforth not to be considered as subjects for future colonization by any European powers."

Addressing the European powers, Monroe declared: "In the wars of the European powers in matters relating to themselves we have never taken any part, nor does it comport with our policy so to do. It is only when our rights are invaded or seriously menaced that we resent injuries or make preparation for our defense." He observed, "The political system of the allied powers [*i.e.*, the European nations] is essentially different in this respect from that of America." Therefore, the United States would "consider any attempt on their part to extend their system to any portion of this hemisphere as dangerous to our peace and safety." Monroe continued, "With the existing colonies or dependencies of any European power we have not interfered and shall not interfere. But with the governments who have declared their independence and maintained it, and whose independence we have, on great consideration and on just principles, acknowledged, we could not view any interposition for the purpose of oppressing them, or controlling in any other manner their destiny, by any European power, in any other light than as the manifestation of an unfriendly disposition toward the United States."

Still later in the message, after reaffirming America's policy of non-interference in Europe's internal concerns, Monroe reiterated the admonition to the European powers: "It is impossible that the allied powers should extend their political system to any portion of either continent [*i.e.*, North or South America] without endangering our peace and happiness. . . . It is equally impossible, therefore, that we should behold such interposition, in any form, with indifference."

Several aspects of the Monroe Doctrine as originally proclaimed require emphasis. First, the doctrine provided a set of principles defining America's relationship toward Europe. Despite later efforts to associate the Monroe Doctrine with Asian affairs (as we shall see in Chapter 2), or even to give it a global application after World War II, Monroe's statement was directed at American-European relations only. In this connection, he enunciated a twofold idea. The United States would not intervene in Europe's wars; and the European powers were enjoined against new colonizing activities—and, more generally, against attempts to "extend their system"—in the New World. Despite considerable misinterpretation on this point, it is essential to note that both of these principles were conditional and qualified. Monroe implicitly admitted the possibility that American rights and security considerations *might* be involved in some future conflict on the European continent. Popular mythology to the contrary, Monroe issued no blanket prohibition against American intervention in European affairs. Similarly, the noncolonization admonition to the European powers was also qualified. In its original form, the doctrine warned the Old World against establishing *new* colonies in North and South America; the Monroe Doctrine did not seek to dismantle the European colonial structures existing in 1823.

Second, the doctrine was a forceful ideological proclamation, as well as a set of diplomatic guidelines reflecting realpolitik calculations by President Monroe and his diplomatic advisers concerning the challenge of maintaining American security and independence. Officials of the Monroe Administration were mindful that the great powers of Europe had the capability of intervention in the Western Hemisphere; and some of them unquestionably had imperial ambitions in the New World.

The impetus for the issuance of the Monroe Doctrine had come initially from Great Britain. British Foreign Secretary Lord Canning suggested a primitive version of the doctrine to the Monroe Administration. His hope—and in this of course he was disappointed—was that it would be issued jointly by Great Britain and the United States.

Several considerations prompted London's suggestion, not the least among which was an underlying British desire to establish a position of commercial, and perhaps even political, dominance in Latin America. By excluding the Holy Alliance from that region, Britain could rely upon its naval superiority to expand its own influence in the area. In addition, Canning also doubtless hoped that, by gaining American acceptance of the noncolonization pledge contained in the doctrine, this principle would inhibit America's own future territorial expansion and influence within the Western Hemisphere.

Thus, the Monroe Administration was conscious of both a positive and negative danger posed by British power. Positively, there was the threat of expanding British power and hegemony throughout the Western Hemisphere. Indeed, according to some authorities, this was the principal danger to the New World which the Monroe Administration identified.[5] Negatively, there was the risk that, by committing itself to an Anglo-American declaration incorporating the ideas embodied in the Monroe Doctrine, the United States would find its future power and territorial limits greatly circumscribed. Because of the disparity in power between the two countries, in time Great Britain would likely emerge as the dominant power of the Western Hemisphere.[6]

This leads to another salient dimension of the realpolitik considerations prompting the Monroe Doctrine, involving two interrelated questions: did the Monroe Administration anticipate the necessity for enforcing the doctrine against potential violators? And if so, what means of enforcement were to be provided when this necessity arose?

According to some commentators, the Monroe Doctrine was prototypical of later diplomatic doctrines (and, as we shall see in Chapter 2, the Stimson Doctrine epitomized the tendency), in that American

5. For further discussion of this point, see Paul A. Varg, *Foreign Policies of the Founding Fathers* (East Lansing: Michigan State University Press, 1963), 249–50; Bemis, *John Quincy Adams and the Foundations of American Foreign Policy*, 400–401; and Arthur P. Whitaker, *The United States and the Independence of Latin America, 1800–1830* (Baltimore: Johns Hopkins University Press, 1941), 493–94.

6. Britain's interests and motivations in proposing the issuance of a set of foreign policy principles jointly with the United States are analyzed in greater detail in Whitaker, *The United States and the Independence of Latin America*, 472; Sir A. W. Ward and G. P. Gooch (eds.), *The Cambridge History of British Foreign Policy, 1783–1919* (3 vols.; New York: Macmillan, 1923), II, 69; and George Morgan, *The Life of James Monroe* (New York: AMS Press, 1969), 398–99.

officials have often relied upon declarations, pronouncements, verbal
principles, and the like—rather than armed force—to safeguard the
nation's vital diplomatic interests. Admittedly, in the early 1800s, the
American Republic was a young, militarily weak nation whose citizens
were overwhelmingly preoccupied with internal problems. Almost a
generation before 1823 (and President Washington's Farewell Address,
September 19, 1796, was a celebrated example), Americans had expressed their desire to avoid foreign "entanglements." Besides, since
these ideas were in conflict with the New World ethos, Americans
were repulsed by realpolitik concepts—like power, balance of power,
and interventionism—actuating the diplomatic conduct of the European powers. Indicative also of the evident indifference of American
officials to the problem of enforcing Monroe's admonitions was the
fact that in the period following his historic message, neither the president nor Congress showed any inclination to expand American naval
power to the level required for effective enforcement of the doctrine's
principles in the Western Hemisphere.[7]

Did these considerations mean that President Monroe, Secretary of
State John Quincy Adams, and other presidential advisers expected
the doctrine to be somehow self-enforcing, and that more broadly,
they were totally oblivious to the role of power in foreign affairs? Although the evidence is clearly mixed, a strong case can be made to the
contrary. The Monroe Administration realized full well that Great
Britain's interests were served by the enunciation and enforcement of
the Monroe Doctrine. On a number of occasions after 1823, the
power of the Royal Navy was crucial in gaining respect for its terms.
American policy-makers also knew that, ominous as President Monroe's public depiction of the threat might be, there was very little actual danger of intervention by the Holy Alliance in the Western Hemisphere. This possibility was largely precluded by two factors: known
British opposition to it, and rivalries among the members of the Holy
Alliance which prevented their collaboration at the expense of the
New World. As for czarist Russia, it showed no inclination to expand
its hegemony beyond its present holdings in the Northwest.[8]

7. Whitaker, *The United States and the Independence of Latin America*, 508–11.
8. While the danger of collective intervention by the European powers in Latin
America seemed remote, American officials were unquestionably apprehensive about
the imperial ambitions of two countries—Britain and France—in the New World. Some

These contingencies aside, other realpolitik calculations underlay the Monroe Doctrine. President Monroe's decision to issue a set of foreign policy guidelines unilaterally—to decline London's proposal for a joint Anglo-American declaration—enhanced the prestige of the young American Republic and was interpreted in London as a blow against British influence throughout the Western Hemisphere, leading Lord Canning to oppose the Monroe Doctrine although he had initially suggested it! In part, Canning's irritation stemmed from a realization that the doctrine's provisions applied to British, no less than to other European, expansionism in the New World.[9]

British officials were also cognizant of another fact about the Monroe Doctrine, and this realization was interpreted as a diplomatic setback for them: by suggesting a joint Anglo-American declaration, London undoubtedly sought to block or impede the future territorial expansion of the United States. Monroe's decision to promulgate his set of foreign policy principles unilaterally, however, undermined this British objective. Future American diplomatic behavior was not conditioned by, nor did it require, British approval; and as the sole interpreter of the doctrine's terms, America avoided any "moral obligation" to apply such provisions as the noncolonization injunction to itself. The Monroe Doctrine, Dexter Perkins wryly observed, accorded well with America's "expansionist ambition" after 1823. It is "not strange that the two go hand in hand."[10]

Most fundamentally perhaps, Monroe's message reflected realpolitik calculations in that, as one commentator noted in 1914, it was "the doctrine of national defense" for the United States.[11] As early as 1823, American foreign policy officials were mindful of the strategic and geopolitical factors which were crucial to national security. They

---

authorities believe the Monroe Doctrine was aimed mainly at Great Britain; others think French expansionism was uppermost in the minds of President Monroe and his advisers. See Varg, *Foreign Policies of the Founding Fathers*, 249–50; Whitaker, *The United States and the Independence of Latin America*, 493–94; and Robert McColley, *Federalists, Republicans and Foreign Entanglements, 1789–1815* (Englewood Cliffs, N.J.: Prentice-Hall, 1969), 2.

9. Bemis, *John Quincy Adams and the Foundations of American Foreign Policy*, 401–403; Varg, *Foreign Policies of the Founding Fathers*, 249–50.

10. Dexter Perkins, *A History of the Monroe Doctrine* (Boston: Little, Brown, 1955), 67.

11. See the views of Professor Callahan, as quoted in Hart, *The Monroe Doctrine*, 351.

knew (or at least sensed) that the establishment of a foreign power in the Western Hemisphere would threaten national independence directly and seriously; and—reluctant as they might be to discuss the likelihood publicly—Monroe and many of his contemporaries were not oblivious to the possibility that the United States might someday have to rely upon armed force to uphold the doctrine's principles. Frequently as it might be cited after 1823 as the embodiment of America's historic isolationist posture, in actuality the Monroe Doctrine did not rule out America's use of armed strength in behalf of diplomatic objectives, nor did it preclude possible joint American action with another country (like Great Britain) in behalf of common goals.

Despite its evident isolationist overtones, Arthur Whitaker has emphasized, the Monroe Doctrine enunciated a basic American security principle: the idea that the United States "would, if necessary, fight for the independence of a foreign nation"—a foreign nation, that is to say, located in the Western Hemisphere.[12] Or to put the matter differently, without using the term, Monroe had expressed one of the oldest realpolitik concepts. In effect, he had proclaimed the region from the Rio Grande to Cape Horn as a *sphere of influence* of the United States and had cautioned other nations to enter it at their peril.[13] Although it may have had several subordinate objectives, Hart has asserted, "The main purpose of the Doctrine was to prevent disturbances of our institutions, and to minimize dangers to the United States."[14]

But if the Monroe Doctrine was undeniably influenced by realpolitik considerations, it was no less an ideological tract as well, proclaiming distinctively American principles. A Latin American observer once likened Monroe's speech to "a peal of thunder" which "paralyzed the Holy Alliance." Another Latin American judgment was that the doctrine served as "the gospel of the new continent." Another commentator has described the Monroe Doctrine as "an ideological challenge" to the Holy Alliance. Monroe's speech postulated an "unbridgeable" gulf between the Old and New Worlds, and "no good

12. Whitaker, *The United States and the Independence of Latin America*, 518. Bemis was convinced that Monroe very clearly understood that enforcement of his doctrine might eventually entail the use of troops to uphold its provisions. Bemis, *John Quincy Adams and the Foundations of American Foreign Policy*, 397–98.

13. For fuller discussion of this point, see Edwin Lieuwen, *U.S. Policy in Latin America: A Short History* (New York: Praeger, 1965), 127.

14. Hart, *The Monroe Doctrine*, 74–75.

American could cross it without losing his political and moral integrity."[15] Originally, President Monroe had favored what Perkins calls "a ringing pronouncement in favor of liberal principles in both the Old World and the New."[16] While such sentiments were ultimately toned down in the message Monroe delivered to Congress, his set of foreign policy guidelines still possessed several important ideological connotations.

In this respect, the key phrase in Monroe's message was the reference to the "political system of the allied powers" which was held to be different from America's and, by strong implication at least, highly inimical to it. Monroe cautioned the nations of Europe against attempts "to extend their system to any portion of this hemisphere." The admonition was designed to serve several ideological purposes.

It was a forceful reaffirmation of the idea that philosophically the political behavior of the New World was fundamentally different from the Old World—and, in the judgment of American officials, that distinction had to be preserved. Implicit in the concept of the New World was also the notion—reiterated many times after 1823 by defenders of America's isolationist stance—that, as the New Society, the United States must be kept free and independent to redeem the world by the power of its example. According to many proponents of isolationism, this was perhaps America's principal contribution to the improvement of human welfare. The Monroe Doctrine also reflected America's deep interest in the future of republican institutions and communicated a conviction that threats to them somehow jeopardized the nation's own democratic way of life.[17] Toward the Holy Alliance, as toward the Axis and Communist threats to hemispheric security over a century later, Americans believed that totalitarian or authoritarian systems of government endangered the future of democracy. Thus, Secretary of State John Quincy Adams viewed the Monroe Doctrine as a deliberate American effort to instruct the European powers in the principles of

---

15. Stuart, *Latin America and the United States*, 54–55. For a discussion of the ideological differences between the Old and New Worlds, which the Monroe Doctrine reflected, see Cushing Strout, *The American Image of the Old World* (New York: Harper and Row, 1963), 22–23.
16. Perkins, *A History of the Monroe Doctrine*, 43–44.
17. The point is developed more fully in Cecil V. Crabb, Jr., *Policy-Makers and Critics: Conflicting Theories of American Foreign Policy* (New York: Praeger, 1976), 1–29.

democratic government.[18] Other commentators have interpreted the doctrine as an American blow against monarchism—if not monarchism in general, then those systems imposed by force upon unwilling societies.[19]

Still other students of the American diplomatic record have interpreted the Monroe Doctrine as an early invocation of a principle conspicuously identified with President Woodrow Wilson during and after World War I: the concept of national self-determination. President Wilson—who called for global acceptance of the Monroe Doctrine's principles—equated it essentially with the right of each nation to determine its own institutions and destiny. In company with President Wilson later, Secretary of State John Quincy Adams was convinced that ultimately the United States might be required to fight in defense of republican institutions; if so, it was essential "to carry the opinion of the nations with us, and the opinion of the world." [20] Adams, that is to say, was aware of a relationship which sometimes eludes disciples of realpolitik: power usually has a vital ideological component. If America is to influence other countries, it must somehow identify with their values and philosophical goals. The Monroe Doctrine was an early step in that direction.

Referring to the *unilateral* issuance of the Monroe Doctrine by the United States, one biographer of President James Monroe concluded that this was the "really important thing" about his doctrine—more so in the long run than its principles. The doctrine's unilateral nature had several significant implications. It meant, for example, that from 1823 to the present day, the United States has remained the doctrine's sole interpreter. The doctrine, Perkins has observed, always possessed a "purely American character"; the United States government has consistently insisted upon the exclusive right of interpretation, in the light of its own diplomatic interests. Or, in the words of the authoritative

18. Hart, *The Monroe Doctrine*, 74–75; Frank Donovan, *Mr. Monroe's Message: The Story of the Monroe Doctrine* (New York: Dodd, Mead, 1963), 215; Ward and Gooch (eds.), *The Cambridge History of British Foreign Policy*, II, 71.

19. This interpretation of the doctrine may be found in the State Department document by J. Reuben Clark, *Memorandum on the Monroe Doctrine* (December 17, 1928), 71st Cong., 2nd Sess., 1930, Document No. 114 (Washington, D.C.: Government Printing Office, 1930), xxiii.

20. Perkins, *A History of the Monroe Doctrine*, 49–50; Stuart, *Latin America and the United States*, 71; Bemis, *John Quincy Adams and the Foundations of American Foreign Policy*, 389.

Clark Memorandum explaining the meaning of the Monroe Doctrine: "No other power of the world has any relationship to, or voice in, the implementing of the principles which the Doctrine contains. It is our doctrine, to be invoked and sustained, held in abeyance, or abandoned as our high international policy or vital national interests shall seem to us, and to us alone, to demand."[21]

Did later efforts to "multilateralize" and "internationalize" the Monroe Doctrine—to make enforcement of its provisions the responsibility of the Organization of American States or the United Nations—basically alter its unilateral character? As we shall see, the evidence strongly indicates that they did not. In the two most serious violations of the Monroe Doctrine in the past generation, for example—the Axis threat to Latin America during World War II and the Soviet Union's installation of offensive missiles in Cuba in 1962—the United States decided upon its response to these threats. Subsequently, it sought the support of the Inter-American System and (in the case of the Cuban Missile Crisis) the United Nations, for its position.

The unilateral quality of the Monroe Doctrine also accorded with and reinforced another element in America's historic isolationist position in foreign affairs: the concept of the "free hand." Isolationist mythology to the contrary, state papers like President Washington's Farewell Address, the Monroe Doctrine, and other sources did not commit the United States absolutely and without qualification to a general position of noninvolvement or "nonentanglement" in the affairs of the world, or even to a blanket policy of nonparticipation in the affairs of continental Europe. Admittedly, nonentanglement in Europe's quarrels was to be the general rule of American diplomatic conduct; but Washington, Monroe, and other chief executives acknowledged exceptional circumstances when the United States might have to abandon its preferred isolationist stance.

Under these circumstances, the concept of the "free hand" perhaps most accurately describes the principle embodied in the Monroe Doctrine. Bemis and other commentators have noted that toward the specific problem of Latin America's newly acquired independence, if London were prepared to recognize the independent status of these

21. Harry Ammon, *James Monroe: The Quest for National Identity* (New York: McGraw-Hill, 1971), 491; Perkins, *A History of the Monroe Doctrine*, 70; Clark, *Memorandum on the Monroe Doctrine*, xxiv.

states, the United States was willing to act "in concert" with Great Britain in maintaining Latin American sovereignty. Yet even in this instance, the United States would engage "*only in separate and parallel, rather than joint action*" with the British government.[22] The basic idea was reiterated by Secretary of State Charles Evans Hughes in 1923, when he declared that under the Monroe Doctrine, the United States had "never bound itself to any particular course of conduct in case of action by other powers." This exemplified the concept of the "free hand": the United States *might* act in concert with other nations—or engage in "separate and parallel" action with them—but American officials alone would ultimately make that decision.[23]

The unilateral promulgation of the Monroe Doctrine also meant that in 1823 and afterwards, other countries viewed it as purely a declaration of American foreign policy principles, having no basis or sanction in international law. Neither President Monroe nor later chief executives asked the concurrence of other nations in the doctrine's original provisions or in the major "corollaries" which came to be attached to it. From time to time, British and other foreign officials expressed the view that the doctrine did not constitute part of the corpus of international law.[24] As long as the doctrine remains a unilateral declaration of American foreign policy—and American officials reserve the right to apply and interpret it—it is difficult to see how it can ever be recognized as part of the law of nations.

Precedents and Policy Antecedents

We turn now to an examination of the process by which the Monroe Doctrine was formulated and the influences affecting its substance and form. Why did President Monroe's historic message of 1823 come to be regarded as constituting a foreign policy *doctrine* of the United States? What was there about his speech which elevated it above the status of an ordinary presidential declaration on foreign affairs and ultimately gave it the qualities associated with a religious dogma or fundamental constitutional principle?[25]

22. Bemis, *John Quincy Adams and the Foundation of American Foreign Policy*, 396, italics in the original.
23. Alvarez, *The Monroe Doctrine*, 420–21.
24. See, for example, the views of British Foreign Secretary Lord Clarendon in 1854, as cited in Perkins, *A History of the Monroe Doctrine*, 100.
25. The Spanish commentator Salvador de Madariaga was but one among many

As many diplomatic historians have pointed out, President Monroe himself did not use the term *doctrine* in his celebrated message, nor is there any evidence that he envisioned his set of foreign policy principles in such terms. Diplomatic historians differ as to when Monroe's principles came to be widely recognized as a diplomatic doctrine of the United States. According to Bemis, for some twenty years after 1823, Monroe's speech was largely "forgotten," along with countless other "ephemeral presidential pronouncements." It was really not until Monroe's principles were invoked vigorously against the French Emperor Napoleon III's incursion into Mexico during America's Civil War that Monroe's precepts became accepted as a major national policy. According to other interpretations, the term *Monroe Doctrine* was first used in a congressional debate in 1853 and began to be employed by executive policy-makers in this same period.[26]

Although Monroe may not have been conscious of having formulated a long-term doctrine of American foreign policy, his message to Congress nonetheless possessed several doctrinal aspects. Both the president and Secretary of State John Quincy Adams, Whitaker has observed, had previously shown a propensity "for frank and manly declarations" in foreign affairs; Adams, whose role in drafting Monroe's message was crucial, was particularly addicted to "trumpet blasts" on diplomatic issues. With regard to the continued independence of Spain's former colonies in the New World, Monroe advocated "vigorous action" by the United States, leading him to speak in a "clear and decisive tone" to the outside world. While, as we shall see, there was nothing very original about most of the ideas contained in his message, Monroe at least made quite explicit what might be called a new principle of American foreign policy: that the continued independence of the nations of the Western Hemisphere was a diplomatic

---

who referred to the Monroe Doctrine in religious phraseology. He said of the Monroe Doctrine that it "is not a doctrine but a dogma . . . not one dogma but two, to wit: the dogma of the infallibility of the American President and the dogma of the immaculate conception of American foreign policy." Dozer (ed.), *The Monroe Doctrine*, title page.

26. Perkins, *A History of the Monroe Doctrine*, 68; Samuel F. Bemis, *The Latin American Policy of the United States: An Historical Interpretation* (New York: Harcourt, Brace, 1943), 98, 112; Julius W. Pratt, *A History of United States Foreign Policy* (Englewood Cliffs, N.J.: Prentice-Hall, 1955), 184; Donovan, *Mr. Monroe's Message*, 4.

vital interest of the United States, for whose protection the nation was prepared to fight if necessary.[27]

In still another important sense, Monroe's message constituted a doctrine of American foreign policy. One of his purposes was to issue a set of diplomatic guidelines which, in the president's own words, formed "parts of a combined system of policy and adapted to each other."[28] His proclamation consisted of several interrelated diplomatic principles. Moreover, it was comprehensive, covering both America's approach to European problems and Europe's behavior in the New World.

In addition—and as time passed, this was one of the Monroe Doctrine's most singular characteristics—Monroe enunciated general and highly flexible diplomatic guidelines susceptible to varying interpretations and applicable to a host of new challenges abroad in the years ahead. Two examples of this characteristic may be cited at this stage. More than a century after Monroe's declaration, one diplomatic historian observed that his principles have "been invoked by isolationists on the one hand and internationalists on the other." After World War I, Secretary of State Hughes asserted that the prohibitions expressed in the Monroe Doctrine applied not just to the European powers but to all nations (e.g., an expansive Japan).[29]

But it was most especially in another respect—the realm of national ethos, psychology, and spirit—that President Monroe enunciated the most influential doctrine in the nation's diplomatic experience. In a unique sense, Monroe's "immortal message," forcefully expressed authentically American ideas vis-à-vis the ideologies and diplomatic practices identified with the Old World. This realization on the part of countless Americans (and not a few foreigners) in time imparted to Monroe's words a quasi-religious, almost sacrosanct quality; as the years passed, most Americans were prepared to accept on faith and *in perpetuo* the set of foreign policy principles proclaimed by their fifth president.

27. Whitaker, *The United States and the Independence of Latin America*, 470, 518; W. P. Cresson, *James Monroe* (Chapel Hill: University of North Carolina Press, 1946), 447.

28. Bemis, *John Quincy Adams and the Foundations of American Foreign Policy*, 364.

29. Pratt, *A History of United States Foreign Policy*, 167; Perkins, *A History of the Monroe Doctrine*, 334–35. See also the views of Hiram Bingham in Hart, *The Monroe Doctrine*, 350.

Originally, and for almost a century thereafter, the Monroe Doctrine was an exercise in American machismo—made all the more appealing to its devotees perhaps by the fact that it emanated from a youthful, militarily weak nation that might have been hard pressed to enforce Monroe's admonitions against a determined violator. It *was* an idealistic, a visionary, in some ways utopian, proclamation. But in that respect, it resembled the Constitution of the United States and, more broadly, the "American way of life." It *did* contemplate fundamental changes in the kinds of political relationships existing within the New World. It *did* postulate also the existence of a political community between North and South America (which some Americans like Secretary Adams at the time doubted really existed or would ever exist). It *did* anticipate the later Wilsonian principle of self-determination and identified America with its maintenance. According to one biographer, President Monroe conceived of his message predominantly in "moral" terms. The doctrine, in W. P. Cresson's words, was "an expression of faith rather than a carefully reasoned exposition of American opposition to European intervention in the New World." It was essentially "a sincere expression of the belief in the superiority of American institutions and ideals." As the embodiment of American ideas and ideals, Hart observed, the Monroe Doctrine became a kind of Ten Commandments of American foreign policy, "which are not questioned or limited or construed, but obeyed."[30]

A doctrine of course can have a legal, as well as a religious or moral, connotation. In the case of the Monroe Doctrine, as well as doctrines associated with later presidents, the legal dimensions have unquestionably loomed large in the minds of public officials and citizens alike. As many commentators have observed, America is a very law-oriented (if not necessarily law-abiding) society. Historically, sooner or later Americans have converted a variety of socioeconomic issues into legal questions. Americans venerate legal concepts and norms like "a government of laws, and not of men," and they look to legal and judicial institutions for the solution of many of their problems. While, as we noted earlier, the Monroe Doctrine was in fact a principle of neither domestic nor international law, undeniably many Americans believed otherwise. To their minds it became tantamount to a kind of

30. Ammon, *James Monroe*, 491; Cresson, *James Monroe*, 448; Hart, *The Monroe Doctrine*, 371.

legal or constitutional edict. At the end of the nineteenth century, the French writer De Beaumarchais stated that as Americans saw it the Monroe Doctrine "includes a solution for all the international complications which could arise." The fact that it was called a *doctrine*, gave "to the decisions which it invokes, a judicial look, which is bound to please a people upon whom the words 'law' and 'legality' exercise so reasonable an influence." To the American mind, Monroe's message had proclaimed principles "of universal range."[31]

President Monroe's message, we have already noted, did not in the main introduce an innovation in the foreign policy of the United States. Instead, it reiterated ideas and principles which were already deeply embedded in the American ethos and which earlier administrations had followed in their approach to diplomatic issues. Space is not available to undertake a lengthy examination of the historical antecedents of the Monroe Doctrine, nor is a detailed survey of precedents necessary for our purposes.[32] It suffices merely to call attention to some of the outstanding landmarks leading to Monroe's message.

In terms of preexisting ideas, the Monroe Doctrine reflected several which were already widely accepted by Americans. A leading example was the notion of the distinctiveness or separateness of the New World, particularly in the realm of political ideologies and behavior— one of the doctrine's most conspicuous themes. Prominent Latin Americans had also expressed this idea before 1823. Interestingly enough, the idea found widespread support—if not always admiration and enthusiasm—on the European continent, as well.[33] In the pre–Revolutionary War era, the writings of Thomas Paine emphasized the uniqueness of the American society, the necessity for its separation from the Old World, and (by implication at least) the need for America to pursue an independent course in its domestic and external policies.

After independence, the unwillingness of the United States to honor

31. Quoted in Hart, *The Monroe Doctrine*, 352–53.
32. On precedents leading to the Monroe Doctrine, see Varg, *Foreign Policies of the Founding Fathers*, passim; Perkins, *A History of the Monroe Doctrine*, 5–26; Clark, *Memorandum on the Monroe Doctrine*, 3–91; and James W. Gantenbein (comp. and ed.), *The Evolution of Our Latin American Policy: A Documentary Record* (New York: Columbia University Press, 1950), 301–22.
33. Arthur P. Whitaker, *The Western Hemispheric Idea: Its Rise and Decline* (Ithaca, N.Y.: Cornell University Press, 1954), 1–21.

the terms of the alliance with France, which would require war with England; the provision of the Constitution (Article II, Section 2) requiring a two-thirds vote of the Senate in the treaty-ratification process; President Washington's Neutrality Proclamation (April 22, 1793) during the Napoleonic Wars; the isolationist sentiments expressed in his Farewell Address (September 17, 1796); America's unilateral chastisement of the Barbary pirates during the Jefferson Administration, along with President Jefferson's embargo of American trade with the European nations in 1807; the decision of the United States to recognize the independence of Latin American nations, taken without consultation with, and in evident defiance of the wishes of, the European powers—these early actions clearly anticipated the provisions of Monroe's message in 1823. A particularly notable development occurred in the period 1810–1811, in connection with Spain's former colonial possession in West Florida (which the United States unquestionably hoped to annex in the future). Early in 1811, Congress passed a resolution stating that the United States could not permit the transfer of any of Spain's colonial possessions to another foreign power. Known as the "no-transfer principle," this concept was sometimes called the "Madison Doctrine," an important forerunner of the Monroe Doctrine.[34]

Awareness of such antecedents led Secretary of State Hughes to declare on the hundredth anniversary of the Monroe Doctrine that it was the "fruition" of national experience and expressed principles "long cherished and made almost sacred by the lessons of experience."[35] The eminent authority on international law, John Bassett Moore, carried this reasoning one step further. In his view, the Monroe Doctrine was an authoritative announcement of a principle already widely accepted by Americans—so much so that Monroe's message was really superfluous: the necessity to limit European power and influence in the Western Hemisphere.[36]

34. For a detailed discussion of the "no-transfer principle," see John A. Logan, Jr., *No Transfer: An American Security Principle* (New Haven: Yale University Press, 1961). Briefer discussions may be found in W. F. Reddaway, *The Monroe Doctrine* (Cambridge, England: Cambridge University Press, 1898), 8–9; and Lieuwen, *U.S. Policy in Latin America*, 6–7.
35. See Secretary Hughes's address, "Observations on the Monroe Doctrine" (August 30, 1923), in Alvarez, *The Monroe Doctrine*, 414.
36. *Ibid.*, 488.

Writing more than a century after 1823, Bailey observed that the Monroe Doctrine is "a crisis doctrine, and it flourishes best when its roots are well manured with insecurity."[37] This underscores one of the outstanding characteristics of the Monroe Doctrine, its corollaries, and virtually all the other diplomatic doctrines promulgated in American diplomatic experience, down to the Carter Doctrine in 1979: the Monroe Doctrine was issued *in response to a foreign policy crisis, in which American policy-makers perceived national security to be directly at stake.* Whether it was in responding to the threat of Holy Alliance intervention in Latin America in the early 1820s or whether it was the danger of Communist control over the Persian Gulf area by the early 1980s, those foreign policy pronouncements which came to be designated *doctrines* were nearly always prompted by an immediate threat to national security. The doctrine thus had a dual purpose: to protect national security in the face of an urgent threat to it; and to provide a general principle (or principles) which would enable policy-makers to deal with more or less comparable threats in the future.

In the case of Monroe's doctrine (as with nearly all others which followed it) the question may legitimately be raised: was the danger to the security of the United States real or was it largely imaginary, existing mainly in the minds of American officials? Considerable evidence exists for believing that President Monroe and his advisers overestimated the likelihood both of Holy Alliance intervention in the New World and Russian expansion in the Northwest. At worst, in 1823, both threats seemed to be only potential dangers. Yet exaggerated or not, the threat to the security of the New World—and ultimately to the continued independence of the United States—was viewed as ominous to President Monroe and his principal aides. His doctrine was America's unique mode of dealing with it then and in the future.

President Monroe's message was the prototype of later foreign policy doctrines in several key respects—none more important than the fact that this landmark in the nation's diplomatic experience was decided upon, and enunciated, by the president. In this respect, it clearly served as a model for the diplomatic doctrines which followed it.

37. Thomas A. Bailey, *The Man in the Street: The Impact of American Public Opinion on Foreign Policy* (New York: Macmillan, 1948), 265.

Authorship and Policy Formulation

Among diplomatic historians, there has long been a debate over the "authorship" of the Monroe Doctrine (one school of thought gives the credit largely to Secretary of State Adams). The evidence supports several conclusions on this general point. Unquestionably, the thinking of Monroe's official and de facto advisers—like James Madison, Thomas Jefferson, and Secretary Adams—influenced the formulation of the Monroe Doctrine profoundly. As we have seen, numerous precedents prepared the way for the president's declaration. That Monroe was cognizant of the gravity and far-reaching consequences of his message is indicated by the fact that both the content and mode of presentation were thoroughly discussed among the principal officers of his administration before its submission to Congress.

After allowing for these facts, it is still historically accurate to refer to the message as the *Monroe* Doctrine. President Monroe himself decided upon the mode of delivery—a public message to Congress vis-à-vis other alternatives, like private diplomatic correspondence with Great Britain and other interested nations. And after listening to the often diverse viewpoints of his advisers, Monroe decided upon the final content of his epochal statement.[38]

In this early stage of the life of the Republic—when the meaning of certain constitutional principles was still not clear, and when the precise responsibilities of the three branches of government had yet to be clearly determined—it was surely a noteworthy fact that the nation's most influential set of diplomatic guidelines was ultimately formulated, issued by, and thereafter identified with, the president of the United States. Barely a generation after the adoption of the Constitution, the Monroe Doctrine thus emerged as a powerful affirmation of executive authority in the foreign policy field. Insofar as other countries heeded the admonitions contained in the doctrine, they were being influenced by the views of the nation's chief executive. Although of course the Monroe Doctrine was in no sense solely responsible

38. For the evidence on Monroe's personal role in the formulation of his doctrine, see Perkins, *A History of the Monroe Doctrine*, 43; Morgan, *The Life of James Monroe*, 394–95; and for detailed treatment, see William A. MacCorkle, *The Personal Genesis of the Monroe Doctrine* (New York: G. P. Putnam's Sons, 1923).

for the phenomenon, the conditions of its formulation and issuance clearly reinforced the tendency toward executive preeminence in foreign relations and provided an authoritative precedent for the idea that the chief executive was the "voice of the nation" in external affairs.

What then was Congress' role in the process culminating in the issuance of the Monroe Doctrine? Implicitly, our treatment has suggested that legislative participation in this crucial foreign policy development was minimal—and that verdict is confirmed by the evidence. (In this respect also, the Monroe Doctrine was typical of those which came after it.) We may conveniently think of the doctrine as involving three important stages: formulation, promulgation, and execution.

In the first two stages—formulation and promulgation—Congress played no significant part whatever. Legislators were unaware of the private correspondence between the Monroe Administration and London which culminated in President Monroe's address. Nor is there any evidence of legislative participation in the deliberations within the administration which produced the final version of the president's message. (The Eighteenth Congress was not in session during this period.) Since no treaty was called for by the president, the "advice and consent" of the Senate was not solicited. While the president delivered his set of foreign policy guidelines in a message to Congress, the House and Senate were not called upon to take any immediate action to implement the principles it contained. Upon receipt of Monroe's address, one student of the period has observed, the dominant reaction within Congress was "relative silence." In that period, the question of possible Holy Alliance intervention in the New World quickly became subordinated to congressional interest in possible American assistance to aid Greece in its efforts to throw off Turkish rule.[39]

Yet, if its role in the formulation and promulgation of the Monroe Doctrine was minimal, there is no evidence that congressional sentiment opposed the content of the president's message or viewed it as a radical departure from preexisting foreign policy guidelines. The lack of explicit congressional approval has led some commentators to assert that the Monroe Doctrine never enjoyed legislative sanction, which was one reason why its provisions could not legitimately be

39. Ammon, *James Monroe*, 490–91.

viewed as legally binding. At best, the doctrine received only implicit and indirect legislative approval in later years, as when the Senate ratified the Hague Convention of 1899, which incorporated the provisions of the Monroe Doctrine.[40]

A more mixed verdict must be rendered on Congress' role in the subsequent implementation of the Monroe Doctrine over the century and a half after 1823. For a number of years after that date, Congress showed no inclination to apply Monroe's principles. As we have already observed, no significant expansion of America's armed forces occurred; neither executive nor legislative officials seemed interested in that result. If the nations of Latin America might reasonably have expected that the Monroe Doctrine would be followed by more vigorous leadership by the United States in behalf of Pan-American cooperation—or that Washington would be willing to incorporate Monroe's principles in a treaty of alliance with the nations of Central and South America—such hopes were quickly doomed to disappointment. Congress, for example, was distinctly hostile to the idea of any new commitment by the United States which might result from the Panama Congress among the American republics in 1826.[41]

Yet, in 1823 and afterwards, executive officials acknowledged that effective implementation of the Monroe Doctrine—especially if it involved the use of military force—depended upon the concurrence of Congress. Any possible concerted (or "parallel") American action with Great Britain to defend Latin America against the Holy Alliance, for example, required congressional approval. Secretary of State Henry Clay declared in 1828, for example, that the Monroe Doctrine had entailed no specific pledge or promise of action by the United States, and that any action taken to enforce its terms required congressional authorization.[42]

If not originally, as time passed Congress' role in all three stages—

40. Secretary of State John W. Foster's view, in 1914, was that Senate ratification of the Hague Convention in effect constituted belated legislative acceptance of the Monroe Doctrine, making it part of the law of the land. Alvarez, *The Monroe Doctrine*, 411–12.

41. Bemis, *The Latin American Policy of the United States*, 70.

42. Bemis, *John Quincy Adams and the Foundations of American Foreign Policy*, 396–98; and see Clay's views, as excerpted in Richard K. Showman and Lyman S. Judson (comps. and eds.), *The Monroe Doctrine: Its Importance in the International Life of the States of the New World* (New York: Oxford University Press, 1924), 43.

but particularly in implementation—tended to increase. As we shall see, the formulation of at least one important corollary of the Monroe Doctrine (the "Lodge Corollary" in 1912) stemmed from legislative initiative. After World War II, the Senate's role in ratifying the Rio Treaty of hemispheric defense (1947)—a pivotal step in the effort to "multilateralize" the Monroe Doctrine and to apply its provisions to new problems like Communist activities in the Western Hemisphere—was vital. In Monroe's era, as in the post–World War II period, whatever authority the Monroe Doctrine possessed depended in the final analysis upon the power of the United States to compel respect for its terms. This in turn involved willingness of Congress to provide the kind of armed forces needed to secure compliance with it under varying conditions. When a powerful adversary was prepared to challenge the doctrine, as in Soviet Russia's efforts to install offensive missiles in Cuba in the early 1960s, this fact obviously heightened the importance of legislative prerogatives, at least in the long run, such as the power to appropriate funds and to provide for the armed forces.

Nevertheless, it seems worth reiterating that the Monroe Doctrine was formulated and issued by the president, in the absence of direct congressional authority. Although in a long-range sense, legislative participation was, and remains, essential in the doctrine's implementation, in a crisis Congress' powers to control implementation of the doctrine are limited. Such decisions as whether and when to apply the doctrine remain presidential determinations. Relying upon his power to influence public opinion and to commit the nation to a predetermined course of action, the chief executive can very largely compel Congress to provide the means for implementation—all the more so when, as in 1823, he can demonstrate that a threat to national security is involved.

In an age when the franchise was still severely limited, and before the era of modern communications media, it is not surprising that public opinion played no significant role in the issuance of the Monroe Doctrine. Certainly in the Old World tradition, if not even in the American ethos, the management of foreign affairs was viewed as the province of an elite. No evidence exists that the Monroe Administration considered the public reaction when the doctrine was formulated or in any meaningful way "consulted" it prior to the president's message to Congress. Nevertheless, public opinion did play a role in the doctrine's emergence, in the sense that nearly all the principles contained in it had long enjoyed widespread public support.

Several years after 1823, Daniel Webster referred to the "general glow of exultation" which Americans exhibited toward the Monroe Doctrine. With the passage of time, Perkins concluded, the Monroe Doctrine won the "widespread, indeed almost unanimous, support in American public opinion." Each extension of it earned "well-nigh universal popularity" among the American people. If not during Monroe's lifetime, then in later years his doctrine came to symbolize American independence, freedom of decision-making, and the distinctiveness of New World political concepts vis-à-vis those of the Old World. The Monroe Doctrine, Thomas A. Bailey has observed, was "intoxicating to the national spirit." Or, as Hart expressed it, Monroe's message greatly enhanced the young Republic's "sense of importance" and reflected its determination to become "a living force in the affairs of mankind." One particular segment of American opinion—business and commercial interests—greeted it with enthusiasm, since adherence to it would assure continued Yankee access to Latin American markets.[43]

Doctrinal Evolution: Corollaries and Adaptations

In 1895, President Grover Cleveland asserted that the Monroe Doctrine had been "intended to apply to every stage of our national existence."[44] Historically correct or not, his view in fact correctly described the *experience* of the Monroe Doctrine. Fully as much in the 1980s as in the 1820s, the United States subscribes to it and expects other nations to abide by its principles. At the same time, like the Constitution itself, the Monroe Doctrine has been applied to innumerable novel circumstances unforeseen by its authors. In the process, its meaning has been modified and expanded to such an extent that the modern version of the doctrine might well be, in some respects, unrecognizable to President Monroe and his contemporaries.

Evolutionary changes in the Monroe Doctrine have been so marked that diplomatic historians like Thomas A. Bailey are convinced in real-

43. Perkins, *A History of the Monroe Doctrine*, 379; Thomas A. Bailey, *A Diplomatic History of the American People* (8th ed.; New York: Appleton-Century-Crofts, 1968), 185; Hart, *The Monroe Doctrine*, 87–88.
44. Quoted in Alvarez, *The Monroe Doctrine*, 412.

ity there have been three rather distinct Monroe Doctrines. The original one—lasting until around 1900—was essentially "defensive" in nature, pledging the United States only to refrain from interfering in Europe's quarrels and to defend the Western Hemisphere against outside threats. The second began with the era of Theodore Roosevelt and the Roosevelt Corollary which, as we shall see, imparted a positive, activist, perhaps even imperialistic, cast to the Monroe Doctrine. Then under President Franklin D. Roosevelt, the third stage—entailing introduction of the Good Neighbor Policy and efforts to "multilateralize" the Monroe Doctrine—was reached in which the doctrine was converted into a collective principle of hemispheric defense. It is not necessary to accept Bailey's threefold classification without qualification (other commentators have used different schemes to characterize the changes in the doctrine) to acknowledge that evolutionary modifications in the Monroe Doctrine since 1823 have been profound. In limited space, we can do no more than take note of the highlights in that process.[45]

A few months after President Monroe's historic address, Senator Henry Clay introduced a resolution in Congress opposing European intervention in Spain's former New World colonies. Closely akin to Monroe's principles, the resolution was called by some the "Clay Doctrine." Yet Congress was indifferent to it, and the resolution died for lack of legislative support.[46] Then in 1826, President John Quincy Adams enunciated what was sometimes referred to as the "Adams Doctrine." Addressed specifically to Mexico, it stated that the United States would not permit the transference of Spain's former colonies (in this instance, Cuba) to another power.

A noteworthy episode in the evolution of the Monroe Doctrine occurred in the late 1840s under the administration of President James K. Polk. Polk was an avowed expansionist, believing that in time the United States was destined to include territories like the Southwest and California. As became evident by the flamboyant and militant manner in which he handled the Oregon controversy with Great Britain, Polk believed in vigorous assertions of American rights in the face of European threats. Polk was also deeply concerned about foreign in-

45. Bailey, *The Man in the Street*, 261.
46. Hart, *The Monroe Doctrine*, 89.

trigue in territories like Texas, Oregon, and California. He was especially apprehensive about efforts (identified particularly with France) to extend the European "balance of power" system to the New World, in part no doubt because it might thwart future expansionism by the United States.[47]

Faced with a crisis in the Yucatan, on April 29, 1848, President Polk stated in a message to Congress that the United States would not henceforth consent to the transfer of "dominion and sovereignty" over the Yucatan to any foreign power, even at the invitation of the inhabitants of the peninsula. Known as the "Polk Corollary" to the Monroe Doctrine, this declaration had far-reaching consequences for its evolution. Henceforth, the European powers were not only enjoined against armed intervention in the New World, but according to President Polk's dictum, they were precluded from diplomatic intrigue and machinations, as well—even with the consent of the American nation concerned.

In effect, Polk closed the door against the importation of the balance of power concept to the American continents. In Perkins' words, his principle constituted an "American veto on European action in the New World." In whatever degree some commentators might regard the Polk Corollary as at variance with the instructions and diplomatic principles of President Monroe, former Secretary of State John Quincy Adams, significantly, believed otherwise and applauded Polk's "extension" of the doctrine. Yet once again, Congress revealed little enthusiasm for Polk's application of the Monroe Doctrine; it refused to pass a resolution approving it (antislavery forces, for example, were convinced that Polk's major purpose was to expand the slaveholding territories of the United States).[48]

On the eve of the Civil War, Secretary of State Lewis Cass declared that the United States would not consent to the establishment of European protectorates in the New World, or to any other "direct political influences" exerted by European powers to subjugate independent

47. Charles A. McCoy, *Polk and the Presidency* (Austin: University of Texas Press, 1960), 110–11; Perkins, *A History of the Monroe Doctrine*, 75–77; Eugene L. McCormac, *James K. Polk: A Political Biography* (Berkeley: University of California Press, 1922), 693.

48. Perkins, *A History of the Monroe Doctrine*, 79, 81–82; Hart, *The Monroe Doctrine*, 114–15.

American states. Known as the "Cass Doctrine," this injunction was enunciated in 1858 and directed specifically at the problem of Spain's faltering authority in the New World.[49]

Down to World War II, the most direct and flagrant challenge to the Monroe Doctrine occurred during the Civil War. Beginning in 1862, Emperor Napoleon III of France used troops to install the alien Maximilian regime on the throne of Mexico. Among the French ruler's several goals, one was to revive the prospects for monarchial government in the New World and to check the expansion of democratic systems. Preoccupied with the bloody contest between North and South, the Lincoln Administration could do little more than protest this intrusion of French power into the Western Hemisphere. Periodic protests were of course made, as in 1862, when Secretary of State William H. Seward declared that no monarchial regime could survive in the New World and that America was not indifferent to its existence in Mexico. As the tide of the Civil War changed, such protests became more pointed. On April 4, 1864, the House of Representatives passed a unanimous resolution condemning French machinations in Mexico. Then as the end of the Civil War approached, American public opinion became increasingly incensed about the issue; the likelihood of direct American military intervention to uphold the Monroe Doctrine increased sharply.

Meanwhile, in a classic instance of rivalries among the European powers promoting American security, France was becoming alarmed about the rising military might and expansionist ambitions of Germany, under its forceful Chancellor Otto von Bismarck. In time, French public opinion also became disenchanted with the Mexican venture. The rising intensity of American protests, therefore, was clearly only one consideration persuading Napoleon III's government to liquidate its presence in Mexico. French troops finally left Mexico early in 1867; the hapless Maximilian and his family were abandoned to their fate.

Curiously enough, throughout the entire Maximilian affair, American officials seldom referred to the Monroe Doctrine by name (it remained highly unpopular in Europe), although they frequently in-

49. Hart, *The Monroe Doctrine*, 133–34.

voked Monroe's original principles and later amplifications of his doctrine. Yet in later years, Secretary Seward boasted that as a result of his diplomacy in the Maximilian episode the Monroe Doctrine had been transformed from a myth into a reality! While its importance in securing a French withdrawal should not be exaggerated, still the Monroe Doctrine—or more correctly perhaps, the growing prospect that the United States would rely upon armed force to uphold its terms—was unquestionably a factor influencing Napoleon III's decision.[50]

Another milestone in the evolution of the Monroe Doctrine occurred at the end of the nineteenth century, in connection with a boundary dispute between Venezuela and British Guiana. Asked by Venezuela to support its request for arbitration, the United States pressed Great Britain to accept this mode of settlement—but to no avail. In 1895, President Grover Cleveland appointed Richard Olney as his secretary of state. Olney promptly applied his considerable talents as a skillful and forceful attorney to the affair. Olney believed that Britain was attempting to expand its influence in Latin America and that only a vigorous invocation of the Monroe Doctrine by the United States would stop the process. President Cleveland shared this conclusion. Olney's militant "brief," addressed to London, asserted that the Monroe Doctrine applied to this controversy; and he contended that its noncolonization principle had been "universally conceded" by all nations. Attempting to justify Washington's active intrusion into the quarrel, Olney based his position on the claim that the United States "is practically sovereign on this continent, and its fiat is law upon the subjects to which it confines its interposition."

Whatever this exercise in legalistic bombast and circular reasoning meant precisely, Olney's outburst accomplished two results. It offended Great Britain, eliciting a lecture from the Foreign Office on the meaning and limitations of the Monroe Doctrine. And it powerfully reinforced a conclusion which many Latin Americans and others had long held about the Monroe Doctrine: the idea that under its guise, the United States sought hegemony throughout the Western Hemi-

---

50. This summary of the Maximilian affair is based upon more detailed accounts in Glyndon G. Van Deusen, *William Henry Seward* (New York: Oxford University Press, 1967), 365–70; and Pratt, *A History of United States Foreign Policy*, 339–44.

sphere. (Late in 1899, the Venezuelan boundary dispute was finally settled by arbitration.)[51]

The Roosevelt Corollary and Its Impact

A few years later, there occurred what was in many respects the most influential and controversial amplification of the Monroe Doctrine—the "corollary" enunciated by President Theodore Roosevelt in the early 1900s. By that period, the United States faced a recurrent problem in inter-American relations, particularly in relations with Caribbean states. Characterized by political instability, and often ruled by self-seeking political regimes, several Caribbean nations had become heavily indebted to European creditors, which threatened to intervene in the Western Hemisphere to collect debts owed them. Alluding several times publicly to America's attachment to the Monroe Doctrine, President Theodore Roosevelt finally declared on December 6, 1904, that any Latin American nation

> whose people conduct themselves well can count upon our hearty friendship. If a nation shows that it knows how to act with reasonable efficiency and decency in social and political matters, if it keeps order and pays its obligations, it need fear no interference from the United States. Chronic wrongdoing, or an impotence which results in a general loosening of the ties of civilized society, may in America, as elsewhere, ultimately require intervention by some civilized nations, and in the Western Hemisphere the adherence of the United States to the Monroe Doctrine may force the United States, however reluctantly, in flagrant cases of such wrongdoing or impotence, to the exercise of an international police power.[52]

As the author of the phrase "speak softly and carry a big stick," President Roosevelt was asserting "an international police power" for the United States in the Western Hemisphere.

For several reasons, the Roosevelt Corollary was a momentous development in the evolution of the Monroe Doctrine. Under its guise, during the next generation the United States actually intervened on some sixty occasions in Latin America (mostly the smaller Caribbean

---

51. Eggert, *Richard Olney: Evolution of a Statesman*, 200–202.
52. Excerpts from Theodore Roosevelt's speeches dealing with problems in Latin America, including his address on December 6, 1904, may be found in Gantenbein (comp. and ed.), *The Evolution of Our Latin-American Policy*, 361–62.

and Central American) states.[53] Interestingly enough, although "big stick" diplomacy is usually associated with Theodore Roosevelt, in fact is was under the administration of President Woodrow Wilson—the advocate of self-determination and of worldwide democracy—that interventionism in Latin America to enforce the Roosevelt Corollary reached its zenith.

Among the forces leading to the promulgation of the Roosevelt Corollary, two deserve special mention. One was the viewpoint exhibited by the permanent personnel of the State Department; according to Perkins, for many years, this group had sought to expand United States influence in the Caribbean area. The other influential force was foreign opinion. As early as the 1860s, for example, British officials had urged Washington to adopt the principles expressed in the Roosevelt Corollary. This fact of course signified ultimate British acceptance of America's unique role in the Western Hemisphere. As President Roosevelt later asserted, if the United States demanded European compliance with the Monroe Doctrine, then Washington had a special responsibility to prevent circumstances from "inviting" European intervention in the New World.[54]

The Roosevelt Corollary also contained the germ of an idea which was to be reiterated by some commentators with regard to the relevance of the Monroe Doctrine for post–World War II American foreign policy. Roosevelt distinguished between two groups of states in Latin America: what he termed the "prosperous civilized commonwealths" (like Argentina, Brazil, and Chile) on the one hand; and the smaller, weaker American republics (like Santo Domingo) which were subject to "misrule" and to "chronic revolution" on the other hand. Literally speaking (although few Latin Americans or other outsiders appeared to grasp the distinction), his corollary was intended to apply to the latter group of states, not to the former.[55]

As with the original Monroe Doctrine, the influence of public and

53. John Gerassi, *The Great Fear in Latin America* (New York: Collier Books, 1965), 231.

54. Perkins, *A History of the Monroe Doctrine*, 258. For examples of British initiative in suggesting the Roosevelt Corollary, see Clark, *Memorandum on the Monroe Doctrine*, xxiii; and Perkins, *A History of the Monroe Doctrine*, 232.

55. For further elaboration of this distinction, see Theodore Roosevelt, *An Autobiography* (New York: Charles Scribner's Sons, 1920), 506–508.

legislative opinion upon the formulation of the Roosevelt Corollary was minimal. There is no evidence that public opinion played any part in the issuance of the Roosevelt Corollary or that it really desired the numerous interventions subsequently carried out to enforce it. (Yet we must remember that the dominant foreign policy sentiment of the American people until World War II—isolationism—was an attitude displayed primarily toward participation in European affairs. The isolationist policy was never applicable to inter-American relations.) Nor did Congress demonstrate any particular fondness for the Roosevelt Corollary or play any discernible role in its formulation. As an example, the Senate refused to approve a treaty with Santo Domingo incorporating the provisions of the Roosevelt Corollary; President Roosevelt later made such an accord in the form of an executive agreement, which did not require senatorial acceptance.[56]

To say that the Roosevelt Corollary was unpopular among Latin Americans would be to understate the matter. In fact, no single action by the United States after 1823 was more instrumental in alienating Latin American opinion than the kind of "big stick" diplomacy which the Roosevelt Corollary epitomized. Later attempts to "multilateralize" the Monroe Doctrine by making its enforcement the common responsibility of the Inter-American System enjoyed, at best, limited success, owing in no small measure to the reservoir of bitterness which the Roosevelt Corollary created.

On the eve of World War I, another important extension of the Monroe Doctrine occurred. Alarmed by the effort of Japanese business interests to acquire port facilities in Lower California, Senator Henry Cabot Lodge (Republican of Massachusetts) introduced a resolution in the Senate calling for full disclosure of Japan's activities; a later Lodge-sponsored resolution prohibited the acquisition of a harbor or naval facility by a foreign power in the Western Hemisphere. The latter resolution was approved by the Senate in August, 1912, by a vote of 51-4. The Lodge Corollary is interesting for several reasons, not the least of which is that the initiative for it came from Congress; President Taft and State Department officials were opposed or lukewarm to the measure. Moreover, as Bailey has noted, the corollary was

56. Roosevelt, *An Autobiography,* 510–11; Perkins, *A History of the Monroe Doctrine,* 242.

also important because, for the first time, the provisions of the Monroe Doctrine were applied to an Asian power and to private groups, no less than to governments. Although it was initially opposed by the State Department, the Lodge Corollary was nonetheless invoked several times after 1912.[57]

By the 1920s even officials in Washington had begun to recognize that adherence to the Roosevelt Corollary paid few dividends for the United States in its relations with the other American republics. Accordingly, in 1923, Secretary of State Charles Evans Hughes "reinterpreted" the Monroe Doctrine so as to exclude the Roosevelt Corollary as a legitimate extension of it.[58]

Hughes's reinterpretation foreshadowed the so-called "Clark Memorandum" on the Monroe Doctrine, prepared by Under Secretary of State J. Reuben Clark in 1928 (not published, however, until 1930). This detailed analysis of the meaning and evolution of the Monroe Doctrine in effect repudiated the Roosevelt Corollary. Its key idea— "The Doctrine states a case of United States *vs.* Europe, not of United States *vs.* Latin America"—meant that the scope of the doctrine was now greatly restricted. It did not, for example, apply to several categories of issues, such as European colonial possessions in the New World held before 1823, to wars among Latin American states, or even to the conduct of warfare by European states against independent Latin American nations.[59]

By repudiating any right of intervention by the United States as defined by the Roosevelt Corollary, it is essential to note, the Clark Memorandum did *not* totally preclude future interventionism in the Western Hemisphere. Hereafter, the Clark Memorandum said in effect, such intervention would have to be based on different concepts (like the inherent right of "self-defense" by the United States) rather than being justified by the provisions of the Monroe Doctrine—a distinction which was not perhaps overly meaningful to the outside world. Yet the salient fact about the Clark Memorandum was that

---

57. Perkins, *A History of the Monroe Doctrine*, 271–75; Bailey, *A Diplomatic History of the American People*, 540.
58. See Betty Glad, *Charles Evans Hughes and the Illusions of Innocence* (Urbana: University of Illinois Press, 1966), 240–41.
59. For these and other exclusions identified by Under Secretary Clark, see Clark, *Memorandum on the Monroe Doctrine*, 180–200.

within the months ahead it was followed by the liquidation of American military forces in Latin America (the last marines left Nicaragua late in 1932) and by the adoption of the Good Neighbor Policy of President Franklin D. Roosevelt.

"Multilateralizing" the Monroe Doctrine

The most serious effort to alter the underlying basis of inter-American relations was made by FDR's Secretary of State Cordell Hull—whose name was synonymous with attempts to change the nation's restrictive tariff laws—and who was especially interested in Latin America. The way had been prepared by the Clark Memorandum for a new era in hemispheric relations, and New Deal efforts to "multilateralize" or "continentalize" the Monroe Doctrine were a vital step in this process. Latin American spokesmen had long urged Washington to make the maintenance of the Monroe Doctrine the common responsibility of the Pan-American movement or (as it was called after 1948) the Organization of American States.

As was true of 1823 and at intervals thereafter, it was a foreign crisis—in the late 1930s, the increasingly grave Axis threat to hemispheric security—that furnished impetus for fundamental changes in the Monroe Doctrine. Curiously enough, the Axis powers offered to accept and respect the Monroe Doctrine—provided that the United States recognized an equivalent German hegemony in Europe and a Japanese sphere in Asia. But the Roosevelt Administration was never prepared to engage in this kind of reciprocity.[60]

In a series of conferences throughout the 1930s and 1940s, President Roosevelt and his advisers sought to convert the Monroe Doctrine into a common responsibility of all the American republics. At Pan-American meetings in Buenos Aires (1936), Lima (1938), and Havana (1940) significant progress was made toward the goal. The culmination of these efforts came with the Act of Chapultepec (1945), and the Rio Treaty of hemispheric defense (ratified by the United States on December 19, 1947). The key provision of the Rio Treaty (Article 3, Section 1) specified that "an armed attack by any State against an American State shall be considered as an attack against all the American

---

60. Charles Wertenbaker, *A New Doctrine for the Americas* (New York: Viking Press, 1941), 19.

States and, consequently, each one of the said Contracting Parties undertakes to assist in meeting the attack in the exercise of the inherent right of individual or collective self-defense recognized by Article 51 of the Charter of the United Nations." [61]

Did the existence of the Rio Treaty now mean that the Monroe Doctrine had been successfully "multilateralized"? Quite a few officials and informed commentators on Latin American affairs thought so. A leading advocate of hemispheric unity, former Under Secretary of State Sumner Welles, was convinced that the goal had finally been accomplished, thereby removing perhaps the most serious impediment to more cooperative inter-American relations. Similarly, Thomas A. Bailey's verdict was that after 1947, "A unilateral anachronism had been changed to conform to multilateral realism." [62]

Other commentators, however, were not so certain that the status of the Monroe Doctrine had been fundamentally changed. From the period of World War II to the present time, efforts to multilateralize the doctrine have been impaired by two contrary tendencies. The first, and (in the light of the United Nations' inability to preserve global and regional peace) the least serious, was America's efforts to make threats to global peace and other controversies among nations the responsibility of the entire international community, as symbolized by the United Nations. The United States of course was the leading sponsor of the new international organization created in 1945. From the inception, therefore, efforts to multilateralize (or, to use a variant phrase, to "regionalize") the Monroe Doctrine were somewhat at variance with parallel efforts to "internationalize" the guarantees of hemispheric security which the doctrine contained.

With regard to this dilemma, the United States encountered a troublesome problem. As occurred in the formulation of the League of Nations nearly a generation earlier, in 1945 Washington insisted that the UN Charter recognize the special ties which bound the nations of the New World. Based on the earlier experience with the League of Nations, considerable domestic opposition could be expected in the

61. For the texts of the Act of Chapultepec and the Rio Treaty, see U.S. Congress, Senate, Committee on Foreign Relations, *A Decade of American Foreign Policy: Basic Documents, 1941–1949*, 81st Cong., 1st Sess., 1950, pp. 414–26.
62. Sumner Welles, *The Time for Decision* (New York: Harper and Row, 1944), 403–404; Bailey, *The Man in the Street*, 260.

United States if an impression existed that the UN Charter imperiled the Monroe Doctrine. Typical of American apprehensions on this point were the views of Sen. Arthur H. Vandenberg (Republican of Michigan), who played an active role in formulating and drafting the UN Charter. Vandenberg viewed the protection of the Monroe Doctrine as one of America's foremost concerns. What would become of hemispheric security, he asked, if measures to protect it were subject to "veto" by the Soviet Union or other countries in the UN? Accordingly, the United States insisted upon the right of regional self-defense, as reflected in Articles 51 through 54 of the charter, a right that Vandenberg saw as "a keystone in the later efforts of the Western Powers against the world-wide expansion of communism." While the Monroe Doctrine was not specifically mentioned, and although all nations might invoke these articles, it was understood by the organization's founders that they had been inserted primarily to accommodate America's historic attachment to the Monroe Doctrine.[63]

At the same time, in 1945 and afterwards officials in the United States were equally opposed to Soviet claims that Moscow possessed a comparable security zone of its own in Eastern Europe which was entitled to international recognition. How could America logically and convincingly demand global acceptance of its own unique regional security system, without according the same right to other powerful states like Soviet Russia and, at a later stage, Communist China? Despite efforts by American policy-makers to differentiate the case of the Monroe Doctrine from Soviet claims to hegemony in Eastern Europe, this was a question to which officials in Washington never provided a convincing answer.[64]

The second and far more serious obstacle hampering efforts to multilateralize the Monroe Doctrine was posed by one of the earliest and most enduring of the doctrine's characteristics: its unilateral nature. By definition, the concept of multilateralization necessarily implied a

63. Arthur H. Vandenberg, Jr. (ed.), *The Private Papers of Senator Vandenberg* (Boston: Houghton Mifflin, 1952), 186.
64. An informative discussion of the conflict between efforts to multilateralize the Monroe Doctrine and attempts to establish a viable international organization after World War II is contained in Barton J. Bernstein (ed.), *Politics and Policies of the Truman Administration* (Chicago: Quadrangle Books, 1970), 154–65. A more detailed analysis is Lloyd Mecham, "The Integration of the Inter-American System into the United Nations," *Journal of Politics*, IX (May, 1947), 178–96.

willingness by the United States to relinquish its hitherto exclusive right to interpret and enforce the doctrine's provisions. In view of the intensive efforts undertaken in the 1930s to improve inter-American relations—and also of the impressive growth in the machinery and responsibilities of the Organization of American States after World War II—was the United States finally prepared to give up its traditional role as sole guardian of the Monroe Doctrine?

As became evident when Washington faced the challenge of Communist penetration of the Western Hemisphere (a subject we shall consider more fully below), considerable evidence existed that in a crisis, the Monroe Doctrine remained what it had been since 1823: a unilateral foreign policy proclamation of the United States, with Washington acting as its authoritative interpreter and enforcer. Typical of the view of Latin American critics on this issue was John Gerassi's verdict that the concept of multilateralization was in reality "a fancy phrase for United States intervention, and the OAS came to represent a new institutional arm of the hated Monroe Doctrine." The United States, Herbert L. Matthews concluded, "has never agreed that any other American nation has a contractual right to invoke the Monroe Doctrine."[65]

The Monroe Doctrine and Postwar Diplomacy

As tended to be true of all other aspects of postwar American diplomacy, after 1945 the evolution of the Monroe Doctrine was concerned predominately with Communist machinations in the Western Hemisphere. As early as April 5, 1947, President Harry Truman related the historic foreign policy principles of Thomas Jefferson and James Monroe to his recently enunciated Truman Doctrine. America's "containment" policy was conceived of by President Truman as a global extension of the ideas embodied in the Monroe Doctrine. Three years later, a high-ranking State Department official stated that the United States would regard Communist efforts to penetrate the Americas as a violation of the Monroe Doctrine.[66]

65. Gerassi, *The Great Fear in Latin America*, 240. See Matthews' chapter on "Diplomatic Relations," in Herbert L. Matthews (ed.), *The United States and Latin America* (2nd ed.; Englewood Cliffs, N.J.: Prentice-Hall, 1963), esp. p. 146.
66. Harry S Truman, *Memoirs: Years of Trial and Hope, 1946–1952* (Garden City, N.Y.: Doubleday, 1956), 107; Matthews, "Diplomatic Relations," 146.

Then in planning for the Tenth Inter-American Conference at Caracas, Venezuela, in 1954, Secretary of State John Foster Dulles asserted that growing Communist activity in the Western Hemisphere posed the same kind of threat to the security of the American republics as the one against which the Monroe Doctrine had been originally directed. In reference to the first major test of the doctrine's applicability to the Communist question—as officials in Washington saw it, successful Marxist efforts to control Guatemala—Secretary Dulles declared, "This intrusion of Soviet despotism was, of course, a direct challenge to our Monroe Doctrine, the first and most fundamental of our foreign policies." [67]

Consonant with its effort to multilateralize the doctrine, early in 1954 the United States urged the Organization of American States to adopt a resolution (ultimately known as the "Caracas Declaration") condemning Communist inroads in the hemisphere; the resolution was finally adopted by the OAS on March 26, 1954, by a vote of 17–1. It is noteworthy, however, that the really decisive step in *enforcing* the Monroe Doctrine—the overthrow of the pro-Communist government of Guatemala headed by Col. Jacobo Arbenz in June, 1954—was financed and instigated by the United States. The Caracas Declaration to the contrary, the anti-Communist coup in Guatemala elicited widespread complaints from Latin America about Yankee "interventionism" in their political affairs. [68]

Yet the successful ouster of a pro-Marxist regime in Guatemala in no sense brought an end to Communist machinations in Latin America. As time passed, one political system above all others—Premier Fidel Castro's Cuba—came to exemplify the challenge and to test the contemporary significance of the Monroe Doctrine. It is not necessary for our purpose to trace the emergence of a Communist regime in

67. Eleanor L. Dulles, *American Foreign Policy in the Making* (New York: Harper and Row, 1968), 247. The ensuing "Guatemalan Crisis" is dealt with at length on pp. 243–68.

68. Dwight D. Eisenhower, *Mandate for Change: 1953–1956* (Garden City, N.Y.: Doubleday, 1963), 421–23. America's role in the overthrow of the Arbenz regime is discussed in *Mandate for Change*, 421–27. Although United States complicity in the overthrow of the pro-Communist government of Guatemala was undeniable, one informed study believes that the crucial factor in its collapse was that President Arbenz lost the support of the Guatemalan military, who were increasingly alienated by his pro-Marxist policies. Ronald M. Schneider, *Communism in Guatemala: 1944–1954* (New York: Praeger, 1958), 314–15.

Cuba. Suffice to say that, following a long and bloody civil war against the oppressive Batista dictatorship, by the end of 1958 rebel forces under Dr. Castro effectively controlled Cuba. Within a few months, Castro's suspected affinity for communism had been explicitly acknowledged in Havana. Despite a brief period of reasonably cordial Cuban-American relations, tensions between the two countries soon developed, leading to a complete diplomatic rupture between them in 1961. Plans were formulated under the Eisenhower Administration, and carried out by the Kennedy Administration, for an American-supported attempt to overthrow Castro's regime. The ill-fated Bay of Pigs invasion in April, 1961, was a diplomatic and military fiasco; its most lasting consequence perhaps was to consolidate Castro's position in Cuba, to worsen Cuban-American relations, and to drive Havana into closer collaboration with Moscow.

Late in 1962, as a result of Cuba's decision to permit the deployment of Soviet missiles on its soil, there occurred what one commentator has described as "the most forceful employment of the [Monroe] Doctrine in the one hundred and thirty-nine years" of its history. The facts concerning the Cuban Missile Crisis are too recent and well known to require more than the briefest recapitulation.[69] As Soviet-Cuban relations became more intimate, reports began to circulate that Moscow was providing massive military assistance to Cuba and that it was constructing offensive missile sites throughout the island. But the White House repeatedly denied the credibility of these reports. Meanwhile influential legislators and segments of public opinion in the United States were becoming increasingly alarmed about this flagrant affront to the Monroe Doctrine. For example, a joint resolution passed by Congress on October 3, 1962, began by saying, "Whereas President James Monroe, announcing the Monroe Doctrine in 1823, declared that the United States would consider any attempt on the part of European powers 'to extend their system to any portion of this hemisphere as dangerous to our peace and safety' . . ." and went on to express American determination to prevent efforts by Cuba to subvert other

69. Donovan, *Mr. Monroe's Message*, 223. Detailed treatments of the crisis may be found in Robert F. Kennedy, *Thirteen Days: A Memoir of the Cuban Missile Crisis* (New York: W. W. Norton, 1968); Arthur M. Schlesinger, Jr., *A Thousand Days: John F. Kennedy in the White House* (Boston: Houghton Mifflin, 1965), 795–830; Theodore C. Sorensen, *Kennedy* (New York: Harper and Row, 1965), 667–719.

American republics and "to prevent in Cuba the creation or use of an externally supported military capability endangering the security of the United States." During the late summer and early fall of 1962, public pressure upon the Kennedy Administration to invoke the Monroe Doctrine mounted steadily.[70]

Then in mid-October—after intelligence photographs left no doubt that Soviet missile installations were indeed being constructed in Cuba—the attitude of President Kennedy and his advisers changed abruptly. While differences of opinion existed within the administration upon the best course to follow, unanimity existed upon one point: this Soviet military intrusion into the Western Hemisphere posed a serious threat to national and regional security, and it could not be tolerated. A prolonged and careful consideration of alternative responses by the United States led to a decision by the Kennedy Administration to institute a blockade of (or, to use the language of President Kennedy, to "quarantine") Cuba. If this limited response to the threat did not produce the desired result, then the administration was prepared to use more forceful measures (not excluding an air strike against the missile sites) to eliminate the danger.

In a dramatic television address to the nation on October 22, President Kennedy announced his plan of action. The existence of Soviet missile sites in Cuba, the president asserted, constituted "an explicit threat to the peace and security of all the Americas"; it violated the provisions of the Rio Treaty of hemispheric defense and "the traditions of this nation and Hemisphere"; it disregarded warnings issued repeatedly during the preceding months by Congress and the White House; and it contravened recent pledges which Moscow had made to Washington on the subject. Moscow had embarked upon a provocative course "in an area well known to have a special and historical relationship to the United States." Kennedy declared that the United States would be willing to present the facts of the case for consideration by the Organization of American States or the United Nations, "without limiting our freedom of action."[71]

70. U.S. Congress, House, Committee on Foreign Affairs, *Inter-American Relations*, 92nd Cong., 2nd Sess., 1972, p. 474. See also Sorensen, *Kennedy*, 669.
71. For the text of Kennedy's address on the Cuban crisis see *Public Papers of the Presidents of the United States: John F. Kennedy, 1962* (Washington, D.C.: Government Printing Office, 1963), 806–809.

Several days of suspense—in which a clear risk of a nuclear confrontation between the two superpowers existed—followed the president's address. In time, however, Moscow and Havana accepted Washington's ultimatum and agreed to withdraw Soviet missiles from Cuba. (For their part, Soviet Russia and Cuba received concessions such as at least a tacit pledge by the United States not to invade Cuba, along with Washington's willingness to forego on-site inspection of suspected missile installations on the island.) On balance, the outcome was a dramatic diplomatic victory for the United States and a humiliating defeat for Moscow and, to a lesser extent, for Havana.

Our interest in the crisis, however, is limited to its relevance for the evolution and contemporary meaning of the Monroe Doctrine. On this question, several points are worth emphasizing. The first is the evident allegiance which the Monroe Doctrine continues to evoke from Congress and public opinion. For reasons we shall identify below, even before 1962 executive department officials were often reluctant to invoke the Monroe Doctrine by name in dealing with threats to hemispheric security. Yet outside the White House, as the experience of the Cuban Missile Crisis indicated, support for the doctrine remains undiminished; as in the past, a flagrant violation of its provisions is apt to be construed publicly as a threat to the existence of the nation itself.[72]

Second, the Cuban Missile Crisis forcefully illustrated the paradoxical role of the Monroe Doctrine in contemporary American foreign policy. On the one hand, it is highly significant that the most serious global Cold War encounter between the United States and the Soviet Union directly, risking possible nuclear devastation, involved a threat to the Monroe Doctrine. Once evidence had been obtained of the Soviet missile buildup in Cuba, President Kennedy was no less determined than President Monroe earlier to remove this threat to hemi-

---

72. One study of the Cuban Missile Crisis notes that America's response to the emplacement of Soviet missiles in Cuba was "the ultimate test of our determination to protect ourselves. . . . no American government could, with domestic impunity, look lightly upon a military threat implanted in the Caribbean." Kahlman H. Silvert, "The Caribbean and North America," in Tad Szulc (ed.), *The United States and the Caribbean* (Englewood Cliffs, N.J.: Prentice-Hall, 1971), 206–207. Similarly, a longtime student of Latin American affairs believed that Soviet machinations in Latin America were almost exactly analogous to those of the Holy Alliance in the early nineteenth century; both threats had to be countered by reliance upon the Monroe Doctrine. Adolf A. Berle, *Latin America—Diplomacy and Reality* (New York: Harper and Row, 1962), 30, 77.

spheric security. In this sense, the Monroe Doctrine has lost none of its salience as a cardinal principle of American foreign policy.

On the other hand, one of the remarkable aspects of President Kennedy's address on October 22 (as was true of executive department pronouncements on the question of Communist activities in Latin America before and after 1962) was that throughout the crisis no direct reference was made to the provisions of the Monroe Doctrine. The closest allusion to the doctrine's provisions was Kennedy's reference to the "traditions of this nation and Hemisphere" and to the terms of the Rio Treaty (which presumably reflected the "multilateralized" Monroe Doctrine). More often than not in recent years, executive officials have gone out of their way to avoid direct allusions to the Monroe Doctrine—even while they have been in the process of enforcing its provisions!

This evident reluctance by executive policy-makers to invoke the doctrine explicitly might—and in the case of Communist nations undoubtedly did—convey the impression abroad that it has somehow been abandoned or superseded, or has otherwise become outmoded as one of the foundations of American foreign policy. Both before and after 1962, for example, Soviet officials expressed this conclusion. Thus, Premier Khrushchev stated publicly that, valuable as it may have been throughout much of America's history, the Monroe Doctrine had "outlived its time . . . has died, so to say, a natural death." Subsequent State Department reaffirmations of the doctrine's continued applicability did little to remove doubts about its contemporary relevance.[73]

Reluctance on the part of executive officials to invoke the Monroe Doctrine publicly may be accounted for by two considerations. Implicit in the long effort to multilateralize the doctrine was the idea that its invocation was no longer the exclusive province of the United States

73. For Soviet interpretations of the history, meaning, and contemporary significance of the Monroe Doctrine, see T. Stephen Cheston and Bernard Loeffke, *Aspects of Soviet Policy Toward Latin America* (New York: MSS Information Corp., 1974), 63–73; and Basil Dmytryshyn and Jesse L. Gilmore, "The Monroe Doctrine: A Soviet View," *Bulletin: Institute for the Study of the USSR* (Munich), XI (May, 1964), 3–14. As always, there is the question of how much Soviet officials believed their own propaganda, leading them to miscalculate America's response. One former Kennedy Administration official believes this occurred in the Cuban crisis. See Roger Hilsman, *To Move a Nation: The Politics of Foreign Policy in the Administration of John F. Kennedy* (Garden City, N.Y.: Doubleday, 1967), 182.

but the common responsibility of the Inter-American System through the OAS. The other, and more decisive, reason was widespread realization in Washington that, to the minds of Latin Americans, the Monroe Doctrine still evoked negative reactions. In Bailey's expressive language, "In the house of a man who has been hanged, the guest does not speak of rope." Accordingly, in dealing with the other American republics, "the representatives of the United States do well not to mention Monroe." Ever since 1823—but particularly since the era of the Roosevelt Corollary—the Monroe Doctrine has been unpopular with many Latin Americans. According to one observer, they often viewed it as "a sinister menace to their national sovereignty and dignity"; its major connotation was the "paramount interest and hegemony" of the United States in the hemisphere vis-à-vis Latin American "political inferiority." A more recent study emphasizes that Latin Americans objected to the Monroe Doctrine as a "patronizing" policy which implicitly cast the United States in the role of "big brother" for the smaller American states. They believed that "it was to be interpreted only for the benefit of the United States." Attempts to legitimatize American diplomatic behavior by overt appeals to the Monroe Doctrine were not, therefore, calculated to win Latin American support and good will.[74]

The third observation about the role of the Monroe Doctrine in the Cuban Missile Crisis involves a subject we have discussed previously: its unilateral nature. This Cold War encounter provided powerful reinforcement for the view that, whatever efforts to multilateralize the Monroe Doctrine may have accomplished down to 1962, one fact about it had not changed. Confronted with a threat to national and regional security, the United States would not hesitate to rely upon the principles of the Monroe Doctrine *unilaterally*. The evidence indicates

74. Bailey, *The Man in the Street*, 269; Clarence H. Haring, *South America Looks at the United States* (New York: Macmillan, 1928), 102; Milton S. Eisenhower, *The Wine is Bitter: The United States and Latin America* (Garden City, N.Y.: Doubleday, 1963), 171. Yet it is also true that, as several commentators have emphasized, the Latin American reaction to the Monroe Doctrine has always been ambivalent. Both in 1823 and afterwards, for example, many groups in Latin America applauded the doctrine's defense of republican institutions and its opposition to European intervention in their affairs. A recent commentator on American foreign policy has said that a schizophrenic quality marked Latin American attitudes toward the United States. "They want us, in other words, to intervene when it suits their purpose, and not to intervene when it doesn't." Ronald Steel, *Pax Americana* (Rev. ed.; New York: Viking Press, 1970), 245.

convincingly that the nation's response to the Soviet missile threat was formulated solely by its own policy-makers. Moreover, if the administration's "quarantine" of Cuba had failed to achieve its intended purposes, there is every reason to believe that the decision to rely upon even stronger measures would similarly have been made by officials in Washington alone.

Once the decision to quarantine Cuba had been reached, it is true, the United States made an intensive effort to enlist the support of the OAS, along with its European allies. In the main, this effort was successful. Perhaps to the surprise of Cuba and the Soviet Union, in time they faced the almost unanimous opposition of the American republics to their provocative behavior—opposition, it is essential to note, which centered on the introduction of Soviet missiles in Cuba, not upon the existence of Marxist ideas or Communist-oriented political movements in the Western Hemisphere.[75]

Yet in his October 22 speech, President Kennedy had stated openly that, desirable as it was, OAS and United Nations involvement in the Cuban controversy would not limit America's freedom of action. In other words, if these organizations were not prepared to enforce the provisions of the Monroe Doctrine, now, as in the past, the United States reserved the right to do so. Even earlier, following the Bay of Pigs misadventure, President Kennedy had said that if the OAS (characteristically) engaged in a "policy of non-action" in its response to Communist activities in the hemisphere, then the United States remained free to protect the security of the Americas.[76]

By the early 1960s, the multilateralization of the Monroe Doctrine amounted to this: President Kennedy and his advisers solicited Latin American support for the containment of communism in the Western Hemisphere; for a number of reasons, they regarded OAS approval of their actions as both diplomatically and legally desirable. But, on the basis of experience, they were far from sanguine about the willingness or ability of the OAS to take effective action in crisis situations, in which case the United States retained the right to apply the Monroe

75. Matthews and other commentators have made the point (not always clearly understood by policy-makers in Washington) that Latin America overwhelmingly supported the United States in dealing with an external military threat to hemispheric security; they were far less prepared to condemn communism in Cuba or Marxism per se. Matthews, "Diplomatic Relations," 144.

76. *Ibid.*, 145.

Doctrine unilaterally. Expressed differently, genuine and meaningful "multilateralization" of the Monroe Doctrine depended upon the degree to which the other American republics were prepared to agree upon a unified policy and to implement it. The Cuban crisis indicated that in Washington's view, after a generation of effort aimed at multilateralization, this vital precondition was still lacking in the Inter-American System. In the years that followed, the Latin American members of the OAS showed no sign of remedying this crucial deficiency.

Another notable characteristic of the Cuban Missile Crisis as a case study in the invocation of the Monroe Doctrine was that, characteristically, it was an exercise in executive decision-making. According to one of his close advisers, in deciding upon his course of action, President Kennedy relied upon "executive Order, presidential proclamation and inherent powers"; his authority was not derived from "any resolution or act of the Congress." A select group of influential legislators was merely informed of Kennedy's decision—and their reaction to it solicited—before he addressed the nation publicly. But there is no evidence that congressional reaction (and several legislators advocated a more militant course than the administration was prepared to follow) in any significant way altered the president's plan of action.[77]

After the resolution of the Cuban Missile Crisis, less serious challenges to the Monroe Doctrine continued to be posed by Communist activities in Latin America. Here we shall take note of only two examples; a third is reserved for more detailed examination of the second Johnson Doctrine in Chapter 6. One of these occurred in the early 1970s, when the Soviet Union attempted to establish a naval base, capable of servicing nuclear submarines, at the Cuban port of Cienfuegos. Negotiations between Washington and Moscow resolved this issue, with the Soviet Union agreeing to suspend construction of the base.[78] Yet Soviet submarines continued to operate rather openly in the Gulf of Mexico and adjacent waters.

Then there was the continuing issue of the Communist system in Cuba. As a result of the missile crisis, the United States spearheaded an

77. Sorensen, *Kennedy*, 702; Schlesinger, *A Thousand Days*, 812.

78. See the testimony of Deputy Assistant Secretary of State Robert A. Hurwitch, in U.S. Congress, Senate, Committee on Foreign Relations, *Hearings on U.S. Policy Toward Cuba*, 93rd Cong., 1st Sess., 1974, pp. 4–5, 17–19.

effort to "isolate" Castro's regime within the hemisphere. American officials successfully persuaded two-thirds of the members of the OAS to impose an economic boycott on Cuban trade, and Washington took the position that, by its own behavior, Castro's government had removed itself from membership in the inter-American community.

According to executive department spokesmen, Washington's stance on the Cuban question was dictated by two considerations— either of which alone was serious enough to guarantee the continuation of tensions in Cuban-American relations. The first was Havana's intimate association with the Soviet Union, which involved massive ideological, economic, and military dependence upon it. Moscow's obvious intention was to make Cuba a model of Marxist-style "Socialist development" for Latin America and for Third World nations generally—a goal whose successful achievement encountered numerous and serious obstacles.

The other source of Cuban-American controversy was the apparent determination of Castro's regime to "export" its revolution to neighboring Latin American societies. After experiencing little or no success in fomenting successful revolution against the governments of Bolivia and Venezuela, by the late 1970s Castro's government had shifted the focus of its revolutionary campaign to Central America. While it would be unwarranted to attribute revolutionary upheaval in this region to Cuban and Soviet intervention alone, it was nonetheless true that leftist political groups throughout Central America (such as the Sandinista movement in Nicaragua and Marxist-oriented rebels in El Salvador) received moral and material assistance from Havana, and possibly from Moscow. As officials of the Reagan Administration assessed the matter, the revolutionary ferment gripping Central America in the early 1980s posed a serious threat to regional peace and security, primarily because it signified a new attempt by the Soviet Union and its Cuban client to impose an alien political system in the Western Hemisphere.[79]

By a literal interpretation, both of these issues—a growing Soviet military "presence" in and adjacent to Cuba, along with joint Cuban

79. For analyses of Marxist-supported revolutionary activities in Central and South America, see the symposium on "Latin America, 1981," in *Current History*, LXXX (February, 1981), especially the discussion of revolutionary conflict in Guatemala and El Salvador, pp. 70–75, 88.

and Soviet sponsorship of Marxist revolutionary movements through-out the hemisphere—involved violations of the Monroe Doctrine. A persuasive case could be made for the idea that the former entailed (in President Monroe's words) the intrusion of a "European power" into the New World. On the premise (admittedly debatable) that Cuba's Marxism had no roots in the Western Hemisphere, it could also be contended that the existence of a Communist order in Cuba—not to mention its imposition on other American states—exemplified pre-cisely the kind of alien "political system" which the original Monroe Doctrine had proscribed.

Yet as we have already observed, in dealing with these issues, policy-makers in the United States remained reluctant to invoke the provi-sions of the Monroe Doctrine publicly and directly. Indeed, even when they denounced Communist interventionism in the Western Hemi-sphere, American officials often appeared to go out of their way to *avoid* references to the Monroe Doctrine; and in some instances, they actually denied the doctrine's applicability to the Cuban problem. There was, for example, an interesting exchange between Senator Aiken (Republican of Vermont) and Deputy Assistant Secretary of State Hurwitch on March 26, 1973. Aiken asked, "Do you think our relationship with Cuba has anything to do with or casts any reflec-tions on the Monroe Doctrine?" Hurwitch replied: "No, sir. I must say, we really sort of regard the OAS and the Rio Treaty in some sense as successors to the Monroe Doctrine." [80]

That consideration aside, does the Monroe Doctrine remain a viable principle of American foreign policy? Insofar as its quintessential meaning—the United States will resist any outside threat to the se-curity of the Western Hemisphere—remains the same today as in 1823, the answer seems evident. Unless and until organizations like the United Nations or the Organization of American States are pre-pared to exercise that responsibility—and by many criteria, prospects seem more remote today than ever—the United States will continue to do so, unilaterally when necessary. A reluctance to rationalize or legit-imatize America's actions by the terms of the Monroe Doctrine thus signifies no fundamental change in its role in the foreign policy of the United States.

80. *Ibid.*, 18.

2 / The Open Door Principle and the Stimson Doctrine
The Policy of "Sticking Pins in Tigers"

The Open Door . . . is the least fundamental of our historic foreign policies. Unlike such guiding stars as the Monroe Doctrine . . . it did not spring from the rugged soil of our needs and aspirations here in the Western Hemisphere, and for this reason it has been a rather sickly plant of hothouse growth. It is one of the most hazily defined and perhaps the most generally misunderstood of all our foreign policies. —Thomas A. Bailey

[The Open Door policy's] effects on popular imagination in the United States were far greater than its influence on world politics and China. As a simple slogan it became a powerful and relatively inflexible domestic influence on American Far Eastern policies in the twentieth century.
—Wayne S. Cole

I was willing to go to war for the preservation of America, but I believed we should not go around alone sticking pins in tigers, or alone impose futile sanctions. . . . I held that one who brandishes a pistol must be prepared to shoot. —President Herbert Hoover

In the year 1784, the Yankee merchant ship *Empress of China* reached Canton, opening one of the most colorful, important, and complex sagas in the annals of American diplomacy. As the years passed, the United States was drawn ever deeper into the vortex of great power rivalries and conflicts in the Far East. The Asian counterpart to the Monroe Doctrine was the policy of the Open Door toward China, initially proclaimed by Secretary of State John Hay in 1899. The Open Door principle was applied and amplified many times thereafter, most forcefully perhaps by Secretary of State Henry L. Stimson in responding to the challenge of Japanese expansionism in Manchuria during the early 1930s.

The Open Door Principle and Its Connotations

There is an interesting, and not altogether explicable, difference in the nomenclature of American foreign policy as applied to Europe and Latin America, on the one hand, and to Asia, on the other hand. As we

noted in Chapter 1, the general body of diplomatic principles governing America's relations with Europe and the Western Hemisphere after
1823 was referred to as a *doctrine*—the Monroe Doctrine. The comparable set of diplomatic guidelines regulating American foreign policy toward China and collateral Asian problems was known after 1899
as the Open Door *policy*. Relatively few commentators, of whom John
K. Fairbank was one, called it the "Open Door doctrine."[1] Yet a specific application of the Open Door policy to the Manchurian crisis in
the early 1930s came to be called the "Stimson Doctrine." The reasons
why usage dictated these semantical differences in America's relations
with various regions are not clear. On the premise that the Monroe
Doctrine serves as the norm—a foreign policy *doctrine* expressing a
set of general principles applicable to varying conditions likely to affect the nation's vital interests—then perhaps the failure to designate
the Open Door policy as a doctrine is understandable. Despite their
avowals of support for the Open Door principle, neither American officials nor the American people were ever really convinced that maintenance of the Open Door in China was a "vital interest" of the United
States.

As a matter of historical accuracy, it is necessary to emphasize that
what came in time to be called the Open Door policy was enunciated
in two stages, as the United States was required to respond within a
relatively brief period of time to changing conditions in China. Accordingly, the Open Door policy contains two reasonably distinct, if
interrelated, ideas. The first stage occurred late in 1899. On September
6, President William McKinley's secretary of state, John Hay, sent
identical diplomatic notes to Great Britain, Germany, and Russia—
and later to France and Japan—asking them to agree to the principle of "perfect equality of treatment" in their commercial and economic relations with China. Anticipating intensified colonial rivalry in
China, Secretary Hay sought to limit it by gaining universal acceptance of the Open Door concept. The Open Door concept precluded
any one foreign country from acquiring a dominant or monopolistic
position, to the detriment of other nations' commercial and financial
interests, in China.[2]

1. John K. Fairbank, *The United States and China* (Rev. ed.; New York: Viking
Press, 1958), 257.
2. The text of the diplomatic notes enunciating the Open Door policy may be found

Hay's initial principle was, therefore, quite limited. Hay did not envision the end of colonial competition in China. A number of important and potentially controversial activities—such as mining and railroad concessions—were altogether omitted from the scope of his original pronouncement. Implicitly at least, Hay's pronouncement assumed the continuation of the "treaty system" of foreign concessions existing in China. Washington's intention was to insure that in the future, one or more foreign countries would not gain concessions that were inimical to American interests.

Another noteworthy aspect of the Open Door policy provides a significant contrast with the Monroe Doctrine earlier. Secretary Hay had requested the concurrence of the foreign powers active in China with the Open Door principle and (according to his interpretation of events) had received it. In its inception at least, America's historic policy toward China was a multilateral undertaking, as distinct from the unilateral character of most other diplomatic doctrines of the United States.

Yet the multilateral character of the Open Door policy was more apparent than real. Hay had engaged in a remarkably successful diplomatic gambit, designed to yield a predetermined result. One of his biographers is convinced that even before he sent the notes, Hay was prepared to assume a positive response to them.[3] In effect, the American secretary of state had asked the foreign powers having concessions in China to join in renouncing sin! Under the circumstances, they were reluctant to refuse, if for no other reason than failure to subscribe to the Open Door principle would be construed as evidence of imperialist ambitions against China. By announcing that the recipients had accepted his principle, Secretary Hay in effect converted the Open Door concept into a unilateral policy declaration by the United States, with Washington serving as the concept's main supporter and interpreter.

---

in U.S. Congress, House, *Papers Relating to the Foreign Relations of the United States, with the Annual Message of the President,* 56th Cong., 1st Sess., 1899, pp. 129–30. For the second series of notes proclaiming the Open Door principle see the same source, 56th Cong., 2nd Sess., 1900, p. 299. The extent to which the United States belonged to the elaborate "treaty system" established by the foreign powers in China by the end of the nineteenth century is discussed in John K. Fairbank, *China Perceived: Images and Policies in Chinese-American Relations* (New York: Alfred A. Knopf, 1974), 83–101.

3. Kenton J. Clymer, *John Hay: The Gentleman as Diplomat* (Ann Arbor: University of Michigan Press, 1975), 147.

A few months later, in the second stage of enunciation of the Open Door policy, Washington significantly broadened Hay's original principle. By the end of 1899, the always volatile Chinese political situation erupted anew, with violence directed at the "foreign devils" having vast concessions within China. Led by a fanatical and xenophobic nationalist group called the Boxers, a rebellion sought both to undermine the Chinese dynasty and to rid China of foreign influence. In time, after an international military force was formed to defeat it, the Boxer Rebellion failed. The result was to undermine the already feeble imperial government of China and to whet foreign appetites for new. concessions by it.

Concerned about what appeared to be a new colonial scramble in China, on July 3, 1900, Secretary Hay dispatched another series of diplomatic notes to the powers. The key concept in them was the idea that the United States called for preservation of the "Chinese territorial and administrative entity." In brief, Hay called upon foreign countries to accept the principle of Chinese political independence—a concept that would be identified with American diplomacy for almost half a century thereafter.

This second stage in the evolution of the Open Door policy represented a substantial broadening of Hay's original principle. As events revealed, its implementation involved far-reaching consequences for the United States, few of which appeared evident to American officials at the turn of the century. As we shall see, Japan particularly found this second stage of the Open Door concept a major impediment to its expansionist goals.

The contrast between the mode of issuance of the first and second series of Hay notes is noteworthy. In the notes dispatched after the Boxer Rebellion, Secretary Hay did *not* solicit the cooperation of the powers in behalf of maintaining Chinese independence. Rather, he informed them that this was now America's diplomatic objective. As Tyler Dennett expressed it, Hay "waited in vain" for the powers to reply to his notes of 1900—but he never received a direct reply to them.[4] Far from interpreting this as disapproval of the Open Door principle, however, the McKinley and later administrations assumed the tacit ac-

4. Tyler Dennett, *John Hay: From Poetry to Politics* (New York: Dodd, Mead, 1933), 303, 307.

ceptance of the Open Door principle by the international community. The lack of overt foreign opposition to it, and the apparent acquiescence of other countries in the principle, convinced Washington that its interpretation of the Open Door policy enjoyed widespread support.

Precedents and Policy Antecedents

Thomas A. Bailey has written, "John Hay took an old principle, dressed it up in bright new clothes, added some jewelry, and gave the whole conception to the American people christened with the catchword 'Open Door.' " Warren I. Cohen's conclusion is that the policy known as the Open Door "came as the natural culmination of over 100 years of American involvement in China." These observations underscore the fact that the Monroe Doctrine and the Open Door policy had a common feature: both expressed ideas already deeply embedded in the American diplomatic tradition and enjoying widespread domestic support. In that sense, neither represented a significant policy innovation for the United States. As early as 1843, for example, the first American commissioner to China, Caleb Cushing, had used the phrase "Open Door" in a public address. For many years also, Great Britain had been identified with the Open Door principle.[5]

Following the voyage of the *Empress of China* to the East, America's commercial ties with China steadily expanded. In the past, no less than today, the lure of the "China market" held a strange fascination for Yankee traders. Exaggerated notions of the wealth to be made in China—perhaps by persuading every Chinese male to buy one necktie or to lengthen his shirttail by an inch—lured American businessmen to the Orient, leading them in time to demand that Washington promote new opportunities for trade with the Chinese mainland.

Owing largely to Caleb Cushing's efforts, in the Treaty of Wanghia (1844) China agreed to place trade concessions granted to foreign nations on a more permanent basis, and the United States obtained a "most-favored-nation" status for its trade (a concept whose meaning

5. Thomas A. Bailey, *The Man in the Street: The Impact of American Public Opinion on Foreign Policy* (New York: Macmillan, 1948), 286; Warren I. Cohen, *America's Response to China: An Interpretive History of Sino-American Relations* (New York: John Wiley and Sons, 1971), 64. For more detailed discussion of the antecedents of the Open Door concept, see Stephen C. Y. Pan, *American Diplomacy Concerning Manchuria* (Boston: Bruce Humphries, 1938), 66–70.

and implications we shall examine more fully below).[6] Cushing's influence also led to adoption of the principle of "extraterritoriality," relied upon by foreign countries in dealing with China. In practice, this meant that foreigners who committed crimes within China would be tried according to the laws of their own country, rather than by China's (presumably backward) legal system. Extraterritoriality proved to be an irritant in Sino-American relations until it was abolished during World War II.[7]

In 1858 the United States gained independent trading privileges from the Chinese government. Following the destructive Taiping Rebellion (1851–1865), Washington used its influence to prevent the foreign powers from "partitioning" China. America's action clearly foreshadowed the pledge to maintain China's "territorial integrity," later affirmed in the Open Door policy.[8]

In the years ahead, the American minister to Peking, Anson Burlingame, played an active role in strengthening Chinese-American ties and in persuading other countries to limit their demands upon China. In 1868, the Burlingame Treaty provided for large-scale Chinese immigration to the United States. In time, the controversy over Chinese "coolie labor" in the United States threatened to cancel out much of the good will that had been created in Chinese-American relations.[9]

Another precursor of the Open Door concept was the "most-favored-nation" principle that had long governed American commercial relations with the Orient. Thus the Treaty of Wanghia (1844) provided that "whatever treaty rights other Powers gained [in China] with respect to trade, residence, religious activity, tariffs, and other commercial regulations would automatically accrue to the United States."[10] In

6. The text of the Treaty of Wanghia (or the "Cushing Treaty"), July 3, 1844, is included as Annex No. 1 in Department of State, *United States Relations with China*, Department of State Publication 3573, Far Eastern Series 30 (Washington, D.C.: Government Printing Office, 1949), 413.

7. Chiang Kai-shek, *China's Destiny and Chinese Economic Theory* (New York: Roy Publishers, 1947), 151.

8. Julius W. Pratt, *A History of United States Foreign Policy* (Englewood Cliffs, N.J.: Prentice-Hall, 1955), 275–76.

9. Robert McClellan, *The Heathen Chinese: A Study of American Attitudes Toward China, 1890–1905* (Columbus: Ohio State University Press, 1971), 112. For a detailed discussion of the "Chinese exclusion" problem, see McClellan, 111–33.

10. Thomas A. Bailey, *A Diplomatic History of the American People* (8th ed.; New York: Appleton-Century-Crofts, 1968), 306; Department of State, *United States Relations with China*, 2.

1882, Washington succeeded in getting the hermit-like kingdom of Korea to accept the most-favored-nation principle. Implicitly, if countries like China and Korea were to grant the United States most-favored-nation status, then Washington had a clear interest in preserving their territorial integrity, as the Open Door policy subsequently provided.[11]

Another parallel between the Monroe Doctrine and the Open Door may be identified: in both cases, Great Britain took the initiative in suggesting the policy to American officials. Some diplomatic historians believe in fact that the Open Door policy accorded more with British, than with American, diplomatic interests in the Far East.[12] That the Open Door concept coincided with British objectives in the Far East can hardly be doubted. Relying upon its naval superiority, Great Britain had steadily expanded its power and influence in East Asia; and officials in London were not enthusiastic about rival colonial and commercial ambitions by countries like France, Russia, and Japan. As in the case of the Monroe Doctrine, however, Washington rejected the suggestion that the Open Door principle be embodied in a joint Anglo-American declaration, since (in Secretary of State Hay's words) American policy would be viewed by the people as "subservience to Great Britain." Hay, one historian has observed, did not wish to appear to be "pulling British chestnuts out of the fire" in American policy toward Asia.[13]

Other forces and developments inducing the United States to issue the Open Door policy may be identified briefly. Some commentators believe that the policy coincided with, and reflected, America's expansionist urge as exemplified by the concept of "manifest destiny" or expansionism across the American continent to the Pacific. According to

11. Dorothy B. Goebel (ed.), *American Foreign Policy: A Documentary Survey, 1776–1960* (New York: Holt, Rinehart and Winston, 1961), 185–86; Pan, *American Diplomacy Concerning Manchuria*, 66–70; and Bailey, *A Diplomatic History of the American People*, 306, 314.

12. For a detailed presentation of this view, see Samuel F. Bemis, *A Diplomatic History of the United States* (Rev. ed.; New York: Henry Holt, 1942), 482–84.

13. William H. Dawson, "Imperial Policy in the Old and the New World, 1885–1899," in Sir A. W. Ward and G. P. Gooch (eds.), *The Cambridge History of British Foreign Policy, 1783–1919* (3 vols.; New York: Macmillan, 1923), III, 229; William R. Thayer, *The Life and Letters of John Hay* (2 vols.; Boston: Houghton Mifflin, 1916), II, 234; Foster R. Dulles, *China and America: The Story of Their Relations Since 1784* (Princeton: Princeton University Press, 1946), 108.

John K. Fairbank, the Open Door policy established a new American "theoretical frontier" in Asia. Alternatively, the policy has been described as promoting the idea of the "American empire," as advocated by Secretary of State William H. Seward after the Civil War. Still another historian has placed the Open Door policy within the context of intensive American "imperialist activity" at the end of the nineteenth century. Conversely (since both during this period and afterward, American diplomacy reflected a strong *anti*-imperialist orientation), Akira Iriye believes that the Open Door policy constituted a form of "nonimperialistic expansionism." If Americans opposed the idea of imperialism and "spheres of influence" abroad, they favored the kind of supposedly peaceful, benign, and liberal extension of American power overseas that the Open Door policy envisioned.[14]

America's acquisition of the Philippine Islands at the end of the Spanish-American War provided another impetus for the Open Door policy. A major motivation in acquiring the Philippines, for example, was to promote growing American trade ties with Asia. Julius W. Pratt believes that the United States acquired the Philippines chiefly as a step toward protecting American interests in China.[15]

China's growing internal weakness and fragmentation—which attracted foreign intervention—also influenced Washington to promulgate the Open Door policy. As the authority of the Chinese imperial dynasty became progressively weaker, foreign encroachments against Chinese sovereignty increased. Significantly, in the case of the Open Door policy—as with every diplomatic doctrine included in our study—Washington believed that Russian expansionism posed the most serious threat to its diplomatic interests.[16]

14. Fairbank, *The United States and China*, 251; Walter LaFeber, "The Preparation," in Thomas G. Paterson (ed.), *American Imperialism and Anti-Imperialism* (New York: Thomas Y. Crowell, 1973), 15–17; Thomas G. Paterson, "Introduction" to Paterson (ed.), *American Imperialism and Anti-Imperialism*, 1; Akira Iriye, *Pacific Estrangement: Japanese and American Expansionism, 1897–1911* (Cambridge, Mass.: Harvard University Press, 1972), 66.

15. Bemis, *A Diplomatic History of the United States*, 483; Pratt, *A History of United States Foreign Policy*, 434; Daniel M. Smith, *The American Diplomatic Experience* (Boston: Houghton Mifflin, 1972), 214.

16. Thomas McCormick, "Insular Imperialism and the Open Door: The China Market and the Spanish-American War," in Gerald Clarfield (ed.), *United States Diplomatic History* (2 vols.; Boston: Houghton Mifflin, 1973), I, 270–72; Dulles, *China and America*, 106–107.

An ancient Chinese tradition—the concept of China as "the Middle Kingdom"—also created a favorable environment for issuance of the Open Door policy. Traditionally, the Chinese government had adhered to the policy of treating all "barbarians" (or foreign powers) *equally*— a behavior pattern that coincided well with the provisions of the Open Door policy.[17]

Moreover, certain forces within American society toward the end of the nineteenth century provided an impetus for the Open Door concept. By that period, despite their continued preference for an isolationist stance toward European affairs, many Americans called for a more active American policy toward Asia. At the same time, a number of ideas that supported the isolationist stance toward Europe—nonintervention in Europe's wars and the avoidance of "power politics"— also colored the American approach to Asian questions. Growing American involvement in Asia ought, therefore, to be essentially benign and peaceful; it ought to be directed at preventing international conflicts; and it ought to focus upon expanding commercial relations among the nations of the world. In brief, it ought to reflect America's interest in fostering an "international community," and the Open Door policy apparently met these criteria.[18]

Policy Formulation and Influences

As a case study in the internal formulation of American foreign policy, the Open Door concept has a number of significant aspects. Ultimately of course, all foreign policy declarations by the United States government are issued under the authority of the president. Secretary of State John Hay's diplomatic notes were no exception to this general rule. The evidence indicates, however, that President William McKinley's role in promulgating the Open Door policy was secondary and largely nominal.

President McKinley approved the initial Hay notes in 1899; and (in part because of the evident popularity of the Open Door concept with

17. The extent to which the Open Door policy derived from China's own cultural traditions is elaborated on in Fairbank, *The United States and China*, 257.

18. Charles E. Neu, *The Troubled Encounter: The United States and Japan* (New York: John Wiley and Sons, 1975), 37. A comparable interpretation of the ideological forces producing the Open Door policy is given in Henry L. Stimson, *The Far Eastern Crisis: Recollections and Observations* (New York: Harper, 1936), 13.

the American people), he approved the second series of notes in 1900, identifying the United States with the maintenance of Chinese territorial integrity. Yet McKinley's passive role in the process is suggested by Dennett's observation that Hay's proposed communications were approved by the president "without the change of a word."[19]

Similarly, Congress played a minimal role in the issuance of the Open Door policy. Fearful that Congress would react negatively to any suggestion of Anglo-American cooperation in Asia, Secretary Hay was careful to formulate his proposed policies so as to avoid any possible congressional involvement in them. Congress was not in session either during the first series of Open Door notes in 1899 or in the following year when Hay sent his second round of notes to the foreign powers active in China. No discernible sentiment existed on these occasions for calling a special session of Congress to deal with this new development in American diplomacy; and scattered complaints that the legislative will was being ignored had no observable effect upon executive officials.[20]

Yet such evidence should not be construed to mean that significant legislative opposition existed toward the Open Door concept. To the contrary, there is every reason to believe that—in conformity with overwhelming popular approval of the idea—members of the House and Senate applauded the policy and commended the White House for adopting it. The *goals* embodied in the Open Door concept enjoyed widespread approval throughout the American society. As we shall see, the *means* for achieving or protecting these goals—especially in the face of Japanese expansionism at China's expense—became an increasingly controversial issue.

Among its other interesting features, the Open Door policy calls attention to the often crucial impact of key personalities upon the American foreign policy process. Two such individuals played a role in the promulgation of the Open Door policy. One of them was W. W. Rockhill, an explorer, expert on Oriental languages, and devotee of Eastern religions. Rockhill was determined to save the Manchu dynasty in

---

19. John Paton Davies, Jr., *Dragon by the Tail: American, British, Japanese, and Russian Encounters with China and with One Another* (New York: W. W. Norton, 1972), 88; Dennett, *John Hay*, 302.

20. Dennett, *John Hay*, 296n; Richard W. Leopold, *The Growth of American Foreign Policy: A History* (New York: Alfred A. Knopf, 1962), 117.

China from what appeared to be its inevitable demise. His close associate was Alfred E. Hippisley, a former British official in China and longtime admirer of Chinese society. Hippisley shared Rockhill's objective of preserving Chinese political stability. Together, they prepared a joint memorandum on the Chinese question that was submitted to Secretary Hay and President McKinley. Their analysis served as an influential source for Hay's initial Open Door notes of 1899.[21]

The Open Door policy was adopted at the turn of the century, some two decades before President Woodrow Wilson inaugurated his "new diplomacy" emphasizing the role of public opinion in the foreign policy process. In the absence of advanced methods for measuring public attitudes during the era of the Open Door policy, judgments about the impact of public opinion upon it must, therefore, be more than ordinarily subjective and imprecise.

In taking account of the public impact upon American policy toward Asia, it is useful to differentiate two stages: the influence of public opinion upon the formulation of the Open Door policy, and the public reaction to it after the Open Door policy was issued. Insofar as mass or general public opinion in the United States toward Asian questions was concerned, it can be described as being apathetic, passive, and pervasively uninformed about foreign policy issues. The same feelings of abhorrence toward Old World diplomatic machinations and conflicts that supported the policy of isolationism (analyzed more fully in Chapter 1) characterized popular attitudes toward Asia. For those Americans who knew about it, the impending "dismemberment" of China appeared to be a typical exercise in Old World diplomatic intrigue and hegemony, directed both against American interests and against weaker societies.

One idea that was prominent in the isolationist credo was particularly relevant for the Open Door policy. This was the idea of American unilateralism or the concept of the "free hand": if the United States acted abroad, it should act alone and not in concert with other countries (least of all, Great Britain). As we have observed, Secretary of State Hay was careful to avoid even the appearance of collaborative action with London in issuing the Open Door policy.

21. For detailed excerpts from the memorandum by W. W. Rockhill to Secretary of State Hay (August 28, 1899), see A. L. P. Dennis, "John Hay," in Samuel F. Bemis (ed.), *American Secretaries of State and Their Diplomacy* (10 vols.; New York: Alfred A. Knopf, 1929), IX, 136–38.

The American people also no doubt implicitly expected that any new departure in their foreign policy would accord with the American society's deeply held values, its ethos, and its traditions. Abroad, no less than at home, national policies should accord with the American belief in freedom, justice, laissez faire, democracy, and other cherished concepts. The Open Door policy appeared to most Americans to satisfy this test.

During the period of the Open Door policy, as during other eras of American diplomacy, there were of course many "publics," holding a wide diversity of opinions on diplomatic questions. Then, as today, American public opinion was highly fragmented and heterogeneous. This fact meant that group opinion often had a decisive impact upon the formulation and implementation of foreign policy. These generalizations applied to the formulation of the Open Door policy.

Toward American diplomacy in Asia around 1900, one group whose influence was noteworthy was the foreign policy "elite" (alternatively the "informed" segment of public opinion). This group comprised those individuals who were seriously interested in foreign policy questions, possessed insights into their complexity, and often espoused a particular point of view which they urged policy-makers to adopt. According to Ernest R. May, a discernible elite—consisting of officials within the State Department and military establishment, businessmen, educators, missionaries, and others having a strong interest in Chinese affairs—was influential in shaping American foreign policy on Asia at the turn of the century.[22] Collectively, this group called upon Washington to pursue a "strong" or activist policy in the Far East; and some members of it avowedly favored a policy of American colonialism in Asia. Each of these groups found that the Open Door policy served its purposes, in some instances admirably.

As we have already noted, American business and commercial interests had been active in China since the late eighteenth century. Not unexpectedly, they favored steps by the American government to expand commercial links with Asia. After the Civil War (when some business interests became concerned about the possibility of overproduction and a "saturated" market at home), a growing overseas market in

---

22. Ernest R. May, *American Imperialism: A Speculative Essay* (New York: Atheneum, 1968). Needless to say, May's views are not universally accepted by diplomatic historians.

China was an especially appealing prospect. President McKinley and Secretary Hay were receptive to the pleas by probusiness groups that new opportunities be provided for American trade with Asia. For this segment of American opinion, one study has concluded, John Hay "came close to being [an] ideal Secretary of State."[23] In her study of the era, Margaret Leech concluded that the "extension of American markets in Asia was a leading policy of the McKinley Administration." Another commentator identifies an "Anglo-American business entente" as a force which vigorously championed the concept of the Open Door. A somewhat cynical, and no doubt oversimplified, judgment is Bailey's verdict that America proposed the Open Door policy not so much because of fear "that China would be cut up, as because our merchants feared that they would be cut out."[24]

American missionaries—supported by their religious organizations and by millions of church members in the United States—constituted another potent force advocating the Open Door principle. The American missionary enterprise began in China in 1830. Thereafter, missionary activity expanded rapidly, although Chinese culture was basically hostile to it; and the results of the missionary enterprise in this alien culture, on the basis of internal Chinese political developments in the twentieth century, appeared to be minimal. As time passed, a kind of symbiosis developed between American missionaries and officials of the United States government. Each group supported the other's goals —a fact that seriously compromised the missionary campaign in the eyes of Chinese officials and citizens. As one study of the American missionary endeavor in China concluded, the venture "could never succeed without the support of Western power."[25]

American missionaries were usually fearful about the impending

23. Charles S. Campbell, Jr., *Special Business Interests and the Open Door Policy* (New Haven: Yale University Press, 1951), 46. Campbell's study provides an informative and objective analysis of the role of business groups in the formulation of the Open Door policy.

24. Margaret Leech, *In the Days of McKinley* (New York: Harper and Row, 1959), 515; Charles S. Campbell, *Anglo-American Understanding, 1898–1903* (Baltimore: Johns Hopkins University Press, 1957), 163; Bailey, *The Man in the Street*, 288.

25. Paul A. Varg, *Missionaries, Chinese, and Diplomats: The American Protestant Missionary Movement in China, 1890–1952* (Princeton: Princeton University Press, 1958), 31. This work provides an illuminating study of the influence of missionary groups both upon China and upon American policy-making. A briefer analysis may be found in Cohen, *America's Response to China*, 52–55.

collapse of the Chinese government, which had granted them the right to proselytize in China. Some nationalist groups in China (like the Boxers) were fanatically xenophobic and antimissionary in their activities. Nor did American missionaries look forward to the division of China into foreign-controlled "enclaves," after which some of their privileges might be withdrawn. Many missionaries also, it must be emphasized, were genuinely concerned about the future and welfare of Chinese society if a new colonial scramble destroyed its political integrity. For these reasons, the Open Door policy usually enjoyed the support of American missionaries and of the churches that sponsored their activities in China.

In time, as China's internal political situation became more unstable, and as the Manchu dynasty became increasingly ineffectual, missionary opinion began to favor sweeping changes in the country's social and governmental structure as the only corrective for its traditional backwardness. Envisioning the emergence of a "friendly and democratic China converted to Christianity," most missionary groups welcomed the Chinese Revolution of 1911 and the new government led by the Christian convert, Dr. Sun Yat-sen. After Dr. Sun's death in 1924 his successor as head of the Kuomintang (Nationalist party) was Chiang Kai-shek, another Chinese Christian whose accession as president was also warmly greeted by missionaries and their supporters.[26] For missionaries and many other Americans, it now appeared that China had finally embarked upon the path of democracy and modernization.

Educators (among whom missionaries were often prominently represented) also championed the Open Door principle in China. On the assumption that Chinese society was "backward" and would benefit from modernization, American educators were convinced that their educational activities within China were essential for its future wellbeing. They joined missionaries, therefore, in calling for the maintenance of the authority of the Chinese government against its internal and external enemies.[27]

Military spokesmen and national strategists also found that the Open Door policy promoted their objectives in East Asia. Among this

26. Varg, *Missionaries, Chinese, and Diplomats,* 81.
27. Jerry Israel, *Progressivism and the Open Door: America and China, 1905–1921* (Pittsburgh: University of Pittsburgh Press, 1971), 17–20.

group, the most influential representative was Captain (later Admiral) Alfred T. Mahan (1840–1914). The author of *The Influence of Sea Power Upon History* and other studies, Mahan was perhaps America's most vocal and capable advocate of sea power and its corollary—a "strong" foreign policy. Constructing, maintaining, and protecting the kind of navy which Mahan and his disciples envisioned inevitably dictated a more dynamic role for the United States in the affairs of the world, especially in Asia. The annexation of Hawaii in 1898, followed by the acquisition of the Philippines the following year, made the United States a Pacific power, giving it new responsibilities in that region. Another consideration loomed large in the thinking of Mahan and his followers: the eventual completion of an intercontinental canal in Central America (the first ship passed through the Panama Canal in 1914) placed a greater premium than ever upon preserving naval superiority and defending the Pacific approaches to this vital waterway. Disciples of "Mahanism," therefore applauded the kind of forceful role for the United States in Asian affairs which the Open Door policy exemplified and which its maintenance required.[28]

Once the Open Door policy had been proclaimed, perhaps no foreign policy declaration in American history elicited such enthusiastic and universal acclaim as Hay's statements. The Chicago *Herald* said that there had never been "a more brilliant and important achievement in diplomacy"; the New York *Times* referred to the policy as "a noble work of peace." Both major political parties endorsed the Open Door policy. In her study of the McKinley Administration, Margaret Leech identifies several reasons why the Open Door policy was greeted with such pervasive enthusiasm. It did not entail a "complicated treaty," riddled with "damaging concessions and dangerous ambiguities," and by promulgating the policy, America had "given nothing away." In addition, the Open Door concept was inherently just, and it reflected "frank, straightforward American methods" in solving a

28. For a discussion of the nature and influence of Mahan's thought, see Margaret T. Sprout, "Mahan: Evangelist of Sea Power," in Edward M. Earle (ed.), *Makers of Modern Strategy: Military Thought from Machiavelli to Hitler* (New York: Atheneum, 1966), 415–46. President Theodore Roosevelt was an enthusiastic disciple of Mahan's theories. In 1902, he said that America's position in the Pacific "is such as to insure our peaceful domination of its waters." He believed America's position in the Pacific was more crucial to its future than its position in the Atlantic. George E. Mowry, *The Era of Theodore Roosevelt, 1900–1912* (New York: Harper and Row, 1958), 181–82.

problem whose solution had thus far eluded the nations of the Old World. Another student of Asian diplomacy has identified a feature of the Open Door policy appealing to imperialists and anti-imperialists alike: while injecting the United States into the affairs of Asia, in reality the policy did not commit the nation to do anything to enforce its terms (or so it appeared to Americans around 1900 and afterwards).[29]

The reactions of foreign governments to the Open Door policy were also interesting, and in some cases paradoxical. As our earlier discussion emphasized, London proposed that Washington join with it in affirming the Open Door principle—a proposal that the McKinley Administration rejected. Characteristically for the doctrines of American foreign policy, the Open Door concept was a unilateral declaration by the United States. Although it had followed the same principle in its own Asian diplomacy, Great Britain greeted the issuance of the Open Door policy with less than total enthusiasm. London had two principal reservations about America's new Asian policy. First, it was not the joint Anglo-American declaration that British officials desired. Second, British officials quickly perceived that—as a unilateral declaration by the United States—the Open Door policy could be invoked to limit British, no less than other foreign, moves threatening China's integrity.[30]

By contrast, the government of Japan, whose policies in the years ahead posed the most serious threat to the Open Door principle, welcomed this new American policy in East Asia. Tokyo also applauded America's subsequent intervention to suppress the Boxer Rebellion, thereby temporarily restoring the authority of the Chinese government.[31]

The Chinese reaction to the Open Door policy was noteworthy and, to the American mind, mystifying. For Americans, the Open Door policy came to be seen as a bold and decisive step by the United States in behalf of Chinese independence, political stability, and (ultimately) democracy—a policy fully consonant with the later Wilsonian concept of self-determination. Americans had no doubt that the principal ben-

29. John G. Stoessinger, *Nations in Darkness: China, Russia, America* (New York: Random House, 1971), 25–26; Leech, *In the Days of McKinley*, 516–17; Dulles, *China and America*, 112.

30. Campbell, *Anglo-American Understanding*, 167.

31. Neu, *The Troubled Encounter*, 35.

eficiary of the Open Door concept was China. Yet the Chinese interpretation of the policy was quite different. The Open Door concept
never had the appeal or mystique for Chinese that it held for Americans. For those few Americans who were aware of Chinese attitudes, it
came as a surprise to discover that after 1911 China's leaders viewed
the Open Door policy as an integral part of the hated foreign-imposed
"treaty system" which infringed upon the country's sovereignty. After
World War I, Chinese dissatisfaction with the Open Door policy and
other aspects of the treaty system became increasingly evident.[32]

The Chinese indictment of the Open Door policy contained four
principal counts. First, neither at the time of its issuance, nor in most
instances of its application after 1899, was the government of China
consulted. Far-reaching decisions had been made by foreign countries
affecting China's future without the participation of the country's
leaders.[33]

Second, China's leaders viewed the Open Door policy as fostering a
spirit of dependency and indolence on the part of the Chinese themselves. As President Chiang Kai-shek said of the policy, "The principles of the 'Open Door' and 'Territorial Integrity' only deepened the
indolent psychology of the Chinese people and increased their dependence upon foreign countries, since they now felt confident that China
would not be partitioned."[34]

Third, despite America's ostensible interest in preserving China's independence by its advocacy of the Open Door policy, America was
seeking above all to promote its own interests; the benefits accruing to
China were secondary. Even President Wilson acknowledged that Sec-

32. The Chinese assessment of the Open Door policy and other foreign concessions
infringing on China's sovereignty was highlighted during the peace negotiations following World War I. At the Paris Peace Conference, for example, the Chinese delegation
demanded sweeping changes in foreign treaty rights; in their view, such changes were
required by the Wilsonian concept of self-determination. Although failing in this broad
purpose, China did succeed in abolishing concessions held by Germany and Austria-
Hungary, thus marking the first breach in the foreign "treaty system" which had been
constructed in China over the years. Dorothy Borg, *American Policy and the Chinese
Revolution, 1925–1928* (New York: American Institute of Pacific Relations and the
Macmillan Co., 1947), 2–7.

33. Cohen has observed: "It is worth noting that Hay at no time consulted with the
Chinese government, at no time sought any expression of China's needs." Essentially,
the Open Door policy was "a means to American ends." Cohen, *America's Response to
China*, 50.

34. Chiang Kai-shek, *China's Destiny*, 124.

retary Hay's policy had envisioned "not the open door to the rights of China but the open door to the goods of America." [35]

Fourth, as other countries infringed upon the Open Door principle—and particularly, as an expansive Japan made one demand after another upon China—it became clear to China that Washington was *not* prepared to enforce the provisions of the policy against possible violators. Much as he epitomized American idealism, for example, President Wilson refused to champion China's cause at the Paris Peace Conference. In the words of one study, Wilson "sacrificed China in order to lure Japan into the League of Nations"; and the irony of course was that his own country refused to join that organization! [36] Then, as we shall see at a later stage, America was unwilling to engage in anything stronger than verbal protests after Japan committed overt aggression against China in the early 1930s.

In the light of such experiences, Chinese were likely to conclude one of two things about the Open Door policy. Either America had never intended to defend it, by force if necessary; in this case the Open Door policy was little more than a pious wish that other countries would refrain from infringing upon China's sovereignty. Or, successive administrations in Washington were basically ignorant concerning the role of power in international politics and the necessity to use it in behalf of a nation's vital diplomatic interests. Whichever interpretation was correct (and diplomatic historians tend to be divided on the question), the Open Door policy had very little value for China.

The Evolution of the Open Door Policy

In common with all general foreign policy principles, the meaning and importance of the Open Door policy were determined fully as much by its subsequent application as by the language of Secretary of State Hay's diplomatic notes. As a major doctrine of American foreign policy (although it was seldom called that), the Open Door concept had to be adapted to a broad range of new and diverse problems in Sino-American relations.

Perhaps the most striking fact about the implementation of the Open Door policy was America's inconsistency in following the prin-

35. Borg, *American Policy and the Chinese Revolution*, 7.
36. Immanuel C. Y. Hse, *The Rise of Modern China* (2nd ed.; New York: Oxford University Press, 1975), 609.

ciple. It was noteworthy, for example, that the United States had never been willing to apply the cherished Open Door concept to trade with its own possessions in the Pacific and the Caribbean. Thus the United States followed a policy of the "closed door" with regard to trade by other countries with Puerto Rico and Cuba. Nor were foreign nations allowed to trade on terms equal to those enjoyed by Americans in Hawaii and the Philippines.[37] Washington also accepted czarist Russia's dominant position in northern China, thereby perhaps making adherence to the policy's requirements impossible. The United States also acquiesced in efforts by Japan to strengthen its commercial position in Manchuria, entailing Tokyo's steady encroachments against the Open Door principle.[38]

Another significant stage in the evolution of the Open Door policy was President Theodore Roosevelt's effort to mediate the Russo-Japanese War (1904–1905). In this conflict, a resurgent Japan defeated an increasingly corrupt and ineffectual czarist government (for half a century or more thereafter, Russian naval power did not recover from the humiliating defeat administered by Japan). An avowed admirer of Japan, Theodore Roosevelt was nevertheless disturbed about the consequences of this decisive Japanese victory in Asia. In TR's view, the most desirable result would be for Japan and Russia to "remain face to face balancing each other, both weakened."[39] In brief, Roosevelt's strategy was to preserve the balance of power in the Orient, in an effort to enhance respect for the Open Door principle. Owing largely to his mediation, the resulting Treaty of Portsmouth (1905) was considerably more favorable to Russia than the military result of the conflict should have dictated.

Toward the end of his administration, President Roosevelt became increasingly concerned about growing Japanese power and its implications for the Open Door principle. Roosevelt's dramatic gesture of sending the American fleet around the world provided a graphic show of force in Japanese waters and was designed to convey Washington's

37. Iriye, *Pacific Estrangement*, 66–67.

38. Pauline Tompkins, *American-Russian Relations in the Far East* (New York: Macmillan, 1949), 20; Pratt, *A History of United States Foreign Policy*, 444.

39. For Roosevelt's views of the Russo-Japanese War, see Raymond A. Esthus, *Theodore Roosevelt and Japan* (Seattle: University of Washington Press, 1967), 37–96; the quotation from Roosevelt is from pp. 38–39. A briefer treatment is Mowry, *The Era of Theodore Roosevelt*, 181–97.

apprehensions about Tokyo's overseas ambitions. On November 30, 1908, Washington and Tokyo arrived at a new accord (called the Root-Takahira Agreement) regulating their relations.[40] In terms of its impact upon the Open Door policy, the results of this accord were clearly mixed. On the one hand, Japan agreed to respect the Open Door principle; on the other hand, the United States accepted Japan's "preferential" position in Manchuria, thereby perhaps encouraging Tokyo to violate the Open Door concept in the years ahead. Once again, Chinese authorities complained that their viewpoints had been ignored in international understandings involving the future of China.

The Chinese Revolution of 1911 was of course a momentous event in Chinese history. The imperial government was finally overthrown, and a new regime led by the prestigious Dr. Sun Yat-sen assumed power in China. President Woodrow Wilson greeted these developments with enthusiasm (the United States was the first nation to extend formal recognition to Dr. Sun's government). Yet America's moral support for the new revolutionary government of China was not translated into financial or other tangible assistance to it—a failure that may have contributed to the Chinese government's subsequent inability to assert its authority effectively and to solve China's age-old problems.[41]

Evidence that American apprehensions about Japanese ambitions in China were not unfounded was supplied by events during the First World War. Taking advantage of the European powers' preoccupation with that conflict, Tokyo chose the opportunity to make new inroads at China's expense. In its notorious "Twenty-one Demands" (1915), Japan presented Peking with a long list of new concessions, acceptance of which would reduce China to a Japanese protectorate, with the almost certain demise of the Open Door policy.

Initially, President Wilson and his advisers were reluctant to intervene in this Sino-Japanese quarrel, despite China's pleas that America uphold the Open Door policy decisively. Official and public opinion in the United States was divided: opposition to Japan's encroachments against China were counterbalanced by fears of a possible Japanese-American conflict. At length, however, the Wilson Administration

40. The text of the Root-Takahira Agreement may be found in Department of State, *United States Relations with China*, 427–28.

41. For fuller discussion of America's relations with China's revolutionary government, see Cohen, *America's Response to China*, 108; Dulles, *China and America*, 139.

concluded that Japan's challenge to the Open Door policy had to be opposed. Early in 1915, therefore, President Wilson informed Tokyo that the United States would uphold Chinese rights in the face of Japan's demands. Foreshadowing the so-called "Stimson Doctrine" of the early 1930s, Wilson notified Tokyo that the United States would not "recognize" territorial changes made in China as a result of the Twenty-one Demands. British opposition was also a significant factor in compelling the Japanese government to withdraw its ultimatum to China.[42]

Seeking to repair the breach in American-Japanese relations caused by this episode, late in 1917 Washington and Tokyo attempted to reach a new understanding delimiting their respective interests in the Orient. On November 2, 1917, the Lansing-Ishii Agreement was signed. This accord acknowledged Japan's "special interests" (although not, as Tokyo desired, its "paramount interests") in China and pledged both nations to adhere to the Open Door principle.[43]

America's "Siberian intervention" at the end of World War I was another important stage in the evolution of the Open Door policy. Following the collapse of the czarist government in 1917, followed by the new Communist government's decision to withdraw from the war, Allied forces entered Russia, ostensibly to prevent military supplies and equipment from falling into German hands. (Some interventionist efforts were unquestionably aimed also at overthrowing the Marxist regime and restoring czarist authority.) America's role in this episode was limited, involving some nine thousand troops in Siberia (vis-à-vis seventy thousand Japanese forces in the area). American intervention was directed primarily at limiting Japanese encroachments in Siberia, to the detriment of the Open Door policy.[44]

For a decade or so after the Paris Peace Conference the dominant concern of American officials with regard to China was gaining international recognition of the Open Door principle and creating conditions under which its enforcement would become a collective responsi-

42. This discussion of the episode of the Twenty-one Demands is based on Cohen, *America's Response to China*, 91–94; Dulles, *China and America*, 141–43; and Neu, *The Troubled Encounter*, 85–88.

43. For the text of the Lansing-Ishii Agreement, see Department of State, *United States Relations with China*, 437–38.

44. Betty Miller Unterberger, *America's Siberian Expedition, 1918–1920* (Durham, N.C.: Duke University Press, 1956), 230–33.

bility of the global community. Two developments during the 1920s were of outstanding importance. One was the Washington Naval Armaments Conference of 1921–1922, culminating in a Five-Power Treaty limiting naval armaments and in other accords aimed at lessening international tensions. Insofar as its relationship to the Open Door policy is concerned, the Washington Conference had a twofold, and somewhat contradictory, impact. One result was that for the first time the most influential nations of the world accepted the concept of the Open Door in China as a principle of international law. Maintenance of Chinese territorial integrity now presumably became the joint responsibility of the international community, not solely an American obligation. Yet the verdict of most commentators on the Washington Conference is that, in the long run, it was a diplomatic victory for Japan. As a result of the particular ratios of naval strength agreed upon—along with America's pledge not to fortify its Pacific possessions—in Pratt's words, Japan gained "supremacy . . . in the waters bordering Asia," thereby greatly enhancing its ability to challenge the Open Door policy in the years ahead.[45]

On August 27, 1928, the United States, France, Great Britain, Italy, Japan, and Germany, along with nine other countries, signed the Pact of Paris, popularly known as the Kellogg-Briand Pact. Eventually, most nations of the world adhered to the accord. Its key provision (Article I) bound the signatories to renounce "recourse to war for the solution of international controversies, and . . . as an instrument of national policy in their relations with one another." The agreement was widely hailed as a milestone toward global peace and international understanding. If adhered to, of course, the pact would obviate the danger that Japan or other countries would violate Chinese sovereignty. Yet the true value of the Pact of Paris was perhaps conveyed by the subsequent action of the United States Senate. After approving the agreement (with but a single dissenting vote), that body next voted a substantial military appropriation for the construction of fifteen new American cruisers to protect national security![46]

45. For a detailed analysis of the Washington Conference, see Pratt, *A History of United States Foreign Policy*, 540–56; the quotation is from p. 554.
46. For commentary on the Pact of Paris, see Pratt, *A History of United States Foreign Policy*, 535–39.

The Stimson Doctrine

The next major development in the evolution of the Open Door policy constituted one of the most complex, controversial, and perhaps least understood chapters in the annals of American diplomacy—culminating in the issuance of the Stimson Doctrine early in 1932. Beginning with the "Mukden Incident" on September 18, 1931, Japanese troops invaded Manchuria. Tokyo's disclaimers to the contrary, it soon became apparent that the ultimate objective was incorporation of China's industrial heartland into the Japanese Empire—a fear confirmed when, on February 18, 1932, Tokyo created the puppet state of "Manchukuo" in Manchurian territory under its control.

Washington's initial reaction to Japanese expansionism in Manchuria was cautious and restrained. Tokyo's action had caught most governments of the world by surprise: policy-makers needed time to decide how to respond to it. Moreover, information about events in far-off Manchuria was sketchy and perhaps unreliable; Chinese claims were contradicted by Japanese counterclaims. Officials in the world's capitals knew that Sino-Japanese relations had witnessed many conflicts; the Manchurian crisis might be simply another "Oriental quarrel" that would quickly be forgotten. American officials also believed that Japan's expansionism in Manchuria was a decision made by the military bloc in Tokyo, against the wishes of the country's "moderate" leadership, which hopefully would reassert its control. Nor did the Hoover Administration and other foreign governments desire to provoke Japan, making its leaders less receptive than ever to a negotiated resolution of the Manchurian affair. Perhaps the strongest constraint upon the Hoover Administration's diplomacy, however, was the fact that during this period policy-makers in America and other countries were increasingly preoccupied with the consequences of the Great Depression. A new regional or global conflict with Japan could only add to worldwide economic instability and distress.[47]

Initially, therefore, American officials urged China and Japan to resolve their differences by negotiations. When this approach yielded no

47. For discussions of the Hoover Administration's initial assessment of, and reaction to, Japanese expansionism in Manchuria, see Richard N. Current, *Secretary Stimson: A Study in Statecraft* (New Brunswick, N.J.: Rutgers University Press, 1954), 69; Henry L. Stimson and McGeorge Bundy, *On Active Service in Peace and War* (New

result—and as Japanese military advances continued unchecked—the administration resorted to stronger measures. As an admirer of President Theodore Roosevelt and a believer in the sanctity of international agreements, Secretary of State Henry Stimson sought British participation in an Anglo-American naval "show of force," designed to persuade Japan to honor its obligations under international law. London's reply to this suggestion was noncommittal and distinctly unenthusiastic.[48]

Concurrently, Washington endeavored to encourage a collective international response to Japanese expansionism, through the League of Nations. The United States of course did not belong to that organization. Yet, as Ferrell has expressed it, Secretary Stimson's "first thought" was to cooperate with the League of Nations in dealing with the Manchurian crisis.[49] This course, however, required the utmost finesse. Two dangers—that public opinion at home would become aroused if the United States became too closely identified with the League, and that other countries would let the United States assume the sole responsibility for dealing with Japanese expansionism—had to be avoided.

In its effort to arouse the League of Nations to take jurisdiction in the dispute, Washington dispatched an official (nonvoting) "observer" to take part in League deliberations; and it declared that the United States would act independently to support and reinforce whatever decisions the League made regarding the Manchurian question. Paradoxically, as a nonmember, in this period the United States became the foremost advocate of collective security through the League of Nations to curb Japanese aggression. In the end, the American effort failed. In the Manchurian case, as in other instances of Axis expansionism during the 1930s, the League of Nations was unable to agree upon a unified and decisive course of action. The League would consent only to the appointment of a committee to investigate Japan's

York: Harper and Row, 1948), 225–27; Herbert Feis, *The Road to Pearl Harbor* (New York: Atheneum, 1963), 7; Stimson, *The Far Eastern Crisis*, 33–34, 239; Robert H. Ferrell, *American Diplomacy in the Great Depression: Hoover-Stimson Foreign Policy, 1929–1933* (New York: W. W. Norton, 1970), 122; Elting E. Morison, *Turmoil and Tradition: A Study of the Life and Times of Henry L. Stimson* (Boston: Houghton Mifflin, 1960), 368–76.

48. Smith, *The American Diplomatic Experience*, 341.
49. Ferrell, *American Diplomacy in the Great Depression*, 139.

conduct in Manchuria and report its findings back to the organization. Beginning its inquiry in November, 1931, this committee required nearly a year to make it report. Its findings, which were highly critical of Japanese behavior, were adopted by the League of Nations Assembly in December, 1932. In the interim, the Hoover Administration concluded that reliance upon the League to engage in collective action against Japan was futile and that some members of the organization were perhaps trying to dump the Manchurian problem in America's lap.[50]

Meanwhile, the government of Japan showed no inclination to be diverted from its aggressive course by global disapprobation. Reluctantly, Secretary Stimson concluded that "mad dogs" now controlled the Japanese government and that, with the failure of League of Nations efforts, some new course was required to counter Japanese expansionism. In identical notes sent to the governments of China and Japan on January 7, 1932, Stimson proclaimed a policy of "nonrecognition" of Japan's aggrandizements in China. Adoption of the Stimson Doctrine meant that for the United States (and for all other countries ultimately accepting the nonrecognition principle), Japan's aggression had no legal or moral legitimacy; Tokyo's puppet state of Manchukuo (created out of Japanese-occupied Manchuria) was accorded no legal recognition or validity by the United States. In brief, the Stimson Doctrine affirmed the continued validity of the Open Door policy and America's devotion to it.[51]

In understanding why the Hoover Administration chose this mode of response to Japanese expansionism, it must be recognized at the outset that the Stimson Doctrine had antecedents in the American diplomatic tradition. One commentator has traced its origins back to the experience of the Inter-American System: during the 1890s, for example, the nonrecognition principle was applied to forcible annexation of Bolivian and Peruvian territories by Chile.[52] A more familiar precedent—one cited by President Hoover and his advisers—was the response of the Wilson Administration to Japan's Twenty-one Demands

50. Morison, *Turmoil and Tradition*, 375–76.
51. Stimson and Bundy, *On Active Service*, 232. The text of the Stimson Doctrine may be found in Department of State, *Foreign Relations of the United States, 1932* (Washington, D.C.: Government Printing Office, 1948), III, 7–8.
52. Pan, *American Diplomacy Concerning Manchuria*, 298–99, 306–307.

upon China during World War I. At length, Secretary of State William Jennings Bryan had declared that the United States would not recognize any change in the status of China which infringed upon American treaty rights.

Several months after the issuance of the Stimson Doctrine, a State Department official said that it had derived in large part from President Hoover's insistence that Japan honor the provisions of the Pact of Paris, outlawing war as an instrument of national policy. The Hoover-Stimson nonrecognition policy stated in effect that nations must adhere to their international legal obligations; when they fail to do so, their actions possess no legal validity or legitimacy.

Executive Officials and Japanese Aggression

An interesting aspect of America's response to the Manchurian crisis was that in time a controversy arose among officials of the Hoover Administration concerning authorship of the Stimson Doctrine. President Hoover evidently desired that the policy of nonrecognition bear his name (every major foreign policy doctrine since 1823, except the Stimson Doctrine, has carried the name of the incumbent president). To his chagrin, however, and despite occasional references to the "Hoover Doctrine" (alternatively, the "Hoover-Stimson Doctrine"), the nonrecognition policy toward Japan was usually referred to as the "Stimson Doctrine." In the presidential election of 1932, President Hoover publicly claimed credit for having promulgated a new doctrine of American foreign policy; and he later asked his cabinet members to attest that he was the real author of it. Ultimate constitutional responsibility for this and all other foreign policy declarations of course belonged to the president. Hoover also based his claim upon the fact that as early as November 9, 1931, he first suggested the nonrecognition policy as America's proper response to Japanese aggression; a few weeks later, Hoover proposed the idea to the cabinet, whose approval led to the doctrine's issuance.[53]

Yet perhaps for three primary reasons, usage decreed that the nonrecognition policy was known as the Stimson Doctrine. By his own admission, President Hoover was minimally interested in foreign af-

53. Herbert Hoover, *The Memoirs of Herbert Hoover: The Cabinet and the Presidency, 1920–1933* (2 vols.; New York: Macmillan, 1952), II, 373; Ferrell, *American Diplomacy in the Great Depression*, 168–69, 353.

fairs. Moreover, the wording of the nonrecognition policy was that of Secretary Stimson, who announced it to the world in diplomatic notes to China and Japan. But most fundamentally, as time passed—as Japanese incursions into China went unchecked—the name of Secretary Stimson became synonymous with an increasingly firm American approach to the challenge of Japanese expansionism. By contrast, President Hoover came to be identified with an isolationist and conciliatory posture toward Japan, which avoided reliance (or even the suggestion of reliance) upon economic sanctions or stronger coercive measures to curb Japanese imperialism.

President Hoover's viewpoint toward developments in Asia, and of America's appropriate response to them, was affected by a number of factors and influences. During the early 1930s Hoover was preoccupied with the consequences of the Great Depression, for the United States and for the world. In 1932, he declared that he would like "to get out" of foreign affairs altogether, in order to devote his full attention to domestic problems. Hoover's viewpoints reflected the deeply ingrained American idea that massive involvement in foreign affairs—and particularly, reliance upon force to resolve international disputes—contributed to economic dislocations and led to worldwide political instability. He was also a Quaker and thus a member of a church whose adherents deplored the use of violence in human relationships.

In Daniel M. Smith's words, President Hoover consequently "recoiled in alarm" at the prospect that the United States would use coercive measures to halt Japanese aggression.[54] To Hoover's mind, little difference existed between relying upon sanctions against Japan and war. Moreover, he believed that to be effective, sanctions had to be applied against Tokyo collectively; and the prospects for concerted international action appeared minimal. Hoover feared provoking the militant Japanese government, and he did not believe that American public opinion would support the use of coercive measures designed to curb Japanese aggression.

For these reasons, Hoover urged caution in the Manchurian crisis. The United States, he was convinced, "should not go around alone sticking pins in tigers," the tiger being the symbol of the expansive

54. Smith, *The American Diplomatic Experience*, 341.

Japanese Empire. So abhorrent was the idea of sanctions to President Hoover that (with Secretary Stimson absent in Europe) he instructed Under Secretary of State William Castle to announce publicly that the United States would refrain from imposing them as a solution to the Manchurian crisis.[55] By doing so, to the minds of many critics, Hoover reduced the Stimson Doctrine to little more than a futile verbal exercise.

Alternatively, President Hoover believed that the United States should rely upon two forces to limit Japanese incursions against China. One was what he called China's "cultural resistance" to foreign invaders and its ability to "absorb" alien influences. President Hoover also believed that "moral sanctions"—such as the condemnation of Tokyo's behavior by official and public opinion throughout the world and the legal obligations Japan had incurred (such as the Pact of Paris, outlawing war)—would ultimately restrain Japanese hegemony.[56]

Although their attitudes toward the Manchurian controversy, and foreign affairs generally, had much in common, President Hoover and Secretary of State Stimson increasingly diverged on the meaning and implications of the Stimson Doctrine—specifically, on the question of reinforcing the nonrecognition policy by imposing sanctions against Japan. For Stimson, the proper American response to Japanese encroachments against China would have been a series of measures, beginning with persuasion and diplomatic protests, followed by efforts to arouse the League of Nations to take collective action (with America acting "independently" of the League), followed next by the Stimson Doctrine, and, if necessary, by coercive measures designed to compel modifications in Japanese conduct. In time, Stimson came to believe sanctions were essential to prevent a larger war (or what President Franklin Roosevelt later called "an epidemic of lawlessness" throughout the global community). Without them—or, at a minimum, without the threat that the Stimson Doctrine might be back-stopped with sanctions—the Hoover Administration's "moral diplomacy" risked becoming little more than an impotent verbal gesture. Under these conditions it would give no real help to China; it would

---

55. Morison, *Turmoil and Tradition*, 398.
56. Hoover, *Memoirs*, II, 366–77; Ray L. Wilbur and Arthur M. Hyde (eds.), *The Hoover Policies* (New York: Charles Scribner's Sons, 1937), 582; Sidney Warren, *The President as World Leader* (New York: McGraw-Hill, 1964), 155.

not restrain Japan's aggressive tendencies; and it would seriously undermine America's own diplomacy. Looking back on the experience of the Manchurian crisis in later years, Stimson lamented that in confronting Japan, he had been armed only with "spears of straw and swords of ice."[57]

Two other factors affected the Hoover Administration's position on the Manchurian question, giving it a cautious and hesitant quality. One was the fact that within the State Department, opinion was divided on the causes of the Manchurian controversy and on how America ought to respond to it. Some State Department officials believed China itself bore a substantial degree of responsibility for the conflict; the conviction also existed that, in view of China's traditional weakness and chronic political instability, Japanese hegemony over portions of the country was "inevitable" and beyond America's control. Other State Department spokesmen, more sympathetic to China, urged their superiors to uphold the Open Door policy and to adopt an increasingly more militant stance toward Japan.[58]

A crucial limitation upon the Hoover Administration's diplomacy toward the Manchurian problem also was the attitude of the nation's military advisers. Ever since the Washington Naval Armaments Conference in the early 1920s the military power of the United States had declined vis-à-vis Japanese strength. American military leaders were plainly apprehensive about the possibility of a Japanese-American conflict. At the very time, for example, when Secretary Stimson was considering the imposition of sanctions against Japan, two admirals visited the State Department to inform him that the navy was in no position to contest Japanese power in the Pacific. In the spring of 1932, President Hoover himself proposed a further reduction in the nation's armed forces. In line with the thinking of many isolationists of the day, Hoover based his approach to national defense upon the concept of "hemispheric supremacy": military superiority within the Western Hemisphere was sufficient to protect the security of the Unit-

57. Current, *Secretary Stimson*, 104–107; Morison, *Turmoil and Tradition*, 398–402.

58. Armin Rappaport, *Henry L. Stimson and Japan, 1931–33* (Chicago: University of Chicago Press, 1963), 37; Current, *Secretary Stimson*, 86–87, 106–107; Pratt, *A History of United States Foreign Policy*, 580; Smith, *The American Diplomatic Experience*, 342.

ed States. Early in his new administration, President Franklin D. Roosevelt decided to begin a program of naval expansion, bringing American seapower up to the level permitted under the Washington Naval Armaments Treaty. Yet the United States did not reach this level of naval strength until 1942.[59]

Congressional and Public Attitudes

What part did Congress play in the Hoover Administration's diplomacy during the Manchurian crisis? As an extension of the president's constitutional power to "receive Ambassadors and other public Ministers," the recognition or nonrecognition of other governments is a prerogative of the chief executive. Yet in exercising this power, incumbent presidents are always sensitive to congressional opinion. Legislative sentiment was a potent influence upon pre–World War II American diplomacy toward Japan.

As every informed student of the modern American diplomatic record is aware, during the interwar period public and congressional opinion within the United States was profoundly isolationist and massively preoccupied with internal problems. While (as we observed in Chapter 1) isolationism defined America's approach to European issues, certain elements in the isolationist credo—such as neutrality toward great-power conflicts and preserving America's freedom of action (or unilateralism)—were clearly applicable to the question of Japanese-American relations. Deeply entrenched isolationist sentiment had prevented American membership in the League of Nations. The controversial issue of American membership in the World Court was at the forefront of President Hoover's mind during the Manchurian crisis.[60] President Hoover and his advisers therefore had to be careful not to trigger a new wave of isolationist or anti–League of Nations sentiment within the United States; nor could they risk the accusation that the American government was entering that organization through "the back door."

Leading congressional isolationists, like Sen. Burton K. Wheeler

59. Neu, *The Troubled Encounter*, 139; Rappaport, *Henry L. Stimson and Japan*, 84; Hoover, *Memoirs*, II, 338; Warren, *The President as World Leader*, 159; Willard Range, *Franklin D. Roosevelt's World Order* (Athens: University of Georgia Press, 1959), 101.
60. Hoover, *Memoirs*, II, 330.

(Democrat of Montana), had long advocated disarmament negotiations and other efforts to reduce military expenditures. Other vocal isolationists, like Sen. William E. Borah (Republican of Idaho), enthusiastically supported the Pact of Paris, in part because it created no obligation by the signatories to enforce its provisions. With President Hoover, Senator Borah had great confidence in the power of "world opinion" to curb international violence. Such spokesmen for the isolationist viewpoint applauded Hoover's desire for peace, his revulsion at the thought of using force in behalf of diplomatic goals, and his reliance upon "moral sanctions" to restrain lawbreakers such as Japan.[61]

Toward China specifically, congressional isolationists believed that traditional European reliance upon armed force to bring stability and peace to that country demonstrated the futility of such a course. Moreover, the United States had to avoid an interventionist policy in China dictated by considerations of "dollar diplomacy" and imperialism. Isolationists were persuaded that in the controversy between China and Japan, the United States ought to adhere to a position of strict neutrality toward the belligerents. As the Manchurian crisis deepened, Senator Borah believed that, if necessary, the United States should *withdraw* from China altogether to avoid giving "provocation" to the Japanese government.[62]

In view of these legislative attitudes, it is interesting to note that the Hoover Administration's decision to adopt the nonrecognition policy stemmed in some measure from a suggestion made to the president in October, 1931, by a member of Congress.[63] Legislative initiative was also important at a later stage when, on February 23, 1932, as part of his effort to intensify pressure upon an unresponsive Japanese government, Secretary Stimson sent a detailed letter to Senator Borah, chairman of the Senate Foreign Relations Committee. In the "Borah letter"—later regarded by Stimson as perhaps his most important state paper—Japan was publicly accused of being an "aggressor" nation,

61. Burton K. Wheeler, *Yankee from the West* (Garden City, N.Y.: Doubleday, 1962), 380; Claudius O. Johnson, *Borah of Idaho* (Seattle: University of Washington Press, 1967), 404; Morison, *Turmoil and Tradition*, 306.

62. For the viewpoints of leading congressional isolationists toward China, see Marian C. McKenna, *Borah* (Ann Arbor: University of Michigan Press, 1961), 345–47; Wheeler, *Yankee from the West*, 383–84; and Hoover, *Memoirs*, II, 375.

63. Rappaport, *Henry L. Stimson and Japan*, 92–93. This source identifies the legislator suggesting the Stimson Doctrine only as an unnamed congressman from Illinois.

and its acts in defiance of international legal norms and world opinion were specified in detail. Stimson's letter contained the implicit threat that, if Japan did not modify its behavior, the United States might strengthen its Pacific defenses. Senator Borah himself had contributed to drafting the letter. Yet in view of Congress' determined attachment to an isolationist position, its effect upon Japan was minimal.[64] In Robert H. Ferrell's opinion, Stimson knew full well—as did the Japanese government—that isolationist sentiment in Congress would preclude strengthening American bases or naval strength in the Pacific.[65]

This leads us to another aspect of congressional involvement in the Hoover Administration's diplomacy during the Manchurian crisis: Congress' actions in support of (or in opposition to) the Stimson Doctrine and the maintenance of the Open Door principle. One study concludes that, in line with American public opinion generally, the congressional reaction to the Stimson Doctrine was overwhelmingly favorable. If so, this was either because legislators did not understand its implications or because they agreed with President Hoover's assessment that the Stimson Doctrine was the strongest measure America was prepared to employ against aggression. As one student of Sino-American relations has observed, during the early 1930s "Congress indicated no willingness to consider Japan's actions a threat to *any* interests of the United States and in the Senate, especially, there was strong opposition to an American stand against Japan."[66]

That this verdict accurately assessed the temper of Congress was indicated by the fact that in the spring of 1932—against the Hoover Administration's expressed desires—the House of Representatives passed a bill granting independence to the Philippines. Although the Senate did not concur in this step, the action of the House conveyed an impression abroad of declining American involvement in Asian affairs and of an unwillingness to assume any responsibilities for peace and security in that region. Moreover, after the Stimson Doctrine was announced, isolationist sentiment within Congress intensified. Subsequently, Congress reduced military appropriations, and Senator Borah

64. For the text and a detailed discussion of the "Borah letter," see Stimson and Bundy, *On Active Service*, 249–54. In his biography of Borah, McKenna (p. 347) asserts that the letter was "the joint work of Hoover and Borah."

65. Ferrell, *American Diplomacy in the Great Depression*, 186.

66. Morison, *Turmoil and Tradition*, 396–97; Cohen, *America's Response to China*, 131.

announced that he would never "support any scheme of peace based upon the use of force."[67]

Shortly after he entered the White House, President Roosevelt asked Congress for authority to embargo armaments sales to aggressor nations. While the House approved this measure, the Senate demanded that arms shipments be embargoed to *all* belligerents in a war; in the Manchurian crisis, this would have prohibited arms sales to China as well as to Japan. Preferring no bill at all to this version, the Roosevelt Administration withdrew its request. Yet Congress refused to modify its position on the question until 1939.[68]

By 1937, leading congressional isolationists called upon the Roosevelt Administration to evacuate China, to relinquish the Philippines, and to avoid any step which might lead to a conflict with Japan. Still later, in 1940, when President Roosevelt sought to appoint the Republican Henry L. Stimson as secretary of war, isolationists opposed the appointment on the grounds that Stimson was an "interventionist," whose policies had led to the breach in Japanese-American relations.[69]

One final influence upon the Hoover Administration's response to the Manchurian crisis remains to be examined: the role of public opinion. A recent study has found that during the 1930s, "the modal response of the American public to the turmoil in Europe and Asia, triggered mainly by the rise of the Nazi Party in Germany and by the militarists' control of Japan, was one of withdrawal and hostility toward any overtures or suggestions of alignments with foreign governments." As late as two months before the Japanese attack against Pearl Harbor in 1941, 79 percent of the people polled said they would vote to "stay out" of any new global conflict. Feis has summarized American public attitudes toward foreign crises by saying that the people "had little hope that we could settle them and much fear that we would be caught in them."[70]

67. Stimson, *The Far Eastern Crisis,* 203; Leopold, *The Growth of American Foreign Policy,* 499.

68. James A. Robinson, *Congress and Foreign Policy-Making: A Study in Legislative Influence and Initiative* (Rev. ed.; Homewood, Ill.: Dorsey Press, 1967), 24–26.

69. Wayne S. Cole, *Senator Gerald P. Nye and American Foreign Relations* (Minneapolis: University of Minnesota Press, 1962), 119–20; Wheeler, *Yankee from the West,* 387.

70. See the polls cited, and the commentary on them, in Rita James Simon, *Public Opinion in America: 1936–1970* (Chicago: Rand McNally, 1974), 123–31. Feis, *The Road to Pearl Harbor,* 6.

With regard to the Hoover Administration's handling of the Manchurian controversy specifically, the overall public reaction to it was predominantly favorable. Japan's expansionism in patent violation of international law had deeply offended American public opinion, particularly in view of the tradition of friendship between the two countries. In Armin Rappaport's words, the Stimson Doctrine had "reflected superbly the sentiments of a majority of Americans" toward Japan's behavior. The doctrine had "voiced their revulsion to the reports of the Japanese advance . . . yet had made no commitment to aid the victims of aggression. He [Stimson] represented the outraged conscience but at no expense, or so it was thought." [71] As construed by President Hoover at least (if not by his secretary of state), the Stimson Doctrine accorded remarkably well with the prevailing temper of the American public: it dramatically registered American opposition to Japan's encroachments against China at the expense of the Open Door policy, without necessarily saying or implying that the United States was prepared to do anything concretely to challenge Japan.

Yet during the isolationist era of the early 1930s, some segments of the public found even President Hoover's approach to Japan too "interventionist" and risky. One study of the election of 1932, for example, concluded that among nine important national issues concerning Americans, only two foreign policy questions were on the list; and only one foreign issue (the tariff) ranked among the top five questions of urgent national concern. A poll by a national magazine late in 1931 showed most American newspaper editors opposed to the use of sanctions against Japan and in favor of American noninvolvement in the Manchurian conflict.[72] In fact, Jules Davids has said, suggestions by Secretary Stimson and other officials that the United States might use force against Japan were interpreted by some Americans as merely efforts by the Hoover Administration to distract attention from the Great Depression.[73]

Despite their traditional sympathy for China, many Americans were cautious about supporting China in this quarrel because of the coun-

71. Rappaport, *Henry L. Stimson and Japan*, 96.
72. Roy V. Peel and Thomas C. Donnelly, *The 1932 Campaign: An Analysis* (New York: Farrar and Rinehart, 1935), 124. See the *Literary Digest* poll taken in December, 1931, as cited in Dulles, *China and America*, 194.
73. Jules Davids, *America and the World of Our Time: U.S. Diplomacy in the Twentieth Century* (New York: Random House, 1960), 130.

try's record of long-standing political instability, economic backwardness, and feeble military resistance to Japanese intrusions. Among influential interest groups, business and commercial interests were generally pro-Japanese, believing that Japan's expansion into Manchuria might ultimately bring expanded benefits to the United States. Agricultural and commercial groups did not want to impair Japanese-American trade, which they expected would increase in the years ahead. One student of Sino-American relations has concluded, "The Stimson Doctrine had carried us as far along the road of open opposition to Japan as most Americans wanted to go, if not somewhat farther."[74]

American public opinion toward the Manchurian crisis was not of course unified. Certain prointerventionist and peace groups within the United States advocated firm resistance to Japanese aggression; to their minds, measures like the Stimson Doctrine were an inadequate response to international lawbreaking. As always, missionaries and their supporters at home sympathized with China and called upon Washington to uphold the Open Door policy. Yet these groups clearly represented a minority segment of American opinion. Their influence upon policy-making was often vitiated by divisions among them concerning the kinds of sanctions which ought to be imposed against Japan and the anticipated Japanese response to them.[75]

The Stimson Doctrine: Gains and Losses

Few episodes in American diplomatic history have elicited such diverse reactions among informed students of American foreign policy as the Hoover Administration's diplomacy toward Japan, climaxed by the issuance of the Stimson Doctrine. To some commentators, the Stimson Doctrine epitomized America's characteristic penchant for "verbal diplomacy," its tendency to engage in "moralizing" in approaching international crises, and its traditional disregard for the principles of realpolitik. At the other extreme, some commentators be-

74. A. T. Steele, *The American People and China* (New York: McGraw-Hill, 1966), 18; Neu, *The Troubled Encounter*, 135; Rappaport, *Henry L. Stimson and Japan*, 89; Foster Rhea Dulles, *Forty Years of American-Japanese Relations* (New York: Appleton-Century-Crofts, 1937), 225.

75. For the viewpoints of prointerventionist groups during the Manchurian conflict, see Rappaport, *Henry L. Stimson and Japan*, 87–89, 96; Varg, *Missionaries, Chinese, and Diplomats*, 253; and Neu, *The Troubled Encounter*, 138.

lieved the doctrine exemplified American "statesmanship" and "moral leadership" in global affairs; under prevailing circumstances, they interpreted it as a realistic, measured, and effective response to Japanese expansionism.

Critics of the Stimson Doctrine have indicted it for several basic reasons. First, in Bailey's words, it exemplified the "diplomacy of condemnation," and he described it as nothing more than a "cheap and conscience-satisfying substitute for armed intervention" by the United States. Dennett believed that the Stimson Doctrine illustrated a recurrent defect in American foreign policy. Americans will neither "put up nor shut up": they will neither "back up" moral pronouncements with force, nor will they abstain from making moral and provocative judgments upon the behavior of other nations. One of America's most experienced diplomats and informed commentators, George F. Kennan, has similarly condemned the Stimson Doctrine as illustrating an affinity for a legalistic-moralistic approach to diplomacy. During the Manchurian crisis, as in other instances of challenges to the Open Door policy, "it was assumed by American statesmen that whatever was uttered or urged in the name of moral or legal principle bore with it no specific responsibility on the part of him who urged it, even though the principle might be of questionable applicability to the situation at hand and the practical effects of adherence to it drastic and far-reaching."[76]

In more specific terms, critics condemned the Stimson Doctrine on several counts. First, it was judged a futile gesture, achieving nothing beneficial and making the United States appear politically naïve and diplomatically maladroit in the eyes of the world. Daniel M. Smith has described the Stimson Doctrine as nothing more than an exercise in "moral wrist-slapping." Elting E. Morison concluded that the doctrine achieved "nothing, even less than nothing" (with other observers, Morison was convinced that the doctrine actually had deleterious consequences for the United States).[77]

Second, the Stimson Doctrine (particularly as it might suggest the

---

76. Bailey, *A Diplomatic History of the American People*, 696; Stoessinger, *Nations in Darkness*, 40–41; George F. Kennan, *American Diplomacy: 1900–1950* (New York: New American Library, 1952), 50.

77. Smith, *The American Diplomatic Experience*, 343; Morison, *Turmoil and Tradition*, 400.

eventual imposition of sanctions against Japan) overlooked what Kennan called the "power realities in the Orient." President Hoover, Secretary of State Stimson, and other high-ranking policy-makers were well aware that the United States was in no position to contest Japanese hegemony in Asia. But even if the United States had possessed the requisite power, Ferrell believes that Secretary Stimson "overestimated the martial ardor of the American electorate."[78] Neither Congress nor public opinion was prepared to support the application of force against Japan. That being the case, advocates of realpolitik have contended, the Hoover Administration should have "accepted" Japan's commitment to an expansionist foreign policy and come to terms with it. Only by doing so—only by allaying Japan's fears and preserving Japanese-American friendship—could Washington hope to maintain the historic Open Door policy in Asia.[79]

Third, critics charged that as a unilateral American foreign policy declaration, the Stimson Doctrine left the United States exposed and "out on a limb," diplomatically. When it adopted the nonrecognition policy, the United States had moved considerably ahead of opinion in the League of Nations and in other foreign capitals. This fact meant that America was now more isolated than ever diplomatically.[80]

Fourth, perhaps the most serious indictment brought against the Stimson Doctrine by its critics was the charge that it actually harmed American diplomatic interests in Asia and elsewhere and that its effect (if certainly not its intention) was to undermine the Open Door policy. One adverse consequence of the policy, for example, was that it alienated China, impairing the long tradition of Sino-American friendship. The Chinese quickly concluded that America was unwilling to do anything tangible to curb Japanese expansionism. As one Chinese source described it, the Stimson Doctrine had the "head of a dragon and the

78. Kennan, *American Diplomacy*, 53; Ferrell, *American Diplomacy in the Great Depression*, 346.
79. This viewpoint was communicated to Washington by W. Cameron Forbes, U.S. ambassador to Japan during the early 1930s. Norman A. Graebner, "The Manchurian Crisis, 1931–32," in Robin Higham (ed.), *Intervention or Abstention: The Dilemma of American Foreign Policy* (Lexington: University of Kentucky Press, 1975), 70–71. See also Smith, *The American Diplomatic Experience*, 342–43.
80. Dorothy Borg, *The United States and the Far Eastern Crisis of 1933–1938* (Cambridge, Mass.: Harvard University Press, 1964), 9; William W. Willoughby, *The Sino-Japanese Controversy and the League of Nations* (Baltimore: Johns Hopkins University Press, 1935), 206.

tail of a rat; [it was] a mere scrap of paper unlikely to be followed by a string of battleships and hardly calculated to halt Japanese aggression."[81] Such judgments served to weaken the position of the Chinese Nationalist government and strengthened the position of anti-Western forces, like the Chinese Communists.

Not unexpectedly, critics asserted, the Stimson Doctrine also deeply offended Japan, widening the breach in Japanese-American relations. If the Hoover Administration hoped to encourage "moderate" elements in the Japanese political system, the Stimson Doctrine had the opposite result. Stimson's increasingly firm posture was, in Neu's words, "pushing Japan toward a defiant nationalism"; from Tokyo, Ambassador Joseph Grew warned his superiors that Stimson's policies were "inflaming" Japanese opinion against the United States. A British diplomat scored the Stimson Doctrine as little more than an exercise in "condemnation" of Japanese behavior; it contributed to forging "a community of the damned"—the Rome-Berlin-Tokyo Axis, formed in 1936.[82]

During the early 1930s and in the years which followed, the Hoover Administration's diplomacy toward Japan had its supporters, as well as its detractors. Defenders of the Hoover-Stimson approach made several cogent points. As Richard W. Leopold and other commentators have noted, "futile" as measures like the Stimson Doctrine might appear, their disabilities stemmed largely from factors over which the administration had little direct control—such as the ingrained isolationist sentiments of the American people, the internal preoccupation with the Great Depression, the inadequacy of the nation's armed forces, and the unwillingness of foreign governments to support the American position. In view of the limitations within which officials of the Hoover Administration operated, real courage was required for the issuance of the Stimson Doctrine. With this pronouncement, the United States took a stand virtually alone against aggression and international lawlessness. Ferrell makes the further observation that in the context of the American tradition and ethos, the Stimson Doctrine re-

81. This (unidentified) Chinese source is quoted in Rappaport, *Henry L. Stimson and Japan*, 104–105. See also Dulles, *China and America*, 201.

82. Neu, *The Troubled Encounter*, 141. See the views of Hugh Wilson, as quoted in Morison, *Turmoil and Tradition*, 369. See also Dulles, *Forty Years of American-Japanese Relations*, 222–23.

alistically and correctly insisted that moral considerations cannot be excluded from the conduct of diplomacy.[83]

Nor was the Stimson Doctrine as "ineffectual" as critics often asserted. Belated as its action was, late in 1932, the League of Nations finally denounced Japanese aggression in Manchuria. By doing so, some forty-two nations of the world in effect accepted the Stimson Doctrine and, in the years ahead, joined America in refusing to accord legitimacy to Japan's conquests.[84]

But the principal impact of the Stimson Doctrine was felt in the realm of international law. Several legal commentators have commended the doctrine as a noteworthy contribution in this field—one which, if adhered to by the members of the global community, would go far toward curbing violence throughout the international system. Thus, as Stephen C. Y. Pan has emphasized, the Stimson Doctrine affirmed that "an illegal accomplished fact [Japan's occupation of Manchuria] can remain only as long as it is physically possible for the aggressor to retain its military supremacy and politically or economically impossible for the non-recognizing state to be in a position to uphold the sanctity of international treaties and justice."[85]

Quincy Wright called attention to several important legal precepts implicit in the Stimson Doctrine, such as the idea that de facto occupation of territory does not confer title to it; that treaties contrary to the rights of third parties are null and void; and that treaties made by non-pacific means are equally void. Dennett concluded that the Stimson Doctrine "held open" the issue of Japanese aggression, preventing the matter from being settled prejudicially to China.[86] The common denominator of these judgments about the Stimson Doctrine is a concept to which political scientists have given increasing emphasis: the idea of the legitimacy of governmental behavior. As the United States discovered many years later in the Vietnam War, when they lack legitimacy, governmental actions are unlikely to be effective or to receive sustained popular support.

---

83. Leopold, *The Growth of American Foreign Policy*, 490; Dulles, *China and America*, 200–201; Pan, *American Diplomacy Concerning Manchuria*, 312; Ferrell, *American Diplomacy in the Great Depression*, 167.
84. Stimson, *The Far Eastern Crisis*, 229–30, 243.
85. Pan, *American Diplomacy Concerning Manchuria*, 317.
86. *Ibid.*, 314, 315–16.

The Demise of the Open Door Policy

The twenty-five years that followed the Manchurian crisis witnessed the steady deterioration of the Open Door policy—initially, because of continuing Japanese encroachments against China, and then as a result of the victory of Communist forces over the Nationalist government in China's civil war. Let us briefly note certain highlights in developments after 1932.

For many years before becoming president, Franklin D. Roosevelt had been fearful of Japanese intentions in Asia. Roosevelt viewed the Japanese as "the Prussians of Asia"; in time, he was convinced Japan would become America's most dangerous adversary in world affairs. Roosevelt's secretary of state, Cordell Hull, was no less apprehensive about Japan. Tokyo's record had been that of a "highway robber"; and its steady expansionism had "created a world danger extending beyond the confines of a conflict between Japan and China." Early in his administration, FDR publicly endorsed the Stimson Doctrine. In 1935, the Roosevelt Administration applied the same "nonrecognition" principle to Italy's conquest of Ethiopia. Down to the Japanese attack on Pearl Harbor on December 7, 1941, the Roosevelt Administration adhered to the position enunciated earlier by the Hoover Administration. Repeatedly, the Roosevelt Administration demanded that Japan respect the Open Door policy and its international legal obligations—demands which the militarists in control of the Japanese government refused to accept, leading them in time to decide upon the Pearl Harbor attack.[87]

Yet on balance, the Roosevelt Administration's conception of the Stimson Doctrine was much closer to President Hoover's than to the viewpoint of Secretary of State Stimson. With Hoover, Secretary Hull also had considerable faith in the ability of "world public opinion" and "moral exhortation" to curb Japanese expansionism.[88] The Roosevelt Administration could count on no public or legislative support

---

87. Range, *Franklin D. Roosevelt's World Order*, 80–81; Cordell Hull, *The Memoirs of Cordell Hull* (2 vols.; New York: Macmillan, 1948), I, 270–71; Current, *Secretary Stimson*, 121–22, 133–34; Bruce M. Russett, "FDR—Unnecessary Intervention and Deception," in Warren F. Kimball (ed.), *Franklin D. Roosevelt and the World Crisis, 1937–1945* (Lexington, Mass.: D. C. Heath, 1973), 37.

88. Neu, *The Troubled Encounter*, 145.

for sanctions against Japan. Public sentiment in the United States remained profoundly isolationist. At the end of 1936, for example, one
analysis of public opinion showed "preserving neutrality" as the *only*
foreign policy issue (out of nine issues cited) which was of urgent concern to the American people.[89] A Gallup Poll taken late in 1937 revealed that 55 percent of the American people favored neither China
nor Japan in the conflict between those two countries. In the same period, 54 percent of the people advocated America's "withdrawal"
from China, rather than intervention to protect American citizens
there; this majority grew to 70 percent by early 1938.[90]

A novel aspect of Japanese-American relations during the 1930s was
Tokyo's proclamation of its own version of a "Monroe Doctrine" for
Asia. Even before World War I, Japan had suggested that, just as the
Monroe Doctrine assured America a dominant position in the Western
Hemisphere, a comparable doctrine ought to recognize Japan's "para-
mount interest" in East Asia, specifically China. As Japanese officials
saw it, Tokyo's diplomatic slogan—"Asia for the Asiatics"—would
merely give Japan the same kind of "free hand" which, according to
Tokyo's interpretation of the Monroe Doctrine, the United States possessed in dealing with Latin America.

For some thirty years before World War II, American officials from
time to time considered Japan's claim to its own "Monroe Doctrine"—
and rejected it. To their minds, no real parallel existed between the
Monroe Doctrine and Japan's attempt to construct a "Greater East
Asia Coprosperity Sphere" at the expense of China and other vulnerable countries. The Monroe Doctrine had been issued to *protect* the
American republics (including of course the United States) from pred-
atory powers. Despite Washington's occasional resort to "big stick diplomacy" in its relations with weaker nations to the south, the United
States had not sought to invade, occupy, and annex Latin American
territory; it had not permanently impaired the sovereignty of other nations in the Western Hemisphere. Even if the Monroe Doctrine might
be interpreted as creating a United States-centered "sphere of influence" in the hemisphere, this was a very different matter from the crea-

89. See the Gallup Poll taken from December 30, 1936, to January 5, 1937, in
George Gallup, *The Gallup Poll: Public Opinion, 1935–1971* (New York: Random
House, 1972), I, 47.
90. See the Gallup Polls, in *ibid.*, 68–70, 85, 193.

tion of an empire, by reliance upon superior military force, existing for the benefit of Japan, and justified in part by Japanese claims of racial superiority.

Tokyo's attempt to rationalize its expansionism by reference to the Monroe Doctrine was of course a logically ingenious gambit. In effect, Tokyo was telling Washington that the two historic foreign policy principles of the United States—the Monroe Doctrine and the Open Door policy—were in contradiction with each other! Once Tokyo's right to its Asian "Monroe Doctrine" was conceded, giving Japan the "free hand" it sought in dealing with China, then the Open Door concept became logically and legally indefensible. American officials consistently rejected the analogy between the Monroe Doctrine and the Open Door policy; they emphasized that the basic purpose of the Monroe Doctrine had been to maintain the independence of nations in the New World.[91]

On December 8, 1941, the day after the debacle at Pearl Harbor, the United States formally declared war on Japan. Once the United States entered World War II, President Roosevelt recognized China as a major ally in the struggle against the Axis powers. In the words of former Secretary of State Dean Acheson, Roosevelt's expectation was "that China, with our help and under our tutelage, would rise from its ashes to the position of a great power and play a beneficent role after the war in bringing stability to Asia."[92] Accordingly, FDR insisted that China be included—along with Soviet Russia, France, Great Britain, and the United States—as a member of the "Big Five." These nations carried the burden of the Allied war effort; and they became the sponsors of the proposed new international order, culminating in the creation of the United Nations organization in 1945. In contrast to all other members of the UN, the Big Five exercised a veto in the organization's principal peace-keeping agency, the Security Council.

Yet if solicitude for China's future characterized American diplomacy during World War II, it is equally true that certain wartime de-

91. For a detailed exposition of Japan's claims to its own "Monroe Doctrine" in Asia, see the views of the Japanese editor Katsuji Inahara, as cited extensively in Donald M. Dozer (ed.), *The Monroe Doctrine: Its Modern Significance* (New York: Alfred A. Knopf, 1965), 139–45. America's official "answer" to Japan's contention is set forth in Hull, *The Memoirs of Cordell Hull*, I, 281–84.

92. Dean Acheson, *Present at the Creation: My Years in the State Department* (New York: W. W. Norton, 1969), 8.

cisions by the Roosevelt Administration made the emergence of a strong, politically unified, pro-Western China very difficult, if not impossible, at the end of the war. In the Chinese government's view, American support of the Chinese war effort was always limited—and inadequate. Even before Pearl Harbor, officials of the Roosevelt Administration had concluded that Nazi Germany posed the most ominous threat to American security; while dangerous, the Japanese threat was secondary. This assumption dominated American strategy during the war. As Gaddis Smith has observed, even after the humiliation of Pearl Harbor, the Roosevelt Administration turned its attention to "the defeat of Germany. This priority was maintained on the sound assumption that Germany without Japan would be as strong as ever, whereas Japan without Germany could not long stand alone."[93]

At the Yalta Conference (February 3–11, 1945)—to which Chinese representatives were not invited—Roosevelt consented to Soviet acquisition of Chinese territories. The decision was justified by officials in Washington on the ground of military necessity: for many months, Soviet entry into the Pacific war had been regarded as essential for the defeat of Japan. (It was not until some six months later that President Truman was notified during the Potsdam Conference that the atomic bomb had been successfully tested.) Yet Roosevelt's diplomacy at Yalta provided rather convincing evidence that in reality China was not a great power, that the United States still was prepared to make decisions directly affecting China's interests without consulting the Chinese government, and that such considerations as winning the war in Asia took precedence over respect for Chinese sovereignty or Chinese participation in decision-making.[94] As events turned out, however,

93. Robert A. Divine, "One World War—Japanese Aggression," in Kimball (ed.), *Franklin D. Roosevelt and the World Crisis*, 109; Gaddis Smith, *American Diplomacy During the Second World War, 1941–1945* (New York: John Wiley and Sons, 1965), 4, 7.

94. For a discussion of the Yalta negotiations as they affected China's future, see John L. Snell (ed.), *The Meaning of Yalta: Big Three Diplomacy and the New Balance of Power* (Baton Rouge: Louisiana State University Press, 1956), 143–52. With regard to Far Eastern issues, not even the State Department played any significant role in discussing them at Yalta; the decisions emerged mainly after "essentially personal talks between Roosevelt and Stalin." Snell (ed.), *The Meaning of Yalta*, 144. A former secretary of state has written, "Military considerations of the highest order dictated the President's signing of the Far Eastern agreement." For a detailed discussion of these considerations, see Edward R. Stettinius, Jr., *Roosevelt and the Russians: The Yalta Conference* (Garden City, N.Y.: Doubleday, 1949), 92–97.

with the development and use of the atomic bomb, Soviet entry into the Pacific war was not a military necessity.

Even before the issuance of the Open Door policy, factionalism and internal strife had characterized the Chinese political system—a weakness that American officials had frequently urged authorities in China to remedy.[95] By the late 1920s, strife had erupted in China between the Kuomintang, led by Chiang Kai-shek, and its principal rival, the Chinese Communist party, led by Mao Tse-tung. This conflict accelerated during the 1930s and continued throughout World War II. As the end of the war approached, each side endeavored to emerge in a politically dominant position. During and after the war, the United States made several unsuccessful efforts to "mediate" the Nationalist-Communist competition within China, culminating in Gen. George C. Marshall's "mission" to China during 1946.[96] Washington's mediatory efforts were somewhat counteracted by the fact, however, that it recognized Chiang's regime as the official government of China and provided it with massive economic and military assistance in the postwar period.

By the end of 1949, the outcome of this internal political contest had been decided: Mao Tse-tung's forces had won, driving Chiang Kai-shek and his followers into exile on Formosa (Taiwan). The Communist victory in China of course marked the end of the era of the Open Door policy. For some twenty years after 1949, Sino-American relations were characterized by extreme ideological hostility, diplomatic tensions, and during some periods (as in the Korean War) armed conflict. To China's new Marxist rulers, the Open Door policy was a relic of the colonialist past; it had been designed mainly to promote America's diplomatic interests at China's expense; it had no place in Peking's "new order" at home and abroad.

America's long attachment to the Open Door concept, however, did not disappear with the communization of China. This was indicated by the abortive attempt during the Kennedy Administration to bring about a "thaw" in Sino-American relations comparable to the détente existing with Soviet Russia. During this period, American officials

95. See the note from the State Department to the Chinese Foreign Office, on June 6, 1917, as quoted in Robert T. Pollard, *China's Foreign Relations, 1917–1931* (New York: Arno Press, 1970), 32–33.

96. America's attempt to "mediate" in the Chinese civil war is described in detail in Department of State, *United States Relations with China,* 561–695.

gave a novel twist to the traditional Open Door concept. If, from a realpolitik perspective, they realized that China was now governed by a Communist system, and that prospects for its disappearance were remote, they nonetheless called upon authorities in Peking to "keep open . . . the possibility of change"; to "foresake its venomous hatreds" of America; and to accept the idea of "a world of diversity." In brief, Washington urged the Chinese government to display greater ideological and diplomatic flexibility in its internal and external policies.[97] While such entreaties had little discernible impact upon Chinese behavior at the time, by the late 1960s (as the end of the Vietnam War could be anticipated), Chinese policies at home and abroad did begin to exhibit the kind of flexibility that American officials had advocated earlier.

It was left to the Nixon Administration to initiate the long-awaited "thaw" in Sino-American relations. This process was carried to fruition when under the Carter Administration on January 1, 1979, the United States and the People's Republic of China reestablished diplomatic relations, after a hiatus of some thirty years.

The Open Door in Retrospect

The Open Door policy is now moribund and is of interest chiefly to diplomatic historians. Although it became outmoded, the policy—and its significant application, the Stimson Doctrine—afford valuable insight into the formulation and conduct of American foreign relations. No serious doubt exists, for example, that the Open Door concept reflected certain deep-seated ideas and attitudes long associated with the American approach to foreign relations—such as a belief in the emerging sense of community among the more powerful nations of the world; the notion that expanding trade and commercial ties among nations reduce the chances of political conflict among them; a faith that "moral suasion" and legal instruments are adequate substitutes for armed force in protecting the nation's vital diplomatic interests; and an uncritical tendency to believe that resounding verbal pronouncements are equivalent to effective actions in the diplomatic realm. For devotees of realpolitik, the Stimson Doctrine, for example,

97. Roger Hilsman, *To Move a Nation: The Politics of Foreign Policy in the Administration of John F. Kennedy* (Garden City, N.Y.: Doubleday, 1967), 351–53.

exemplifies "moralism," posturing, and innumerable other deficiencies in the American approach to external problems.

From the beginning, a fundamental difference existed between the Monroe Doctrine and the Open Door policy as pillars of American foreign relations before World War II. The former, for example, expressed America's vital interest in preserving the security of the Western Hemisphere. The latter, however, expressed an imagined vital interest of the United States in the destiny of China. As we have seen, this assumed interest rested upon a number of affinities—such as American missionary and educational activities in China, trade ties between the two countries, and (after 1911) American expectations that China was evolving democratically.

Yet time and again after 1899, successive administrations in Washington made clear their unwillingness to uphold the Open Door principle by reliance upon force if necessary. In part, this reluctance stemmed from America's belief in the rapid emergence of an international community based upon "the rule of law." Down to World War II, few American officials seriously contemplated the use of force to compel respect for the Open Door policy. On one occasion, even Secretary of State John Hay actually informed the Russian ambassador that the United States had no intention of using armed force to protect China's territorial integrity.[98] Under these circumstances, the wonder is that the Open Door policy had any impact at all upon great power relationships in Asia. In John Paton Davies' words, the Open Door policy exemplified the practice of "diplomacy by incantation." More often than not after 1899, the policy degenerated into little more than verbal "exorcisms of imperialism" by indignant American officials. The policy, therefore, became a "stalactite monument of precedents, a marvel to behold but not really a workable proposition." America, concluded Bailey, was never willing to wage war in behalf of the policy, "although our government tried to act as though we would." In Foster R. Dulles' words, the Open Door policy amounted to little more than a "diplomatic posture."[99]

98. Neu, *The Troubled Encounter*, 37, 44; Dulles, *China and America*, 160–61; Cohen, *America's Response to China*, 65; Clymer, *John Hay*, 152.

99. Davies, *Dragon by the Tail*, 94; Bailey, *The Man in the Street*, 289; Dulles, *China and America*, 160.

These criticisms of the Open Door policy cannot be ignored or dismissed lightly. Throughout the policy's history, abundant evidence can be found of diplomatic naïveté, ignorance, and ineptitude by the United States. The Stimson Doctrine has been cited in the past—and it may well be cited in the future—as a leading example of how *not* to conduct foreign relations and as illustrating pitfalls to be avoided in defining and protecting the nation's vital interests abroad. Diplomatic posturing that confuses the nation's friends and encourages its enemies has little to recommend it. As was the case with the "appeasement" policies that governed the behavior of the Western powers toward the Axis powers during the late 1930s, attempts to conciliate and to "understand" aggressors may do little in the end beyond whetting their appetite for territory and insuring the outbreak of an even more destructive military conflict in the future.

Yet after taking note of its defects, it can still be said that the Open Door policy made a more positive contribution to American foreign policy—and to overall peace and security—than is sometimes supposed. Ineffectual as the Stimson Doctrine was, for example, it is noteworthy that neither the Hoover nor Roosevelt administration was willing to abandon it for the sake of harmonious relations with Japan. For ten years, Washington reiterated the Stimson Doctrine, although this contributed directly to a condition—involvement in an overseas war—which the American people obviously desired to avoid.

On numerous occasions during the 1930s, the United States might have avoided this result by taking a twofold step: rescinding the Stimson Doctrine, and recognizing Japan's "new order" in Asia. According to many critics of Hoover-Roosevelt diplomacy, relinquishing something as apparently "ineffectual" as the Stimson Doctrine would seem a small price to pay for that outcome. Yet the nation's leaders consistently refused to follow this course, even at the risk of a direct military clash with Japan.

Two explanations of this intriguing phenomenon are possible. One, widely held by diplomatic historians, is that American officials had a distorted and highly romanticized view of America's stake in preserving China's security. This led them to approach Asian questions from an emotional and sentimental, rather than from a logical and realistic, perspective.

But there is another possible explanation—one which seems fully as defensible and perhaps even more in conformity with the underlying ideological and ethical values of the American civilization. Its basic premise is that during the 1930s national policy-makers were much less politically ignorant, naïve, and blind to the "realities" of political relationships than is often supposed. (If that criticism might legitimately be made of President Hoover, it seems much less applicable to one of the master politicians of the modern age, Franklin D. Roosevelt.) American officials were not unmindful of the fact that insistence upon the Stimson Doctrine was widening the breach in Japanese-American relations. Nor were they oblivious to the Japanese government's alienation and its growing reliance upon armed force to achieve its external objectives. Why then did Washington persist in reiterating the Stimson Doctrine?

The answer is to be found in the nature of the American ethos and the ethical-ideological values intrinsic to "the American way of life." While Americans may well have romanticized their involvement in China's security, this criticism of the Open Door policy, especially given the fact that it was threatened by Japan's expansiveness, misses the main point. The crucial point often overlooked by detractors of the doctrine is that China was a kind of "test case" for the viability of international principles with which the United States has become identified in modern history and that are viewed by most Americans as fundamental to an orderly and peaceful international system. They were essentially reiterated, for example, at the end of the 1970s, when President Jimmy Carter vigorously denounced the Soviet attempt to subjugate Afghanistan (as analyzed more fully in Chapter 8). World War II was fought to vindicate the principle against the Axis powers. After the war, the ideas implicit in the Stimson Doctrine were largely embodied in the United Nations Charter and in a host of other agreements among the members of the international system in the years ahead.

What were the principles involved in America's insistence upon Japanese compliance with the Open Door policy? Several may be mentioned. There was the idea that the defenseless nations, no less than great powers, are entitled to the security and inviolability of their frontiers. There was the precept that international agreements must be adhered to in good faith; or if circumstances require changes in them, they must be modified in accordance with procedures acceptable to the international community, rather than by the unilateral actions of a militarily superior state. Still another principle integral to the Stimson Doctrine—enunciated even more forcefully when the United States issued the Truman Doctrine in 1947—was that aggression cannot be countenanced by the international community. The idea, for example, that Soviet aggression threatens the security of the United States directly may be regarded as a common denominator of every diplomatic doctrine promulgated by the United States after World War II. In whatever degree the power of the United States became "overextended" before and during and the Vietnam War, adherence to this principle has been a consistent theme of American foreign policy since World War II.

As expressed by the Stimson Doctrine, the Open Door concept called attention to another component of modern diplomacy, whose role has become increasingly pronounced in the postwar period. Amorphous and indefinable as it may be—and prone as devotees of realpolitik are to dismiss it—"world public opinion" does serve as a greater or lesser constraint upon the diplomatic activity of most nations today. The Declaration of Independence called upon the government of King George III to demonstrate "a decent respect for the opinions of mankind"; in effect, this admonition was reiterated in the Stimson Doctrine; and during the Vietnam War, the same injunction was directed at the diplomacy of the United States. A nation's "image," events since World War II have increasingly made clear, is a part of its power to influence developments abroad. As we have previously emphasized, the external policies of Japan and other nations must possess legitimacy, if they are to be accepted, rather than continually contested, by the members of the international system.

Another reason why, despite its seeming futility, the Stimson Doctrine continued to govern American relations with Japan during the 1930s was a belief that has been identified with the American Republic since its foundation. For two centuries or more, citizens of the New World have been convinced that moral principles are (or should be) applicable to political decision-making. As much as any other tenet, this idea differentiated the political ideology of the New World from that of the Old World, where realpolitik considerations frequently dictated political behavior.[100] In his famous foreign policy doctrine, President James Monroe had emphasized the difference between political concepts guiding the actions of nations in the New and the Old Worlds; and this distinction was preserved in the Stimson Doctrine.

The Stimson Doctrine, therefore, reflected America's unique political ideology and values, among which was the notion that moral and ethical canons should constrain the behavior of states, no less than of individuals. Although (as in the 1930s) it may not always be possible for the United States to *enforce* compliance with moral standards, the United States can at least insist upon the distinction between moral and immoral behavior by the members of the international system. For if this distinction is lost, most Americans believe profoundly, then insecurity will in time become the lot of every nation within the international community. Finally, we may take note of a supreme irony with respect to the Open Door policy that had become evident by the 1970s. As we have seen, at the end of the decade, the United States and the People's Republic of China decided to "normalize" their relationships. By the early 1980s, if they were not formal allies, increasingly close ties bound the two countries.

For some fifty years after 1899, as our treatment has emphasized, the Chinese were skeptical about the Open Door policy for a variety of reasons. For almost two decades after the Communist victory on the Chinese mainland, Sino-American relations were tense, and in some periods (as in the Korean War) actively hostile. Yet by the end of the 1970s, Chinese authorities had decided to broaden their diplomatic options. Having become deeply suspicious of Soviet intentions, Chinese officials became more receptive to American influence. As time passed, they concluded that China's interests were best served by opening the door to a variety of foreign influences from the United States, Japan, Western Europe, and other countries. Belatedly, the rulers of China had concluded that the earlier policy of "leaning to one side"—or exclusive reliance upon the Soviet Union—conferred few benefits upon the Chinese society. Ultimately, they concluded—as the

---

100. This is the basic thesis of Hans J. Morgenthau's *In Defense of the National Interest* (New York: Alfred A. Knopf, 1951). See especially p. 34.

Open Door policy had assumed—that China would ultimately gain from a policy of exposure to a broad range of foreign contacts. At the same time, China's leaders were determined to preserve the nation's independence and to evolve their own distinctive ideology and system of government. This development—widely applauded in the United States—represented at least a partial vindication of America's historic approach to China, as reflected in the Open Door policy.[101]

101. Dispatch by John B. Oakes, New York *Times*, December 29, 1978.

3 / The Truman Doctrine: Cold War and the Containment Strategy

*[The Truman Doctrine was] the soberest foreign policy the American peo-
ple ever undertook. . . . Promising ourselves the least glory, we won the
most permanent honor.* —Edmund Stillman and William Pfaff

*In one way or another, the pragmatic ideas of the containment thesis have
permeated Western policy ever since 1947.* —David Rees

*[After the issuance of the Truman Doctrine] Americans sensed a radical
new departure in foreign policy, and one with perhaps untold implications
for the future. Some called it the most significant development in American foreign relations since the Monroe Doctrine.*
—Sen. Arthur H. Vandenberg

On March 12, 1947, President Harry S Truman addressed a
joint session of Congress. His address—directed specifically at political and economic crises existing in Greece and Turkey—involved the
issuance of one of the most influential diplomatic principles in the nation's history. The "Truman Doctrine," as it quickly came to be called,
officially reversed America's long-standing "isolationist" stance toward European affairs, and it committed the nation to a variety of interventionist policies and programs, from Western Europe to East.
Asia.[1] The key idea in Truman's historic address was his assertion that

1. The text of Truman's address may be found in *Public Papers of the Presidents of
the United States: Harry S Truman (1947)* (Washington, D.C.: Government Printing Office, 1963), 176–80. The containment strategy, which the Truman Doctrine adopted,
was identified particularly with the ideas of the State Department official and expert on
the Soviet Union, George F. Kennan. See his widely circulated article, "The Sources of
Soviet Conduct," written under the pseudonym of X, in *Foreign Affairs*, XXV (July,
1947), 556–83; the article is also an appendix to Kennan's study on *American Diplomacy: 1900–1950* (New York: New American Library, 1952), 102–21.

"I believe that it must be the policy of the United States to support free peoples who are resisting attempted subjugation by armed minorities or by outside pressures."

The Truman Doctrine, it is no exaggeration to assert, ranks with the Monroe Doctrine as one of the two most influential foreign policy pronouncements in the annals of American diplomacy. The doctrine expressed and epitomized America's "internationalist" or "globalist" approach to foreign relations since World War II, particularly its preoccupation with the Soviet challenge. Despite the retrenchment occurring in American foreign policy for several years following the Vietnam War, the election of a Republican slate headed by Ronald Reagan in 1980 made it clear that a majority of the American people still believed in the containment principle and were, in many respects, as concerned about the problem of Soviet expansionism in the 1980s as in the late 1940s.

The Containment Policy: Context and Rationale

In common with the Monroe Doctrine and the Open Door policy, the Truman Doctrine was issued in response to a particular set of immediate and urgent circumstances confronting the United States abroad. The immediate challenge was twofold: an internal political crisis, accompanied by the threat of Soviet interventionism, in Greece; and Soviet pressure directed against the government of Turkey, aimed at achieving Moscow's centuries-old goal of controlling the Dardanelles and expanding its influence throughout the Middle East.

Traditionally, Greece had been in the British sphere of influence. Close ties had existed between the Greek monarchy and London, with the latter sometimes playing a decisive role in preserving Greek political stability. Even before World War II ended (Germany surrendered on May 7, 1945), political turmoil had erupted within Greece, between left-wing and right-wing (promonarchial) forces. Known as the National Liberation Front (or EAM), the leftist rebels contained Marxist elements, although even today doubt exists on the question of whether EAM was Communist-controlled or the degree of Soviet influence over it. Meanwhile, Great Britain emerged from World War II debilitated and on the verge of bankruptcy. In Greece, Palestine, and other settings, Britain was no longer able to assume its traditional overseas commitments. Confronted with an accelerating political crisis in Greece, as early as the fall of 1945 London had asked Washington's assistance in maintaining Greek independence against what Western officials believed was a Soviet-instigated threat. At the end of 1946, the United States sent a technical-aid mission to Greece; and in the same period the Greek government complained to the United Nations about Soviet intervention in its affairs.

Then on February 3, 1947, the American embassy in Athens notified the State Department of an impending British withdrawal from the country—a fact confirmed by the British government on February 21. Following an intensive study of the problem, the Truman Administration concluded that Greece needed assistance urgently and that only the United States was in a position to provide it.[2] In his speech to Congress, therefore, President Truman asked Congress to appropriate $250 million for aid (mainly economic assistance) to Greece.

Turkey's situation was different and presented a less urgent challenge to American policy-makers. Turko-Russian enmity of course has deep historical roots. Control over the strategic Dardanelles has been a centuries-old goal of Russian foreign policy. (In the Nazi-Soviet Pact of 1939, for example, Stalin's government had reiterated that longstanding ambition.) After the war, Soviet political intervention in the nearby Iranian provinces of Kars and Ardahan created anxieties within Turkey; and in this period, Moscow called for a revision of the Montreaux Convention of 1936, whose provisions gave the U.S.S.R. only limited access to the Mediterranean through the Turkish straits. In the early postwar period also, intensive Soviet propaganda was directed at the Turkish government. American officials discerned a steady increase in Soviet pressure against Turkey and concluded that a moderate program of aid to it was needed to preserve Turkish security.[3] On March 12, therefore, President Truman asked Congress to provide $150 million for assistance to Turkey.

2. A detailed account of the political conflict in Greece at the end of World War II and the early postwar period may be found in Hugh Seton-Watson, *The East European Revolution* (New York: Praeger, 1964), 131–39.

3. For more detailed discussion of Turkey's postwar situation, see Harry S Truman, *Memoirs: Years of Trial and Hope, 1946–1952* (Garden City, N.Y.: Doubleday, 1956), 98. An informative study of the postwar diplomatic crisis in Turkey is Bruce R. Kuniholm, *The Origins of the Cold War in the Near East: Great Power Conflict and Diplomacy in Iran, Turkey and Greece* (Princeton, N.J.: Princeton University Press, 1980). See especially pp. 359–78.

To the minds of President Truman and his advisers, the threats faced by Greece and Turkey could not be viewed in isolation. Rather they formed part of a larger and continuing pattern of postwar Soviet expansionism and interventionism throughout the non-Communist world. In France and Italy, for example, the Communist party (with Soviet backing) sought to gain political dominance. Throughout the Afro-Asian world, the Kremlin sought to identify with, and support, nationalist movements directed against Western colonial systems (Western policy-makers recalled Lenin's observation that the capitalist world would be undermined in its colonial possessions). According to Adam B. Ulam, the concept of "international communism"—or a tightly knit worldwide Communist network controlled by Moscow—was justified in the early postwar era. President Truman's advisers believed that Communist activities in Greece, along with pressures against Turkey, were Soviet-instigated. Significantly, after Marxist Yugoslavia "broke" with Stalin's government in 1948, and the Greek rebels could no longer use Yugoslavia as a "sanctuary" in their insurrection against the monarchy, the left-wing rebellion in Greece soon collapsed. As the former American ambassador to Moscow, W. Averell Harriman, expressed the prevailing viewpoint, the Greek insurrection exemplified the Kremlin's strategy of "supporting Communist parties in other countries to be in a position to take control in the postwar turmoil."[4]

In time, President Truman concluded that the United States faced as grave a challenge to its security as it had confronted during World War II. The failure to formulate an effective response to it, Truman informed Congress, would amount to "handing to the Russians vast areas of the globe"; it would jeopardize the security of the Mediterranean area; and it would directly imperil the security and well-being of the United States. Truman believed that the challenge was global in scope, and it had to be countered with a global strategy.[5]

A few weeks after his historic address to Congress, President Truman elaborated the rationale of his new foreign policy doctrine by

4. Adam B. Ulam, *The Rivals: America and Russia Since World War II* (New York: Viking Press, 1971), 278; Joseph M. Jones, *The Fifteen Weeks* (New York: Viking Press, 1955), 77; Martin F. Herz, *Beginnings of the Cold War* (New York: McGraw-Hill, 1966), 192.

5. Truman, *Memoirs: Years of Trial and Hope,* 96–106.

relating it to the principles enunciated in 1823 by President James Monroe. Truman quoted from a letter from Thomas Jefferson urging President Monroe to enunciate what came to be called the Monroe Doctrine: "Nor is the occasion to be slighted which this proposition offers of declaring our protest against the atrocious violations of the rights of nations by the interference of any one in the internal affairs of another." [6]

What purposes did President Truman hope to accomplish by issuing the foreign policy doctrine bearing his name? Most immediately of course, the paramount objective was to strengthen the security of Greece and Turkey, thereby keeping these countries out of the Soviet orbit. By the end of the 1940s—owing primarily to American assistance and to the defection of Yugoslavia from the Soviet satellite system—the internal threat to Greece had largely disappeared. By the end of the decade also, Moscow had largely abandoned its overt efforts to dominate Turkey (although of course various indirect and subtle Soviet pressures against the country continued throughout the years that followed).

Within a broader global perspective, the Truman Doctrine also attempted to redress the balance of power. According to a number of commentators, this was the dominant goal of President Truman's new foreign policy strategy. As Dean Acheson and other American officials assessed the matter, the defeat of Germany and Japan—together with the decline of British power after World War II—created a serious global imbalance that could only be corrected by adoption of a new American diplomatic strategy. In George F. Kennan's view, Soviet power was like a "fluid stream" that threatened to fill up "every nook and cranny available to it in the basin of world power." [7] Only countervailing power applied by the United States—as envisioned by the policy of containment—would curb Soviet expansionism.

John W. Spanier has interpreted the goals of the containment policy in somewhat different terms. After World War II, expansionist Soviet

6. *Ibid.*, 107.
7. Robert W. Tucker, "The American Outlook," in Robert E. Osgood, *et al.*, *America and the World: From the Truman Doctrine to Vietnam* (Baltimore: Johns Hopkins University Press, 1970), 43; George F. Kennan *Memoirs (1925–1950)* (New York: Bantam, 1969), 262; Ronald J. Stupak, *The Shaping of Foreign Policy: The Role of the Secretary of State as Seen by Dean Acheson* (Indianapolis: Odyssey Press, 1969), 3; Kennan, "The Sources of Soviet Conduct," in *American Diplomacy*, 102–21.

moves threatened to give Moscow control of the "heartland" of Eurasia. As was true of the Axis (particularly the German) threat, this development would seriously endanger the security of the West. The Truman Doctrine was, therefore, promulgated to avert this ominous prospect.[8]

Another goal implicit in the Truman Doctrine was to notify the world that (in contrast to American behavior after World War I) the United States was prepared to accept the "leadership" position that its power and influence demanded. The Truman Doctrine signified realization that the long-standing American dream of "one world" was moribund. After World War II, it was evident that "two worlds" existed: a Communist-controlled system directed by Moscow; and a hitherto leaderless and dispirited non-Communist world whose security and independence were in grave jeopardy.[9]

Expressed differently, a dominant purpose of the Truman Doctrine was to announce to the world—and even perhaps to many Americans—that the historic era of American isolationism had ended. At first glance, this might seem an unnecessary development. The United States, for example, had taken the lead in planning and creating the United Nations and (vis-à-vis American behavior toward the earlier League of Nations) was an active member of it. Yet under both the Roosevelt and Truman administrations, many Americans unquestionably believed that America could now "turn over" troublesome international questions to this nascent organization—thereby relieving the United States of any further direct responsibility for them! Moreover, once the war had ended, the demobilization (more accurately perhaps, the disintegration) of America's armed forces presaged a return to America's classical isolationist position. By contrast, Soviet diplomatic moves in this period were based upon Moscow's maintenance of a large and powerful military establishment to support its political objectives.[10]

Down to early 1947 also—as exemplified by attitudes in the Repub-

8. John W. Spanier, *American Foreign Policy Since World War II* (4th ed.; New York: Praeger, 1971), 3, 21–39.
9. Walter Millis (ed.), *The Forrestal Diaries* (New York: Viking Press, 1951), 307.
10. See, for example, the discussions of Soviet assessments of the forces shaping American postwar foreign policy in Ulam, *The Rivals*, 32–33; and in Frederick C. Barghoorn, *The Soviet Image of the United States* (New York: Harcourt, Brace, 1950), 87–113.

lican-controlled Eightieth Congress, elected in 1946—Americans were once again preoccupied by internal problems. Consequently, in his address to Congress President Truman believed it necessary to warn Americans about reverting to a "Fortress America" concept, whose basic premise was that the United States could successfully preserve its security and well-being while insecurity and political upheaval characterized the rest of the world. This concept was identified with ex-President Hoover and other right-wing neoisolationists in the years ahead.[11] As Ernest Lefever has expressed it, by announcing the Truman Doctrine the United States signified its willingness to accept "the leadership of the free world" and to build "a viable Western coalition."[12]

Yet in conformity with earlier doctrinal pronouncements in American diplomacy—such as the Monroe Doctrine and the Open Door policy—the Truman Doctrine was also consonant with certain deeply held ideas and traditions identified with the American society. While the doctrine admittedly committed the United States to an "internationalist" or "interventionist" foreign policy, for example, a conspicuous feature of it was its essentially defensive nature. As Kennan, Truman, and other officials recognized, America was not prepared to play the kind of hegemonial role in global affairs comparable to Soviet behavior in Eastern Europe and other settings. Accordingly, the containment strategy contemplated America's use of counterforce to restrain Soviet expansionist moves. In effect, this approach left the diplomatic initiative to the Kremlin; Soviet officials would largely determine whether the United States invoked the Truman Doctrine.

Moreover, the containment policy anticipated the selective and eclectic application of American power overseas. The policy thus reflected another typically American behavior pattern: pragmatism, or the formulation of national policy largely in response to concrete and changing circumstances. To the mind of its principal architect, George F. Kennan, containment was not envisioned as a static policy; he urged policy-makers to utilize American power selectively and adroitly abroad, presumably under conditions favoring a successful outcome.

11. Truman, *Memoirs: Years of Trial and Hope*, 102. A more detailed analysis of the "Fortress America" idea may be found in Cecil V. Crabb, Jr., *Policy-Makers and Critics: Conflicting Theories of American Foreign Policy* (New York: Praeger, 1976), 228–30.

12. Ernest Lefever, *Ethics and United States Foreign Policy* (New York: Meridian Books, 1957), 42.

Implicitly, his strategy acknowledged that American power was limited; that the United States was not (as some Americans after 1947 apparently believed) omnipotent; and that the nation's power must be applied abroad with discrimination and acumen, if Washington's purposes were to be achieved.

As "negative" as the Truman Doctrine might appear, the coin of containment clearly had another side. The logical corollary of Kennan's ideas was that the United States would *not* engage in "preventive war" or some other kind of diplomatic "offensive" against its ideological enemy. By adopting containment as its diplomatic principle, the United States did *not* seek to dismantle the Soviet empire; it did not embark upon a campaign to "liberate" Eastern Europe or other areas from Communist domination. In effect, the doctrine committed the United States to contest any new effort by the Soviet Union to enlarge its orbit, at the expense of the non-Communist world. One authority has said of the Truman Doctrine as it was originally conceived, that it was "not only defensive in character but was also motivated by the traditional liberal principles of self-government, self-determination, and non-interference. American power was to be employed in a discriminating fashion on behalf of the independence and self-esteem of established powers in Europe and Asia."[13]

In other respects also, the Truman Doctrine reflected underlying American ideological concepts and values. It was not a provocative or "adventurist" foreign policy: it did not contemplate establishment of American hegemony over Greece, Turkey, and other countries threatened by Soviet expansionism. On a global basis, it did not anticipate creation of a *Pax Americana* or an American empire over weaker societies. The proclaimed goal of the Truman Doctrine was the independence of nations not currently within the Soviet orbit—an idea clearly harmonious with the older Wilson doctrine of self-determination and with the goals contained in the United Nations Charter. At intervals after 1947, for example, both Greece and Turkey time and again demonstrated their independence from dictation by the United States.

As the oldest functioning democracy on the globe, the United States has always been interested in the future and growth of democracy throughout the international system. This concern was not missing

13. Michael H. Armacost, *The Foreign Relations of the United States* (Belmont, Calif.: Dickenson Press, 1969), 58.

from President Truman's historic foreign policy proclamation. The Truman Administration was aware that Greece was governed by a monarchy; and a political victory by right-wing political forces within the country was not likely in the short run to enhance the prospects for democracy within the society. Nor was Turkey a democratic country according to criteria normally applied by Americans. Ever since the era of "Ataturk" (Mustafa Kemmal) after World War I, the reform of Turkish society had been carried out by authoritarian methods; and periodically, the Turkish armed forces had served as the arbiters of the Turkish political system.

Under these circumstances, why then did President Truman pledge the United States to defend "free peoples" in Greece, Turkey, and other settings? President Truman and his advisers were convinced of two pivotal facts. First, the democratic ideal existed in both countries, and it was in America's interests to encourage its realization. Second, however deficient the governments of Greece and Turkey might be in meeting democratic tests in 1947, they would have no chance of becoming more democratic if they passed behind the Iron Curtain. Neither in these nor other countries did the Truman Doctrine guarantee the emergence of democracy. What could be guaranteed, as the Truman White House assessed the problem, was that America's failure to help these countries would result in the imposition of Soviet hegemony over them, giving them no chance of evolving in a democratic direction.[14]

Another striking feature of the Truman Doctrine was its emphasis upon economic reconstruction as the key to political stability and enhanced security for endangered countries. Most of the funds under the Greek-Turkish Aid Program were devoted to this purpose; American military aid was limited in scope and duration. An underlying premise of America's new strategy was the idea that a country's ability to withstand internal and external threats derived ultimately from its economic and social stability. American assistance was designed to pro-

---

14. The interested reader is encouraged to read the full text of Truman's speech to Congress on March 12, 1947, as reprinted in *Public Papers of the Presidents of the United States: Harry S. Truman*, 176–80. The leitmotif of Truman's approach on the question of democracy within Greece and Turkey is conveyed by his statement that America must assist Greece "*to become* a self-supporting and self-respecting democracy" (italics inserted). Again, he noted in reference to Greece: "No government is perfect. One of the chief virtues of a democracy, however, is that its defects are always visible and under democratic processes can be pointed out and corrected."

mote such stability, thereby enhancing the ability of the society itself to maintain its independence.

Two more long-range goals of containment remain to be identified. As former Secretary of State Acheson later observed about the Greek crisis: "Like apples in a barrel infected by one rotten one, the corruption of Greece would infect Iran and all [countries] to the east. It would also carry infection to Africa through Asia Minor and Egypt, and to Europe through Italy, and France. . . . The Soviet Union was playing one of the greatest gambles in history at minimal cost. . . . We and we alone were in a position to break up the play."[15]

As a logical extension of its conviction that the threats to Greece and Turkey were part of a coordinated Soviet effort to expand its hegemony wherever possible, the Truman Administration expected that successful implementation of the Greek-Turkish Aid Program would have a general deterrent effect upon Soviet behavior. In Kennan's words, one purpose of the containment strategy was to convey the impression broadly to other societies that communism was not "the wave of the future" or in any wise "inevitable."[16] Insofar as reality—rather than blind fanaticism, ideological rigidity, or other factors—guided Soviet foreign policy, the successful frustration of Soviet designs against Greece and Turkey ought to convince the Kremlin that it could not pursue its expansionist course without grave risks to itself and to the civilized world. As a later concept expressed it, the United States sought to convince the Kremlin that its interests were better served by a policy of détente toward non-Communist countries.

Far off in the future lay another goal of containment, as formulated by Kennan. This was what he called the "gradual mellowing" of Soviet power, leading perhaps ultimately to the total disappearance of the Communist regime within the U.S.S.R. The successful frustration of expansionist Soviet foreign policy goals would produce "strains" in the Soviet system accelerating this decay. At a minimum, containment would "force upon the Kremlin a far greater degree of moderation and circumspection than it has had to observe in recent years"; it would "promote tendencies which must eventually find their outlet in either the break-up or the gradual mellowing of Soviet power."[17]

15. Dean Acheson, *Present at the Creation: My Years in the State Department* (New York: W. W. Norton, 1969), 219.
16. Kennan, *Memoirs*, 335.
17. Kennan, "The Sources of Soviet Conduct," in *American Diplomacy*, 119–20.

Antecedents of the Containment Policy

The Truman Doctrine, one student of postwar American diplomacy has said, "represented no abrupt departure in U.S. policy; rather, [it] marked the culmination of trends that had begun as early as 1945." Other commentators are convinced that the antecedents of the Truman Doctrine can be traced back before World War II. As with any war, the Cold War had both long-range and short-range causes. David Rees believes that the Cold War grew out of the Bolshevik Revolution of 1917 and the Western response to it. Its more immediate outbreak occurred after the decisive Battle of Stalingrad in 1943, when the Soviet Red Army began the westward advance which eventually carried it into the center of Europe.[18]

Before and during World War II, a number of prominent Americans—such as Henry Luce, the publisher of *Time* magazine—called for the creation of a *Pax Americana* to preserve global peace and security after the Axis defeat. Other influential Americans, cognizant of the nation's failure to contain Axis expansionism during the 1930s, believed that in the postwar era, the United States must play a decisive role in global decision-making. The lessons of the "appeasement era" made an indelible impression upon American policy-makers for a generation or so after World War II.[19]

Among certain "revisionist" historians of the Cold War, the Soviet-American conflict could be traced to the alleged change in American foreign policy occurring after Harry S Truman entered the White House on April 12, 1945. This interpretation, however, overlooks the fact that the Truman Doctrine was plainly foreshadowed by the viewpoints and deeds of President Franklin D. Roosevelt in the months immediately preceding his death. As early as 1942, for example, FDR had cautioned the British government against possible Soviet demands in Europe during and after the war. President Truman asserted that FDR had formulated a rudimentary containment strategy some two

18. Susan M. Hartmann, *Truman and the 80th Congress* (Columbia, Mo.: University of Missouri Press, 1971), 53; David Rees, *The Age of Containment: The Cold War* (New York: St. Martin's Press, 1967), 9.

19. Lloyd C. Gardner, *Architects of Illusion: Men and Ideas in American Foreign Policy, 1941–1949* (Chicago: Quadrangle Books, 1970), 3–25; Arthur H. Vandenberg, Jr. (ed.), *The Private Papers of Senator Vandenberg* (Boston: Houghton Mifflin, 1952), 342.

years before the policy was officially promulgated.[20] After the Yalta Conference early in 1945, Roosevelt wondered whether Stalin's government had perpetrated a "monstrous fraud" against the Allies.[21] On the day he died, FDR wrote British Prime Minister Winston Churchill that the United States and Britain must be "firm" in resisting Stalin's demands and must insist that Moscow honor its wartime pledges.[22]

As a United States senator, Harry Truman had long been known for his suspicions of Soviet motives and behavior. (Early in World War II, Senator Truman called for the Nazi and Soviet dictatorships to fight it out, hopefully ridding the world of two expansive totalitarian systems![23]) After observing Soviet machinations in Eastern Europe, Iran, and other locales, a few months after he assumed the presidency Truman had a face-to-face meeting with Soviet Foreign Minister V. M. Molotov. In remarkably blunt language, Truman informed Molotov that the United States expected the Kremlin to honor its wartime pledges. Molotov later complained that, in his entire diplomatic career, he had never been talked to so forthrightly![24] From Moscow, Ambassador Harriman cautioned his superiors about the possibility of a "barbarian invasion" from the east and urged them to formulate a policy for responding effectively to it. Harriman's subordinate, George F. Kennan, also repeatedly warned Washington about Moscow's postwar ambitions.[25]

By the period of the Potsdam Conference (July 17–August 2, 1945) the existence of serious Soviet-American differences could hardly be concealed. According to one high-ranking official of the Truman Ad-

20. Gardner, *Architects of Illusion*, 33–34, 54–55.

21. See the discussion of the Yalta Conference and its aftermath in Robert E. Sherwood, *Roosevelt and Hopkins* (2 vols.; New York: Bantam, 1950), II, 490–531.

22. Herbert Druks, *Harry S. Truman and the Russians: 1945–1953* (New York: Robert Speller, 1966), 31; William E. Griffith, *Cold War and Coexistence: Russia, China, and the United States* (Englewood Cliffs, N.J.: Prentice-Hall, 1971), 36.

23. On the day following the German attack against Soviet Russia, Senator Truman urged the Roosevelt Administration to support Germany, if Russia were winning the war, and to support the U.S.S.R., if Germany were winning the war. That way, both totalitarian regimes might be eliminated. D. F. Fleming, *The Cold War and Its Origins: 1917–1960* (2 vols.; Garden City, N.Y.: Doubleday, 1961), I, 135.

24. Druks, *Harry S. Truman and the Russians*, 36–37, 106, 115; Gardner, *Architects of Illusion*, 206.

25. Gardner, *Architects of Illusion*, 60. See the various dispatches which Kennan sent to the State Department during and after World War II, dealing with the Soviet Union's foreign policy goals and tactics, as reproduced in his *Memoirs*, 531–604.

ministration, this meeting brought "into world focus the struggle of two great ideas—the Anglo-Saxon democratic principles of government and the aggressive and expansionist police-state tactics of Stalinist Russia. It was the beginning of the 'cold war.' " As a result of the conference, President Truman became persuaded that Soviet Russia expected an American economic collapse after the war. On that premise, the Kremlin had adopted a policy of global expansionism. Faced with this prospect, Truman believed America had only one choice. Its policy had to be based on the principle that "force is the only thing that the Russians understand."[26]

Antecedents of the Truman Doctrine can also be found in the increasingly firm stance which the Truman Administration took in the prolonged negotiations of the peace treaties for the minor Axis powers throughout 1945 and 1946. Confronted with Moscow's intractability and a series of one Soviet demand after another in these sessions, American officials became convinced that expansionism was the keynote of Soviet foreign policy. Asserting that "I'm tired of babying the Soviets," Truman instructed Secretary of State James F. Byrnes that Moscow's expansionist behavior must be countered "with an iron fist and strong language"; otherwise, "another war is in the making." Sen. Arthur H. Vandenberg, who played a leading role in negotiating these treaties, believed that America faced "Communism-on-the-march" throughout the world; the Kremlin expected nothing less than America's "unconditional surrender" to its policy of "ruthless expansionism." On February 28, 1946, Secretary of State Byrnes delivered what amounted to an ultimatum to the Kremlin regarding Communist intrigues in Iran. In a statement clearly anticipating the Truman Doctrine, Byrnes asserted that America "will not and cannot stand aloof if force or threat of force is used contrary to the purposes and principles of the [UN] Charter."[27]

Throughout 1946 and early 1947, both official and public opinion in the United States visibly hardened toward the Soviet Union. A landmark on the road to the Truman Doctrine was former British Prime Minister Winston Churchill's speech at Fulton, Missouri, on March 8,

26. William D. Leahy, *I Was There* (New York: McGraw-Hill, 1950), 429; Gardner, *Architects of Illusion*, 56.
27. Gardner, *Architects of Illusion*, 103; Vandenberg (ed.), *The Private Papers of Senator Vandenberg*, 262, 269, 286; Jones, *The Fifteen Weeks*, 54.

1946. In unusually graphic language, Churchill urged Americans to acknowledge that an Iron Curtain had descended across Europe. To Churchill's mind, the contest between communism and democracy had now become the pivotal fact of contemporary global politics— and he urged Americans to respond decisively to that challenge.[28] A few months later, Churchill's views were largely confirmed by the former Soviet foreign minister, Maxim Litvinov (who had been an indefatigible champion of "collective security" at the League of Nations). In Litvinov's view, "a conflict between the Communist and capitalist worlds is inevitable." Failure by the West to counter Soviet demands would merely result in even more ambitious Soviet demands in the future. In the same period, President Truman advised both Turkey and Iran to resist Soviet pressures; and he ordered units of the U.S. Navy to the Mediterranean, as a symbol of American concern about Soviet expansionism. By August, 1946, Truman's State Department advisers had concluded that Moscow was seeking to subjugate Turkey as an initial step in its effort to gain control over Greece.[29]

By the latter part of 1946, therefore, many of the elements later contained in the Truman Doctrine were already present in American foreign policy. In October President Truman declared that the continued independence of Greece was vital to the security of the United States. A few weeks later, Under Secretary of State Dean Acheson recommended that Washington undertake a limited program of arms-aid to Greece and Turkey. By the end of 1946, Susan M. Hartmann has said, the Truman Administration "had developed a policy of verbal and diplomatic firmness toward the Soviet Union but had reached no decisions about deploying U.S. power to bolster this approach." This view was echoed by President Truman himself, who later said that the doctrine bearing his name had not emerged suddenly and without forewarning. In reality, "it had been developing ever since the Germans surrendered. And it finally got to the point where we had to state our

28. For commentary on Churchill's speech, see Robert G. Kaiser, *Cold Winter— Cold War* (New York: Stein and Day, 1974), 136–37; and Gardner, *Architects of Illusion*, 105.

29. Kaiser, *Cold Winter—Cold War*, 12–13; Druks, *Harry S. Truman and the Russians*, 118–20; Millis (ed.), *The Forrestal Diaries*, 192; Jones, *The Fifteen Weeks*, 59–62.

case to the world."[30] By early 1947, it seems accurate to say, a kind of tacit understanding existed among Great Britain, the United States, Greece, and Turkey, that the latter two countries should henceforth look to Washington for economic and military assistance for the preservation of their independence.

Traumatic as it was for many members of Congress and some segments of American public opinion, the Truman Doctrine could hardly be called a major innovation in American foreign relations. For over two years—as Soviet-American relations steadily deteriorated—American diplomacy had been evolving toward the adoption of a counterstrategy for dealing with Soviet expansionism. Moreover (as our later discussion of public opinion will show), the doctrine enjoyed the overwhelming support of the American people. Hartmann's verdict—that the Truman Doctrine "represented no abrupt departure in U.S. policy" but was instead "the culmination of trends that had begun as early as 1945"—must, therefore, be viewed as substantially correct.[31]

The Formulation of the Truman Doctrine

An official of the Truman Administration who was intimately involved in decision-making on the Truman Doctrine said that in its final form the doctrine was the product of "many minds." President Truman's message to Congress "reflected a unanimity and spontaneity of view rare in the government."[32] On all sides the president's advisers urged him to respond decisively to the crises facing Greece and Turkey. Long known as a foe of communism, Truman was inherently receptive to the viewpoints of those advisers who urged him to resist further Communist inroads; and in some instances, his own predelictions in the direction of "patience and firmness" were even more pronounced than those of his subordinates (such as Secretary of State James F. Byrnes).[33] In early drafts of his speech enunciating the Truman Doctrine, for ex-

30. Kaiser, *Cold Winter—Cold War*, 181; Millis (ed.), *The Forrestal Diaries*, 216; Hartmann, *Truman and the 80th Congress*, 48; Gardner, *Architects of Illusion*, 206.

31. Hartmann, *Truman and the 80th Congress*, 53.

32. Jones, *The Fifteen Weeks*, 148.

33. See, for example, Barton J. Bernstein, "American Foreign Policy and the Origins of the Cold War," in Barton J. Bernstein (ed.), *Politics and Policies of the Truman Administration* (Chicago: Quadrangle Books, 1970), 23.

ample, the president changed the language from it "should" be the policy of the United States to resist aggression, to it "must" be the policy of the United States to adopt this policy. In his own words, Truman wanted "no hedging" in his forthcoming message to Congress concerning America's intended course of action.[34]

Moreover, in accordance with his constitutional role as manager of American foreign relations, President Truman himself made the historic decision to assist Greece and Turkey. At the end of February, Truman met with congressional leaders, informing them of "the situation and of the nature of the decision I had to make. . . . I told the group that I had decided to extend aid to Greece and Turkey and that I hoped Congress would provide the means to make this aid timely and sufficient." As Truman envisioned it, assistance to Greece and Turkey would be "only the beginning" of a new era in American foreign relations.[35]

As our discussion has suggested, President Truman's inclinations encountered little or no opposition from his advisers. State Department experts on Soviet behavior—like George F. Kennan and Charles E. Bohlen—supported Truman's increasingly firm stance in dealing with Moscow as consonant with their own policy recommendations. Former ambassador to Moscow Averell Harriman joined in urging the White House to resist Soviet Russia's hegemonial moves in the postwar era. Secretary of State James Byrnes was convinced that after the war, the Soviet state had reverted to traditional czarist behavior patterns in dealing with other countries. In his view, "Only the personalities and the tactics" of the Kremlin had changed. Byrnes referred to the verdict of a former newspaper reporter—Karl Marx—who had urged the great powers of Europe to "hold firm" against czarist encroachments.[36] Byrnes's successor, Secretary of State George C. Marshall, echoed this judgment. To Marshall's mind, if the United States "stood up" to the Kremlin, in time this would induce significant changes in Soviet external behavior. Another influential presidential

34. Truman, *Memoirs: Years of Trial and Hope*, 105.

35. *Ibid.*, 102–104.

36. See Byrnes's memoirs, *Speaking Frankly* (New York: Harper and Row, 1947), 283–97; and W. Averell Harriman and Elie Abel, *Special Envoy to Churchill and Stalin, 1941–1946* (New York: Random House, 1975), 370, 414–15. Harriman's views are set forth more fully in Averell Harriman, *Peace with Russia?* (New York: Simon and Schuster, 1959).

adviser, Clark Clifford, believed that Russia must be made to understand that Americans "are too strong to be beaten and too determined to be frightened." Clifford called for primary reliance upon the provision of economic assistance to endangered countries to contain Soviet influence.[37]

Spokesmen for two other groups of executive officials—the president's military and economic advisers—advocated a comparable response to the Soviet challenge. Fleet Admiral William D. Leahy, for example, had long expressed concern about the ominous strategic implications of Soviet expansionism and urged unequivocal American opposition to it. Secretary of Defense James Forrestal similarly favored American resistance to communism in Greece, Turkey, and other locales.[38]

Economic considerations also provided a rationale for the Truman Doctrine. During World War II, several executive officials expressed the conviction that a peaceful and secure international order required an "open world" economically, providing maximum opportunity for American trade and investment. President Truman's economic advisers urged him to reject a "spheres of influence" division of the world with the Soviet Union that would, in effect, close Eastern Europe to trade and commerce with the West.[39] (This reasoning was remarkably similar to that advanced in earlier years to support the Open Door policy toward China, as explained more fully in Chapter 2.)

In view of this consensus among his advisers, it is not surprising that at a meeting on March 7, 1947, President Truman's cabinet agreed that the United States must assist Greece and Turkey, provided Congress and public opinion approved this course. As Truman candidly admitted, he ultimately made the decision to adopt the containment strategy.[40] It remained to communicate the proposed course of action to the American people and Congress.

By many criteria, the congressional environment for this momentous turnaround in historic American foreign policy could hardly have been less favorable. Difficult as it may be for contemporary Ameri-

37. Kaiser, Cold Winter—Cold War, 151, 179–80, 192.
38. Fleming, The Cold War and Its Origins, I, 440–41; Millis (ed.), The Forrestal Diaries, 263.
39. Gardner, Architects of Illusion, 28, 71–73, 212.
40. The Forrestal Diaries, 251; Hartmann, Truman and the 80th Congress, 58.

cans to comprehend it, President Truman's speech on March 12, 1947, stunned the assembled House and Senate. Three groups of legislators were especially dismayed by the president's message.

Political conservatives—who, after the congressional elections of 1946, comprised a majority of the legislature—were interested above all in reducing taxes and the level of governmental spending. Curtailing military expenses would go a long way toward achieving the goal. A second group of legislators (that of course included some members of the first group) had long been concerned about the Truman Administration's "softness" in dealing with the Soviet Union. While they approved of any step by the administration to resist Soviet demands, they were nonetheless skeptical about two aspects of the Truman Doctrine. Right-wing critics, for example, complained that the doctrine did not go far enough in committing the United States unequivocally to an anti-Communist course (some critics called containment a "no win" policy for America). Other critics of containment applauded this new "toughness" in America's stance toward Moscow; but they were reluctant to provide the Truman Administration with the means needed to implement the Truman Doctrine successfully.[41]

A third group of legislators—consisting mainly of political liberals—expressed different reservations about the Truman Doctrine. Among this group, a fear had long been expressed that the United States was becoming an "imperial" power. The idea that America was assuming Britain's age-old commitments in Greece and elsewhere reinforced this apprehension. A variant fear was that by adopting containment, the United States was really seeking to establish a dominant position economically in the Mediterranean and ultimately perhaps in the Middle East oil industry.[42]

Legislative doubts about the Truman Doctrine were exemplified by the skepticism exhibited by Sen. Robert A. Taft (Republican of Ohio), popularly known as "Mr. Republican." Acknowledging that he was no expert in foreign affairs (Taft's role in this regard was overshadowed

41. Paul Y. Hammond, *The Cold War Years: American Foreign Policy Since 1945* (New York: Harcourt, Brace and World, 1969), 22; Hartmann, *Truman and the 80th Congress*, 58, 215; Druks, *Harry S. Truman and the Russians*, 124; H. Bradford Westerfield, *Foreign Policy and Party Politics: From Pearl Harbor to Korea* (New Haven: Yale University Press, 1955), 205–22.
42. Acheson, *Present at the Creation*, 221–22.

by his colleague, Sen. Arthur H. Vandenberg, Republican of Michigan, who was a tireless advocate of "bipartisan" cooperation between Republicans and Democrats in foreign affairs), Senator Taft had long been an outspoken opponent both of communism and of what he viewed as the Truman Administration's ineffectual response to the Communist global challenge. Even so, Taft had many reservations about the containment strategy. Taft did not, for example, favor long-range American commitments to Greece, Turkey, and other countries facing a Communist threat. (In later years, Taft advocated the "Fortress America" concept proposed by ex-President Herbert Hoover.) Senator Taft also opposed military conscription and other measures he believed would be required to implement the containment policy.

Yet in the end—in company with a majority in the House and Senate—Taft supported the Greek-Turkish Aid Program and the overall containment strategy. Taft and other Republicans acknowledged that the program was a bipartisan measure in which his colleagues, like Senator Vandenberg, had participated. As his biographer observed, Taft also lacked a "cogent alternative" to President Truman's proposal. Most crucially perhaps, Taft and other legislators recognized that— after President Truman's dramatic presentation to a joint session of Congress—Congress could not reject his request without repudiating presidential leadership in the eyes of the world. Neither Senator Taft nor other critics of containment were prepared to face the consequences of this action.[43]

Favorable legislative action on the president's request was also assured by intensive White House efforts to build a bipartisan foundation under the Truman Doctrine. On February 27, for example, congressional leaders were summoned to the White House for a briefing on conditions in Greece and Turkey and on the administration's proposed response to them. Although then and later, legislators complained that President Truman had presented Congress with a diplomatic *fait accompli*, they also realized that they had little choice except to approve his program. The United States, said Senator Vandenberg, confronted "a condition and not a theory" in Greece and Turkey. Prolonged legislative debate and indecision would intensify

43. James T. Patterson, *Mr. Republican: A Biography of Robert A. Taft* (Boston: Houghton Mifflin, 1972), 369–72; Herz, *Beginnings of the Cold War*, 194.

the crises in both countries; and, as Vandenberg declared on the floor of the Senate, it would likely set in motion a "chain reaction," resulting in Communist-instigated threats to other countries as well. No legislators present at the White House meeting challenged the conviction of executive officials that American security was directly affected by events in Greece and Turkey; nor did they contest the corollary idea that the United States must make some positive response to these crises.[44]

Yet legislative influence upon the Truman Doctrine was significant in one important respect. In view of the fundamental change in the nation's diplomatic role contemplated by the president's proposal, legislators advised President Truman to "scare hell" out of the country when he addressed Congress. To no inconsiderable degree, therefore, the "crisis atmosphere" and the stridently anti-Communist tone of Truman's speech could be attributed to legislative influence upon the policy-making process. Senator Vandenberg, for example, urged the president to emphasize "today's world-wide cleavage between democracy and communism."[45] As Vandenberg viewed it, the president must convince the American people that they faced a global and continuing danger and persuade them that his administration possessed a strategy for meeting it successfully.

After lengthy hearings by the Senate Foreign Relations Committee and by the House Foreign Affairs Committee, in late April, the Senate approved the Greek-Turkish Aid Program by a vote of 67–23. Early in May, the measure won House approval by a majority of 287–108. It is significant that—despite vigorous support by Senator Vandenberg and a concerted bipartisan effort by the White House—in the end, approximately one-third of the members of Congress opposed this epochal undertaking in American diplomacy. Before giving its approval, Congress had insisted that American aid to Greece and Turkey must be terminated if either country requested it, or if the UN General Assembly or Security Council opposed it, or if the president determined that aiding these countries no longer served American interests.[46]

44. Vandenberg (ed.), *The Private Papers of Senator Vandenberg*, 339–42; Jones, *The Fifteen Weeks*, 142; Acheson, *Present at the Creation*, 222.

45. Vandenberg (ed.), *The Private Papers of Senator Vandenberg*, 340–47; Acheson, *Present at the Creation*, 225.

46. See the provisions of "An Act to Provide Assistance to Greece and Turkey, 1947" (Public Law 75, 80th Cong., 1st Sess.), as reprinted in U.S. Congress, Senate, Committee

Public Opinion and Containment

As is nearly always true in a democratic setting, the public opinion context of decision-making was extremely important, if not ultimately decisive. At the same time, American public attitudes toward the containment policy were characteristically marked by fundamental inconsistencies, contradictions, and inadequate understanding of containment's implications.

By 1947, the American public's attitude toward Soviet Russia's diplomatic behavior was in some respects more apprehensive and adverse than the viewpoints of executive officials. Yet, President Truman and his advisers were clearly concerned about the public reaction to the proposed containment strategy. For most Americans, the "war was over"; the Allied victory was expected to usher in a new era of international peace and stability; and the United Nations had been created to deal with threats to the peace, thereby relieving the United States of the responsibility for doing so. Psychologically, the American people were unprepared for the kind of extensive, continuing, and unforeseen overseas commitments contemplated by the Truman Doctrine.

Throughout most of World War II, American public opinion had been favorably oriented toward the Soviet Union. Gradually, however, by the end of the conflict, public sentiment shifted, reflecting deep anxiety about Moscow's wartime and early postwar behavior. By the time Japan was defeated in August, 1945, a national poll revealed that 50 percent of the people believed that Stalinist Russia sought world domination. Studies of public attitudes throughout the months that followed showed that from one-half to two-thirds of the American people were troubled about the goals and methods of Soviet foreign policy.[47]

---

on Foreign Relations, *A Decade of American Foreign Policy: Basic Documents, 1941–1949*, 81st Cong., 1st Sess., 1950, pp. 1259–61. For commentary on congressional action on the Greek-Turkish Aid Program, see Cecil V. Crabb, Jr., *Bipartisan Foreign Policy: Myth or Reality?* (New York: Harper and Row, 1957), 56–61.

47. John L. Gaddis, *The United States and the Origins of the Cold War: 1941–1947* (New York: Columbia University Press, 1972), 356–61. See the results of public opinion polls, as cited in Gabriel A. Almond, *The American People and Foreign Policy* (New York: Harcourt, Brace, 1970), 95–97. Additional evidence of changing American attitudes toward Russia is provided by the results of public opinion polls cited in Peter G. Filene (ed.), *American Views of Soviet Russia* (Homewood, Ill.: Dorsey Press, 1968), 161–67.

By early 1946, Gabriel A. Almond has concluded, American public opinion "overwhelmingly favored a firm policy" toward the U.S.S.R. A few months later, some 80 percent of the public now *opposed* the withdrawal of American armed forces from Europe (a remarkable finding, in view of the American people's insistence upon rapid demobilization after the war). Democrats particularly found themselves under repeated attack for being "soft on communism." In Michael H. Armacost's words, the "emotional climate" in the American society was decisively influenced by the "memory of Munich" before World War II and by axioms such as the idea that the appetite of dictators for territory is never satisfied by engaging in "appeasement." In Ulam's view, the Truman Doctrine satisfied an essential criterion of successful public policy in the United States: it was "highly acceptable to the vital center" of the American political spectrum.[48] This fact was of decisive importance both in accounting for Congress' approval of the containment strategy and for public support for later programs adopted for implementing the containment principle.

Press opinion also tended to be predominantly favorable to Truman's decision. The Washington *Post* described his speech as "one of the most momentous ever made by an American Chief Executive." The New York *Times* correctly judged that the "epoch of isolation and occasional interventionism is ended" for the United States. President Truman had "called for action which will launch the United States on a new and positive foreign policy of world-wide responsibility for the maintenance of peace and order." The *Christian Science Monitor* characterized the speech as "one of the most momentous decisions in American history."[49]

If officials of the Truman Administration received overall public endorsement of the president's new foreign policy doctrine, some aspects of the public reaction caused concern among policy-makers. In America (as perhaps in all societies), the specific attitudes reflected by public opinion are notoriously ambivalent and incongruous. The American people favored a firmer stand against communism abroad—but they also wanted lower taxes and reduced federal spending. Immediately

---

48. Almond, *The American People and Foreign Policy*, 97; Kaiser, *Cold Winter—Cold War*, 168–69; Armacost, *The Foreign Relations of the United States*, 57; Ulam, *The Rivals*, 124.
49. Jones, *The Fifteen Weeks*, 172–73.

after the war, public opinion had demanded the rapid demobilization of the nation's armed forces, indicating that few citizens perceived a connection between the successful "containment" of the Soviet Union and the application of military power abroad. In brief, it was doubtful that a majority of citizens in any realistic sense grasped the implications of their enthusiastic endorsement of the containment policy.

Against this background, the Truman Administration undertook a systematic campaign to inform the press and public opinion about the containment policy. Special efforts were directed, for example, at explaining the policy to business leaders and interest groups. That the campaign was successful was indicated a few months later, when organizations representing the "big three"—industry, labor, and agriculture—supported the multibillion-dollar Marshall Plan to promote European recovery.[50]

President Truman and his advisers clearly recognized the importance of public approval for his new foreign policy undertaking. For example, several motifs in the president's speech to Congress emphasized traditional American concepts and values—such as repeated allusions to the promotion of democracy within Greece; the concept of the "free world" (which some commentators believed was closely akin to the traditional concept of the New World, prominent in the Monroe Doctrine earlier); and America's historic opposition to tyranny and oppression. Coincidentally, the existence of a political crisis in Greece was bound to elicit a sympathetic American response: for more than a century, the American society had been identified with the principle of Greek independence.[51] Moreover, the Greek-Turkish Aid Program contemplated a small-scale and limited foreign commitment; it involved no noteworthy military obligation or threat of involvement in military hostilities by the United States. Americans still devoted to isolationism could support the program as a short-run or "emergency" measure, entailing no permanent overseas commitments. By contrast,

50. Hartmann, *Truman and the 80th Congress*, 57–58; Millis (ed.), *The Forrestal Diaries*, 252; Almond, *The American People and Foreign Policy*, 167–71. For a detailed discussion of the attitudes and activities of an influential segment of the labor movement toward the Greek crisis, see Ronald Radosh, *American Labor and United States Foreign Policy* (New York: Random House, 1969), 337–47.

51. Paul Seabury, *The Rise and Decline of the Cold War* (New York: Basic Books, 1967), 40–45. For background on American attitudes on the Greek independence movement in the early nineteenth century, see Crabb, *Policy-Makers and Critics*, 38.

"internationalists" could endorse the Truman Doctrine because if and when the new United Nations became capable of doing so, in the future the preservation of international peace and security could become a responsibility of that agency.

We may summarize our discussion of the role of public opinion in this case by referring to John E. Mueller's concept of a "rally point." The issuance of the Truman Doctrine was a noteworthy example of this phenomenon in the postwar period. A rally point is associated with an event which meets three criteria: it relates to an issue in international affairs; it involves the United States, and specifically the president, directly; and it entails a "specific, dramatic, and sharply focused" issue. The promulgation of the Truman Doctrine satisfied these requirements. The result was a policy winning the overwhelming approval of the American people and their leaders.[52]

Containment as a Diplomatic Doctrine

Former Secretary of State Dean Acheson once described the Truman Doctrine as a natural outgrowth of the Monroe Doctrine. President Truman's own assessment of his speech to Congress on March 12, 1947, was that "the policy I was about to proclaim was indeed as much required by the conditions of my day as was Washington's ['Farewell Address,' September 19, 1796] by the situation in his era and Monroe's doctrine by the circumstances which he then faced."[53]

By many criteria, the Truman Doctrine was the most influential foreign policy declaration in American diplomatic history. Certainly in terms of its immediate impact upon American diplomatic conduct, it would be difficult to think of a more momentous development in the nation's foreign policy record. Truman's pronouncement ranks as a major doctrine of American foreign policy for several fundamental reasons.

First, there was the "universal" nature of the foreign policy principles Truman enunciated. As Ronald J. Stupak has expressed it, "The Truman Doctrine . . . became a universalistic open-ended policy for United States intervention, rather than a specific policy decision to aid

52. John E. Mueller, *War, Presidents and Public Opinion* (New York: John Wiley and Sons, 1973), 208–10.

53. Gardner, *Architects of Illusion*, 229; Truman, *Memoirs: Years of Trial and Hope*, 102.

Greece and Turkey." Or as Norman A. Graebner has phrased it, "The Truman Doctrine seemed to promise salvation to the world."[54]

Implicit in this "universalistic" aspect of the Truman Doctrine are several specific ideas. For example, President Truman and his advisers were convinced that the United States, and what Truman designated the "free world" (*i.e.*, the non-Communist world), faced a threat which had no geographical limits. The challenge to American security was global in scope. In his appearance before the House Foreign Affairs Committee on March 20, for example, Under Secretary of State Dean Acheson noted that the Communist threat was "even wider" than the context of merely Greece and Turkey; it extended to "the east and south of Turkey" and throughout the Middle East generally. Still later, Acheson alluded to the vulnerability of "the vast area from the Dardanelles to the China Sea." And at a later point, he informed legislators that disastrous consequences "for the world" would be incurred if the United States failed to assist Greece and Turkey.[55]

The Truman Doctrine was also a universalistic message in the sense that it envisioned the existence of a threat to American security for an indefinite period of time in the future. It would no doubt exaggerate to say that officials of the Truman Administration viewed containment as a timeless strategy of American foreign policy. They did, however, regard the threat eliciting that doctrine as emanating from an opportunistic and determined opponent, who was prepared to exploit any future circumstances deemed favorable for enhancing Soviet power and influence abroad.

The Truman Doctrine enunciated an extremely broad principle of American foreign policy in another sense: geographically, no limits existed upon the scope of the commitments to be assumed by the United States under it. George F. Kennan had urged his superiors to adopt "a long-term policy of firmness, patience and understanding," designed to confront the Russians with superior counterforce "at every junc-

54. Ronald J. Stupak, *American Foreign Policy: Assumptions, Processes, and Projections* (New York: Harper and Row, 1976), 87; Norman A. Graebner, *Cold War Diplomacy, 1945–1960* (Princeton, N.J.: Van Nostrand, 1962), 41.

55. See Acheson's testimony in U.S. Congress, House, Committee on Foreign Affairs, *Hearings on Assistance to Greece and Turkey*, 80th Cong., 1st Sess., 1947, pp. 62–74. George F. Kennan also tended to depict the threat in global terms. Soviet behavior jeopardized "the interests of a peaceful and stable world." See "The Sources of Soviet Conduct," in *American Diplomacy*, 112, 119.

ture" where the Kremlin threatened the security interests of the free world.[56] President Truman acknowledged to his cabinet on March 7, 1947, that the Greek-Turkish Aid Program represented "only the beginning" of a new era in American foreign relations.[57]

As some informed Americans interpreted it, the Truman Doctrine was a universal principle in another sense. To resist Soviet expansionism successfully, the United States must be prepared to use its resources totally and unconditionally. In effect, the containment strategy was viewed as akin to the concept of "total war" adopted by the United States during World War II.[58] The extent of this campaign was suggested in a passage in Truman's speech to Congress, when he declared, "The seeds of totalitarian regimes are nutured by misery and want. They spread and grow in the evil soil of poverty and strife. They reach their full growth when the hope of a people for a better life has died."

As events over the next generation or more after Truman's message to Congress indicated, to implement the containment strategy successfully the United States was required to engage in two separate (if sometimes related) courses of action. It had to respond to immediate threats to the security of endangered countries, as in Greece and Turkey, and subsequently in Korea and Southeast Asia. Then it had to wage a prolonged and costly campaign against what are sometimes described as the "long-term causes of war" and upheaval in the international system. A conspicuous example of the latter was the Marshall Plan to promote the postwar recovery of Western Europe, formally initiated early in June, 1947. Some eighteen months later, President Truman announced his Point Four Program of American assistance to countries throughout the Third World.

From an ideological and metaphysical perspective, President Truman's pronouncement also qualifies as a doctrine of American foreign policy. His speech clearly had religio-moral connotations. It grew out of a conviction by President Truman and his advisers that after World

56. Kennan, "The Sources of Soviet Conduct," in *American Diplomacy*, 102–21. Later, Kennan reiterated the same idea in his *Memoirs* (p. 595), where he called for American resistance to Soviet encroachments "at every point" they are encountered.

57. Truman, *Memoirs: Years of Trial and Hope*, 104. See also Jones, *The Fifteen Weeks*, 158–59.

58. Henry L. Stimson, "The Challenge to Americans," in Philip E. Mosely (ed.), *The Soviet Union: 1922–1962* (New York: Praeger, 1963), 187–96.

War II international politics were dominated by a clash between two totally dissimilar and antithetical value systems—alternatively described as a contest between freedom and tyranny or democracy and totalitarianism. Nations of the world, Truman believed, were being compelled to choose "between alternative ways of life" represented by the United States and the Soviet Union. Some informed commentators are convinced that in essence, Truman had proclaimed a new diplomatic "crusade"—a recurrent phenomenon in American diplomatic experience.[59] Truman believed, for example, that the Communist menace was as dangerous for the American society as the earlier Axis threat. Dean Acheson was persuaded that after World War II, Western civilization faced a "barbarian onslaught from the East." Senator Vandenberg depicted the struggle as an effort by the Kremlin to achieve "complete encirclement" of the non-Communist world; failure to resist Soviet expansionism would almost certainly lead to a new global war.[60]

Just as the Crusades of the Middle Ages were designed to "save" the Holy Land from the infidels (i.e., the Moslems), so the Truman Doctrine held out the hope of salvation from the Communist menace. Replacing the "Grand Design" formulated earlier by President Roosevelt (who envisioned a stable international order based upon Allied cooperation in the postwar era), President Truman's strategy also contemplated fundamental changes in the nature of the international system. Successful containment of the Soviet Union, in Anatol Rapoport's words, would not only save the world from "a ruthless, savage enemy."[61] In time, it would also (as George F. Kennan envisioned it) produce permanent modifications in Soviet internal and external policies—thereby making the international system itself more stable and peaceful. For a people who were rapidly becoming disillusioned with the results achieved by World War II, this was indeed a new grand design worthy of congressional and public support.

59. For a detailed discussion of the American tendency to engage in diplomatic crusades (followed by isolationist interludes), see F. L. Klingberg, "The Historical Alternation of Moods in American Foreign Policy," World Politics, IV (January, 1952), 239–73.

60. Truman, Memoirs: Years of Trial and Hope, 101; Gardner, Architects of Illusion, 209; Vandenberg (ed.), The Private Papers of Senator Vandenberg, 340–42.

61. Anatol Rapoport, The Big Two: Soviet-American Perceptions of Foreign Policy (New York: Pegasus, 1971), 112.

From a legal point of view also, President Truman's statement warrants being called a doctrine of American foreign policy. As Kennan and other students of American diplomacy have repeatedly emphasized, Americans are very law-oriented people; and their approach to diplomatic questions is nearly always characterized by an emphasis upon legal norms and principles.[62] American initiative, for example, had been largely responsible for the creation of the United Nations, as it had been in formulating the League of Nations more than two decades earlier. It is instructive to recall (as explained more fully in Chapter 2) that the Stimson Doctrine incorporated one or more principles of international law which the American government reiterated, even at the risk of war with Japan.

To the minds of countless Americans, frequent and flagrant Soviet violation of international law was viewed as a primary cause of the Cold War. Time and again in Eastern Europe, for example, Moscow patently violated wartime agreements designed to assure freedom and democracy in this zone. Like the Nazi regime, Stalin's government apparently believed that treaties and international understandings were "scraps of paper" that could be violated whenever Soviet diplomatic interests dictated this course.

Against this background, it is not surprising that President Truman's message to Congress emphasized certain legal principles long venerated by Americans. Earlier, Goerge F. Kennan had called attention to the absence of legal restraints inhibiting Soviet relations with other countries. The Kremlin, said Kennan, recognized no "community of aims" with non-Communist states: "If the Soviet Government occasionally sets its signature to documents which would indicate the contrary, this is to be regarded as a tactical maneuver permissible in dealing with the enemy . . . and should be taken in the spirit of *caveat emptor* ['let the buyer beware']."[63]

In the State Department, Kennan's superior, Dean Acheson, also emphasized the international law dimensions of the Cold War. Communist expansionism, for example, clearly collided with the principles of the UN Charter. To Acheson's mind, the "heart" of the Soviet-American conflict was "the right of free determination [or what Presi-

62. Kennan, *Memoirs*, 340–41.
63. Kennan, "The Sources of Soviet Conduct," in *American Diplomacy*, 106–109, 112–13.

dent Wilson called self-determination] of peoples, not only in Greece, but throughout the world." Conversely, the containment strategy was designed to uphold the principles embodied in the UN Charter.[64]

President Truman also related his new doctrine to traditional international law principles and America's determination to enforce them. By adopting his strategy, America would be "giving effect to the principles" of the Charter. When it enacted the Greek-Turkish Aid Program, Congress emphasized that its purpose was to "contribute to the freedom and independence of all members of the United Nations."[65]

After examining certain "universalist" features of the Truman Doctrine, let us also take note of some characteristics that make the containment strategy a more limited and qualified principle of American diplomacy than is often supposed. (As will be explained more fully in Chapter 9, nearly all the doctrines of American foreign policy have a paradoxical quality—in some cases, perhaps deliberately.) Broad as its terms may have been, the Truman Doctrine cannot be correctly understood as a diplomatic "blank check," permitting or justifying indiscriminate American interventionism throughout the world after 1947.

Some commentators on postwar American diplomacy—and George F. Kennan is a prominent spokesman for this view—have denied that President Truman enunciated a new foreign policy, applicable to a broad range of diplomatic problems. Former Secretary of State James Byrnes similarly doubted that President Truman intended to issue a "permanent doctrine" of American diplomacy. Nor did Senator Vandenberg believe that the Truman Doctrine constituted a "universal pattern" for guiding American diplomatic activity in the years ahead. In his congressional testimony, Under Secretary of State Dean Acheson emphasized that in the future, the United States would respond to crises as they arose abroad; American officials would judge them on their merits; and they would tailor a response designed to fit the circumstances of each case.[66] Again, Acheson appeared to be denying

64. See Acheson's testimony before the House Foreign Affairs Committee in *Hearings on Assistance to Greece and Turkey*, 35, 40.

65. Public Law 75, 80th Cong., 1st Sess., reprinted in Senate Foreign Relations Committee, *A Decade of American Foreign Policy*, 1257–61.

66. Charles Gati (ed.), *Caging the Bear: Containment and the Cold War* (Indianapolis: Bobbs-Merrill, 1974), 36; Byrnes, *Speaking Frankly*, 303; Hartmann, *Truman and the 80th Congress*, 61; Acheson's testimony to the House Foreign Affairs Committee, in *Hearings on Assistance to Greece and Turkey*, 14–15; Jones, *The Fifteen Weeks*, 190–93.

that President Truman had announced a universally applicable formula for American diplomacy throughout the world.

The evidence indicates that the Truman Administration indeed had in mind certain criteria that would govern or limit application of the containment strategy in the future. First, spokesmen for the administration emphasized that American assistance had to be requested by governments seeking it, as had been the case with Greece and Turkey.

Second, as President Truman stated in his congressional message, "There is no other country to which democratic Greece can turn." American officials determined that the United Nations, Great Britain, or other possible sources were unable to extend the needed assistance. Only America was in a position to provide the aid required by these countries.

Third, in the key passage in his speech, the president stated that "it must be the policy of the United States to support free peoples *who are resisting attempted subjugation* by armed minorities or by outside pressures" (italics inserted). On this basis, a major criterion was that the endangered country must be making some effort to preserve its own security and independence. Based upon the precedents of Greece and Turkey, American aid would have to be matched by a considerable degree of "self-help" on the part of recipients (a principle that was given even greater emphasis in the Nixon Doctrine). This limitation in the original Truman Doctrine appeared largely to have been forgotten or overlooked during the 1960s, when the United States assumed the primary responsibility for preserving the independence of South Vietnam.

Fourth, in President Truman's words to Congress, American aid was available to governments that were "unable to cope with the situation" confronting them. By implication at least, American assistance was to be viewed as a kind of "last resort" by nations confronting a challenge to their security.

Fifth, while it cannot be said that this qualification was made unequivocally in Truman's address to Congress, the containment strategy was envisioned by most officials of the Truman Administration as directed at the threat of external aggression against vulnerable nations. Secretary of State Byrnes, for example, believed that Washington should differentiate between the forcible takeover of a country by Soviet-directed communism and a Communist internal victory achieved without external support.[67] As explicated by George Kennan and other defenders of containment, the strategy was designed as a counter-measure to *Soviet expansionism and interventionism* in the affairs of other countries.

In the case of Turkey, the threat of external Soviet pressure and intimidation seemed clearcut and unambiguous. The Greek case was considerably more complicated and ambiguous. As officials in Washington viewed it, the left-wing insurgents there were basically instruments of Soviet foreign policy. To use the nomenclature of the later Khrushchev era, the Kremlin appeared to be waging a "war of national liberation" in Greece, relying upon "proxies" like the Greek rebels and the Marxist states of Eastern Europe to achieve its goals. Presumably, for the Truman Doctrine to be invoked, some significant degree of Soviet intervention within a threatened country had to exist and to be evident to officials in Washington.

The sixth and seventh limitations on the application of the Truman Doctrine were suggested by Under Secretary Acheson in his testimony to Congress. In deciding upon future cases of American assistance, he informed legislators, the United States would give careful attention to the "conditions" prevailing in the countries making such requests. Two questions would be of paramount importance: was it possible for the United States to provide the kind and amount of assistance needed by these countries? And would the recipient countries be in a position to utilize American aid effectively?[68]

Eighth, insofar as the cases of Greece and Turkey served as a precedent for assisting other countries, American aid was restricted largely to providing financial assistance, supplemented by a small-scale program of military aid and advice. The United States intervened with military force in neither Greece nor Turkey.

Ninth, as we have already noted, largely at the instigation of Congress, the Greek-Turkish Aid Program contained several provisions for its possible termination—if such termination was requested by either country; or if the United Nations determined that American aid was no longer necessary; or if the president determined that the purposes of the program had been achieved; or if the president determined that

67. Byrnes, *Speaking Frankly*, 302.
68. Acheson's testimony to the House Foreign Affairs Committee, in *Hearings on Assistance to Greece and Turkey*, 43.

assurances given by Greece and Turkey relative to the use and administration of American aid were not being carried out.

Tenth, executive officials were careful to note that the containment strategy did not apply to countries already behind the Iron Curtain. Although a reading of President Truman's speech might possibly suggest otherwise, the administration did not interpret the concept of "free peoples" as applying to the peoples of countries like Hungary, Poland, the Baltic states, or other societies where Soviet influence was already dominant. By this stage also, a Communist victory in the Chinese civil war appeared to be inevitable. The Truman Doctrine did not propose to "roll back" the Iron Curtain. While George F. Kennan was convinced that the successful application of containment would eventually produce fundamental changes in the Soviet system, these changes were expected to come about gradually over a long period of time. In brief, the Truman Doctrine challenged neither the existence of the prevailing Soviet satellite system nor the legitimacy of communism within Soviet Russia itself.

One other and more general limitation upon the Truman Doctrine remains to be noted. Several commentators have called attention to a marked dichotomy between the rather militant rhetoric of the Truman Doctrine and the actions taken by the United States to implement it. From the text of his speech, it is clear that President Truman accepted the advice of legislators to "scare hell" out of the country. In nearly every paragraph, Truman alluded to the existence of crises abroad and to the dangerous consequences for American security if they were not dealt with decisively. The menace of Communist expansionism in the eastern Mediterranean and elsewhere was depicted graphically, and the conflict between the two opposing systems of democracy and totalitarianism was vividly drawn.

At the same time, the action undertaken by the United States to aid Greece and Turkey was very limited. It involved a relatively small allocation of economic assistance, together with an even more limited military aid program. Even this modest program could be terminated for a variety of reasons already identified. The president and his advisers were fully cognizant that Congress undertook this commitment with considerable reluctance, and legislative concurrence stemmed from the belief that the president's speech had given legislators no choice. For these reasons, Ronald Steel was convinced that President

Truman "probably did not envisage the extreme ends toward which this policy would eventually be applied." His conclusion is that "the language of the Truman Doctrine was sweeping, but its application was limited."[69]

The Truman Doctrine in Perspective

No postwar American foreign policy principle, it seems safe to say, outranks the Truman Doctrine in terms of its impact upon the diplomacy of the United States. Despite some evidence that containment had been abandoned as the foundation stone of the nation's foreign policy after the Vietnam War, the election of Ronald Reagan to the White House in 1980 was a forceful reminder that the American people remained as concerned about Soviet expansionism abroad as ever; and they were no less insistent that their leaders continue to oppose it. As much as any other single concept, the containment idea expressed in the Truman Doctrine was the integrating principle of American postwar diplomacy toward the Soviet Union, toward Western Europe, toward the Middle East, toward the Third World, and toward almost every other major challenge confronting the United States in foreign affairs.

President Truman's address to Congress on March 12, 1947, was followed within a few weeks by congressional passage of the Greek-Turkish Aid Program. In early June, there followed the Marshall Plan or European Recovery Program, entailing American assistance of some $12 billion for European reconstruction (with the European recipients contributing some eight times that amount to achieve the goal). To the minds of legislators at least, the Marshall Plan was viewed as a crucial measure in implementing the containment principle.[70] Still later (on July 21, 1949), the United States, Canada and ten European nations joined in the North Atlantic Treaty Organization (NATO), providing a defensive shield against Communist aggression.[71]

Under the Eisenhower Administration, other alliance systems, with

69. Ronald Steel, *Pax Americana* (Rev. ed.; New York: Viking Press, 1970), 22–23.
70. ERP emerged as an anti-Communist measure, although Soviet Russia and the smaller Communist satellite countries of Europe were invited to participate in the program. After an initial expression of interest, however, Moscow declined participation and refused to permit its satellites to take part as well. Acheson, *Present at the Creation*, 226–35; Crabb, *Bipartisan Foreign Policy*, 61–72.
71. Crabb, *Bipartisan Foreign Policy*, 74–81.

countries like Australia and New Zealand, the Philippines, the Republic of China (Taiwan), and the Republic of Korea, were established. Successful alliances of course require well-equipped and trained military forces at their disposal. Late in July, 1949, Congress enacted the Mutual Defense Assistance Program (MDAP)—later called the Mutual Security Program (MSP)—providing American arms-aid to the European allies.[72] Thereafter, military aid to vulnerable countries became a permanent feature of American foreign policy. Another landmark in the evolution of the containment policy was the Point Four Program of aid to the developing countries inaugurated by the Truman Administration early in 1949. Designed to aid needy societies to achieve goals like modernization and national development, this program also clearly reflected the American conviction that to the extent that these objectives were achieved, the vulnerability of Third World societies to Communist control would be significantly reduced.[73]

These were the highlights in the evolution of the Truman Doctrine after 1947. Space is not available in which to present a history of the Truman Doctrine, since this would involve nothing less than a detailed chronicle of American postwar foreign relations. Nor is such treatment necessary for our purpose. In the remainder of the chapter, discussion will focus upon certain questions and criticisms raised about the doctrine in 1947 and in the years that followed, beginning with indictments of the Truman Doctrine made by members of the "revisionist" or "re-examinist" school of thought concerning the origins and nature of the Cold War.[74] Among the criticisms made of the Truman

72. For more detailed discussion of the MDAP, see *Ibid.*, 81–87.

73. The evolution of the American foreign aid program since World War II is discussed more fully in Cecil V. Crabb, Jr., *American Foreign Policy in the Nuclear Age* (3rd ed.; New York: Harper and Row, 1972), 405–23. Helpful interpretive studies are Robert E. Hunter and John E. Rielly, *Development Today: A New Look at U.S. Relations with the Poor Countries* (New York: Praeger, 1972); Herbert Feis, *Foreign Aid and Foreign Policy* (New York: Dell, 1966); and John D. Montgomery, *Foreign Aid in International Politics* (Englewood Cliffs, N.J.: Prentice-Hall, 1967).

74. The revisionist viewpoint is here interpreted to mean that school of thought which rejects the "official" or orthodox point of view holding Soviet Russia mainly accountable for the emergence of tension and conflict among the great powers after World War II. While the revisionist school is far from monolithic, its common denominator is perhaps the idea that American diplomatic behavior might have been even more crucial than Soviet conduct in producing the Cold War. Representative expressions of this viewpoint are Fleming, *The Cold War and Its Origins*; William A. Williams, *The Tragedy of*

Doctrine by this group of interpreters, the most serious indictment perhaps is the charge that President Truman and his advisers misconstrued the threat facing American security after World War II. The containment strategy was, therefore, the wrong prescription for a misdiagnosed diplomatic malaise; and as is usually the case under such circumstances, Truman's new foreign policy prescription made the condition worse rather than better! In brief, many revisionist interpreters have asserted, the Truman Doctrine committed the United States to a policy of indiscriminate, emotionally based "anti-Communism" in the postwar era; and the culmination of this policy was America's tragic involvement in the Vietnam War. In reality, some of these commentators believe, under the guise of the Truman Doctrine, the United States actually sought to impose a *Pax Americana* upon the world. Since this was the "real" purpose of the Truman Doctrine, the alleged struggle between democracy and communism, or between freedom and tyranny, had no meaning; it served merely as a rationalization for America's own hegemonial tendencies.

Some re-examinists attribute America's postwar hegemony to economic forces, stemming from Washington's desire to impose a capitalist order upon weaker societies. Alternatively, the United States sought to obtain access to "raw materials and markets" abroad and to "destroy those who dare to resist" this new form of American imperialism. To Bertrand Russell's mind, the "free world" which Washington proposed to defend under the Truman Doctrine was in reality "the American Empire." D. F. Fleming was convinced that the doctrine signified America's determination to make capitalism the universal model for all societies. The basis of America's objection to Soviet behavior in Eastern Europe, as Stephen E. Ambrose assessed it, was that the United States wanted to impose its own economic hegemony on this

---

American Diplomacy (Cleveland: World Publishing Co., 1959); David Horowitz, *The Free World Colossus: A Critique of American Foreign Policy in the Cold War* (New York: Hill and Wang, 1971); John M. Swomley, Jr., *American Empire: The Political Ethics of Twentieth-Century Conquest* (New York: Macmillan, 1970); Richard J. Barnet, *Roots of War: The Men and Institutions Behind U.S. Foreign Policy* (Baltimore: Penguin, 1972); Amaury de Riencourt, *The Coming Caesars* (New York: Capricorn Books, 1957); N. D. Houghton (ed.), *Struggle Against History: United States Foreign Policy in an Age of Revolution* (New York: Simon and Schuster, 1968).

region, as part of its global strategy of imposing "democratic capitalism" on other countries. In the same vein, America's security interests in Greece and Turkey were an outgrowth of Washington's desire to establish a dominant position in the Middle East.[75]

A variant criticism is the assertion that the Truman Doctrine was issued mainly as an instrument for promoting America's own diplomatic self-interests and for achieving the long-term objective of making the United States the political arbiter of the world. The Truman Administration, Rapoport has said, was determined to see that the world "was properly organized, in accordance with American precepts." The real purpose of the Truman Doctrine, Isaac Deutscher was convinced, was to achieve the "rollback" of Soviet power from the heart of Europe, and to replace it with American power. Or, as another study contended, the Truman Doctrine signified that the British Empire had been replaced by the American Empire.[76]

A logical corollary of such interpretations is that the Truman Doctrine inescapably committed the United States to an antirevolutionary orientation in its foreign policy. Under the doctrine, critics charged, America became inevitably "allied" with reactionary political and social systems, identified with the status quo throughout the world, and compelled to support dictatorships from Latin America to East Asia. The unfortunate results were twofold: by doing so, America forgot its own "revolutionary heritage"; and Washington permitted Marxism and other extremist movements to become the agents of political change throughout the Third World.[77]

Such criticisms of the Truman Doctrine are formidable and are not easy to answer convincingly in limited space. To no inconsiderable de-

75. See the Preface by Bertrand Russell, in David Horowitz (ed.), *Containment and Revolution* (Boston: Beacon Press, 1967); Carl Ogleby and Richard Shaull, *Containment and Change* (New York: Macmillan, 1967), 73; Fleming, *The Cold War and Its Origins*, I, 437; Stephen E. Ambrose, *Rise to Globalism: American Foreign Policy, 1938–1970* (Baltimore: Penguin, 1971), 118; Richard J. Barnet, *Intervention and Revolution: America's Confrontation with Insurgent Movements Around the World* (New York: World Publishing Co., 1968), 118–19.

76. Rapoport, *The Big Two*, 91; Isaac Deutscher, "Myths of the Cold War," in Horowitz (ed.), *Containment and Revolution*, 17; Lloyd C. Gardner, "Dean Acheson and 'Situations of Strength,'" in Gary R. Hess (ed.), *America and Russia: From Cold War Confrontation to Coexistence* (New York: Thomas Y. Crowell, 1973), 49–50.

77. Fleming, *The Cold War and Its Origins*, I, 446–47.

gree, these indictments derive from subjective interpretations of the "real motives" or clandestine objectives of President Truman and his advisers (not excluding influential members of Congress) vis-à-vis their publicly declared or apparent motives. If it is admittedly very difficult to fathom correctly the "real motives" of policy-makers, this challenge confronts re-examinists no less than other schools of thought about the Cold War. Such quests more often than not become little more than highly subjective evaluations based upon fragmentary and inferential evidence; and in many cases, they prove more about the ideological orientation of the interpreter than they do about the well-springs of national policy.

In the case of the Truman Doctrine, no convincing evidence exists that the actual motives of President Truman and his diplomatic advisers differed fundamentally from their announced objectives. By 1947, national leaders had incontestably become genuinely apprehensive about Soviet expansionism and interventionism throughout the world. Moreover, as we have seen, public and congressional anxieties about the Soviet challenge reinforced the concerns of executive policy-makers. To no inconsiderable extent, the Truman Doctrine was a response to a rising public and congressional demand that the White House toughen its position in dealing with the Soviet hierarchy. Far from engaging in some kind of conspiracy to foist an unwelcome diplomatic strategy upon the American people, the Truman Administration adopted the containment policy much later than many Americans desired; and it was a more limited response to the Communist challenge than many critics preferred.

Revisionist criticisms of the Truman Doctrine also overlook another key fact about the context of the Truman Doctrine. As late as 1947, isolationism still exercised a powerful attraction for millions of Americans, including some of their representatives in Congress. Despite America's crucial role in World War II—followed by energetic American efforts in planning and creating the United Nations—relatively few Americans were enthusiastic about the kind of internationalist diplomatic role implied by the Truman Doctrine. Far from seeking to establish an *imperium* throughout the world, Americans were skeptical about assuming the responsibility for the security of Greece and Turkey; they did so most reluctantly; and even then, they surrounded the containment principle with numerous limitations and qualifications in an effort to avoid indiscriminate interventionist behavior abroad.

Yet the most effective refutation of the idea that the underlying motive of the Truman Doctrine was an American empire is to be found in the nature of the international system after 1947. For Greece and Turkey, for Western Europe, and for approximately one hundred new nations comprising the Third World today, national independence has become an evident reality of the postwar political system. Within NATO, for example, for a generation or more after its creation, the United States had encountered the phenomenon sometimes known as "disarray." While the problem of disunity within NATO has multiple origins, one of them clearly is the unwillingness of the European partners to serve as compliant "satellites" of the United States on key diplomatic issues like the future of détente with the Soviet Union or the Arab-Israeli conflict. Throughout the Third World, most nations subscribe to the concept of diplomatic nonalignment; they refuse to be diplomatically or militarily allied with either of the two superpowers.[78] After a period of initial skepticism about nonalignment during the 1950s, in time Washington accepted this diplomatic posture and came to terms with the existence of what the Kennedy Administration called a "pluralistic" international system. By the 1980s, it was evident that neither the United States nor the Soviet Union had been able to successfully dominate or control the Third World; and after Vietnam, American officials largely abandoned efforts to do so. In a number of Third World countries (and under President Anwar Sadat, Egypt was a prominent example), the impetus for greater American involvement in the nation's affairs frequently came from the indigenous government itself, rather than from hegemonial impulses in Washington.

A more moderate and defensible criticism of the Truman Doctrine is the charge that from the beginnings, its instigators were unclear about

78. For a detailed analysis of the emergence of the concept of nonalignment and the major tenets of this diplomatic posture, see Cecil V. Crabb, Jr., *The Elephants and the Grass: A Study of Nonalignment* (New York: Praeger, 1965). A discussion of the American response to this concept is contained in the same work, pp. 168–98, and in the same author's "The United States and the Neutralists: A Decade in Perspective," *Annals of the American Academy of Political and Social Science*, CCCLXII (November, 1965), 92–102.

he precise nature of the threat faced by Greece and Turkey after World War II, and by other countries in the years thereafter. As a result, implementation of the doctrine was often ineffectual, if not mpossible.

Informed students of international politics have often given highly divergent answers to the question of the nature and severity of the threat confronting the United States in the early postwar period. Did it stem mainly from the historic and traditional expansionist impulses of the Russian state, irrespective of its system of government? Was the non-Communist world jeopardized chiefly by Marxist ideological goals, such as sponsorship of revolutionary activities in other countries or communism's proclaimed antagonism to capitalism? Alternatively, was the real danger in Greece, Turkey, and other locales posed by the Soviet Union to alter the global balance of power in its favor? In the case of Greece, was the true source of its instability an internal civil war, involving right- and left-wing factions vying for control of the government? Conversely, in the instance of Turkey, did the country face chiefly an external threat, deriving from Russia's age-old determination to control the Dardanelles? More broadly after 1947, was American security jeopardized by a variety of ethnic, tribal, religious, and other conflicts that kept the Third World in turmoil and (as officials in Washington viewed it) enhanced the opportunities for Communist adventurism abroad?

Admittedly, at one time or another President Truman and his advisers depicted the threat confronting the United States in the early postwar period by reference to all of these possibilities. Yet this fact does not necessarily prove that executive officials were deliberately distorting external reality, or that they consciously deceived the American people and Congress about developments overseas and their effect upon the security of the United States. In 1947 and afterward, in some instances more than one threat actually existed in individual cases. (Castro's Cuba, for example, both served as a conduit for external Soviet influence in the Western Hemisphere and as an active agent of Communist-sponsored revolutionary activities in other American republics.) The fact that American officials emphasized different dimensions of the danger facing the United States abroad also stemmed in some measure from the nature of the audience or constituency toward which explanations of the Truman Doctrine were directed. As was emphasized in Chapter 1, historically the American people have been conditioned to react negatively to Old World concepts like the preservation of the balance of power (no matter how much in fact the containment strategy sought to achieve that goal). They could, however, understand and support the idea that containment was necessary to protect "the American way of life" against an expansionist, ideological enemy.[79] Alternatively, in view of their recent experience in World War II, some Americans conceived of Soviet communism as a form of Red fascism: the conduct of Stalinist Russia was equated in their minds with the behavior of Hitler's Germany, and both imperiled the security of other countries.[80]

It remains true, however, that in 1947 and throughout the years that followed successive chief executives and their advisers defined the threat against which the containment policy was directly aimed differently, primarily because they perceived it differently. In turn, this result may have stemmed from the fact that after World War II, the United States confronted several essentially different conditions abroad that adversely affected its security and well-being.

Paul Seabury has raised another troublesome question about the underlying rationale of the containment strategy. For some proponents of containment, the external challenge facing the United States after World War II derived principally from the nature of the Soviet internal system, which was totalitarian and inherently expansionist. Under the oppressive Stalinist regime that existed in the U.S.S.R. until 1953, Soviet policies were viewed by many Americans as inimical both to the Russian people and to vulnerable societies abroad. George F. Kennan had predicted that as the Soviet regime "mellowed"—and the process of de-Stalinization after 1953 might be regarded as an example of what Kennan anticipated—Soviet external behavior would presumably become more benign and less dangerous to the security of non-Communist nations. Yet Seabury has called attention to the basic fallacy of such reasoning: as liberalization has taken place internally

79. See the views of Paul Seabury, as cited in Philip W. Quigg, *America the Dutiful: An Assessment of U.S. Foreign Policy* (New York: Simon and Schuster, 1971), 47–48.
80. Les K. Adler and Thomas G. Paterson, "'Red Fascism' and the Development of the Cold War," in Hess (ed.), *America and Russia: From Cold War Confrontation to Coexistence*, 62–74.

within the Soviet society, this prospect has often *enhanced* Soviet influence abroad, especially in the Third World.[81] At any rate, by the 1980s it seemed questionable whether internal political developments within the U.S.S.R. had *any* clear or direct correlation with the problem of Soviet aggressiveness abroad. As we shall see more fully in Chapter 8, the Carter Administration believed that after 1979, the United States and its allies faced an extremely serious threat deriving from the Soviet invasion of Afghanistan and the consequent insecurity to the Persian Gulf area.

In summary, it is possible to say that the Truman Doctrine left a troublesome area of vagueness and uncertainty about the external threat confronting the United States. More specifically, the doctrine failed to provide unambiguous answers to four crucial questions. First, was it overt Soviet aggression? Was it what was later called "indirect aggression" or Soviet "proxy wars," in which the Kremlin's role was more or less successfully concealed behind the facade of an internal political struggle? As in Turkey, was it some combination of Soviet pressures and intimidation directed against a vulnerable country? In particular cases, was it perhaps several of these threats against which the Truman Doctrine was directed?

The second problem was highlighted by what the Truman and Eisenhower administrations frequently described as the machinations of "international communism." This concept posed a number of difficult questions. Even in the early postwar period, for example—not to mention the international system as it had evolved by the 1960s—it is doubtful that the Communist movement was ever as monolithic and as subject to Soviet dictation as the concept suggested. By the period of the Truman Doctrine, a novel variety of Marxism had evolved in Yugoslavia; and within a decade, deep fissures had appeared in the wall of Sino-Soviet solidarity. Was the Truman Doctrine really applicable to the distinctively Chinese version of "Maoism" that shaped China's political course? What relevance did the Truman Doctrine have as a foreign policy guideline toward a wide range of crypto-Marxist and socialist regimes throughout the Afro-Asian world? How useful was it as a benchmark for American diplomacy toward Western Europe, where Marxist groups (Euro-communism) sometimes had

81. Seabury, *The Rise and Decline of the Cold War*, 77–81.

wide political appeal? If the doctrine had any real relevance for such situations, then it had to be revised and modified—to the point of being unrecognizable to President Truman and his advisers.

Third, the Truman Doctrine—along with the rationale presented in its behalf—provided little guidance for the United States in responding to what in time became a pervasive challenge in the global environment: revolutionary upheaval within the Third World. The Truman Administration justified the containment principle by reference to "armed minorities" challenging the authority of established governments (an unmistakable allusion to the Greek political struggle). Moreover, in the administration's view the Greek rebels were unquestionably incited and assisted by the Soviet Union.

As a general phenomenon, revolutionary ferment became a recurrent feature of the international milieu in the years ahead. When and under what circumstances did it adversely affect American security interests? When rebel groups were "armed" (few insurgent movements in the modern world forego reliance upon arms)? When a revolutionary movement is externally assisted, by the Soviet Union or its satellites (such as Cuba)? Throughout history, revolutionary movements have had foreign support—as in the prominent case of French support for the American Revolution. Did issuance of the Truman Doctrine mean that the United States opposed *all* attempts to overthrow incumbent governments by revolutionary methods? In that case, America in effect would be saying that its own successful revolutionary struggle against England lacked legitimacy. (Paradoxically, America's "revolutionary heritage" was one of its most appealing features for many newly independent societies in the contemporary world.) Did the region in which revolutionary upheaval occur perhaps determine its impact upon the security interests of the United States (*i.e.*, might Washington evaluate revolutionary ferment in Latin America differently from the same phenomenon in East Asia)? The Truman Doctrine left such important questions largely unclarified, and to that extent it served the nation poorly as a general foreign policy dictum.

Fourth, the Truman Doctrine also left several crucial questions unresolved with regard to the global balance of power. On the assumption that the doctrine was an exercise in realpolitik—that above all, the Truman Administration was attempting to maintain the global balance of power—a number of problems confronted American diplomacy in the years ahead.

Did issuance of the Truman Doctrine mean that the United States was now required to maintain the balance of power *anywhere* it was jeopardized by the Soviet Union or other countries? Did maintenance of the balance of power have a higher priority for the United States in some regions (such as the eastern Mediterranean) than others (such as sub-Saharan Africa)? Was the emergence of a Marxist or crypto-Marxist system in *any* region a threat to the global balance of power per se? And, as the threat of overt military conflict between the United States and the Soviet Union receded, what did the classical concept of balance of power have to do with Soviet-American rivalry in the Third World or economic competition?

Many of these deficiencies of the Truman Doctrine are reflected in John L. Gaddis' judgment that its effect in time was "to imprison American diplomacy in an ideological strait jacket almost as confining as that which restricted Soviet foreign policy." Among its other defects, it prevented Washington from making "conciliatory gestures" to Moscow that would have resolved at least some underlying causes of Cold War animosity. Other commentators are convinced that the doctrine fostered a "Maginot Line" complex in the American approach to foreign affairs, inducing Washington to engage in a form of "static warfare" against communism after 1947.[82] George F. Kennan later complained that his containment strategy had been misinterpreted and misapplied by his superiors: although his early conceptions of the idea do not indicate it, Kennan contended that he envisioned containment mainly as a *political*, rather than a military, response by the United States to the Communist challenge.[83] (What Kennan meant precisely by "political containment" was never very clearly specified.)

82. Gaddis, *The United States and the Origins of the Cold War*, 352; Edmund Stillman and William Pfaff, "Cold War and Containment," in M. Donald Hancock and Dankwart A. Rustow (eds.), *American Foreign Policy in International Perspective* (Englewood Cliffs, N.J.: Prentice-Hall, 1971), 136–37.

83. Thus, Kennan observed in 1967 that a "serious deficiency" of his analysis of the Soviet challenge and the American response to it "was the failure to make clear that what I was talking about when I mentioned the containment of Soviet power was not the containment by military means of a military threat, but the political containment of a political threat." Kennan, *Memoirs*, 378.

Other telling criticisms of the Truman Doctrine may be made. Even today, perhaps the most searching and cogent critique of the containment strategy was the analysis by Walter Lippmann, published a few months after Truman's speech to Congress.[84] Lippmann's evaluation identifies most of the defects of the Truman Doctrine emphasized here, as well as others creating problems for American officials in the future. In briefest form, Lippmann's contention was that the doctrine had done nothing really to *resolve* Soviet-American tensions; and in some respects, it perhaps assured their continuation in the years ahead.

Yet our extended treatment of the defects of the Truman Doctrine should not be construed to mean that it was devoid of positive features or that its contribution to American diplomacy was entirely negative. To the contrary, the Truman Doctrine has a number of significant gains to its credit. Paul Y. Hammond, for example, has asserted that "the standard of achievement in foreign relations that Truman set has not been surpassed by another postwar President." Rostow's verdict is that the containment policy served as "the cement of the world" and constituted its "hope for peace" in the postwar era.[85]

For all its weaknesses and ambiguities, the Truman Doctrine did successfully achieve its goal: the security of Greece and Turkey was preserved, and the former at least evolved in a more democratic direction after 1947. Except for Cuba and Vietnam, and most recently Afghanistan, no other country was brought within the Soviet orbit after 1947. Conversely, Yugoslavia and China ultimately broke away from dependency on Moscow, and as the years passed, Soviet rule over Eastern Europe was subject to at least partially successful challenge. In the Third World, the Soviet Union as a rule experienced no greater success than the United States in imposing its hegemony; and in a number of countries (like Egypt, the Sudan, Algeria, and Indonesia) Soviet-supported Communist forces were less influential now than in the early postwar period.

Second, to the degree that the Truman Doctrine sought to preserve a stable balance of power between the nuclear giants, that objective also

---

84. Walter Lippmann, *The Cold War: A Study in U.S. Foreign Policy* (New York: Harper and Row, 1947). Even today, this book would repay careful study by the student of postwar American foreign policy.

85. Hammond, *The Cold War Years*, 10; Eugene V. Rostow, *Law, Power and the Pursuit of Peace* (New York: Harper and Row, 1968), 42.

has been largely accomplished. As our earlier treatment indicated, under containment the United States did not attempt to "dismantle" the Iron Curtain or to liquidate the Soviet satellite regime in Eastern Europe. In effect, American officials "accepted" the existence of the Soviet satellite system. The Truman Doctrine cautioned the Kremlin against attempts to enlarge or expand it. On the basis of this balance, a new global war between the superpowers has been successfully averted.[86]

A third positive feature of the Truman Doctrine was that it was an essentially moderate and limited response by the United States to the Soviet challenge. Containment did not envision that the United States would initiate "preventive war" against the Soviet adversary or even undertake the kind of diplomatic offensive that some critics of the Truman Administration demanded. As Gaddis has emphasized, the Truman Doctrine avoided two potentially ruinous extremes in American postwar diplomacy: preventive war and a possible retreat into traditional American isolationism. For all its inadequacies, the containment strategy was preferable to either of these two alternatives.[87]

A fourth positive contribution of the containment principle was that—despite its "universal" quality as a general foreign policy dictum—it was applied selectively and pragmatically after 1947. In practice, the Truman Doctrine did *not* serve as a diplomatic straitjacket for the United States. With the possible exception of the early and mid-1950s, the United States did not embark upon an indiscriminate and worldwide "anti-Communist crusade." As the years passed, Washington accommodated itself to a wide variety of Marxist, crypto-Marxist, socialist, and other species of leftist political systems throughout the world. American aid, for example, was extended to Communist Yugoslavia and Poland; and by the late 1970s, the People's Republic of China sought large-scale American assistance as a vital element in its modernization campaign. Throughout the Afro-Asian world, most societies sought to *increase* American (along with Western European) economic assistance and investment—in some cases, because experience with Soviet aid had proved a disillusioning experience. As it was

86. Rees, *The Age of Containment*, 7; Rostow, *Law, Power and the Pursuit of Peace*, 40; Sir William Hayter, "The Cold War and the Future," in Evan Luard (ed.), *The Cold War: A Re-Appraisal* (New York: Praeger, 1964), 318–27.
87. Gaddis, *The United States and the Origins of the Cold War*, 358–60.

actually applied, Seabury contends, the containment strategy was in fact a remarkably "undogmatic" and flexible concept. In essence, it was a kind of diplomatic "Micawberism": by adopting it, the United States hoped that in time "something would turn up" to lower the temperature of the Cold War and reduce the prospect of a global nuclear conflagration.[88] After the Vietnam War, détente produced some alleviation of Soviet-American tensions and reduced the risks of nuclear war.

The Truman Doctrine, in Ulam's words, may well have "provoked" the Kremlin—but not in the sense that revisionist interpreters usually employ the term. America's adoption of containment provoked Moscow to limit its hegemonial tendencies; to avoid direct encounters between the superpowers; and in time to advocate détente in Soviet-American relations. Or, as Rostow has asserted, the Truman Doctrine contributed to the emergence of a set of de facto ground rules regulating relations between the nuclear giants. After 1947, both superpowers sought to avoid disastrous "miscalculations" likely to trigger a nuclear conflict; and in their relations with each other (if not always with other countries) their diplomatic behavior became more rational and restrained.[89] This was a noteworthy accomplishment, not only for American foreign policy, but for the entire international community as well.

88. Seabury, *The Rise and Decline of the Cold War*, 81–82. See also Rees, *The Age of Containment*, 24.

89. Ulam, *The Rivals*, 126; Rostow, *Law, Power and the Pursuit of Peace*, 39–43.

4 / The Eisenhower Doctrine: America Becomes a Middle Eastern Power

By means of the Monroe Doctrine the United States affirmed its rights over the whole of the American continent. Through the Truman Doctrine it took the initiative in Greece and Turkey. Through the Eisenhower Doctrine it designated itself as the policeman of the Middle East.
—Claude Julien

[The Eisenhower Doctrine was] nothing that is sufficiently tangible to be "embraced," you might say. It is an attitude, a point of view, a state of mind. —Secretary of State John Foster Dulles

The Eisenhower Doctrine . . . was a desperate attempt to formulate American policies in the Middle East in the only terms which at the time could secure popular support, i.e., anti-Communist rhetoric.
—Adam B. Ulam

A decade after President Truman enunciated the containment strategy, his successor, President Dwight D. Eisenhower, promulgated a new doctrine of American foreign policy which bore his name. Addressing a joint session of Congress on January 5, 1957, Eisenhower called for a fundamental reorientation in American policy towards the volatile Middle East, and he requested the collaboration of Congress in this undertaking. In due course, the House and Senate granted the president a modified version of the authority he requested as embodied in the joint resolution (popularly called the "Middle East Resolution") which passed on March 9, 1957. The joint resolution gave legislative sanction to what came to be known as the Eisenhower Doctrine for the Middle East.[1]

1. The text of Eisenhower's speech may be found in Department of State, *United States Policy in the Middle East: September, 1956–June, 1957*, Near and Middle East Series 25 (Washington: D.C.: Government Printing Office, 1957), 15–23. The congressional resolution supporting it may be found on pp. 44–46.

Elements of the Eisenhower Doctrine

President Eisenhower's new approach to the problems of the Middle East contained three basic components. First, he requested legislative approval for new bilateral and multilateral foreign aid programs designed to bolster the independence of nations in the Middle East. Second, the administration proposed to extend American military aid and cooperation to Middle Eastern countries requesting it. Third, in what came to be viewed as the crux of his new doctrine, Eisenhower asked Congress to authorize "employment of the armed forces of the United States to secure and protect the territorial integrity and political independence of such [Middle Eastern] nations, requesting such aid, against overt armed aggression from any nation controlled by International Communism."

Underscoring the importance he attached to his new Middle Eastern strategy, President Eisenhower had presented it personally before a joint session of Congress. Subsequently, the White House let it be known that the president regarded his proposal as the "first order of business" for the new Congress.[2] For President Eisenhower and his advisers, this new policy statement was designed to restore Western prestige and influence in the Middle East. After the Suez Crisis of 1956, these were lower than at any time in recent memory. By relying upon three components—economic aid, military assistance, and the possible use of American armed forces in the area—the Eisenhower Administration hoped to promote long-term political stability and security in the region. The Eisenhower foreign policy team was also aware that, as one of the most volatile areas on the globe, the Middle East was subject to sudden and unpredictable political crises. Accordingly, as Eisenhower said on a later occasion, the resolution he requested from Congress "confers on the President discretion to determine what action should be taken by the United States in any given circumstances."[3]

Two of the three principal provisions of the Eisenhower Doctrine seemed clear enough. The first empowered the president to enter into agreements for the extension of economic assistance to nations in the

2. Dwight D. Eisenhower, *Waging Peace, 1956–1961* (Garden City, N.Y.: Doubleday, 1965), 178.
3. See Eisenhower's statement on August 5, 1957, in Department of State, *American Foreign Policy: Current Documents, 1957* (Washington, D.C.: Government Printing Office, 1961), 863.

Middle East requesting it. As we observed in Chapter 3, this step represented merely a new application of the principles embodied in the Truman Doctrine and set forth more explicitly in President Truman's Point Four Program in 1949. The Eisenhower White House proposed to allocate the modest total of $200 million for assistance to Middle Eastern governments. In Secretary of State John Foster Dulles' view, this was the most crucial aspect of the Eisenhower Doctrine, in terms of promoting the long-range stability of the region.[4]

The second feature of Eisenhower's new Middle Eastern strategy provided for the extension of American arms-aid to nations in the Middle East requesting it. Again, precedent for this step could be found in the modest military assistance program provided to Greece and Turkey in 1947 and in the much larger program of military aid to NATO countries in the months that followed. The intention of the Eisenhower White House was to give nations of the Middle East an alternative to exclusive reliance upon Soviet arms-aid (Egypt's acquisition of Communist arms, for example, had been a key factor leading to the Suez Crisis of 1956). In contrast to the administration's earlier position, no longer would states in the Middle East be required to join a Western-sponsored regional defense system (like the Baghdad Pact, renamed the Central Treaty Organization after 1958) before they were eligible to receive American arms-aid.

The intention and meaning of the third provision of the Eisenhower Doctrine were initially more troublesome—and they remained so in the years ahead. The language of the Middle East resolution passed by Congress provided that "if the President determines the necessity thereof, the United States is prepared to use armed forces to assist any such nation or group of nations [in the Middle East] requesting assistance against armed aggression from any country controlled by international communism."

Some aspects of this provision were clear enough. The president (not Congress) determined whether the armed forces of the United States would be committed in the Middle East. This might be done, if their use were requested by a Middle Eastern state. But it was the last

---

4. See Dulles' testimony on the rationale of the Eisenhower Doctrine, in U.S. Congress, Senate, Committees on Foreign Relations and Armed Services, *Hearings on the President's Proposal on the Middle East*, 85th Cong., 1st Sess., January 14–February 4, 1957, Pt. 1, p. 8. This source will be hereafter cited as Senate *Hearings on the Middle East*.

proviso of this resolution—identification of the threat arising from "armed aggression from any country controlled by international communism"—that proved the most controversial feature of the Eisenhower Doctrine.

What, for example, did the doctrine mean by "armed aggression"? The term had three possible, and somewhat conflicting, connotations. It might, for example, mean overt aggression or military intervention by the Soviet Union or one of its Communist satellites in the Middle East. The world had witnessed this form of aggression recently when the Soviet Union invaded Hungary in 1956. One interpretation of the Eisenhower Doctrine, therefore, was that it was designed to prevent "another Hungary" in the Middle East. Yet even executive officials conceded that this seemed an unlikely prospect.[5]

Alternatively, the "aggression" against which the Eisenhower Doctrine was directed could be envisioned chiefly as subversion by Communist groups against some Middle Eastern state. (The term sometimes employed for this phenomenon is *indirect aggression*.) By relying upon a variety of methods—revolutionary activities, economic and military arms-aid programs, terrorism, propaganda campaigns, and other means—Communist groups might seek to gain control over one or more countries within the Middle East. To President Eisenhower's mind, this was the principal threat to the security of the Middle East and to Western influence in the region.[6]

Yet, in obvious recognition of Middle Eastern anxieties about overly close identification with powerful Western nations, the Eisenhower Administration and its supporters in Congress initially de-emphasized this danger.[7] As a report by the House Foreign Affairs Committee on the Eisenhower Doctrine stated:

> The resolution avoids any specific statement of policy or any outline of a course of action with respect to subversion from within. The committee

5. Secretary of State Dulles informed the House Foreign Affairs Committee that the "principal value" of the Eisenhower Doctrine "is its deterrent effect." U.S. Congress, House, Committee on Foreign Affairs, *Hearings on Economic and Military Cooperation with Nations in the General Area of the Middle East*, 85th Cong., 1st Sess., January 7–22, 1957, p. 31. This source will be hereafter cited as House *Hearings on the Middle East*.

6. Eisenhower, *Waging Peace*, 178.

7. Roscoe Drummond and Gaston Coblentz, *Duel at the Brink: John Foster Dulles' Command of American Power* (Garden City, N.Y.: Doubleday, 1960), 192.

recognizes that the greatest danger of Soviet aggression lies in this direction. Nevertheless, the committee is convinced that most nations of the Middle East would regard a formal commitment to oppose subversion as an assumption by the United States of a right to interfere in their internal affairs. Subversion has to be fought from within. A nation which has the money and the equipment to maintain an effective internal security force, which is able to carry on a program for improving the living conditions of its people and which is protected against overt aggression from across its borders should be able to defend itself against subversion. The resolution provides for making such assistance available. The United States can contribute best to the prevention of subversion by making it possible for sovereign nations to fight their own battles effectively rather than by intervention.[8]

As the months passed, however—and as events made it clear that subversion was perhaps the main Communist-instigated threat to the stability of the Middle East—this connotation of "aggression" became more pronounced in official explanations of the Eisenhower Doctrine. Thus, in reference to the deepening crisis in Lebanon, on July 1, 1958, Secretary of State Dulles said that the Eisenhower Doctrine's reference to "armed attack" did not "preclude . . . an armed revolution which is fomented abroad, aided and assisted from abroad." As a precedent, Dulles noted that this comprehensive interpretation of "armed aggression" had also been employed earlier, when the Senate Foreign Relations Committee had approved the terms of the North Atlantic Treaty in 1949; and the same construction of the term *armed aggression* was given to the language of the Japanese peace treaty in 1951. In her discussion of the Eisenhower Doctrine, Eleanor Dulles (who served in the State Department, while her brother was secretary of state) was even more forthright: "The Eisenhower Doctrine was designed to thwart aggression, whether direct or indirect."[9]

A third contingency possibly requiring application of the Eisenhower Doctrine was the peaceable or voluntary accession to power by a Communist regime in the Middle East. How would the Eisenhower Administration respond to such a development? President Eisenhower stated that his doctrine was not aimed at the overthrow of Communist

8. House Report No. 2, 85th Congress, January 25, 1957, in Department of State, *American Foreign Policy: Current Documents, 1957*, p. 813.

9. Department of State, *American Foreign Policy: Current Documents, 1958* (Washington, D.C.: Government Printing Office, 1962), 951; Eleanor L. Dulles, *American Foreign Policy in the Making* (New York: Harper and Row, 1968), 144.

regimes in the Middle East which had come into power "by peaceful means." What would happen, he was asked by a member of Congress, if Soviet troops entered a country in the Middle East *by invitation* of the government of that country? Eisenhower's reply was that in that event, "there will be time to consult with Congress" before the administration reached a decision on the proper response.[10]

Another ambiguous feature of the Eisenhower Doctrine was the determination of the source of the threat to Middle Eastern security. As defined by the doctrine, the United States would protect the security of the region from a threat posed by "any nation controlled by international communism." Executive officials conceded that the criteria for making such a determination were inexact and subjective.[11] As Secretary of State Dulles acknowledged, there was "no precise formula" for making such a judgment; and for several countries in the Middle East, it would be a "close question" as to whether they confronted such a threat. In any individual case, the White House would examine "a whole complex of actions or lack of action" in determining whether a particular state faced the kind of threat the Eisenhower Doctrine contemplated. To skeptical legislators, Dulles pointed out that Congress itself had used the phrase "a government dominated by international communism" in earlier cases. Dulles also promised that in deciding individual cases, the president would consult with congressional leaders.[12]

Several months after his speech to Congress, President Eisenhower narrowed the scope of his new doctrine considerably. He observed, for example, that such varieties of Marxism as practiced in Yugoslavia were not included in "international communism." Eisenhower conceded that "independent communism" existed and posed no threat to American security interests. In effect, Eisenhower equated "international communism" with Soviet Marxism or Communist movements *directed from Moscow.*[13]

In the Middle Eastern context, however, such explanations left a

10. Eisenhower, *Waging Peace*, 178–79, 181.
11. See, for example, Sherman Adams, *Firsthand Report: The Story of the Eisenhower Administration* (New York: Harper and Row, 1961), 272.
12. Senate *Hearings on the Middle East*, 29.
13. See Eisenhower's statement at his news conference of August 21, 1957, in Department of State, *American Foreign Policy: Current Documents, 1957*, p. 1036. His remarks were made within the context of growing Communist influence in Syria.

number of crucial questions unanswered. Was a nation (like Egypt under President Nasser) that received substantial economic and military assistance from behind the Iron Curtain controlled by "international communism"? Did an Arab state (like Syria in the late 1950s) that was vocally anti-Western, and in which Communist elements were gaining strength, meet the criteria embodied in the Eisenhower Doctrine? No one (perhaps not even officials of the Eisenhower Administration themselves) could be certain of the answers in 1957. As a "doctrine" of American foreign policy, the meaning of Eisenhower's pronouncement would have to be supplied in the light of experience, as the United States confronted a series of tests in its Middle Eastern diplomacy.

Background and Antecedents

The Eisenhower Doctrine shared a common characteristic with the Monroe, Stimson, and Truman doctrines which preceded it. It was issued in response to what executive policy-makers perceived as a threat to the nation's security and diplomatic interests abroad. The locale in this instance was the turbulent Middle East—a region that threatened to become the Balkans of the post–World War II era. The political instability that pervaded the Middle East showed no sign of diminishing—and some crises within the area appeared to be becoming more intense than ever. As a congressional report expressed it, President Eisenhower's policy proposals were designed to serve as "an emergency stopgap" measure to prevent conditions in this region from deteriorating adversely to American interests.[14] Other steps—like ongoing efforts to resolve the vexatious Arab-Israeli conflict—would also be taken to restore political stability to the area.

In the Eisenhower Administration's view, the volatility of the Middle East stemmed from three interrelated causes. The first was the graphic and precipitous decline of Western power and influence in the Middle East, highlighted by the Suez Crisis of 1956. This crisis had been precipitated by Egyptian President Nasser's nationalization of the Suez Canal on July 26, 1956. In turn, this act was followed (on October 29) by an Israeli invasion of Egyptian territory; and a few days later (on November 5) French and British forces also entered Egypt.

---

14. Senate Report No. 70, 85th Congress, February 14, 1957, in Department of State, *American Foreign Policy: Current Documents, 1957*, p. 823.

Although the goals of this foreign incursion into Egypt were never totally clear, one objective was to discredit Nasser's leadership and perhaps to topple his regime. To President Eisenhower's mind, the Anglo-
French-Israeli venture was indefensible, differing little from the Soviet
Union's reliance upon armed force in the same period to suppress dissent in Hungary.[15]

A detailed discussion of the Suez Crisis and of the events that followed it is not necessary for our purpose. Suffice to say that—despite
the military success of the Anglo-French-Israeli invasion of Egypt—
the results were not what its instigators anticipated. Owing primarily
to Washington's opposition to the venture—ultimately resulting in the
evacuation of foreign troops from Egyptian soil—the affair resulted in
a serious diplomatic and psychological defeat for the West and its
Middle Eastern ally, Israel. President Nasser emerged from the crisis
with his prestige at home and abroad greatly enhanced; the Arab-
Israeli controversy was escalated to a new level of acrimony and violence; a serious breach developed among the NATO allies; and after
1956, the United States emerged as an active participant in the affairs
of the Middle East.[16] The results for Great Britain were especially traumatic: Prime Minister Anthony Eden was humiliated and compelled to
resign from office; and the Suez Crisis left a reservoir of ill-feeling between Washington and London that lasted for many months thereafter. Israelis were also disaffected by the Eisenhower Administration's
diplomacy during this episode. In the Israeli view, Washington had
"robbed" them of the fruits of victory and had denied them an opportunity to get rid of one of their chief antagonists, Egypt's Nasser. Israel
was ultimately required to return the conquered Sinai to Egypt, while
official Egyptian attitudes toward Israel became more hostile than
ever. In brief, the Western position in the Middle East deteriorated
sharply. Already in retreat before the forces of anticolonialism, British
and French power all but disappeared from the Middle East. To the
chagrin of American officials, the Suez Crisis appeared to offer new
opportunities for Soviet mischief-making and intervention in this
troubled region.

15. Eisenhower, *Waging Peace*, 20–58.
16. For a brief and objective discussion of the Suez Crisis of 1956, see Fred J. Khouri,
The Arab-Israeli Dilemma (Syracuse, N.Y.: Syracuse University Press, 1968), 210–19.
An excellent commentary is Peter Calvocoressi (ed.), *Suez: Ten Years After* (New York:
Random House, 1967).

Accordingly, in the weeks following the crisis, Secretary of State Dulles was reported to be "harassed and unreassuring" about the prospects for peace and stability in the Middle East. Although it had disagreed with its allies in this episode, the Eisenhower Administration did not wish this fact to be interpreted as signifying indifference toward the area; nor did it denote any weakening of America's resolve to prevent Communist inroads in the region. As President Eisenhower informed Congress, the existing power vacuum "must be filled by the United States before it is filled by Russia."[17]

This leads to the second cause of anxiety in Washington about Middle Eastern security: the rapid growth of Soviet power and influence within the region. Down to the mid-1950s, Moscow had paid relatively little attention to the Middle East. When it began to play an active role in the area, Soviet influence grew rapidly. The door was opened to Soviet intervention when in 1955–1956, after prolonged (and, in the Egyptian view, deliberately dilatory) study, Washington rejected Cairo's request to finance the proposed Aswan High Dam. To Nasser's mind, Washington's refusal to extend the needed aid was not only an unfriendly act; the method of communicating the decision to Nasser was insensitive and insulting. Nasser's response was to nationalize the Suez Canal, thereby triggering the foreign invasion of Egypt.

During the months that followed, the Kremlin took advantage of other opportunities to enhance its influence among Arab states. Soviet Premier Nikita Khrushchev, for example, offered to send Russian "volunteers" to join in the defense of Egypt during the Suez Crisis—an offer which President Nasser wisely declined. After hostilities had ended, Moscow resupplied the Egyptian armed forces. In other Arab states (such as Syria) Communist elements were actively seeking to acquire political power. Secretary of State Dulles believed that a combination of three factors—Moscow's military capabilities, its readiness to use force for political ends, and the lack of moral and ethical restraints on Soviet behavior—created a favorable environment for Communist inroads in the Middle East.[18]

17. Emmet John Hughes, *The Ordeal of Power: A Political Memoir of the Eisenhower Years* (New York: Atheneum, 1963), 178; Eisenhower, *Waging Peace*, 178.

18. Patrick Seale, *The Struggle for Syria: A Study of Post-War Arab Politics, 1945–1958* (London: Oxford University Press, 1965), 285.

To officials of the Eisenhower Administration, Soviet ambitions in the Middle East were related to Moscow's global objectives, which caused deep concern in Washington. Internally, the Communist hierarchy had successfully engaged in "de-Stalinization." The U.S.S.R. had become a nuclear power and was adding to its nuclear arsenal each year. On October 4, 1957, the first Soviet "Sputnik" was launched—giving the Russians an initial lead in space competition and greatly adding to their prestige. On the basis of such developments, at the end of 1956 Khrushchev had defiantly informed the West: "We will bury you!"[19] Although he later explained that the boast meant that the U.S.S.R. would in time surpass the United States *economically*, at the time Khrushchev's statement was interpreted as authoritative evidence of Soviet expansionism and global interventionism.

Officials of the Eisenhower Administration attributed the instability of the Middle East to a third influential factor: the movement known as "Nasserism" which (to some Americans, like Secretary of State Dulles) was regarded as "the next thing to communism." The Nasser-led "Free Officer" movement had led a successful revolution against the monarchy, seizing power on July 23, 1952. As time passed, Egyptian-American relations steadily deteriorated. Nasser became an outspoken and tireless opponent of the West in the Middle East—as in his sharp denunciations of the Baghdad Pact (a defense network for the Middle East, favored by Secretary Dulles). Nasser's decision in mid-1956 to accept Communist arms-aid was interpreted in Washington as providing convincing evidence of Cairo's pro-Soviet orientation. Concurrently, Nasser had emerged as an active leader of the "neutralist" movement that was rapidly attracting adherents among the nations of the Third World. In addition, Americans had great difficulty understanding certain goals and concepts—such as "Arab Socialism" and "Pan-Arabism"—identified with Nasser's regime. Lacking experience in Middle Eastern affairs, Americans widely concluded that such concepts were inimical to Western interests in the region.

Nasser of Egypt also alienated Western opinion because of two other campaigns directed against Western influence in the Middle

19. Drummond and Coblentz, *Duel at the Brink*, 191. Dulles' views on the rapid growth of Soviet influence in the Middle East are set forth in Senate *Hearings on the Middle East*, 4–7; for President Eisenhower's views on this subject, see *Waging Peace*, 177–78.

East. One was Cairo's leading role in rallying Arab opposition against Israel; the other lay in Nasser's support for anticolonial movements (directed against the continued British presence in Egypt and against the French colonial regime in Algeria).

Although in contrast to some Western critics, Secretary of State John Foster Dulles did not view President Nasser as a Communist or a deliberate agent of Soviet imperialism, the increasingly close relationship between Cairo and Moscow engendered deep concern among officials of the Eisenhower Administration.[20] Deliberately or not, Dulles said, Nasser had become a "standard-bearer of the 'immoral' Khrushchev-promoted neutralist tide spreading through the Afro-Arab-Asian world." According to Eleanor Dulles, American officials in time concluded that "the troubles in North Africa and in other parts of the East were linked with the subversion originating in Moscow, but often found a congenial 'launching pad' in Egypt." By early 1957, therefore, even President Eisenhower appeared to share the British government's highly critical assessment of Nasserism—and this fear was at least implicitly reflected in the president's new foreign policy doctrine. Unless the president's proposals were adopted, said Secretary of State Dulles, "the probabilities are that the [Middle East] will be lost to international communism." In his view, the Eisenhower Doctrine would "provide an atmosphere in which other measures can be brought to bear" that would restore lasting stability and security to the region.[21]

To this list of factors eliciting the Eisenhower Doctrine must be added another that (as we noted in Chapter 3) was an influential force in the issuance of the Truman Doctrine. In company with the Truman Administration earlier, President Eisenhower and his advisers were under sharp political attack because of their alleged indifference to

20. The official American assessment of Nasser was perhaps best conveyed by President Eisenhower's verdict that if Nasser were not a Communist, "he certainly succeeded in making us very suspicious of him." Quoted in Townsend Hoopes, *The Devil and John Foster Dulles: The Diplomacy of the Eisenhower Era* (Boston: Little, Brown, 1973), 431.

21. Drummond and Coblentz, *Duel at the Brink*, 171; Eleanor L. Dulles, *John Foster Dulles: The Last Year* (New York: Harcourt, Brace and World, 1963), 67; William R. Polk, *The United States and the Arab World* (Cambridge, Mass.: Harvard University Press, 1965), 279–80; Dulles' testimony in Senate *Hearings on the Middle East*, 72–73; Senate Report No. 70, 85th Congress, in Department of State, *American Foreign Policy: Current Documents, 1957*, p. 823.

Communist gains abroad. The Democratic party had won control of both houses of Congress in the elections of 1956—in no small measure because of attacks upon the diplomatic record of the Eisenhower Administration. Leading Democrats charged that under the Eisenhower White House, American power had declined; the nation's alliances were in serious disarray; friends of the United States (like Israel) had been alienated; and the Soviet Union was rapidly making gains in the Middle East and other regions. Even Republican members of Congress joined the chorus, some of whom asserted that Secretary of State Dulles had "lost the confidence" of the nation. Inside and outside Eisenhower's own party, critics demanded fundamental changes in American policy toward areas like the Middle East.[22]

The internal political context of American diplomacy provided another incentive for the issuance of the Eisenhower Doctrine. President Eisenhower and his advisers believed that it would facilitate the emergence of a new "national consensus" in foreign affairs and would impart a new sense of national unity to American diplomatic efforts. The doctrine would provide forceful evidence to foreign governments that the United States was determined to protect its diplomatic interests and that it had a relevant strategy for doing so. As a symbol of unity, the doctrine would be most effective if it reflected an executive-legislative consensus concerning American goals in the Middle East.[23]

The Formulation of the Eisenhower Doctrine

In common with nearly all other doctrines in American diplomatic experience, several forces played a key role in the Eisenhower Doctrine's formulation. Initially, the doctrine enunciated certain ideas and principles with which Americans were already familiar in different contexts. In that sense, Eisenhower's foreign policy dictum represented no significant innovation in American foreign relations.

The Eisenhower Doctrine, for example, was clearly harmonious with the overall trend of American foreign policy since World War II. Indeed, spokesmen for the administration related the president's new

22. For discussions of the domestic political environment influencing the issuance of the Eisenhower Doctrine, see Drummond and Coblentz, *Duel at the Brink*, 189–90; Charles A. H. Thomson and Frances M. Shattuck, *The 1956 Presidential Campaign* (Washington, D.C.: Brookings Institution, 1960), 259; Stephen E. Ambrose, *Rise to Globalism: American Foreign Policy, 1938–1970* (Baltimore: Penguin, 1971), 248.
23. Eisenhower, *Waging Peace*, 179, 182.

Middle Eastern strategy to the diplomatic principles enunciated by President Monroe in 1823 (see Chapter 1). As Secretary of State Dulles viewed it, the Eisenhower Doctrine was simply an "extension" of Monroe's historic principles; both entailed a "declaration of peace" and were designed to prevent war.[24] Much the same assessment was made by the Washington *Post*, which said of the Eisenhower Doctrine, "Much of the importance of this policy . . . is psychological. It seeks to bolster the independence of the area [the Middle East] by telling the Russians, in the manner of the Monroe Doctrine of 130 years ago, that American power will be used to keep them out. By implication this is designed to cover not only the Near East but Africa as well."[25]

If other commentators on American diplomacy might regard the connection between the Monroe and Eisenhower doctrines as tenuous, less doubt existed about the precedent afforded by the Truman Doctrine. Secretary of State Dulles, for example, cited President Truman's precedent; the Eisenhower Doctrine was merely an application of the containment principle to the Middle East. Throughout a series of measures—beginning with the Greek-Turkish Aid Program in 1947, continuing with the Marshall Plan a few months later, followed by the establishment of NATO in 1949—the United States had time and again expressed its opposition to Communist encroachments against the non-Communist world. Essentially, President Eisenhower was asking Congress to defend the "free peoples" of the Middle East, just as President Truman had sought to preserve the security of Greece and Turkey a decade earlier.[26]

Other precedents for the Eisenhower Doctrine could be found in the "Tripartite Declaration" (May 25, 1950), according to which the United States, Britain, and France had guaranteed the security of the nations of the Middle East against aggression.[27] Early in Eisenhower's administration also, largely at Secretary Dulles' instigation, the United

24. Dulles' testimony in House *Hearings on the Middle East*, 35.
25. Editorial in Washington *Post*, January 7, 1957, reprinted in House *Hearings on the Middle East*, 27. Basically this same view of the Eisenhower Doctrine is taken by Walter LaFeber in *America, Russia, and the Cold War, 1945–1966* (New York: John Wiley and Sons, 1968), 198.
26. Dulles' testimony in the House *Hearings on the Middle East*, 1–6, 149, and in the Senate *Hearings on the Middle East*, 6, 75–76, 133–34.
27. For a discussion of this document, see Harry N. Howard, "The United States," in Tareq Y. Ismael (ed.), *The Middle East in World Politics* (Syracuse, N.Y.: Syracuse University Press, 1974), 123.

States had proposed the creation of a "northern tier" defense zone against Communist penetration, consisting of Turkey, Iraq, and Pakistan. Because of both adverse Israeli and Arab reaction to this security network, the United States refrained from joining what came to be called the Baghdad Pact. Yet his effort clearly conveyed American interest in the "northern tier" zone of the Middle East.[28]

Pointing to these antecedents of the Eisenhower Doctrine, Secretary Dulles declared that eventually there might emerge what he called a "universal doctrine reflected by multilateral treaties or multilateral worldwide authority from the Congress," patterned after the Truman and Eisenhower doctrines.[29]

As is nearly always true with major diplomatic decisions, the president and his advisers played an important—not to say decisive—role in the issuance of the Eisenhower Doctrine. More than any chief executive in modern history perhaps, President Eisenhower leaned heavily upon his secretary of state, John Foster Dulles, whose advice he tended to trust implicitly. Even though the president seldom played an active role in foreign affairs while Dulles was alive, both officials realized that Eisenhower bore the ultimate constitutional authority for the conduct of foreign affairs. In that sense of course, the Eisenhower Doctrine was accepted and promulgated by the chief executive.

Much as he tended to give Secretary Dulles wide latitude in the foreign policy field, the Eisenhower Doctrine bore the president's imprint in four important respects. First, President Eisenhower became convinced that a reformulation of American policy toward the Middle East was necessary. The president called for "more fresh and concrete programs from the State Department, especially for the Middle East."[30] Second, after a detailed study by the State Department leading to the desired policy reformulation, the decision to adopt a new policy

---

28. The Baghdad Pact was initially signed between Turkey and Iraq on February 24, 1955. Great Britain adhered to it a few months later; and subsequently, Pakistan and Iran joined it. Iraq withdrew from the pact early in 1959, after which this defense network was renamed the Central Treaty Organization (CENTO). Although the United States never adhered to the pact, Washington preserved a close working relationship with CENTO. A detailed discussion of the establishment of this "northern tier" defense line may be found in Rouhollah K. Ramazani, *The Northern Tier: Afghanistan, Iran, and Turkey* (Princeton, N.J.: Van Nostrand, 1966), 113–32.

29. Senate, *Hearings on the Middle East*, 74.

30. Hughes, *The Ordeal of Power*, 232–33.

was made by President Eisenhower, in conformity with constitutional requirements. Third, the new policy, as expressed in the Eisenhower Doctrine, was publicly announced and presented to a joint session of Congress personally by President Eisenhower. Fourth, the congressional joint resolution (popularly called the "Middle East Resolution") giving legislative sanction to the doctrine had to be signed by the president before it became law.

Not unexpectedly, Secretary of State Dulles played a pivotal role in the formulation of the Eisenhower Doctrine. As our earlier discussion has emphasized, Dulles had become progressively apprehensive about the "power vacuum" that was developing in the Middle East, especially after the Suez Crisis. As he assessed the problem, the Middle East was caught in the grip of two forces—Nasserism and communism—keeping it in a state of turbulence and insecurity. Moreover, Dulles was fully mindful of the domestic criticism surrounding his diplomatic leadership and of the need to win broader congressional and public support for the administration's diplomacy.

The concerns of the president and the secretary of state were also shared by several ambassadors of the United States, who informed their superiors in Washington late in 1956 that a clear and firm American statement of policy on the Middle East was overdue. By the end of 1956, the State Department had undertaken intensive study of conditions in the Middle East and of the most effective way the United States might respond to them. Secretary Dulles' participation in these studies was limited, however, by two developments: his hospitalization (necessitating a long recuperative period) in November; and his preoccupation with an important meeting of the NATO Council scheduled for mid-December.[31]

Even more than was the case with earlier doctrines of American foreign policy, the role of Congress in the formulation and promulgation of the Eisenhower Doctrine was highly influential. Moreover, as we shall see in later chapters, the mode of legislative participation in the doctrine established a significant precedent in the conduct of American diplomacy.

31. Senate *Hearings on the Middle East*, 76–77; Adams, *Firsthand Report*, 271; Herman Finer, *Dulles over Suez: The Theory and Practice of His Diplomacy* (Chicago: Quadrangle Books, 1964), 467; Peter Lyon, *Eisenhower: Portrait of the Hero* (Boston: Little, Brown, 1974), 725–26.

A unique feature of the Eisenhower Doctrine was the extent to which the president, Secretary of State Dulles, and other executive officials *actively solicited* legislative involvement in the proposed reformulation of American policy toward the Middle East. In a number of respects, their approach was patterned after an earlier measure—the "Formosa Resolution," which passed Congress on January 29, 1955.

While a rough parallel existed between the resolutions providing for the defense of Formosa (Taiwan) and the Middle East, there were also some crucial differences between these two cases. In the instance of the "Formosa Resolution," Congress had acted promptly to give President Eisenhower the authority he requested. As we shall see, by contrast legislative action on the "Middle East Resolution" had emerged in the form of a concurrent resolution of Congress, rather than a joint resolution, as in the case of the Eisenhower Doctrine. (The former is merely an expression of legislative opinion and, as such, is not subject to presidential veto; the latter is an enactment or, after it is signed by the president, a law.) In addition (and we shall note specific examples below), in the case of the "Middle East Resolution," Congress modified the president's request in a number of significant particulars. Finally, although it was intended as a dramatic gesture of "national unity" in foreign affairs, in the end the Eisenhower Doctrine itself proved productive of intense partisan controversy.

The Eisenhower-Dulles foreign policy team was determined that the new Middle Eastern strategy would emerge as the result of joint executive-legislative efforts. At a time when Republicans controlled the White House, and both houses of Congress were under Democratic control, the resulting doctrine would provide a visible symbol of national unity in the diplomatic field. Or, as a report by the House Foreign Affairs Committee expressed it, a declaration supported by the executive and legislative branches would dramatically affirm "the plenary power and authority of the United States" in foreign affairs.[32] Secretary Dulles believed that the principal value of the declaration lay in its "deterrent effect" upon Soviet behavior—a result that would be greatly enhanced if the Kremlin knew in advance that Congress would support White House moves in the Middle East. Congress, said Dulles,

---

32. Eisenhower, *Waging Peace*, 179. See the full report of the committee, in Department of State, *American Foreign Policy: Current Documents, 1957*, pp. 803–16.

should have no reluctance to approve the Eisenhower Doctrine, just as it had supported the Formosa Resolution earlier. Experience had shown that when America faced a threat from "international communism" the two branches of the government had collaborated to meet it, and "when that happened, the danger subsided."[33]

The Eisenhower Administration launched its effort to assure full congressional support for the president's doctrine by summoning legislative leaders to the White House on January 1, 1957. At this session lasting four hours, the rationale and provisions of the proposed Middle East doctrine were fully explained. Legislators present asked numerous questions about the doctrine's provisions and its implications. From the White House's perspective, a major purpose was to impress upon congressional leaders the urgency of legislative approval for the Eisenhower Doctrine.[34]

On the same day that President Eisenhower delivered his speech to a joint session of Congress (January 5, 1957), the House of Representatives began its deliberations on the Eisenhower Doctrine. Hearings on the president's proposal were conducted by the House Foreign Affairs Committee, at which Secretary Dulles and other executive officials and witnesses testified. With reasonable dispatch, on January 30, the House passed its version of the "Middle East Resolution" by a vote of 355–61. This resolution substantially conferred upon the president the authority which he had requested.[35]

Senate disposition of the Eisenhower Doctrine, however, was another matter. Events quickly revealed that in the upper chamber, the president's request for authority to use armed force in the Middle East faced substantial opposition. So outspoken and influential were Senate critics of the proposal that an amended version of the resolution was not approved until March 5—thereby largely vitiating Eisenhower's contention that the protection of American interests in the Middle East required "urgent" support by Congress. In the words of one commentator, Senate consideration of the doctrine was characterized by

33. Dulles' testimony in House *Hearings on the Middle East*, 31, and in Senate *Hearings on the Middle East*, 7, 47.

34. Eisenhower, *Waging Peace*, 178.

35. House Joint Resolution 117, 85th Cong., 1st Sess., in Department of State, *American Foreign Policy: Current Documents, 1957*, pp. 816–17. The House version of the Eisenhower Doctrine differed in several key respects from the Senate version—chiefly in the direction of giving the president the wide latitude in the Middle East he requested.

"nine weeks of acrimonious wrangling." Secretary of State Dulles spent hours on Capitol Hill answering the objections of legislative critics. To his sister, Dulles complained that when he testified before congressional committees, legislators acted "as if I were a criminal at the bar."[36]

Senate objections to the Eisenhower Doctrine were numerous and wide-ranging. Some senators believed that the doctrine provided merely another example of Secretary Dulles' anti-Communist phobia. With that crucial defect, the doctrine left the main causes of Middle Eastern instability (like the Arab-Israeli conflict) unresolved. Other senators objected to the fact that in effect the White House had requested a "blank check" from Congress: Congress was expected to approve *in advance* whatever action the administration chose to take under the president's highly flexible foreign policy guidelines. As some Democrats assessed the matter, the Eisenhower Doctrine was a White House gambit, whereby executive officials sought to "share political responsibility with a reluctant Congress" for an inept Middle Eastern policy.[37] Or, as one outspoken critic of the doctrine—Sen. J. William Fulbright (Democrat of Arkansas)—expressed it, the White House "asks for a blank grant of power over our funds and Armed Forces, to be used in a blank way, for a blank length of time, under blank conditions with respect to blank nations in a blank area. . . . Who will fill in all these blanks?"[38]

Along with a number of other senators, Fulbright regarded the procedures employed by the White House to make the Eisenhower Doctrine a "bipartisan" measure as inadequate. Sen. John F. Kennedy (Democrat from Massachusetts) believed true bipartisanship was lacking in the case of the Eisenhower Doctrine: to his mind, the administration's intention had been to solicit Democratic support for the doctrine without giving the opposition party any real voice in its formulation.[39]

36. Richard Goold-Adams, *John Foster Dulles: A Reappraisal* (New York: Appleton-Century-Crofts, 1962), 241; Dulles, *John Foster Dulles*, 40.

37. Paul Y. Hammond, *The Cold War Years: American Foreign Policy Since 1945* (New York: Harcourt, Brace and World, 1969), 117.

38. On January 24, 1957, Fulbright delivered a lengthy speech on the Senate floor in opposition to the Eisenhower Doctrine. For the text of his speech, see *Congressional Record*, 85th Cong., 1st Sess., Pt. 2, pp. 1855–57.

39. John F. Kennedy, *The Strategy of Peace* (New York: Harper and Row, 1960), 210–11. He regarded the doctrine as one of the more conspicuous American foreign policy failures in the Middle East in recent years (p. 219).

In view of the partisan discord that was to surround the Johnson Doctrine toward Asia (as explained more fully in Chapter 5), one aspect of congressional viewpoints toward the Eisenhower Doctrine was unusually interesting. A number of senators believed that President Eisenhower *already possessed* ample constitutional and legal authority to safeguard American security and diplomatic interests in the Middle East. On that basis, some senators thought Congress ought to withhold approval of the Eisenhower Doctrine. Thus, Senator Fulbright contended that passing the resolution would weaken the chief executive's authority in the foreign policy field; it could similarly erode Congress' constitutional power to "declare war." In marked contrast to his later complaints about diplomatic moves carried out by the "imperial presidency," Fulbright informed the Eisenhower Administration in 1957 that: "Experience tells us that when the highest interests of the country are at stake, an Executive who is timid represents a far greater danger to the preservation of our constitutional system than does one who exceeds the letter of the law in a vigorous use of Executive power to defend the Government, the Nation, and the Constitution." [40]

Critics of the Eisenhower Doctrine called attention to other defects and problems associated with it. To some senators, the doctrine would necessarily weaken America's long-standing ties with Israel. Other senators feared that it would diminish the power and prestige of the United Nations. A small minority was fearful that the doctrine would provoke Moscow into some new adventuristic action in the Middle East or elsewhere. Former Secretary of State Dean Acheson informed senators that the doctrine had innumerable weaknesses—not the least of which was that it was "vague, inadequate, and not very useful." [41] Despite such objections, on March 5, 1957, the Senate voted (72–19) in favor of a modified version of the resolution requested by the White House; and on March 9, President Eisenhower signed the joint resolution into law.

In the end, two considerations above all overrode legislative objections to the Eisenhower Doctrine. The first—as Secretary of State

40. Fulbright's speech on January 24, 1957, in *Congressional Record*, 85th Cong., 1st Sess., Pt. 2, pp. 1855–57.
41. Acheson's testimony to the House Foreign Affairs Committee, in House *Hearings on the Middle East*, 159–68. For other criticisms, see Eisenhower, *Waging Peace*, 180; and Adams, *Firsthand Report*, 273.

Dulles reminded legislators almost daily—was that the White House was merely asking Congress to express its opposition to Communist expansionism, thereby reaffirming the basic continuity of American foreign policy. The second pivotal consideration was that—as in the case of the Truman Doctrine earlier—congressional repudiation of the president's role of diplomatic leadership could have had highly damaging consequences for America's position in international relations.[42]

Yet if legislative critics could not block passage of the Middle East Resolution, their objections were not without influence upon the outcome. Secretary Dulles himself acknowledged that the doctrine reflected congressional viewpoints in several respects. Before consenting to it, for example, the Senate demanded a thorough "review" of American foreign policy toward the Middle East. The House Foreign Affairs Committee urged the White House to formulate "positive and comprehensive measures" for promoting American diplomatic interests in the strife-torn Middle East. Other legislators demanded that the executive branch submit periodic "reports" to Congress on efforts to implement the Eisenhower Doctrine.[43] Congressional sentiment was also reflected in provisions for the Eisenhower Doctrine's termination: it could be terminated by a concurrent resolution of Congress (a measure that could be adopted by simple majorities in both houses and that did not require the president's signature).

Yet these were relatively minor changes in the Middle East Resolution as submitted by the White House. It will be recalled that the House of Representatives had acted on the resolution fairly promptly and had given the president substantially the authority he requested. The Senate, however, refused to follow suit. At Senate insistence, the language of the Middle East Resolution stated that the United States was "prepared to use armed forces" to safeguard the security of the Middle East from Communist encroachments. Senators were unwilling to "authorize" the president to use the armed forces for that purpose, believing that he already possessed sufficient authority to do so if a new Communist-instigated crisis in the Middle East required such a commitment. The Senate's phraseology thus avoided the contentious

42. Dulles' testimony in Senate Hearings on the Middle East, 133–34, 340.
43. House Hearings on the Middle East, 6; House Report No. 2, 85th Congress, January 25, 1957, in Department of State, American Foreign Policy: Current Documents, 1957, p. 807.

constitutional issue of whether the president *needed* legislative approval to commit the armed forces abroad. Politically, the Senate's language also left Congress free to exercise its own prerogatives in the future—including the right to criticize presidential diplomatic moves in the Middle East if these miscarried! To President Eisenhower's mind, Congress had substantially granted him the authority he had requested and had demonstrated the unity of American foreign policy in approaching Middle Eastern questions.[44]

What role did public opinion play in the promulgation of the Eisenhower Doctrine? No evidence exists that the Eisenhower Administration made any overt effort to "consult" public opinion, or to take it directly into account, during the stage of policy formulation. The evidence does indicate, however, that the doctrine accorded with the prevailing sentiments of the American people and enjoyed at least their tacit support. As late as May, 1957, a Gallup Poll found that the issue of dealing with Russia headed the list of the most important problems identified by the American people. Another national poll, taken early in 1957, showed that 62 percent of the people approved of Eisenhower's performance as president, while 23 percent disapproved, and 15 percent had no opinion. By late February, some 72 percent of the people indicated approval for President Eisenhower's performance, while 18 percent disapproved, and 10 percent had no opinion.[45]

After the president's speech to Congress on January 5, a Gallup Poll was taken specifically on the public's reaction to his new foreign policy doctrine for the Middle East. The results showed that 70 percent of the people approved of United States economic assistance to friendly countries in the Middle East; 19 percent disapproved; and 11 percent had no opinion. On the question of American arms-aid to Middle Eastern nations, 53 percent of the sample approved this step; 36 percent disapproved, while 13 percent had no opinion. Asked if they would support the use of American military forces to defend Middle Eastern countries which might be attacked by the Soviet Union, 50 percent of the sample answered "yes"; 34 percent answered "no"; and

44. See Eisenhower's first report to Congress on the Eisenhower Doctrine, submitted on August 5, 1957, in Department of State, *American Foreign Policy: Current Documents, 1957*, p. 863.

45. George H. Gallup (ed.), *The Gallup Poll: Public Opinion, 1935–1971* (New York: Random House, 1972), II, 1476, 1492, 1493.

16 percent expressed no opinion on the matter.[46] Public opinion polls throughout the months ahead showed two tendencies. The American people basically approved of Eisenhower's performance as president; and they continued to view the problem of Cold War tensions with the Soviet Union as an urgent national issue.[47]

Although we may conclude that the Eisenhower Doctrine enjoyed a wide degree of public suport, as always public opinion revealed ambiguous and anomolous characteristics. Some groups within the United States, for example, were outspokenly opposed to the doctrine. Israel's supporters feared that the anticipated program of American arms-aid to Arab countries would upset the regional balance of power. Other groups complained that the doctrine was but another manifestation of the Eisenhower Administration's anti-Communist fixation, leading it to attribute the major causes of instability in the Middle East and elsewhere exclusively to Soviet machinations. In some degree, Congress' skepticism about the doctrine stemmed from the fact that congressional mail analyses showed that public sentiment was running eight to one against the Middle East Resolution. (In this and other instances of public policy, of course, the "negatives" on an issue were more inclined to express their viewpoints forcefully than the "positives.")[48]

The Eisenhower Doctrine provides perhaps a classic case study in what is sometimes called the "malleability" of mass public opinion.[49] As has been almost consistently true since World War II, the American people have supported measures designed to contain communism (or, more broadly, to protect American security interests) abroad. Whenever a chief executive asserts that the security of the United States is endangered, he normally receives whatever degree of public support he requires to protect it. In the face of this tendency, Congress is extremely reluctant to "cripple" the president or to create the impression

46. *Ibid.*, 1467.
47. See, for example, the Gallup Polls conducted on June 6–11, 1957, in early January, 1958, and on October 1, 1958, in *ibid.*, 1492.
48. For evidence of adverse public sentiment toward the Eisenhower Doctrine, see Goold-Adams, *John Foster Dulles*, 240–41; Lyon, *Eisenhower: Portrait of the Hero*, 728; and LaFeber, *America, Russia, and the Cold War*, 197–98.
49. This is the basic thesis of Bernard C. Cohen's study on *The Public's Impact on Foreign Policy* (Boston: Little, Brown, 1973). See especially his conclusions on pp. 184–208.

of an internally divided government in the face of an impending foreign crisis.[50]

Overseas, the Eisenhower Doctrine encountered a mixed reception. As had been true of the Monroe Doctrine earlier, after the Suez Crisis the British government proposed a joint Anglo-American declaration on the Middle East to Washington; as was also true of the earlier case, Washington declined London's suggestion. The Eisenhower Doctrine thus became another unilateral policy statement by the United States. Secretary of State Dulles asserted that the ideas contained in the doctrine had been discussed with the NATO allies prior to its announcement; and according to his tally, some fifteen European nations supported this new American policy statement.[51] Yet these facts did not change the doctrine's essentially unilateral nature.

Among certain pro-Western governments in the Middle East—notably, Turkey, Pakistan, Lebanon, and Iran—the doctrine also enjoyed substantial support. Indeed, Secretary Dulles contended that the Eisenhower Doctrine had been promulgated in some measure in response to overtures by these governments. Dulles was also confident—and in this assumption, of course, he erred—that the doctrine would subsequently be approved by the governments of Syria and Egypt. As some commentators pointed out, those Middle Eastern governments that were most enthusiastic about the doctrine were also those that could be expected to benefit most directly from American economic and military aid programs under it. Yet it was equally clear that predominant Arab opinion was hostile to the Eisenhower Doctrine, fearing that it presaged a new era of Western hegemony in the Middle East. The endorsement of the doctrine by the pro-Western Iraqi government of Nuri es-Said, for example, was one reason why that regime was overthrown in August, 1958. King Hussein's government in Jordan—always sensitive to adverse Arab opinion toward it—ultimately denied that the aid received by Jordan from the United States was provided under the Eisenhower Doctrine.[52]

50. Michael H. Armacost, *The Foreign Relations of the United States* (Belmont, Calif.: Dickenson Press, 1969), 124.

51. Hughes, *The Ordeal of Power*, 209; Dulles' testimony in Senate *Hearings on the Middle East*, 82–98.

52. Dulles' testimony in House *Hearings on the Middle East*, 9; Eisenhower, *Waging Peace*, 181; Polk, *The United States and the Arab World*, 281; Charles D. Cremeans, *The*

In the Middle Eastern context, it was clear that the Eisenhower Doctrine had injected the United States directly into intra-Arab conflicts and rivalries. Iraq's initial acceptance of the doctrine, for example, aroused deep suspicions by its traditional rival, Egypt. Collectively, most Arab states believed that the doctrine was irrelevant to the most critical issue engendering regional tensions: the Arab-Israeli conflict. As Arabs assessed it, the latter also offered the main opportunities for Soviet adventurism in the area. As one commentator expressed it, Arab reactions to the doctrine reflected "the deepest suspicion," since it offered protection against a threat they did not fear (the Soviet Union), but no real protection against the most dangerous force jeopardizing their security (Israel).[53]

Applying the Eisenhower Doctrine to Jordan and Syria

In the months following the promulgation of the Eisenhower Doctrine, there were three cases involving its applications. Two of these—involving Jordan and Syria—were relatively minor. The third instance—entailing the entry of American troops into Lebanon—was highly important and requires more detailed analysis.

Created as a new political entity in 1923, the Emirate of Transjordan or Jordan always had close ties with Great Britain. In the wake of the Suez Crisis of 1956—in which Jordan joined other Arab states in condemning Western military intervention in the Middle East—King Hussein dismissed the British Commander of the Jordan (later renamed the Arab) Legion. Thereafter, Jordan looked mainly to the United States as a source of external economic and military assistance. For officials in Washington, King Hussein was a voice of "moderation" in the Arab-Israeli conflict and in intra-Arab controversies generally. Yet, aware that his grandfather, the Emir Abdullah, had been assassinated by Palestinian nationalists, King Hussein was mindful of his always precarious political position both within Jordan and among the Arab nations.

Arabs and the World (New York: Praeger, 1963), 157; Malcolm H. Kerr, *The Arab Cold War: Gamal 'Abd al-Nasir and His Rivals* (3rd ed.; London: Oxford University Press, 1971), 5.

53. Richard H. Nolte, "United States Policy and the Middle East," in Georgiana G. Stevens (ed.), *The United States and the Middle East* (Englewood Cliffs, N.J.: Prentice-Hall, 1964), 166.

By the spring of 1957, Jordan experienced another internal political crisis—this one caused mainly by opposition to the monarchy from the large number of Palestinians living within the country. Palestinian opposition to Hussein was in turn encouraged by Arabs in other Middle Eastern countries (such as Syria and Egypt). Fearful of the political future of his country if the Jordanian monarchy was toppled, President Chamoun of Lebanon urged Washington to invoke the Eisenhower doctrine.

In time, President Eisenhower concluded that Jordan's security was endangered and that the country faced a threat posed by "international communism." (This judgment of course necessarily implied that Egypt, Syria, and other governments spearheading the campaign against the Jordanian monarchy were Communist-controlled.) On the basis of that finding, Eisenhower ordered units of the U.S. Sixth Fleet to move into the eastern Mediterranean. Within a few days, the Jordanian crisis had subsided and the monarchy appeared stable. Subsequently, Jordan received $10 million in American economic assistance under the Eisenhower Doctrine. (A later threat to Jordan's political stability, occurring concurrently with the American intervention in Lebanon, was successfully countered by Great Britain. On that occasion, Washington promised to support British efforts to protect Jordan's security if that became necessary, which it did not.)[54]

Richard H. Nolte believes that there were two residual effects of this initial application of the Eisenhower Doctrine. As a result of it, Jordan became "an American client under the authoritarian rule of King Hussein"; British influence in Jordan correspondingly declined. And for most of the Arab states, American behavior appeared to conform to Soviet descriptions of it: Washington had relied upon "gunboats, bribes, and puppet regimes" to maintain Western influence in the Middle East. It was highly significant that—even though he had been a beneficiary of it—King Hussein publicly denied that Jordan had "accepted," or was being protected by, the Eisenhower Doctrine.[55]

The second case involving the application of the Eisenhower Doc-

54. The details of this first application of the Eisenhower Doctrine are set forth at length in Eisenhower, *Waging Peace*, 194–95, 279–82.

55. Nolte, "United States Policy and the Middle East," 167; Leila M. T. Meo, *Lebanon, Improbable Nation: A Study in Political Development* (Bloomington, Ind.: Indiana University Press, 1965), 190.

trine concerned Syria. Among the Arab states, Syria was distinctive in several respects. The country had a long history of chronic political upheaval—so much as to be described by some commentators as "ungovernable." Damascus was also at the forefront of Arab opposition to Israel and of anti-Western sentiment in the Middle East. Authorities in Damascus, for example, outspokenly condemned the Eisenhower Doctrine.[56]

By mid-1957, Syria appeared to be on the verge of another internal political crisis. Anti-Western propaganda reached a new high, as Syrian sources contended they had evidence of intervention by the Central Intelligence Agency (CIA) in their domestic affairs. On the basis of such evidence, Damascus expelled several American officials from the country.[57] During this period, two developments within Syria caused anxiety in Washington: the influence of Marxist groups within the country appeared to be growing; and Syria was becoming increasingly dependent upon the Soviet Union for external economic and military assistance. President Eisenhower became convinced that a Communist takeover of Syria was imminent; Secretary Dulles indicated that the administration was considering invoking the Eisenhower Doctrine. Late in August, the White House sent a former State Department official, Loy Henderson, to the Middle East to investigate conditions in Syria. On September 5, Henderson (who did not actually visit Syria) reported to Secretary Dulles that Syria was in danger of succumbing to Communist control.[58] Officials in other countries—including Turkey, Lebanon, and Jordan—urged Washington to avert a Communist seizure of power in Syria. Yet even these governments were cautious about American *military* intervention in Syria, unless the Syrian government committed aggression against a neighbor (which seemed unlikely).

The possibility of invoking the Eisenhower Doctrine against Syria posed a troublesome policy dilemma for the Eisenhower Administration. Just a year earlier, Washington had severely condemned Britain,

56. Seale, *The Struggle for Syria*, 289.
57. Lyon, *Eisenhower: Portrait of the Hero*, 746. One of the best informed students of Syrian affairs has said that it is difficult to dismiss Syria's accusations against American intervention in its affairs as "fabrications." Seale, *The Struggle for Syria*, 293.
58. Eisenhower, *Waging Peace*, 196–97; Department of State, *American Foreign Policy: Current Documents, 1957*, p. 1040. For a discussion of Henderson's mission to the Middle East, see Seale, *The Struggle for Syria*, 295–96.

France, and Israel for using force against Egypt; and in the same period, it had castigated the Kremlin for relying upon armed might to
crush the Hungarian revolt. Not very convincingly, President Eisenhower explained that reliance upon the Eisenhower Doctrine in the
Syrian case was "different," since an alien force—"international communism"—had already "invaded" the country; and America's assistance to protect Syrian security had been "requested" by other
countries, because they feared for their own security.[59] Yet American
officials were also aware that Arab sentiment was overwhelmingly opposed to Washington's reliance upon the Eisenhower Doctrine in dealing with Syria.

On September 10 Secretary Dulles specified a number of criteria
that would have to be met before Washington invoked the Eisenhower
Doctrine toward Syria—the principal one being that Syria had to
commit aggression against a neighboring state. Dulles added that in
his view, this was an unlikely development. The administration was
obviously attempting to reduce the likelihood of American military intervention in Syria. As events turned out, Washington did not actually
invoke the Eisenhower Doctrine in the Syrian case. It did, however,
take several other steps short of military intervention in the country,
such as increasing American arms-aid to Syria's neighbors and trans-
ferring naval units to the area. Concurrently, the government of Turkey (which had long had tense relations with Syria) was warned not to
use its own armed forces against Syria. Seeking to inflame this potential conflict in the Middle East, the Kremlin joined Syria in denouncing possible American intervention. Premier Khrushchev pointedly
warned Turkey: "If the rifles fire, the rockets will start flying." Secretary Dulles' answer to this threat was to say that if there were a Soviet
attack upon Turkey, the United States might retaliate directly against
Soviet territory![60]

Throughout the remainder of 1957, the Syrian political crisis ebbed
and flowed—and the prospect of American intervention in the country steadily diminished. Then early in 1958, a new development seriously weakened Communist influence within Syria, further reducing
the likelihood of American intervention. This was formation of the

59. Eisenhower, Waging Peace, 198–99.
60. Department of State, American Foreign Policy: Current Documents, 1957, p.
1040; Eisenhower, Waging Peace, 203–204.

United Arab Republic, a union between Syria and Egypt, on February 1, 1958. (The UAR lasted until September 29, 1961, when Syria withdrew from it.) If few Americans realized it at the time, the evidence indicated that the impetus for this union came from the militantly anti-Communist Syrian Ba'ath Party, whose leaders sought to counter growing Marxist influence within the country.[61] Policy-makers in Washington, however, misconstrued the meaning of the UAR, interpreting it primarily as an effort by Egypt's Nasser to expand his hegemony. In turn, the Eisenhower White House feared this was equivalent to enhanced Soviet influence in this key Arab state.[62]

A dominant conclusion which emerges from the Syrian case is that officials in Washington acted with considerable *restraint* in their response to events in Syria. The administration was obviously reluctant to invoke the Eisenhower Doctrine, and American influence played a key role in de-escalating an emerging crisis between Syria and Turkey. Yet it is also true that even this moderate American response inflamed Syrian and Arab opinion generally against the Eisenhower Doctrine. Even the possibility that the United States would invoke the doctrine against Syria created Arab resentment. Washington's negative reaction to the creation of the United Arab Republic convinced Arabs that Americans had a most imperfect understanding of political developments in the Middle East. Conspicuous among these American misconceptions was failure to appreciate the Arab determination to resist Communist domination.

Yet official misunderstandings and misinterpretation of motives with regard to the Eisenhower Doctrine were not confined to the United States. Syrian and other Arab leaders tended to overlook the fact that American behavior during the Syrian crisis was restrained and that Washington's influence was cast in the direction of preventing other countries (like Turkey) from interfering in Syria's internal affairs. As a result of America's behavior, a still independent Syria was left free to solve its "Communist problem" in its own way—by union with Egypt.[63] Under the Ba'athist government that emerged after the dissolution of the UAR, Syria not only retained its independence but

---

61. For an authoritative study of the creation of the United Arab Republic, see Kerr, *The Arab Cold War*, 1–44.
62. For an illustration of this view, see Hughes, *The Ordeal of Power*, 262.
63. Meo, *Lebanon*, 192.

in time became one of the most outspokenly anti-Israeli and anti-Western states in the Middle East—a fact that American officials did not necessarily like, but made no concerted effort to change.

American Intervention in Lebanon

The major test of the meaning and utility of the Eisenhower Doctrine for the United States came in Lebanon—climaxed by the landing of American marines in the country during the summer of 1958. Sometimes called "the improbable nation," Lebanon stands as an exception to almost every general rule of Middle Eastern politics. Throughout modern history, Lebanon has experienced a series of conflicts and internal political crises among its religious minorities. After receiving nominal independence in 1941 from France, in 1943 representatives of the major Christian (Maronite) and Moslem factions agreed to establish a "confessional state," in which political power would be allocated according to a formula reflecting the assumed size of each religious faction (as determined by a French census taken in 1932). This unusual arrangement more or less preserved political stability in the country until the early 1970s, when a large number of Palestinians (after being driven out of Jordan) took sanctuary in Lebanon. Thereafter, the hapless country was plunged into the most destructive, and seemingly interminable, conflict in its history.[64]

Although modern Lebanon has been subject to chronic political instability, developments during the late 1950s—especially the creation of the United Arab Republic—provided a new source of political turbulence for the country. Many Lebanese, especially the Maronite segment, were concerned that the UAR was the forerunner of an even larger, new Arab state incorporating Lebanon, in which the Maronites would lose their identity and privileged position. A new political crisis in Lebanon was precipitated in April, 1958, when pro-Western President Chamoun announced that he planned to seek reelection—a decision his critics inside and outside the country believed violated Lebanon's National Charter (or constitution).[65] Chamoun's announce-

64. More detailed discussion of the political development of Lebanon, with emphasis upon the period since World War II, may be found in Leonard Binder (ed.), *Politics in Lebanon* (New York: John Wiley and Sons, 1966); Meo, *Lebanon*; and Fahim Qubain, *Crisis in Lebanon* (Washington, D.C.: Middle East Institute, 1961).
65. Eisenhower, *Waging Peace*, 265.

ment was followed by insurrections throughout the country. The Lebanese Army—reflecting the religious and ethnic divisions existing within the country—was powerless to impose the government's authority against dissident elements. President Chamoun complained to the UN Security Council that Syria and Egypt were fomenting revolution against his government; in the same period, Chamoun raised the possibility with Washington of American intervention in Lebanon under the Eisenhower Doctrine.

American officials were sympathetic to Chamoun's request. Secretary of State Dulles believed that Lebanon faced a threat (via Syria and Egypt) stemming from the machinations of "international communism." Yet it cannot be said that the Eisenhower Administration acted precipitously in responding to Beirut's pleas. Initially, the White House awaited the outcome of a United Nations investigating team sent to Lebanon; and Secretary Dulles urged all factions involved in Lebanon's political strife to settle their differences peacefully.[66]

The political turmoil in Lebanon, however, showed no sign of disappearing. Despite United Nations efforts, the crisis in Lebanon was intensifying. President Chamoun reiterated his charge that Syria and Egypt were actively intervening in Lebanon's political affairs. Then on July 14, 1958, there occurred an event that sent shock waves throughout the Middle East and precipitated new political strife in Lebanon: the Iraqi Revolution that toppled the pro-Western monarchy and brought in a new regime, led by the Iraqi military under Gen. Abdel Karrim Kassim. To say that officials in Washington were traumatized by this event would be to understate the reaction. President Eisenhower feared "a complete elimination of Western influence in the Middle East" as a result of developments in Iraq; and he believed that American power must be used "to stop the trend toward chaos" in the region.[67] No less alarmed by the Iraqi Revolution, President Chamoun immediately and urgently requested American military intervention in Lebanon under the Eisenhower Doctrine (a request the Lebanese cabinet had approved approximately a month before it was relayed to Washington).[68] Meanwhile, other governments in the region (such as

---

66. *Ibid.*, 266, 268; Dulles' statement on May 20, 1958, in Department of State, *American Foreign Policy: Current Documents, 1958*, pp. 939, 951.
67. Eisenhower, *Waging Peace*, 269–70.
68. Robert McClintock, *The Meaning of Limited War* (Boston: Houghton Mifflin,

Turkey, Iran, and before its revolution, Iraq) had urged Washington to preserve the independence of Lebanon.[69]

Before receiving Chamoun's request, Washington had already informed Beirut that if it became necessary, the United States would defend the country's security under the Eisenhower Doctrine. This pledge, however, was conditional: for example, American troops would not enter Lebanon in order to guarantee President Chamoun a second term in office, and the forces of the United States would be used mainly to protect American life and property in the country. On May 14, the American ambassador to Lebanon specified two additional conditions: Lebanon's independence had to be in jeopardy; and the nation's own armed forces had to be incapable of preserving internal order and national security.[70]

A complex sequence of events in Washington followed President Chamoun's urgent (not to say frantic) request for American intervention in Lebanon. Hurriedly, State Department officials—in collaboration with those from the Defense Department and the Central Intelligence Agency—assembled data on the situation in Lebanon; Secretary of State Dulles solicited the views of some seventy high-level State Department and other governmental officials, as well as the views of key American embassies in London, Paris, and Beirut. Out of such consultations, a consensus developed that American intervention in Lebanon was essential—a step ultimately approved by President Eisenhower.[71]

Once the decision had been made, President Eisenhower summoned twenty-two congressional leaders to the White House to inform them of it. Legislative viewpoints reflected a belief that (although there was little enthusiasm for it) a *limited* American intervention in Lebanon would be supported by Congress, if the president believed it necessary. Legislative spokesmen also believed that the chief executive possessed the constitutional authority to take this step.

1967), 105–107. McClintock is a former State Department official who was directly involved in the Lebanese crisis of 1958.

69. Qubain, *Crisis in Lebanon*, 127.

70. Eisenhower, *Waging Peace*, 267; McClintock, *The Meaning of Limited War*, 101.

71. Eisenhower, *Waging Peace*, 270–71; Dulles, *American Foreign Policy in the Making*, 274–77. One study has found that the decision to intervene in Lebanon was "pure Dulles." It was taken "on his direct recommendation to the President." Drummond and Coblentz, *Duel at the Brink*, 191.

Accordingly, by the president's order at 3:00 P.M. on July 15, U.S. Marines from the Sixth Fleet landed on the Lebanese coast. Within a matter of hours, there occurred what one commentator has called "the largest peacetime concentration of American military power ever assembled" to that time: some nine thousand marines and paratroopers, seventy warships, and four hundred navy and air force planes comprised the force supporting the Lebanese operation.[72]

On the day the marines landed in Lebanon, President Eisenhower addressed the American people on radio and television. American forces had entered Lebanon, he declared, in order to safeguard American lives and property and to defend the political integrity of the country. As he had done several times in the recent past, Eisenhower called upon the United Nations to assume responsibility for preserving Lebanon's independence; and he promised that, if the organization did so, American troops would be withdrawn from the country. Eisenhower assured the American people that the commitment of troops in Lebanon would be temporary; if their use did not achieve political stability within a brief time, then "we are backing up a government with so little popular support that we probably should not be there."[73]

The landing of U.S. Marines in Lebanon was bloodless and unopposed. As one observer has expressed it, American troops were met only by "curious Beirut sunbathers and Coca-Cola vendors." The principal opposition to American intervention came from outside Lebanon. As Secretary Dulles had anticipated, pro-Nasser sentiment throughout the Middle East was incensed by the American landing. Nasser denounced the expedition and expressed his displeasure by immediately traveling to Moscow to appeal for Soviet assistance in countering this latest Western intrusion in the Middle East.[74] Predictably, the new revolutionary government of Iraq denounced "American imperialism" in Lebanon—and warned that American troops would next invade Iraq! Within Lebanon, anti-Chamoun groups accused the

72. Hughes, *The Ordeal of Power*, 263.
73. Eisenhower, *Waging Peace*, 270–75. For the full text of Eisenhower's speech, see Department of State, *American Foreign Policy: Current Documents, 1958*, pp. 969–72.
74. Herbert K. Tillema, *Appeal to Force: American Military Intervention in the Era of Containment* (New York: Thomas Y. Crowell, 1973), 49. For a discussion of Nasser's efforts to involve the Soviet Union in the Lebanese crisis, see John Lukacs, *A New History of the Cold War* (Garden City, N.Y.: Doubleday, 1966), 168–69.

United States of trying to "save" President Chamoun and dictate Lebanon's political future.[75]

After the marines landed, the Lebanese crisis quickly subsided. The presence of American forces—and even more crucially perhaps, the diplomatic skill displayed by presidential envoy Robert Murphy in deescalating the crisis—restored stability at least temporarily to the country. Murphy's diplomatic acumen—utilized fully as much in dealing with his superiors in Washington, as in negotiating with the factions within Lebanon—was decisive in the outcome.[76] His principal contribution perhaps lay in convincing officials in Washington that the root of Lebanon's political turmoil lay in ongoing conflict and suspicion among the country's heterogeneous religious and ethnic groups, rather than in the machinations of "international communism" in the Middle East.[77]

This did not mean of course that foreign intervention was totally lacking in Lebanon (Syrian and Egyptian officials had, for example, called for the overthrow of Chamoun's government).[78] Yet Chamoun's enthusiastic endorsement of the Eisenhower Doctrine had also seriously undermined his credibility with Arabs inside and outside Lebanon.[79] Murphy and other informed students of Lebanese affairs were convinced that foreign intervention remained a relatively subordinate and collateral problem. In his view, the conflict in Lebanon could be attributed to "concerned personalities and rivalries of a do-

75. Tillema, Appeal to Force, 48; Qubain, Crisis in Lebanon, 119.
76. Robert Murphy, Diplomat Among Warriors (Garden City, N.Y.: Doubleday, 1964), 408; Qubain, Crisis in Lebanon, 131.
77. For a detailed discussion of this aspect of the Lebanese political crisis, see Arnold Hottinger, "Zu'ama and Politics in the Lebanese Crisis of 1958," Middle East Journal, XV (Spring, 1961), 127–40.
78. See, for example, Richard J. Barnet, Intervention and Revolution: America's Confrontation with Insurgent Movements Around the World (New York: World Publishing Co., 1968), 144. See also J. C. Hurewitz, "Lebanese Democracy in its International Setting," in Binder (ed.), Politics in Lebanon, 231–32. Another critic of the Eisenhower Doctrine who concedes there was Syrian and Egyptian intervention in Lebanon is Melvin Gurtov in The United States Against the Third World: Antinationalism and Intervention (New York: Praeger, 1974), 28.
79. For reaction inside and outside Lebanon to Chamoun's acceptance of the Eisenhower Doctrine, see Nolte, "United States Policy and the Middle East," 169; and Cremeans, The Arabs and the World, 164. The Syrian and Egyptian reaction is discussed in M. S. Agwani (ed.), The Lebanese Crisis, 1958: A Documentary Study (New York: Asia Publishing Co., 1965), 107.

mestic nature, with no relation to international issues. Communism was playing no direct or substantial part in the insurrection, although Communists no doubt hoped to profit from the disorders." Or, as a well informed student of Lebanese affairs put it, the 1958 crisis was "fundamentally caused by a division in the soul of Lebanese society. All other factors are either external manifestations or subsidiary derivatives." [80]

Robert Murphy in time negotiated a successful resolution of the Lebanese internal crisis; and the first contingent of American troops left the country on October 25, 1958. President Chamoun was persuaded not to seek reelection, and his political opponents requested American assistance in maintaining public order. Despite his anti-American rhetoric, Egypt's President Nasser obviously desired a peaceful settlement of the Lebanese problem and did not impede Murphy's efforts toward that end. The formula for ending the crisis called for Lebanon's return to the provisions of the National Charter—including the stipulation that it preserve its customary "neutrality" in foreign affairs. This meant that Lebanon would no longer adhere to the Eisenhower Doctrine; American forces would be evacuated from the country; under the aegis of the United Nations, the Arab League would assume responsibility in the future for preventing new threats to Lebanese independence. After American forces left Lebanon, in Ulam's words, politics in Lebanon returned to "normal"—that is, from a condition of "acute crisis" to a "lingering and less acute one." [81]

A major casualty of American military intervention in Lebanon was the Eisenhower Doctrine. The new Lebanese government under General Chehab publicly announced it would no longer accept the doctrine, thereby joining most other Arab governments in repudiating it. As one authority on Lebanon has stated, with the evacuation of American forces from Lebanon, the United States "abandoned the Eisenhower Doctrine as a policy for the Arab Middle East." [82]

80. Murphy, *Diplomat Among Warriors*, 404; Qubain, *Crisis in Lebanon*, 28.
81. Keither Wheelock, *Nasser's New Egypt: A Critical Analysis* (New York: Praeger, 1960), 262–63; Adam B. Ulam, *The Rivals: America and Russia Since World War II* (New York: Viking Press, 1971), 280.
82. Meo, *Lebanon*, 189. See also Hoopes, *The Devil and John Foster Dulles*, 439.

Diplomatic Profit and Loss

Many of the positive and negative consequences of the Eisenhower Doctrine may be more meaningfully discussed in our examination of American diplomatic doctrines collectively (Chapter 9). Here certain unique and significant implications of the Eisenhower Doctrine may be identified briefly.

The Eisenhower Doctrine is classified among the "minor" doctrines of American foreign policy primarily because of its short life-span. With most Arabs—and some critics of Eisenhower-Dulles diplomacy at home—it was unpopular from the beginning; and that fact did not change while it was in effect. For many years after President Eisenhower left office, his doctrine remained an impediment to cordial Arab-American relations.

Critics of the doctrine often overlook the point, emphasized in this chapter, that the Eisenhower Administration invoked it most reluctantly in Lebanon—and only after it had unsuccessfully attempted to get the United Nations to preserve the peace in Lebanon.[83] Moreover, America's involvement in Lebanon under the doctrine went far toward healing the breach in Anglo-American relations caused by the Suez Crisis of 1956. (Concurrently with the marine landing in Lebanon, British troops entered Jordan to protect the Hashimite monarchy from its political enemies). Once more, the United States and Britain appeared to be pursuing parallel policies in the Middle East.

American military forces were also used in Lebanon to achieve a peaceful and orderly transfer of political power within the country. Washington's diplomacy confounded critics at home and abroad: avowedly pro-Western figures (like President Chamoun) did *not* benefit from the presence of American troops in the country. Instead, the new Lebanese government reiterated the country's neutral position in foreign affairs—including its renunciation of the Eisenhower Doctrine! The orderly transfer of power in Lebanon contributed to another gain for American foreign policy in the Middle East: a gradual improvement in Egyptian-American relations.[84]

83. This point is emphasized by Qubain, *Crisis in Lebanon*, 113.
84. This point is stressed by J. C. Hurewitz in "Lebanese Democracy in its International Setting," 233.

While the application of the Eisenhower Doctrine in Lebanon did little to cure its underlying political malaise, it did preserve the country's independence. Lebanon's unique system of democracy was maintained, in the face of efforts by some groups inside and outside the country to dismember it. This paramount goal of the Eisenhower Doctrine was achieved; and as events during the 1970s and 1980s demonstrated, this was no insignificant accomplishment.

The Lebanese affair also communicated a reality to the Kremlin that, during the late 1950s, was a needed reminder: the United States possessed both the determination and the ability to honor its international commitments. Against a background of rising Soviet prestige and power—vis-à-vis declining Western influence in the Middle East—this was a beneficial result of the Eisenhower Doctrine as it was applied in Lebanon. As one study concluded, America's action in Lebanon "demonstrated to exposed American allies throughout the world that they could count on swift American help regardless of Soviet ICBMs, with American troops withdrawing after the mission was accomplished." Or, as Fahim Qubain concluded: "The American involvement in Lebanon was a good example of a limited war to achieve political objectives." President Eisenhower viewed it as a demonstration of America's ability to react to "brush fire" threats throughout the world. American firmness in Lebanon, another study observed, could not fail to influence Soviet behavior in other global trouble spots, like Berlin and the Far East.[85]

A related gain for the United States was that, in the end, the Lebanese crisis resulted in a deterioration in Soviet influence among the Arab states. Predictably, the Kremlin denounced the Eisenhower Doctrine as a flagrant example of "American imperialism" and reiterated its own devotion to the cause of Arab independence. Yet if Cairo, Damascus, and other Arab capitals had expected tangible Soviet assistance (including perhaps the introduction of Soviet troops into the Middle East) to oppose American intervention in Lebanon, they were sorely disappointed. To the contrary, Premier Khrushchev urged President Nasser to be "patient" and not to expect any Soviet move that

85. Drummond and Coblentz, *Duel at the Brink*, 238; Qubain, *Crisis in Lebanon*, 130; Eisenhower, *Waging Peace*, 290; Hughes, *The Ordeal of Power*, 272.

might lead to a direct encounter with the United States. In view of such developments, as a former American State Department official observed, a major result of the Lebanese affair was to destroy "the myth in Arab eyes of Soviet invincibility." Throughout the Lebanese episode, "Khrushchev was nowhere to be found."[86]

Note must also be taken of the fact that ultimately, the United States relinquished responsibility for peace-keeping in Lebanon to the United Nations, and its designated agent, the Arab League. By doing so, Washington expressed its moral and tangible support for the principle of effective international organization and gave the UN an opportunity to demonstrate its ability to deal with a serious regional crisis.[87]

The Eisenhower Doctrine was not of course without diplomatic liabilities for the United States—and some were serious enough to raise questions about whether the doctrine was on balance a positive development for American foreign policy. As we have already observed, in the Lebanese context particularly, the doctrine was a stopgap measure, doing little to remedy the underlying causes of upheaval and vulnerability to Communist penetration in the Middle East. At best, the Eisenhower Doctrine provided time in which Lebanon's problems might be solved (or at least attenuated), within an atmosphere of relative calm and freedom from foreign domination.[88] As the subsequent political history of Lebanon indicated, it was at least questionable whether the United States, the factions within Lebanon, or other parties to the conflict used the time available constructively.

As an exercise in the containment strategy, the Eisenhower Doctrine exemplified certain weaknesses (some of which were analyzed in detail in Chapter 3). Whether, in the long run, the doctrine inhibited the growth of Soviet influence throughout the Middle East is clearly debatable. Adverse Arab reaction to the doctrine provided new opportunities for the Kremlin to win goodwill among disaffected states. The doctrine's basic premise—that a "power vacuum" existed in the Mid-

---

86. McClintock, *The Meaning of Limited War*, 121. For a detailed discussion of the Soviet response, see Lukacs, *A New History of the Cold War*, 168–69.

87. By a resolution on August 21, 1958, the UN General Assembly assigned primary responsibility for peace-keeping in Lebanon to the Arab League. Department of State, *American Foreign Policy: Current Documents, 1958*, pp. 1047–48.

88. Adams, *Firsthand Report*, 293.

dle East which ought to be filled by the United States—was offensive to Arabs and contravened their cherished principle of diplomatic nonalignment.

More than most doctrinal pronouncements, President Eisenhower's policy guidelines for the Middle East suffered from acute vagueness and imprecision. Foreign governments did not always understand the provisions of the Eisenhower Doctrine; and in time, it seemed questionable whether American officials were clear about its terms. By the late 1950s, for example, fundamental questions existed about whether the principal adversary identified in the doctrine—"international communism"—really existed as a monolithic political force. Moreover, the identity of interests between some Arab and Soviet goals in the Middle East could in many cases be explained as Arab efforts to use the Soviet Union, as logically as concluding that Arab governments were controlled by "international communism." As an example, Arab opposition to Israel was authentic; it needed no instigation or encouragement by the Kremlin. Many Arab states would have been suspicious of American motives in the Middle East even if Moscow had no diplomatic interests in the region.

As with all diplomatic doctrines, President Eisenhower's dictum also suffered from inconsistency in application. The United States, for example, intervened militarily to preserve the security of Lebanon. It did *not* intervene to prevent the emergence of a radical and anti-Western regime in Iraq—a much more influential Arab state, where Soviet involvement in time became extensive.[89]

As our treatment has emphasized, the Eisenhower Doctrine was a unilateral policy declaration by the United States. This fact raised questions about the doctrine's compatibility with international law and (as Washington had emphasized to its allies in the earlier Suez Crisis) the responsiveness of governments to world public opinion. Washington, it goes without saying, differentiated in several fundamental respects between America's reliance upon armed force in dealing with Lebanon, and the Soviet Union's military invasion of Hungary to sup-

89. Charles C. Alexander, *Holding the Line: The Eisenhower Era, 1952–1961* (Bloomington, Ind.: Indiana University Press, 1975), 234; Seale, *The Struggle for Syria*, 284; Meo, *Lebanon*, 104.

press political opposition in that country. A key difference was that within a fairly short period of time, American troops were evacuated from Lebanon; another difference was that the United States did not seek to impose a pro-Western political regime upon the country. The fact remains, however, that under the Eisenhower Doctrine, Washington alone determined when American armed force would be used abroad and the purposes their use would serve.[90]

Mention must also be made of the effect of the Eisenhower Doctrine upon Franco-American relations. Since 1800 or earlier, Lebanon has had close ties with France. As the Lebanese crisis intensified, some evidence existed that Paris desired to act collaboratively with Washington in responding to the crisis. Again, however, America exhibited its traditional preference for acting unilaterally. This fact was subsequently cited by French President Charles de Gaulle as evidence of America's "neglect" of French interests and of the "subordinate" role which an increasingly prosperous France played in the NATO alliance. De Gaulle's demand for a "reorganization" of NATO—and France's subsequent withdrawal from the NATO command structure, although not from the alliance per se—was in some measure a result of the Eisenhower Doctrine.[91]

Finally, in achieving one of its dominant goals—the creation of a sense of national unity within the United States in behalf of the nation's foreign policy—the Eisenhower Doctrine must be judged a failure. The doctrine did not lead to a revival of bipartisanship in foreign affairs. After the Lebanese intervention, critics of the doctrine were still convinced that the Eisenhower Doctrine remained largely irrelevant to the central causes of political turbulence in the Middle

90. For one contention that the Eisenhower Doctrine was in violation of international law, see Quincy Wright, "United States Intervention in Lebanon," *American Journal of International Law*, LIII (January, 1959), 112–26; and for other discussions of the legal aspects of the Eisenhower Doctrine, see Finer, *Dulles over Suez*, 499–500; Eisenhower, *Waging Peace*, 271–72. See also Ambassador Henry C. Lodge's defense of the doctrine before the UN Security Council on July 15, 1958, in Department of State, *American Foreign Policy: Current Documents, 1958*, pp. 960–64.

91. The French response to American intervention in Lebanon is discussed at greater length in W. W. Kulsi, *DeGaulle and the World: The Foreign Policy of the Fifth French Republic* (Syracuse, N.Y.: Syracuse University Press, 1966), 171–72; Edward A. Kolodzeij, *French International Policy Under DeGaulle and Pompidou* (Ithaca, N.Y.: Cornell University Press, 1974), 47–48, 72–73, 76.

East. Indeed, many of them were persuaded that the doctrine was itself a new source of regional ferment and anti-Western sentiment.[92] The Eisenhower Doctrine's detractors brought another indictment against it. Presented by the White House as a "bipartisan" undertaking, in reality the doctrine was an example of what might be called *pseudo*bipartisanship. In effect, the president and his advisers sought to share responsibility for this new Middle Eastern strategy with the political opposition, without really according the opposition party a meaningful voice in policy formulation. In time, this became a familiar lament—revived (as we shall see more fully in Chapters 5 and 6) when the Johnson Administration attempted to deal with the Vietnam War and with revolution in the Dominican Republic.

92. See, for example, Sen. John F. Kennedy's assessment of American policy in the Middle East under the Eisenhower Administration in Kennedy, *The Strategy of Peace*, 106–18. Democratic presidential candidate Adlai E. Stevenson called American foreign policy generally under the Eisenhower Administration "a thing of wonder and mirth" to the world's political leaders. Among its other defects, American diplomacy in the Middle East had sharply divided the NATO partnership. Theodore H. White, *The Making of the President: 1960* (New York: Atheneum, 1961), 120–21. Another Democratic critic believed that, as a result of the Eisenhower-Dulles diplomatic record in the Middle East, there was now "grave danger that the Russian penetration there will increase to the point of controlling the greater part of the area." In his view, the Eisenhower Administration's efforts had left the real problems of the Middle East as critical as ever. Thomas K. Finletter, *Foreign Policy: The Next Phase* (New York: Harper and Row, 1958), 123–41.

5 / The First Johnson Doctrine
Tonkin Gulf and the Vietnam War

That [Tonkin Gulf] resolution became the principal constitutional instrument by which he [President Johnson] altered the character of U.S. involvement in Vietnam six months later. —Townsend Hoopes

The trouble with the sweeping foreign policy resolution [like the Gulf of Tonkin resolution] as a governmental technique is simply that it has no place in a democracy. —Eric F. Goldman

We [Americans] have tended since World War II to respond to seeming emergencies with an anxious and uncritical disregard for normal constitutional procedure. . . . Time after time, until recently, Congress concurred, without protest or question, in the executive's accounting of the facts of a situation and in its judgment as to whether the case at hand constituted a genuine national emergency. —Sen. J. William Fulbright

According to information made public by officials of the Johnson Administration, the American destroyer *Maddox* was attacked on August 2, 1964, in international waters, in the Gulf of Tonkin, by North Vietnamese torpedo boats. Despite an immediate and sharp warning from Washington, the same ship, along with the destroyer *C. Turner Joy*, was attacked again two days later by North Vietnamese PT boats. The second attack precipitated two responses by the Johnson Administration: the president ordered a retaliatory air strike against selected targets in North Vietnam; and on August 5, President Johnson sent a message to Congress enunciating what came to be known as the Johnson Doctrine for Southeast Asia, which received formal expression in the "Gulf of Tonkin Resolution" (passed by Congress on August 7, and signed into law by the president on August 11).[1]

1. For the texts of Johnson's speeches dealing with the crises in the Tonkin Gulf and

The Gulf of Tonkin episode was a crucial stage in America's participation in the Vietnam War. More broadly, it was a highly significant development in the conduct of American foreign relations, particularly as it related to the powers of the presidency and Congress in external affairs. After this naval encounter, America's role in the Vietnam conflict escalated rapidly, with the United States assuming an ever larger burden of the military commitment. These incidents in the Gulf of Tonkin also brought to a head a long-standing congressional resentment and frustration about what came to be called the "imperial presidency." Legislative disaffection with unilateral presidential decision-making received forceful expression in the War Powers Resolution (November 7, 1973), designed to limit the authority of the chief executive to use the armed forces for diplomatic ends.[2] The episode also convinced critics of the Johnson Administration that the White House routinely relied upon secrecy and deception in the management of foreign affairs.

The Doctrine's Issuance and Meaning

What came to be known as the Johnson Doctrine for Southeast Asia (as we shall see in Chapter 6, there was a second Johnson Doctrine, regarding Latin America) was expressed in more than one presidential policy statement. It received its most forceful expression in the "Gulf of Tonkin Resolution," requested by the president and passed by overwhelming majorities in the House and Senate.

Immediately after the second North Vietnamese attack on American naval units in the Gulf of Tonkin (on August 4), President Johnson informed the American people that the United States was determined "to take all necessary measures in support of freedom and in defense of peace in Southeast Asia." Subsequently, Johnson declared that "aggression unchallenged is aggression unleashed" and that "there can be no peace by aggression and no immunity from reply." The president asked Congress to join him in affirming that "all such attacks will be

Southeast Asia, see *Public Papers of the Presidents of the United States: Lyndon B. Johnson, 1963–1964* (Washington, D.C.: Government Printing Office, 1965), II, 927–32. The Tonkin Gulf Resolution was House Joint Resolution 1145, and after receiving Johnson's signature it became Public Law 88-408.

2. For an analysis of the War Powers Act, see Harry C. Thomson, "The War Powers Resolution of 1973: Can Congress Make It Stick?" *World Affairs*, CXXXIX (Summer, 1976), 3–10.

met" and that the United States would "continue in its basic policy of assisting the free peoples of the area to defend their freedom."

Congress responded by approving the Gulf of Tonkin Resolution, stating that "the Congress approves and supports the determination of the President, as Commander in Chief, to take all necessary measures to repel any armed attack against the forces of the United States and to prevent further aggression [in Southeast Asia]." In sweeping language, the resolution expressed the conviction of Congress that "the United States regards as vital to its national interest and to world peace the maintenance of international peace and security in Southeast Asia. . . . the United States is therefore, prepared, as the President determines, to take all necessary steps, including the use of armed force, to assist any member or protocol member of the Southeast Asia Collective Defense Treaty requesting assistance in defense of its freedom."[3] The resolution would expire under one of two conditions: by a presidential decision that the peace and security of Southeast Asia had been assured; or by a concurrent resolution of Congress terminating it.

When he signed the Tonkin Gulf Resolution into law, President Johnson interpreted it to mean: "To any armed attack upon our forces, we shall reply. To any in Southeast Asia who ask our help in defending our freedom, we shall give it." This, in essence, constituted the Johnson Doctrine for Southeast Asia.[4]

Several points about the issuance and meaning of the doctrine require brief emphasis. First, as has been true of all other major diplomatic doctrines discussed thus far, it was issued in response to a perceived crisis abroad. As policy-makers in Washington assessed it, North Vietnam (perhaps with Soviet encouragement) had chosen to escalate the conflict in Southeast Asia by carrying out unprovoked attacks against American ships in international waters. The Johnson

3. The Southeast Asia Treaty Organization (SEATO) was created as a result of a mutual defense treaty signed on September 8, 1954. Members included the United States, the United Kingdom, France, New Zealand, Australia, the Philippines, and Thailand. The key provision of the treaty was that in the event of an armed attack against any member, each signatory would "act to meet the common danger in accordance with its constitutional processes." Unlike its counterpart in Europe (NATO), SEATO did not bind the signatories automatically to regard an attack against one as an attack against all. After the withdrawal of American forces from Vietnam on June 30, 1977, SEATO was dissolved. See New York *Times*, July 1, 1977.

4. See Johnson's statement on August 10, 1964, as quoted in Eugene G. Windchy, *Tonkin Gulf* (Garden City, N.Y.: Doubleday, 1971), 25.

White House interpreted this as a Communist effort to "frighten" the president; and they believed that the national honor and credibility of the United States had been called into question by events in the Gulf of Tonkin.[5]

Second, the essence of President Johnson's doctrine toward Asia— the idea that the United States would respond to this and other forms of "aggression" in the region—was initially enunciated by the president. As was true of the Eisenhower Doctrine earlier, Congress subsequently gave its approval to this commitment; but the House and Senate were in effect merely ratifying a policy already proclaimed by the chief executive. (At a later stage, both President Johnson and President Richard M. Nixon were to contend that they did not "need" legislative authority to respond to aggression in Southeast Asia.)

Third (as had also been the case with the Eisenhower Doctrine), a leading purpose of the first Johnson Doctrine was to present a united American posture to the world. The Tonkin Gulf Resolution, reinforcing President Johnson's policy statements, would demonstrate "unity and determination of the American people to preserve the nation's security interests in Southeast Asia"—and presumably, in other areas in which they might be threatened.[6]

Fourth, the language of the Tonkin Gulf Resolution stated that "Congress approves and supports" efforts by the president "to take all necessary measures" designed to repel attacks upon American military units and "to prevent further aggression." Later, the same idea was expressed even more broadly, when the resolution affirmed America's readiness "as the President determines" to support the freedom of its allies in Southeast Asia. This provision constituted the so-called "blank check" which many critics later believed Congress gave the White House in the Johnson Doctrine. In effect, Congress granted the White House *advance approval* for steps it might take thereafter to prosecute the war in Vietnam. Despite the disaffection which the Gulf of Tonkin Resolution ultimately generated on Capitol Hill, this was the plain and natural meaning of the language of the resolution.

---

5. Philip Geyelin, *Lyndon B. Johnson and the World* (New York: Praeger, 1966), 113.
6. See Secretary of State Dean Rusk's testimony in U.S. Congress, Senate, Committees on Foreign Relations and Armed Services, *Hearings on Southeast Asia Resolution*, 88th Cong., 2nd Sess., 1964, pp. 4–5. This source will hereafter be cited as Senate *Hearings on Southeast Asia Resolution*.

Broad as the language of the Tonkin Gulf Resolution was, in his testimony to Senate committees, Secretary of State Dean Rusk noted that the resolution was limited in three respects: (1) it applied only to defense of America's SEATO allies in Asia; (2) the United States would only provide assistance to maintain the security of those states requesting it; and (3) the powers of the resolutions would be invoked only to cover cases of aggression committed by Communist countries.[7]

The Johnson Doctrine for Asia emerged as one in a series of steps by which the United States became massively committed to the defense of South Vietnam. This process began in 1954 when (on October 1) the Eisenhower Administration pledged that the United States would support the South Vietnamese regime of Ngo Dinh Diem; the following year, the Southeast Asia Treaty Organization (SEATO) was established, in an effort to make this commitment a collective responsibility of other states in the region.

Late in 1961, for the first time American military "advisers" fought with South Vietnamese forces against the Communist insurgents, the Viet Cong. By 1963, the United States had stationed some sixteen thousand American troops in Vietnam. Yet during this period, President Kennedy insisted that the government of South Vietnam bore the primary responsibility for preserving the country's security.[8]

After he entered the White House, President Lyndon B. Johnson, on November 27, 1963, pledged that his administration would keep the nation's foreign policy commitments from South Vietnam to West Berlin. Johnson echoed Kennedy's earlier view—that ultimately, South Vietnam had to take the lead in safeguarding its security—and pledged America to assist Saigon in doing so.[9]

7. Senate *Hearings on Southeast Asia Resolution*, 3.
8. For background to the involvement of the Johnson Administration in the Vietnam conflict, see Rowland Evans and Robert Novak, *Lyndon B. Johnson: The Exercise of Power* (New York: New American Library, 1966), 531; Richard N. Goodwin, *Triumph or Tragedy: Reflections on Vietnam* (New York: Random House, 1966), 29. Kennedy's views on the extent of American commitment to South Vietnam may be found in Theodore C. Sorensen, *Kennedy* (New York: Harper and Row, 1965), 639–61; and Arthur Schlesinger, Jr., *A Thousand Days: John F. Kennedy in the White House* (Boston: Houghton Mifflin, 1965), 320–43, 532–51.
9. Lyndon B. Johnson, *The Vantage Point: Perspectives of the Presidency, 1963– 1969* (New York: Holt, Rinehart and Winston, 1971), 197–98; Tom Wicker, *JFK and LBJ: The Influence of Personality upon Politics* (New York: William Morrow, 1968), 219; Eric F. Goldman, *The Tragedy of Lyndon Johnson* (New York: Alfred A. Knopf, 1969), 175.

During the six months or so which preceded the issuance of the doctrine, three dominant themes were evident in American foreign policy toward Southeast Asia. One was the relatively low priority which the Vietnam conflict had with the Johnson Administration and with the American people. The second was the confidence existing among leading officials of the administration that America's limited commitment in Vietnam, coupled with South Vietnam's own defense efforts, would result in the defeat of Communist forces. The third (a theme which was of course in some contradiction to the second) was the rapidly deteriorating position of South Vietnam in terms of providing an effective barrier against Communist penetration and control of the country.

Former Senator Lyndon B. Johnson assumed the presidency with little direct knowledge of—or discernible interest in—foreign affairs. As a senator, Johnson had been immersed mainly in domestic policy and in forging the necessary legislative consensus needed to win support on Capitol Hill for the president's programs. This perspective colored LBJ's approach to foreign relations. The new president, in Hoopes's words, had "a passion for consensus"; and he tended to view foreign policy as "an integral and subordinate element of domestic politics." During the early months of his administration, LBJ was preoccupied chiefly with learning his job as chief executive, with assuring a Democratic victory in the forthcoming national elections, and with selecting a vice presidential running mate.[10]

Under the Johnson presidency, conditions within South Vietnam deteriorated rapidly, with the Viet Cong steadily expanding the area under its effective control. Official optimism in Washington about the progress of the campaign against the Communists was almost daily contradicted by reports from Southeast Asia depicting Communist gains and South Vietnamese setbacks. By early 1964, political instability within South Vietnam had become acute; several political coups and attempted coups were carried out; and public morale sagged. Meanwhile, to the north in Hanoi, Communist officials confidently predicted victory in their attempt to unite the whole of Vietnam under their auspices. As their military position became stronger, Communist

10. Townsend Hoopes, *The Limits of Intervention* (New York: David McKay, 1969), 24; and see the views of Walter Lippmann, as cited in Geyelin, *Lyndon B. Johnson and the World*, 229.

spokesmen also became increasingly resistant to the idea of a negotiated settlement of the conflict.[11]

In company with chief executives before him, President Johnson related Communist gains in Southeast Asia to a larger pattern of expansionism, ultimately instigated by the Soviet Union (and, Americans believed in this period, Communist China). The U.S.S.R. had already become a nuclear giant; Red China was acquiring a nuclear arsenal; and Moscow and Peking alike were fomenting and aiding revolutionary activities throughout the Third World. Communist efforts to gain control of the government of Indonesia (ultimately frustrated by military elements in that country) provided disturbing evidence of worldwide Communist aggrandizement.[12]

Officials of the Johnson Administration were becoming increasingly concerned about the deteriorating situation in Vietnam and they considered a number of proposals for reversing that process. One suggestion—American air strikes against North Vietnam—was consistently rejected by President Johnson, for two primary reasons: they might provoke Soviet and/or Chinese direct intervention into the conflict; and LBJ was determined that America's role in the war would remain limited.[13]

For several months preceding the Gulf of Tonkin episode, South Vietnamese PT boats had conducted raids against North Vietnamese coastal villages; in doing so, the South Vietnamese Navy had enjoyed U.S. naval protection. On July 31, 1964, Hanoi officially protested to Washington concerning American involvement in these raids.[14] During the first half of 1964, as the situation in South Vietnam worsened, the Johnson Administration had augmented U.S. naval strength in the waters adjacent to Vietnam. As a part of this naval buildup, American destroyers were ordered to patrol the Gulf of Tonkin. The purpose was twofold: this exercise in "showing the flag" was obviously designed to underscore America's commitment to the independence of South Viet-

11. More detailed discussion of conditions in Southeast Asia during this period may be found in: Johnson, *The Vantage Point*, 64–67; Neil Sheehan, *et al.* (eds.), *The Pentagon Papers* (New York: Bantam, 1971), 240–42; and Goodwin, *Triumph or Tragedy*, 29–31.

12. Johnson, *The Vantage Point*, 134–35.

13. *Ibid.*, 119.

14. Franz Schurmann, Peter D. Scott, and Reginald Zelnik, *The Politics of Escalation in Vietnam* (Boston: Beacon Press, 1966), 39–40.

nam and its other Asian allies; and—in one of the most controversial aspects of the Gulf of Tonkin affair—the administration later admitted that certain U.S. naval units were engaged in gathering intelligence data by monitoring Communist radio and radar transmissions and other activities. As long as they were carried out in international waters (as the Soviet Union's "fishing trawlers" had done for years off the coast of the United States), these intelligence operations were not illegal, nor could they be used to justify an attack by one nation against the naval forces of another. The question also arose concerning whether American naval units in the Gulf of Tonkin actually violated the "territorial waters" of North Vietnam. Washington denied this assertion, while of course North Vietnamese contended there had been an American intrusion justifying its assault. Both the facts on the question and relevant international law covering it are debatable. No general consensus exists within the international community concerning the definition of a nation's "territorial waters."[15]

On August 2, the U.S. destroyer *Maddox* reported that it was under attack in the Gulf of Tonkin by North Vietnamese PT boats.[16] Among officials in Washington, considerable uncertainty surrounded both the details and the purpose of the attack (some officials were inclined to attribute it to a "miscalculation" by a North Vietnamese naval commander). Although Hanoi's motivations were unclear, the president and his advisers were convinced of three things: a Communist attack

---

15. In this case, the United States insisted upon the right to approach within three miles of the North Vietnamese coastline, whereas Hanoi contended that its national jurisdiction extended for twelve miles into the adjacent waters. The legal complexities of the issue are underscored by one authority's observation that—while the "three-mile limit" came to be the accepted rule of international law (primarily because coastal defense guns had a range of three miles)—in time the prevailing concept was that "a state could claim ownership over such waters as it was able to command with its armament." In time, many states claimed territorial jurisdiction wider than three miles from their shores. Under the Carter Administration, the United States proclaimed a "two-hundred-mile limit," prohibiting foreign fishing activities along the eastern seacoast. Gerhard von Glahn, *Law Among Nations: An Introduction to Public International Law* (2nd ed.; Toronto: Collier-Macmillan, 1970), 309–14.

16. For a detailed recapitulation of events during early August, as officials of the Johnson Administration understood and interpreted them, see the testimony of Secretary of Defense Robert McNamara in Senate *Hearings on Southeast Asia Resolution*, 6–9. More detailed and critical accounts of the Gulf of Tonkin episode are Windchy, *Tonkin Gulf*; Schurmann, *et al.*, *The Politics of Escalation in Vietnam*; and Sheehan, *et al.* (eds.), *The Pentagon Papers*.

against an American naval vessel had occurred; the *Maddox* had been in international waters when it was attacked; and the initiative for the engagement had come entirely from Hanoi. Nevertheless, Washington's response to the attack on the *Maddox* was restrained. Hanoi was warned against a repetition of such behavior; orders were issued to the U.S. Navy to maintain its patrols in the Gulf of Tonkin, to be on the alert for future attacks, and to repel them if there was a recurrence; and naval reinforcements were sent to the Tonkin Gulf area. From the evidence available, the Johnson Administration apparently concluded that the first Tonkin Gulf incident was an "accident" or isolated event not likely to be repeated.[17]

Then on August 4, the American destroyers *Maddox* and *C. Turner Joy* were again attacked by North Vietnamese PT boats in the Gulf of Tonkin. While the exact sequence of events even today remains in some respects unclear, and certain contradictory evidence about the attack has never been satisfactorily explained, the second Tonkin Gulf incident was viewed by the Johnson Administration as an extremely serious matter. A second attack within a two-day period, under almost identical circumstances as the first, could hardly be regarded as an accidental naval encounter or "miscalculation" by Hanoi. Although Hanoi's purpose in undertaking this new assault was difficult to discern, President Johnson was convinced that this new attack was designed to intimidate the United States and to inflict at least a psychological defeat upon it. In LBJ's view the honor and prestige of the United States were at stake.[18]

The response agreed upon by officials of the Johnson Administration consisted of two different, but interrelated, actions. Militarily, President Johnson ordered American aircraft to carry out retaliatory raids against selected villages in North Vietnam. Johnson personally selected target sites for these raids in order to produce minimum civilian casualties. The raids were designed to have both a punitive and a deterrent purpose. They were intended to punish Hanoi for its two attacks upon U.S. naval units; and their purpose was to "deter" North Vietnam from further escalation of the conflict in Southeast Asia.[19]

17. Sheehan, *et al.* (eds.), *The Pentagon Papers*, 259–60.
18. Geyelin, *Lyndon B. Johnson and the World*, 113; McNamara's testimony in Senate *Hearings on Southeast Asia Resolution*, 9.
19. Wicker, *JFK and LBJ*, 226. For discussion of the rationale of the American air

Diplomatically, and for our purposes more significantly, the administration answered Hanoi's behavior in the Gulf of Tonkin episode by formulating, and gaining congressional support for, the first Johnson Doctrine. The enunciation of the doctrine under these circumstances also had several purposes. It was designed to have a deterrent effect upon Hanoi and other Communist states supporting its campaign in Vietnam. The doctrine was intended to underscore the determination of the Johnson Administration to honor American commitments in Southeast Asia by obtaining an overwhelming congressional majority in support of these commitments. Moreover, the Gulf of Tonkin crisis occurred during a period of partisan discord, surrounding the forthcoming national elections in November. (As we shall see, the Johnson Administration faced sharp criticism from its Republican opponents, many of whom accused it of following a "no-win" policy in Southeast Asia. We shall deal more fully with the political implications of the first Johnson Doctrine at a later stage.) Passage of the Gulf of Tonkin Resolution by overwhelming majorities in the House and Senate conveyed the unified position of the American government on the Vietnam issue, serving as a dramatic symbol of "bipartisan" cooperation in the foreign policy field.

As time passed, critics of America's involvement in the Vietnam War attributed three other motivations to the Johnson Administration in its response to events in the Gulf of Tonkin. Some commentators believed that the so-called attacks upon American naval vessels off Vietnam (the facts concerning which came to be hotly contested) provided the administration with the pretext it had long desired for escalating the war. According to this view, officials of the Johnson Administration had known for several months that a significantly expanded American military effort would be required to save Vietnam from communism. The Tonkin Gulf episode provided a long-awaited and fortuitous opportunity for doing so. (This view was of course contested by President Johnson and his supporters, who contended that any escalation of the war during this period would likely result in the

---

attacks against North Vietnam, see Herbert K. Tillema, *Appeal to Force: American Military Intervention in the Era of Containment* (New York: Thomas Y. Crowell, 1973), 128–29.

collapse of the government of South Vietnam and would risk direct Soviet and/or Chinese intervention in the conflict).[20] Critics of the Johnson Administration's diplomacy detected another purpose in the president's Asian doctrine: it (along with expanded American air strikes against Communist-held territory) was intended to communicate Washington's opposition to a negotiated settlement of the war and its determination to win a decisive "victory" over communism. In effect, critics charged, the doctrine constituted a negative American reply to efforts by United Nations Secretary General U Thant and others who advocated a diplomatic resolution of the conflict in Southeast Asia.[21] Needless to say, President Johnson and his advisers rejected this interpretation. They contended that on numerous occasions in the past, they had endeavored to interest Hanoi and its foreign sponsors in a diplomatic settlement—but to no avail.[22]

Other critics believed that the Johnson Administration was actually looking for a pretext to invoke for testing certain theories of "limited war" current among American strategists. The Gulf of Tonkin provided the desired rationale for engaging in the "restrained" use of force which, some strategists believed, would ultimately compel Hanoi and other Communist capitols to favor an end to the war.[23] Spokesmen for the administration also of course disagreed with this interpretation, pointing out that American air strikes in retaliation for the assault on American ships were not repeated; were not designed to enlarge the war; were limited in their destructiveness; and were undertaken only in response to Hanoi's own aggressive behavior.[24]

20. Louis Heren, *No Hail, No Farewell* (New York: Harper and Row, 1970), 52; Morton Berkowitz, P. G. Bock, and Vincent J. Fuccillo, *The Politics of American Foreign Policy: The Social Context of Decisions* (Englewood Cliffs, N.J.: Prentice-Hall, 1977), 220; Johnson, *The Vantage Point*, 120.

21. This view is expressed by Schurmann, *et al.*, *The Politics of Escalation in Vietnam*, 35–36.

22. Arnold Beichman, "Lowenthal's Errors: The Vietnam Argument," in Welley R. Fischel (ed.), *Vietnam: Anatomy of a Conflict* (Itasca, Ill.: F. E. Peacock, 1968), 726–27.

23. See the views of Theodore Draper, in Richard M. Pfeffer (ed.), *No More Vietnams? The War and the Future of American Foreign Policy* (New York: Harper and Row, 1968), 27.

24. See President Johnson's explanation of the rationale of the retaliatory air strikes against North Vietnam, as given in Goldman, *The Tragedy of Lyndon Johnson*, 234–35.

Formulating the First Johnson Doctrine

In common with other foreign policy doctrines in American history, President Johnson's pronouncement toward Southeast Asia was the product of a long and complex sequence of developments. A number of significant influences affected the timing, mode of issuance, content, and application of the Johnson Doctrine for Southeast Asia.

As an experienced and influential legislator, Lyndon B. Johnson was of course sensitive to congressional viewpoints and aware of the importance of constructive executive-legislative relations. While serving in the Senate, he had become convinced that during the early 1950s President Truman had made a serious error in the conduct of the Korean War. Deliberately or indeliberately, Truman had failed to involve Congress in the decision to defend South Korea against Communist attack. As a result, the conflict became known as "Truman's war." Acrimonious wrangling between Democrats and Republicans over America's role in it produced considerable internal disunity and contributed in some measure to the election of Republican President Dwight D. Eisenhower in 1952. Johnson was determined to avoid Truman's mistake in handling the Korean War. Accordingly, after he became president, Johnson instructed his advisers that any new proposal submitted to him concerning the conduct of the Vietnam War must also include provisions "for assuring the backing of Congress."[25]

A former official of the Johnson Administration has said that "contingency planning" for massive air strikes against North Vietnam (first undertaken after the Gulf of Tonkin incidents, but not carried out repeatedly until early 1965) were considered as early as 1961. State Department officials had prepared preliminary drafts of congressional resolutions, to be submitted to Congress when the president determined. One purpose of these draft resolutions was to "dramatize" America's opposition to communism and its unified resolve to resist it. During the first half of 1964, for example, the evidence indicates that the United States was engaged in carrying out clandestine military operations against North Vietnam. Executive officials had prepared a draft congressional resolution expressing legislative support for this idea. In his testimony before the Senate Foreign Relations Committee

25. Goldman, *The Tragedy of Lyndon Johnson*, 176–77; Johnson, *The Vantage Point*, 115.

some two years after the Gulf of Tonkin crisis, Assistant Secretary of State William P. Bundy declared that such preliminary drafts actually bore little resemblance to the Gulf of Tonkin Resolution which Congress approved in August, 1964.[26]

Any discussion of the antecedents of the first Johnson Doctrine must also take note of earlier congressional resolutions, upon which the Gulf of Tonkin Resolution was patterned. One of these, dealing with the Middle East, was analyzed in Chapter 4. Even earlier, there was the Formosa Resolution (January 29, 1955) and the Cuba Resolution (October 3, 1962). While the circumstances surrounding, and the language of, each of these earlier resolutions varied, they had a common purpose: to provide dramatic evidence of agreement between the executive and legislative branches to defend a vital security interest of the United States. Two of these resolutions (the Formosa and the Middle East resolutions) "authorized" the president to use the armed forces alone, or in concert with other nations, to protect the nation's diplomatic interests. Alternatively, the Cuba Resolution stated that America was "determined" to prevent the use of Cuba as a base for communizing Latin America or as a foreign military installation jeopardizing the security of the United States. In still different language, the Tonkin Gulf (or Southeast Asia) Resolution provided that Congress "approves and supports the determination of the President, as Commander-in-Chief, to take all necessary measures to repel any armed attack against the forces of the United States and to prevent further aggression." In Section 2, the resolution affirmed that "the United States is . . . prepared, as the President determines, to take all necessary steps, including the use of armed force" to support its Asian allies requesting such assistance to maintain their security. It is worth noting that, in contrast to the Formosa and Middle East resolutions, the Tonkin Gulf Resolution did not "authorize" the president to employ armed force in Southeast Asia. It approved and supported his determination to do so and stated that the United States (not merely the president alone) was "prepared" to use armed force to defend its security interests.[27]

26. Hoopes, *The Limits of Intervention*, 21–23; Sheehan, *et al.* (eds.), *The Pentagon Papers*, 257; Wicker, *JFK and LBJ*, 225.

27. The text of these earlier resolutions, along with the Gulf of Tonkin Resolution, is included in U.S. Congress, Senate Committee on Foreign Relations, *Background*

Before the events in the Tonkin Gulf early in August, 1964, President Johnson had personally directed the preparation of draft resolutions to be submitted to Congress when he determined the time and circumstances propitious. These early draft resolutions remained within the executive branch prior to the Gulf of Tonkin crisis. Within a few hours after the first North Vietnamese attack on American ships, Lyndon B. Johnson summoned the members of the National Security Council into session. After discussion, the National Security Council recommended that the United States undertake "retaliatory" air strikes against North Vietnam and that the president seek congressional support for this step in the form of an appropriate resolution.[28] Yet, as we have noted, after the first attack the president rejected this recommendation, choosing instead merely to warn Hanoi against a resumption of hostilities in the Tonkin Gulf.

The second Tonkin Gulf incident (August 4) changed President Johnson's appraisal of the situation and induced him to follow the steps recommended earlier by the National Security Council. In the events which followed, the president's influence was direct and decisive. Immediately after the second Tonkin Gulf incident, in his role as commander-in-chief of the armed forces, Lyndon B. Johnson ordered retaliatory American air strikes against North Vietnam. He also summoned a group of legislative leaders to the White House to discuss the Tonkin Gulf crisis with them and to urge their support for the measures the administration had taken, or proposed to take, in response to it. When these legislators met with the president and his advisers, they learned that plans for a retaliatory air strike against North Vietnam were already under way. Johnson requested their support for a congressional resolution expressing the unified determination of the government to resist Communist expansionism in Southeast Asia. Emphasizing his desire to work closely with Congress, he asked the

---

Information Relating to Southeast Asia and Vietnam, 90th Cong., 1st Sess., 1967, pp. 127–28.

28. Berkowitz, *et al.*, *The Politics of American Foreign Policy*, 220–21. The National Security Council is the highest presidential advisory agency on national security questions. Its members are the president (as chairman), the vice president, the secretary of state, and the secretary of defense. Other officials may be, and frequently are, "invited" to attend meetings of the NSC and express their views. The NSC, it is important to bear in mind, is a civilian-controlled advisory body, whose composition reflects the American tradition of civilian supremacy over the military establishment.

cooperation of legislators in passing a resolution containing three main elements: it would indicate congressional approval of retaliatory air strikes against North Vietnam; it would authorize the president to take whatever steps were necessary to combat aggression in Southeast Asia (with the definition of "aggression" left to presidential determination); and the resolution would remain in force either until the president decided it was no longer necessary, or until it was repealed by a majority in the House and Senate.[29]

At this meeting, however, Johnson emphasized an idea which he and other executive officials were to state publicly a number of times in the months ahead: the president did not "need" congressional authorization to retaliate militarily against North Vietnam or, presumably, to take whatever steps were required to protect American security interests abroad. As interpreted by the White House, the Tonkin Gulf Resolution would merely provide dramatic confirmation and reinforcement of the president's powers by Congress. Despite a later denial that he had sought to "hurry" congressional approval of the Tonkin Gulf Resolution, in his special message to Congress on August 5, LBJ did call upon the House and Senate to pass the resolution "promptly." Such a request by the president for expeditious congressional action seems logically in keeping with the context of the Tonkin Gulf crisis; and it is also comfortable with presidential actions in earlier instances involving similar congressional resolutions.[30]

President Johnson's personal involvement in the formulation and issuance of his first doctrine did not end with submission of a draft resolution to Congress. For example, the chief executive urged the congressional leadership to schedule full hearings on the resolution by the Senate Foreign Relations and Armed Services committees, and by the House Foreign Affairs and Armed Services committees, before each chamber considered the measure. He also asked the congressional leadership to require "roll-call votes" on the resolution, so that "the record will be complete and indisputable" concerning the nature and

29. Goldman, *The Tragedy of Lyndon Johnson*, 178.
30. Allan S. Nanes, "Congress and Military Commitments: An Overview," in Ronald C. Moe (ed.), *Congress and the President: Allies and Adversaries* (Pacific Palisades, Calif.: Goodyear, 1971), 254; Henry F. Graff, *The Tuesday Cabinet: Deliberation and Decision on Peace and War Under Lyndon B. Johnson* (Englewood Cliffs, N.J.: Prentice-Hall, 1970), 168–69.

extent of legislative support for it. In the Senate, LBJ urged the floor leader (Senator Fulbright) to accept no "amendments" to the resolution as recommended by the Foreign Relations and Armed Services committees; otherwise, the impression of "national unity" regarding America's position in Southeast Asia would be impaired.[31]

As personal and crucial as his own role was in the formulation and promulgation of the first Johnson Doctrine, LBJ also leaned heavily upon his advisers in the executive branch in dealing with the Gulf of Tonkin crisis. As we have noted, State Department officials had prepared several early drafts of what came to be called the Tonkin Gulf Resolution—as in February, 1964, when the idea was proposed to Secretary of State Dean Rusk by W. W. Rostow (who served as chairman of the State Department's Policy Planning Council). Again in June, Secretary Rusk proposed such a resolution to the president since (in any planned escalation of the Vietnam War) congressional approval for an expansion of the armed forces would be required.[32]

The resolution which was ultimately presented to Congress was prepared by Secretary of State Rusk, Under Secretary of State George Ball, and leaders of both political parties in Congress. That draft was personally approved by the president and then submitted for legislative passage. The recommendation for a retaliatory air strike against North Vietnam had similarly emanated from the nation's highest military leaders, the Joint Chiefs of Staff, who unanimously proposed it to the secretary of defense and to the president. The recommendation was considered by the National Security Council, which also unanimously recommended this step to the president, who approved it.[33]

Congress also played a pivotal role in the formulation and issuance of the Johnson Doctrine for Southeast Asia. We have already called attention to President Johnson's legislative background and his concern with cooperative executive-legislative relations. On several occasions prior to the Tonkin Gulf crisis, legislators had been informed of developments in Southeast Asia. In the early summer, 1964, for example, certain members of Congress had been "briefed" concerning U.S.

---

31. Johnson, *The Vantage Point*, 118; Anthony Austin, *The President's War* (Philadelphia: J. B. Lippincott, 1971), 103.
    32. Sheehan, *et al.* (eds.), *The Pentagon Papers*, 245, 251.
    33. Johnson, *The Vantage Point*, 114, 117–18; and Senate *Hearings on Southeast Asia Resolution*, 10.

intelligence operations in the area, including American support for South Vietnamese military strikes against the north.[34]

As we have already observed, following the second North Vietnamese attack against American ships (on August 4) in the Tonkin Gulf, President Johnson immediately summoned a representative group of legislators (including nine senators and seven representatives) to the White House to discuss the crisis and to inform them regarding the administration's intended response. As the Vietnam crisis intensified, critics of the Johnson Administration's policies later raised serious questions about the timing and circumstances of the White House meeting. In their view, it had been designed to yield a predetermined result: overwhelming legislative endorsement of the steps already taken or contemplated by the Johnson Administration for dealing with the crisis in Southeast Asia. The president informed the legislators present that retaliatory air strikes had already been ordered against North Vietnam. He also asked for their cooperation in preparing and passing a congressional resolution expressing the unified determination of the United States government to resist new Communist inroads in Southeast Asia. Each legislator attending the meeting was invited to express his viewpoints frankly, and most did so. After discussion, in President Johnson's words, each congressman "expressed his wholehearted endorsement of our course of action and of the proposed (Tonkin Gulf) Resolution."[35]

After examining the evidence, more impartial observers have expressed basically the same conclusion. Executive and legislative leaders at this White House meeting were "in accord" on the main elements of the response to be made to the Tonkin Gulf crisis. The legislators present called for "strong action" by the United States against North Vietnam and favored the kind of congressional resolution which the president requested. In brief, LBJ *received* the kind of support from members of Congress which he sought.[36]

Reflecting its traditionally subordinate role in the foreign policy process, the House of Representatives engaged in only perfunctory de-

---

34. For more detailed documentation on this point, see Johnson, *The Vantage Point*, 113; and the testimony of Secretary of State Rusk in Senate *Hearings on Southeast Asia Resolution*, 3.
35. Johnson, *The Vantage Point*, 116–17.
36. Austin, *The President's War*, 29–30; Windchy, *Tonkin Gulf*, 11.

bate on the Tonkin Gulf Resolution. After a total of only some forty minutes of floor discussion, the House adopted the resolution by a vote of 414-0.

One of the ironies surrounding the Vietnam War controversy is that in the Senate, the floor manager for the Tonkin Gulf Resolution was the chairman of the Foreign Relations Committee, Sen. J. William Fulbright (Democrat from Arkansas). At the time, Fulbright seemed an excellent choice for this assignment. He headed perhaps the most influential committee in Congress on foreign policy issues. In addition, he had been LBJ's nominee for the position of secretary of state under President Kennedy in 1960. During the early 1960s, Fulbright had taken an avowedly "hawkish" position on Cuba, calling for the use of American armed force to overthrow Castro's regime. Fulbright had repeatedly stated that the independence of South Vietnam was vital to the security of the United States and its Asian allies. With a political campaign in progress within the United States, Fulbright was persuaded that the president needed the bipartisan support of both political parties to achieve the nation's objectives in Southeast Asia.[37]

Defending the Gulf of Tonkin Resolution to the Senate on August 6, Senator Fulbright overwhelmingly urged approval of it on several grounds. In his view, President Johnson's response to Hanoi's aggressiveness had been limited and restrained; the United States was acting in "self-defense," as was its right under international law; the administration was reacting to "unambiguous aggression" and was seeking to communicate the idea that aggression "cannot be tolerated or ignored"; the rulers of North Vietnam must be made to understand that they "must confine their ambitions within their own frontiers." The United States, Fulbright asserted, sought to avoid a "land war in Asia," but it was determined to protect its security interests in the region. Moreover, to Fulbright's mind the proposed resolution presented no constitutional problems. Ample precedent could be found in similar resolutions earlier. In asking for congressional support, President Johnson was determined to continue the same "moderate" and restrained policies that had guided his approach to Southeast Asia in the past.[38]

37. Alan M. Jones, Jr., *U.S. Foreign Policy in a Changing World* (New York: David McKay, 1973), 14; Goldman, *The Tragedy of Lyndon Johnson*, 182.
38. See Fulbright's detailed speech to the Senate on August 6, 1964, in *Congressional Record*, 88th Cong., 2nd Sess., CX, 18398–18430.

Senate Majority Leader Mike Mansfield (Democrat of Montana) also urged the Senate to support the White House. Mansfield was convinced that there must be "no doubt" in the minds of Communist officials that the United States was prepared to defend itself. Such retaliatory action should be supported by "an entire Nation united in their trust and in their support of the President."[39]

Despite such entreaties by pro-Johnson forces, the Senate decided to make certain changes in the provisions of the Gulf of Tonkin Resolution. For example, the measure took the form of a joint resolution, rather than a concurrent resolution. In contrast to the earlier Middle East Resolution (which had "authorized" the president to use armed forces for foreign policy objectives), the Asian resolution expressed "congressional support and national unity" for the Johnson Administration's position on the Vietnam question.[40]

After some eight hours of debate, on August 7, the Senate approved the Tonkin Gulf Resolution by a vote of 88-2; on the same day, President Johnson signed the resolution into law. "Once again," said Senator Fulbright, "Congress was asked to show its support for the President in a crisis; once again, without question or hesitation, it did so." The judgment of James Reston was that "Congress complied with very little debate and with only two dissenting votes [with the president's request]. It could scarcely have done otherwise. . . . it is hard to imagine any Congress—even one dominated by the opposition party—doing otherwise."[41]

39. See Mansfield's speech in *ibid.*, 18399.
40. For a more detailed discussion of the semantical and substantive differences between the Tonkin Gulf Resolution and those which preceded it, see U.S. Congress, Senate Committee on Foreign Relations, *National Commitments*, S. Rept. 797, 90th Cong., 1st Sess., 1967, p. 19. A *concurrent resolution* requires the approval of both houses of Congress for passage, but does not require the president's signature. Normally, it is employed for the purpose of making (or amending) Congress' own procedural rules or for expressing the sentiment of the House and Senate on some issue. By contrast, a *joint resolution* requires the approval of both the House and Senate, but it must also have the president's signature before becoming law. This device has frequently been used by Congress in dealing with foreign policy questions. Occasionally (as in legislative action on the annexation of Texas and Hawaii), it has been employed to circumvent the Senate's role in the ratification of treaties. Jack C. Plano and Milton Greenberg, *The American Political Dictionary* (New York: Holt, Rinehart and Winston, 1967), 132, 143.
41. J. William Fulbright, *The Arrogance of Power* (New York: Random House, 1966), 50; James Reston, "The Press, the President and Foreign Policy," *Foreign Affairs*, XLIV (July, 1966), 560.

Public Opinion and Escalation in Vietnam

As with all recent diplomatic doctrines of the United States, public opinion also had an impact upon President Johnson's Asian doctrine. Three aspects of public opinion, as it relates to the first Johnson Doctrine, seem significant. The first is that on the question of American military involvement in Southeast Asia—as on nearly all other foreign policy issues—public attitudes were marked by evident inconsistencies, anomalies, and contradictions. The level of overall public understanding and awareness of developments in Southeast Asia was low; and public sentiment concerning the course of action the United States should take toward them was coi sed and ambiguous. Not untypically for foreign policy ques is, national officials were hard-pressed to draw any firm or consistent conclusions about what citizens "wanted" their government to do in the realm of Asian policy. For example, public opinion polls showed that (as had been consistently true since the end of World War II) the people wanted their leaders to "defeat communism" and to protect the nation's security and diplomatic commitments. At the same time, a majority of the people opposed unlimited military escalation in the Vietnam War, and they were in favor of settling the conflict by negotiations.[42]

A second noteworthy feature of public opinion as it affected the first Johnson Doctrine was that, despite such anomalies and inconsistencies in popular attitudes, the predominant stance of the American public toward the Vietnam War was "hawkish." President Johnson stated repeatedly that a larger number of Americans favored expanding than curtailing the war in Southeast Asia; still less did the American people advocate an American retreat from Southeast Asia.

Down perhaps to the closing months of his administration, the evidence supplied by public opinion polls indicated President Johnson's judgment was correct. If they were compelled to choose between the stark alternatives of "defeat" at the hands of communism, or a decisive "victory" in Southeast Asia, a majority of Americans preferred the latter. (It is equally true that relatively few Americans really understood

42. The contradictory and incompatible elements present in American public opinion toward the Vietnam conflict are highlighted clearly in Seymour M. Lipset, "The President, the Polls and Vietnam," in Robert J. Lifton (ed.), *America and the Asian Revolutions* (New Brunswick, N.J.: Transaction Books, 1970), 101–16.

the consequences of, or price to be paid for, "victory" in the Vietnam War.) As merely one example, a poll taken early in August, 1964, showed that citizens interviewed were divided over a wide range of eight options which confronted the United States in Southeast Asia. The largest response (27 percent of those polled) favored keeping American troops in Southeast Asia and resisting Communist efforts to defeat them. On the combined options, some 48 percent of the people advocated various kinds of "hawkish" solutions to the Vietnam conflict; some 14 percent favored "dovish" solutions (such as American withdrawal from the area); while some 30 percent were undecided about the best American course of action. On the basis of such evidence, and his own subjective and intuitive understanding of American attitudes, President Johnson was certain that the American people did not favor—nor would they countenance—an American withdrawal from, or defeat in, the Vietnam War.[43]

The two qualities of public opinion we have identified—its conflicting and ambiguous nature, and the predominantly "hawkish" coloration of American attitudes—reinforced, and help explain, a third characteristic of public sentiment. This was the public's readiness to accord the president *wide latitude* in responding to events in Southeast Asia and to give *massive public support* to whatever course of action the chief executive believed was necessary to protect American security interests. After analyzing numerous public opinion polls on American attitudes toward the Vietnam War, Seymour M. Lipset advanced the general observation that "national policy-makers, particularly the President have an almost free hand to pursue any policy they think correct and get public support for it." The strong underlying anti-Communist cast of American public opinion served "to support any actions which the President can argue need to be taken to defeat this enemy." In Lipset's opinion, "the American people know that they do not know, and feel they must trust the President" to safeguard the diplomatic and security interests of the nation.[44] In company with other chief executives before him, within limits President Johnson possessed a "free hand" to respond to foreign crises in whatever manner

43. John E. Mueller, *War, Presidents, and Public Opinion* (New York: John Wiley and Sons, 1973), 81; Lipset, "The President, the Polls and Vietnam," 116; Jack Valenti, *A Very Human President* (New York: W. W. Norton, 1975), 300–301.
44. Lipset, "The President, the Polls and Vietnam," 102, 108, 115.

he was convinced the security interests of the United States dictated; and in doing so, he could be reasonably confident of overwhelming public support.

After the promulgation of the first Johnson Doctrine, opinion surveys consistently showed strong public support for the president's response to the Gulf of Tonkin crisis. A Harris Poll, for example, showed that 72 percent of the American people approved President Johnson's handling of the Vietnam conflict (vis-à-vis 58 percent who had approved in July). Approximately the same majority (71 percent) thought LBJ could deal with the Vietnam problem more effectively than his political opponent, Sen. Barry Goldwater. Both during and in the weeks after the Tonkin Gulf crisis, one commentator has observed, public opinion polls consistently reflected a high degree of public endorsement for the policies of the Johnson Administration in Southeast Asia. One study concluded that the "vast majority of Americans applauded President Johnson's firm and decisive action" during the Tonkin Gulf affair. The president's "restraint" in responding to Communist provocations was widely applauded. Another study found that, as a result of President Johnson's handling of the Gulf of Tonkin crisis, public support for his overall performance in the White House increased. That Johnson's response to the Gulf of Tonkin episode had a firm foundation in public support was indicated by a national poll taken in the fall of 1964, which showed that 37 percent of the people favored a continuation of present American policy in Vietnam; 29 percent favored increased American military activity in Southeast Asia; 16 percent advocated American withdrawal from Vietnam; and 18 percent had no opinion on the subject. Some 66 percent of the people responding, in other words, either supported the existing level of American involvement in Southeast Asia or advocated greater involvement (which was actively under consideration by the Johnson Administration during this period).[45]

As one of President Johnson's later critics about the conduct of the Vietnam War, Sen. George McGovern (Democrat from South Dakota), conceded early in 1965: the results of public opinion surveys indicated that almost two-thirds of the American people *favored* retaliatory

45. Windchy, *Tonkin Gulf*, 12, 25; Wicker, *JFK and LBJ*, 228; Sheehan, *et al.* (eds.), *The Pentagon Papers*, 270; Mueller, *War, Presidents, and Public Opinion*, 82–83.

American air strikes against North Vietnam. Illustrating the ambiguous nature of public attitudes, the same poll indicated that some 81 percent of the people desired a negotiated settlement of the Vietnam conflict! But this mixed finding reflected McGovern's own position. In his view, President Johnson should be commended for defending American security interests in Southeast Asia, but he should also make a renewed effort to settle the Vietnam conflict by negotiations.[46] A further indication of public approval of the administration's policies during the Tonkin Gulf episode and afterward was that, irrespective of their particular political orientation, the reaction of the nation's leading newspapers was overwhelmingly favorable to the first Johnson Doctrine. The Washington *Post*, for example, commended LBJ's "careful and effective handling" of the crisis, while the New York *Times* applauded the administration's restrained behavior and endorsed Congress' approval of the Gulf of Tonkin Resolution.[47]

Foreign opinion about the Johnson Doctrine for Southeast Asia was divided. Predictably, Soviet Russia, Communist China, North Vietnam, and other Marxist nations vociferously opposed it. By contrast, official and unofficial opinion in most Western nations was favorable—with British opinion perhaps most enthusiastic about it. The French government was silent on the matter. America's treaty allies in Asia—Thailand, Australia, Nationalist China, and the Philippines—expressed varying degrees of support for it. The Latin American reaction to the first Johnson Doctrine was extremely restrained, almost undetectable. Among Third World nations (and the country was an acknowledged "leader" of this group) opinion in India was highly critical; the Indian government condemned the presence of U.S. warships in the Gulf of Tonkin. Anti-American demonstrations of greater or lesser intensity erupted in New Delhi, Tokyo, Stockholm, Glasgow, Toronto, Melbourne, and Algiers.[48]

We may conclude our discussion of the role of public opinion in the formulation and issuance of the first Johnson Doctrine by making five brief observations. First, as one study of the Johnson Administration's

46. "The United States and the Situation in Vietnam," *Congressional Digest*, XLIV (April, 1965), 121–25.
47. These and other examples of newspaper reaction to the first Johnson Doctrine may be found in Austin, *The President's War*, 83; and Windchy, *Tonkin Gulf*, 22.
48. Austin, *The President's War*, p. 74.

diplomacy has concluded, "It is doubtful that public opinion was ever regarded [by policy-makers] as more than a very insignificant factor in the actual determination of policy [toward Vietnam]."[49] In the Gulf of Tonkin episode, as in other critical developments involving America's role in the Vietnam War, there is no evidence that American public opinion served as a direct policy determinant or major "input" in the decision-making process.

Second, the overall public opinion environment in the United States was, however, clearly favorable for the issuance of the doctrine. In no sense could the Johnson Administration accurately be accused of "flouting" or otherwise disregarding public sentiment in the action it took after the incidents in the Gulf of Tonkin. When he issued the doctrine, LBJ had no reason to fear an adverse public reaction, nor did one occur in the United States. Third, the eruption of the Tonkin Gulf crisis—and LBJ's prompt disclosure of the facts concerning it to the American people and to Congress—further strengthened his hand in dealing with public opinion. (We shall deal at a later stage with the question of whether the Johnson Administration "misled" the American people and Congress about events in the Tonkin Gulf.) As almost always occurs, once the people became aware of the existence of a crisis—dramatized by the president's personal disclosure of it in a national radio and television speech—they turned to the White House for the expected leadership in dealing with it, and they accorded the president with latitude in formulating his response.

Fourth, as the evidence of public opinion polls reveals, LBJ's response to the Tonkin Gulf episode may well have been more restrained and limited than a substantial segment of American public opinion desired. Quite clearly, in the months after August, 1964, the president was free to pursue a more militant course in opposition to communism in Southeast Asia, without reaching the limits of public tolerance for his policies. Fifth, despite later complaints among legislators that they had been manipulated into passing the Gulf of Tonkin Resolution, overwhelming congressional support for Johnson's Asian doctrine was perhaps inevitable, given the high level of public approval expressed for the administration's policies. Even in the complete absence of such alleged "manipulation," under prevailing circumstances, it is

49. Nelson W. Polsby, "Hawks, Doves and the Press," in Lifton (ed.), *America and the Asian Revolutions,* 77.

difficult to imagine significant congressional opposition to the first Johnson Doctrine.

The Political Environment of the First Johnson Doctrine

No understanding of the Johnson Doctrine for Southeast Asia is possible without placing the doctrine within the domestic political context existing at the time of its issuance. During the period of campaigning which preceded the national elections in November, 1964, President Johnson and his Democratic supporters found themselves subjected to a barrage of criticism—identified specifically with Sen. Barry Goldwater (Republican of Arizona) and his followers—for their alleged "failure" to prosecute the war in Southeast Asia vigorously and victoriously. To the minds of such critics, this failure symbolized a long-standing and continuing lack of leadership by Democratic policy-makers in dealing with a number of international issues—like communism in Cuba, the Communist threat to Laos, Soviet pressures on Berlin, Marxist penetration of the Congo and other African countries, and now the threatened communization of Indochina. As the administration's Republican opponents assessed it, under the Democrats American diplomacy had been marked by "drift, deception, and defeat." Senator Goldwater and his supporters clearly understood, and were exploiting politically, the deeply ingrained anti-Communist proclivities of the American people and were echoing the demands of many citizens that their leaders "stand up" to communism abroad.[50]

To such accusations, President Johnson and his supporters made a twofold reply. The Johnson White House was merely continuing American policies in Southeast Asia that were inaugurated by the Kennedy Administration; and Democratic policy-makers were determined to keep America's involvement in the Vietnam conflict limited, leaving the main responsibility for defending the security of South Vietnam to the leaders and people of that country.[51]

Undeniably, the two crises in the Gulf of Tonkin were opportune developments for the Johnson Administration from a political perspective. They afforded LBJ an opportunity to "answer" political oppo-

---

50. Evans and Novak, *Lyndon B. Johnson*, 531–32; Goldman, *The Tragedy of Lyndon Johnson*, 176; Paul Tillett, et al., *The National Election of 1964* (Washington, D.C.: Brookings Institution, 1966), 54–55.
51. Wicker, *JFK and LBJ*, 227; Heren, *No Hail, No Farewell*, 48–49.

nents, while at the same time reiterating basic American policy toward Southeast Asia. At the president's initiative, the Gulf of Tonkin Resolution conveyed a forceful and unified American response to Communist aggressiveness; yet this was a "restrained" response (in contrast to Senator Goldwater's avowedly "hawkish" position on the Vietnam War). Two basic ideas having wide popular appeal—the administration's determination to resist Communist hegemony, combined with the restrained application of American power abroad—were central in Johnson's diplomacy. In terms of its domestic political impact, one observer asserted, the first Johnson Doctrine was a "shrewd political act, shoring up Johnson against the Republican campaign charge that he was 'soft on Vietnam.'" Armed with the Gulf of Tonkin Resolution, LBJ could cultivate the image of himself as a leader who could not, and would not, be "taken advantage of" by Communist nations.[52]

An unusual feature of the Johnson Doctrine for Southeast Asia was the fact that it was officially terminated—it would be no exaggeration to say, "repudiated"—by act of Congress. Insofar as the doctrine was embodied, and approved by Congress, in the form of the Tonkin Gulf Resolution, this legislation was repealed, as an amendment to the Foreign Military Sales Act signed by President Nixon on January 14, 1971. Thus, the first Johnson Doctrine remained in effect some six and a half years, covering the period of maximum American military involvement in the Vietnam War.[53]

Efforts to bring about the termination of the doctrine began within less than a year after its passage. They were led by Sen. Wayne Morse (Democrat of Oregon, one of the few original opponents of the resolution) and by Senator Fulbright (the latter having "broken" with the Johnson Administration over the Vietnam issue and over LBJ's diplomacy in dealing with the Dominican crisis, as explained more fully in Chapter 6). Initially, these attempts to repeal the Tonkin Gulf Resolution were unsuccessful. During 1966, for example, the Senate voted 92-5 *against* its abrogation. In the same period, however, under Fulbright's leadership as chairman, the Senate Foreign Relations Committee began to conduct widely publicized hearings on the Vietnam War. Prominence was given to the Gulf of Tonkin incidents, with sev-

52. Evans and Novak, *Lyndon B. Johnson*, 533.
53. For the text of the legislation repealing the Tonkin Gulf Resolution, see Public Law 91-672, *U.S. Statutes at Large* (Washington, D.C.: Government Printing Office, 1971), LXXXIV, 2053.

eral witnesses challenging the administration's version of events. As a result, considerable doubt existed in Congress concerning the administration's credibility in providing the public the facts about the Gulf of Tonkin affair and about legislative approval of the resolution based upon information supplied by executive officials. Unquestionably, the hearings contributed significantly to rising public discontent over America's role in Vietnam and its dissatisfaction with the diplomacy of the Johnson Administration.[54]

The language of the Gulf of Tonkin Resolution expressly provided for its appeal at any time, by a concurrent resolution passed by majorities within the House and Senate. Within two or three years after the resolution's approval by massive majorities in both houses of Congress, it was evident that legislative dissatisfaction with it had become pervasive. For reasons that we shall examine more fully at a later stage, many members of Congress believed that the resolution exemplified the "credibility gap" characteristic of the administration's statements about the progress of the war in Vietnam; the resolution became a symbol of LBJ's "manipulation" of Congress and public opinion to achieve his purposes. One observer is convinced that, as early as 1965, possibly a majority of the Senate actually favored repeal of the resolution. Yet it was not until the end of 1970 that a majority in both houses voted to terminate the Gulf of Tonkin Resolution.[55]

Two factors largely explain this phenomenon. One was the fact that—disaffected as many legislators became with the Gulf of Tonkin Resolution—Congress was reluctant to repeal it, as long as the United States remained heavily committed to the defense of South Vietnam. Termination of the resolution under these circumstances would amount to (or would be widely interpreted as signifying) a repudiation of presidential leadership during time of war. Such an action by Congress was not only unprecedented, but it might give rise to totally unforeseen consequences which legislators were unprepared to face. Even Senator Fulbright was aware of the risk; and the realization unquestionably deterred many of his colleagues from voting for the resolution's repeal.[56]

The second factor constraining Congress against repeal of the

---

54. For a discussion of these initial efforts to terminate the first Johnson Doctrine, see Windchy, *Tonkin Gulf*, 40–44; and Wicker, *JFK and LBJ*, 227.

55. Wicker, *JFK and LBJ*, 227.

56. *Ibid.*; Fulbright, *The Arrogance of Power*, 51.

Tonkin Gulf Resolution was the change in the position of executive policy-makers under the Johnson and Nixon administrations concerning its necessity and value. For several years after passage of the resolution, executive officials cited it as a major source of presidential authority for the steadily increasing American military presence in the Vietnam War. As the White House interpreted it, the Tonkin Gulf Resolution was the "functional equivalent of a declaration of war," authorizing the president to take any steps he deemed necessary to achieve victory in Southeast Asia. The text of the resolution unquestionably supported such an interpretation. It gave congressional approval for the president to "take all necessary measures to repel any armed attack against the forces of the United States and to prevent further aggression." It further provided that the United States was "prepared as the President determines" to defend the security of its Asian allies.

Concurrently and somewhat contradictorily, however, executive officials also maintained that the president did not "need" the authority conferred by the Gulf of Tonkin Resolution to protect the nation's security interests in Southeast Asia or presumably, any other region. Thus, on August 18, 1967, President Johnson asserted that the resolution had been "desirable," but that it was not "necessary to do what we did and what we're doing" in Southeast Asia. Its major contribution lay in giving Congress an opportunity to be in on the "takeoff" of national policy in Vietnam.[57] Both President Johnson and President Nixon believed that the Constitution conferred ample authority upon the chief executive to prosecute the war in Southeast Asia. Since this authority did not derive from an act of Congress, it could not be abrogated by withdrawal of the Tonkin Gulf Resolution.

But President Johnson and his advisers in time ceased opposing, and ultimately advocated, repeal of the Tonkin Gulf Resolution for two reasons. The first was that the Johnson Administration was committed to reducing the American military presence in Southeast Asia and, ultimately, to ending America's role in the Vietnam War. Thus, the resolution was no longer needed to justify involvement in the Vietnam conflict. The second reason was that, along with the Johnson Administration before it (and other administrations prior to 1963), the

57. See President Johnson's statement on August 18, 1967, as cited in Senate Foreign Relations Committee, *National Commitments*, 22.

Nixon Administration contended that presidential authority to use the armed forces for the preservation of national security did not depend upon an affirmative grant of power by Congress, in the form of the Tonkin Gulf Resolution. Hence, repeal of the resolution would not inhibit the president from responding to foreign threats.[58]

The First Johnson Doctrine in the Diplomatic Balance

On the basis of two major criteria—the deterrence of Communist expansionism in Southeast Asia, and the creation and maintenance of a strong sense of national unity toward the Vietnam War—only one verdict about the first Johnson Doctrine is possible. As a long-run development in American diplomacy, *the doctrine was a failure.* It was unsuccessful in accomplishing its twofold objective; and with regard to the problem of national unity, in time the doctrine itself became a focal point of the internal dissension which erupted within the United States over the Vietnam War.

When evaluated by more short-range criteria, however, a somewhat different and more favorable verdict must be rendered upon the first Johnson Doctrine. One purpose of the doctrine was to deter new aggressive moves by North Vietnam. For a period of several months after the doctrine was issued, there was no recurrence of direct Communist assaults against American military units in Southeast Asia. This fact of course does not prove that the first Johnson Doctrine alone inhibited Communist expansionism (the government of South Vietnam, for example, experienced no lessening of Communist efforts to control the south). Nevertheless, for a period of several months Hanoi seemed reluctant to repeat its assaults directly against American forces in Southeast Asia. To whatever degree the doctrine was responsible for this result, it proved to be short-lived. No evidence exists that it had any lasting effect in deterring Communist determination to control Vietnam.

As a measure intended to promote national unity on the Vietnam question, the Johnson Doctrine for Southeast Asia also enjoyed considerably greater short-term, than long-term, success. Admittedly, criteria for measuring the degree of national unity existing before and

---

58. Windchy, *Tonkin Gulf*, 337; *The Power of the Pentagon* (Washington D.C.: Congressional Quarterly, 1972), 72.

after issuance of the doctrine are imperfect and somewhat subjective. Yet according to two which might be employed—the degree of public support for the administration's Vietnam policies, and the apparently high level of executive-legislative cooperation on measures required to prosecute the Vietnam War—the doctrine did serve for a time as a unifying device.

Public support for Johnson's approach to the Vietnam problem increased after the Tonkin Gulf episode. Until the late 1960s, public approval for the administration's "restrained" response to communism in Southeast Asia (vis-à-vis the "hawkish" and "dovish" alternatives offered by LBJ's critics) remained high. Irrespective of their subconscious and unexpressed feelings about the first Johnson Doctrine, a majority in the House and Senate remained reluctant to change it—or even to criticize it directly—until the late 1960s. By such actions as its almost automatic approval of funds requested by the administration to prosecute the Vietnam War, Congress as a whole gave no sign of underlying dissatisfaction with the president's management of the war or his specific response to the Gulf of Tonkin crisis.

Yet these temporary gains for the first Johnson Doctrine were largely nullified by certain long-term problems and objections which the doctrine raised. Even today some of these questions remain unresolved. A number of constitutional and other issues exemplified by the doctrine still impede the unified conduct of American diplomacy. Four such questions surrounding the doctrine merit detailed examination.

The first relates to the accusation made by one group of critics against President Johnson and his advisers that the first Johnson Doctrine was issued in response to a crisis which was entirely "fabricated" by executive policy-makers. In short, the indictment charges that the alleged Communist attacks on units of the U.S. Navy in the Gulf of Tonkin on August 2 and 4, 1964, never occurred. Some critics asserted that the entire episode was "invented"—or that the crisis was greatly exaggerated—by the administration to achieve its covert and longstanding objective: escalation of the conflict in Vietnam. This theme became prominent in the views of several "dovish" critics of America's role in Southeast Asia and more generally, in the analyses of "New Left" and revisionist commentators who denounced the "overextension" of American power in Asia, and the nation's hegemonial impulses globally.[59] As a result of the hearings conducted by the Senate Foreign Relations Committee, Senator Fulbright in time came to believe that the whole Tonkin Gulf matter had been "deliberately staged" by the Johnson Administration in order "to gain public support for military action" which the White House was already determined to take in Southeast Asia.[60]

According to this view, the administration's purpose in inventing the Gulf of Tonkin crisis was not only to create national support for a vastly expanded American military effort in Southeast Asia. A related and necessary goal was also to undermine initiatives by individuals like UN Secretary General U Thant and French President Charles de Gaulle to promote a negotiated settlement of the Vietnam conflict. Citing the Gulf of Tonkin episode as evidence, the Johnson Administration could "prove" Hanoi's aggressiveness and its lack of interest in a peaceful resolution of the dispute. Moscow's and Peking's support of the North Vietnamese position in the crisis constituted proof of overall Communist determination to "win" the struggle in Southeast Asia. Conversely, the administration's decisive response to the Tonkin Gulf crisis strengthened the government of South Vietnam and renewed its determination to defeat the Communist enemy.[61]

A number of critics of the Johnson and Nixon administrations are convinced that the White House routinely engaged in duplicity, not only in connection with the Vietnam War, but more generally with regard to a wide range of foreign and domestic policy questions. Even more broadly, some of these commentators have discerned a pattern of duplicitous behavior by executive officials since World War II. Executive policy-makers have been motivated by an obsessive anti-Communism, compelling them to "win" the Cold War and to take any steps—not excluding deceiving the American people—required to

---

59. A detailed indictment, charging the Johnson Administration with duplicity in the Gulf of Tonkin affair, is Joseph C. Goulden, *Truth is the First Casualty: The Gulf of Tonkin Affairs—Illusion and Reality* (Chicago: Rand McNally, 1969). A shorter treatment in this vein is John M. Swomley, Jr., *American Empire: The Political Ethics of Twentieth Century Conquest* (New York: Macmillan, 1970), 207–11.

60. Fulbright's views are quoted in Haynes Johnson and Bernard M. Gwertzman, *Fulbright: The Dissenter* (Garden City: N.Y.: Doubleday, 1968), 198.

61. Schurmann, *et al.*, *The Politics of Escalation in Vietnam*, 35–43; Swomley, *American Empire*, 211; Geyelin, *Lyndon B. Johnson and the World*, 203.

achieve that objective. In this interpretation, the Johnson Administration's behavior in early August, 1964, was merely one episode in a long record of deceit by national officialdom.[62]

Such an interpretation of the Gulf of Tonkin episode, and of the first Johnson Doctrine issued as a result of it, it may as well be stated frankly, is all but impossible to refute persuasively. How is it ever possible to "prove" convincingly that public officials are "not lying" or that they are revealing their "true motives" in policy decisions? The precondition for such proof would seem to be access to governmental archives providing a complete record of what transpired, and a comparison of the evidence with the statements issued by officials involved in decision-making. Even then, doubts and uncertainties are likely to remain, particularly as these involve interpretive and judgmental questions based upon the evidence. (Over a century later, for example, historians still differ over the "causes" of the Civil War and over the respective responsibilities of the North and the South for producing that conflict!) The kind of conspiratorial interpretation of the Tonkin Gulf episode and the Johnson Administration's response to it, set forth briefly above, forms part of a more comprehensive "devil theory" of American diplomatic behavior since World War II, which attributes the preponderance of blame for the Cold War to the decisions of American policy-makers. Proponents of that theory often seem oblivious to contrary evidence and uninterested in an objective examination—involving the same standard of behavior for Western and for Communist policy-makers—of the facts.

With regard to the Tonkin Gulf affair, congressional and private investigations of the evidence unquestionably *have* produced a number of ambiguities, inconsistencies, and unanswered questions about events occurring off the coast of Vietnam on August 2 and 4, 1964. Incomplete, confusing, and sometimes conflicting reports *were* received by American commanders on the scene and by officials in

---

62. See, for example, David Wise, *The Politics of Lying: Government Deception, Secrecy, and Power* (New York: Random House, 1973), 61–62. Senator Fulbright also cited the Tonkin Gulf Resolution as "one of the clearest examples" of a "very disastrous distortion" by executive policy-makers in their presentation of events abroad. In his view, there had been "a clear misrepresentation of facts" in the Tonkin Gulf crisis. John C. Stennis and J. William Fulbright, *The Role of Congress in Foreign Policy* (Washington, D.C.: American Enterprise Institute, 1971), 80–81.

Washington. A number of questions (such as how many attacks occurred against American naval units, or whether these assaults were accidental or deliberate) may never be answered satisfactorily. Admittedly, during the first week of August, the evidence available to President Johnson and his advisers was fragmentary, puzzling, and incomplete, in many respects. (Yet as often as not, this fact is also true of other foreign policy crises confronting executive policy-makers. President Kennedy and his advisers, for example, were never certain about many aspects of the Cuban Missile Crisis of 1962. Interpretations of Soviet motivations in that instance still vary widely. As we shall see in Chapter 8, the question of Soviet intentions was a crucial issue—evoking widely conflicting interpretations—with regard to the Carter Doctrine.) Even today, pieces of the puzzle of what actually occurred in the Gulf of Tonkin are missing—and some of them may never be found.

Enough is known, however, to warrant several reasonably firm conclusions about the Gulf of Tonkin affair. Some kind of Communist-instigated assault on American naval units did occur on August 2 and 4, 1964. Physical evidence of such assaults was available at the time and in the months which followed. Even Hanoi admitted that it had attacked American naval units (ostensibly, on the grounds that they had violated North Vietnamese territorial waters).[63] To accept the idea that the entire episode was fabricated by officials of the Johnson Administration requires that we believe in the existence of a conspiracy reaching from the White House to the crews of American ships off the Vietnamese coast. Such a conspiracy would involve literally hundreds of American civilian and military officials at home and in Asia—none of whom at the time, or later, was prepared to reveal the existence of it to congressional investigative committees, to journalists, or to the American people. Given the propensity of the American news media, for example, for prompt and dramatic disclosures of official wrongdoing by the White House, by the Central Intelligence Agency, and other agencies of government, it is inconceivable that such a conspiracy could exist without being revealed at some point.

63. George McT. Kahin and John W. Lewis, *The United States in Vietnam: An Analysis in Depth of the History of America's Involvement in Vietnam* (New York: Dell, 1969), 157.

Thus far, no credible evidence has yet been produced that such a pattern of duplicity characterized the Johnson Administration's diplomacy during the Gulf of Tonkin affair. Admittedly, numerous unanswered questions and contradictions in the record remain (but routinely, that is also true of accounts by credible witnesses of traffic accidents, bank robberies, and "unidentified flying objects"). The weight of the evidence available clearly supports the conclusion that the Johnson Administration responded to what it perceived to have been a genuine crisis in the Gulf of Tonkin. The White House sincerely believed that Hanoi had embarked upon a new course of militancy, involving direct assaults against American naval forces in the area. The first Johnson Doctrine was issued as a result of, and as an effort to respond effectively to, this crisis.

A second important question associated with the Tonkin Gulf affair and the first Johnson Doctrine is: did the Johnson Administration use this crisis deliberately to carry out a preconceived strategy, entailing a significant escalation in America's role in the Vietnam conflict? A number of commentators believe the question must be answered affirmatively. David Wise has written that for the United States, the Gulf of Tonkin episode was equivalent to President James K. Polk's military occupation of disputed territory with Mexico in 1846: "It provided the excuse to go to war." [64]

If this verdict is extreme (de facto by mid-1964 the United States was already at war in Southeast Asia), a variant conclusion is that the Tonkin Gulf crisis and the first Johnson Doctrine resulted in a fundamental change in America's role in the Vietnam conflict. Eric F. Goldman is convinced that the events of early August, 1964, marked a "turning point" in United States policy toward Vietnam. The authors of another study have asserted that in its response to the events in the Gulf of Tonkin, the Johnson Administration "set a precedent" which "marked a new stage of active intervention" by the United States in the Vietnam conflict. Or as another work on the Vietnam conflict has put it, armed with the authority of the Gulf of Tonkin Resolution, President Johnson altered the nature of America's involvement in the war, from merely sending military "advisers" and equipment (as the

64. Wise, *The Politics of Lying,* 35.

Kennedy Administration had done) to direct American military intervention to defeat communism in Southeast Asia.[65]

According to this school of thought, even if it is granted that the Johnson Administration did not actually fabricate the incidents purportedly occurring in the Gulf of Tonkin, the administration found these two naval encounters an extremely useful development for the purpose of carrying out a new American strategy in Southeast Asia. Sometimes described as a policy of "incrementalism," the strategy envisioned a step-by-step buildup and application of American military power in Southeast Asia, with primary reliance upon American air power, in an effort to compel the Communist enemy to negotiate an end to the Vietnam conflict. Skillfully exploiting the Communist assaults against American ships in the Tonkin Gulf, LBJ was able to secure congressional support for this planned escalation of the war and, thereafter, to assert that the new strategy represented the "unified" approach of the United States Government to the Vietnam conflict.[66]

As many critics of the Johnson Administration see it, the Tonkin Gulf crisis and the first Johnson Doctrine marked a turning point in America's role in the Vietnam War. Not only did it witness the adoption of a new American strategy for dealing with the conflict. For the first time, President Johnson became personally and actively involved with the Vietnam problem. Moreover, as a result of the retaliatory American air strikes conducted against North Vietnam the government of South Vietnam became more aggressive and confident of America's support in its response to the Communist challenge; it also became more authoritarian in dealing with its own citizens. Within a few days after the Gulf of Tonkin crisis, for example, the new regime of General Khanh had invoked sweeping "emergency power," giving it virtually a free hand to prosecute the war more vigorously.[67]

65. Goldman, *The Tragedy of Lyndon Johnson*, 175–76; Schurmann, *et al.*, *The Politics of Escalation in Vietnam*, 42; Kahin and Lewis, *The United States in Vietnam*, 159.

66. Sheehan, *et al.* (eds.), *The Pentagon Papers*, 268–69; John McDermott, "Vietnam is No Mistake," in Marvin E. Gettleman and David Mermelstein (eds.), *The Great Society Reader: The Failure of American Liberalism* (New York: Random House, 1967), 446–47.

67. Kahin and Lewis, *The United States in Vietnam*, 159; Jean Lacouture, *Vietnam: Between Two Truces* (New York: Random House, 1966), 258–59.

It is true that for several months preceding the Tonkin Gulf crisis, the Johnson Administration had prepared various "contingency plans," which included two major elements later incorporated into its response to that crisis: retaliatory air strikes against North Vietnam and a congressional resolution giving the president wide latitude to oppose communism in Southeast Asia. According to one commentator, by late spring, LBJ's principal advisers had agreed upon "a thirty-day scenario culminating in full scale bombing" of the north.[68]

Earlier in our discussion, however, we noted that prior to August, President Johnson had refused to approve such plans. Moreover, in responding to the two North Vietnamese naval attacks, he did not order retaliatory air strikes until after the second Communist assault on American ships. Even then, these air strikes were launched against carefully selected targets, in order to minimize civilian casualties. American air strikes were not carried out against Communist-held territory on a regular basis until early in 1965. Both before and after the Tonkin Gulf crisis, President Johnson and his advisers were constrained from escalating the war because they feared such a step might provoke direct intervention by North Vietnam's powerful allies (like Soviet Russia and Communist China); they were also apprehensive about South Vietnam's ability to resist intensified Communist military pressures.[69] In his message to Congress recommending the Gulf of Tonkin Resolution, President Johnson stated his hope that the administration's response to events in the Gulf of Tonkin would induce more restrained behavior by Hanoi and the Viet Cong.

Events showed that his hope by the Johnson Administration was illusory. During the months following the Tonkin Gulf incidents, Communist forces in Southeast Asia made new gains. Meanwhile, political conditions in South Vietnam continued to deteriorate. Within the United States, the election of President Johnson in November constituted a crude popular mandate for his middle-of-the-road approach to the Vietnam problem vis-à-vis Senator Goldwater's more "hawkish" stance. Confronted with continuing Communist gains in Southeast

68. John C. Donovan, *The Cold Warriors: A Policy-Making Elite* (Lexington, Mass.: D. C. Heath, 1974), 218–19.

69. Johnson, *The Vantage Point*, 119. See also U.S. Congress, Senate, Committee on Foreign Relations, *Hearings on Supplemental Foreign Assistance: Fiscal Year 1966—Vietnam*, 89th Cong., 2nd Sess., 1966, p. 606.

Asia, early in February, 1965, therefore—some six months after the Gulf of Tonkin imbroglio—the administration finally adopted the strategy of sustained air strikes against North Vietnam. This approach, the administration erroneously believed, would enable the United States to avoid a large commitment of ground forces in Southeast Asia and would induce Hanoi to settle the Vietnam controversy by negotiations.[70]

A pattern of massive and repeated aerial bombardment of North Vietnam, it needs to be repeated, was not employed by the Johnson Administration until after two developments: the retaliatory air strikes against North Vietnam in August had failed to achieve their purpose; and Communist elements in Southeast Asia began to pursue their goals with new militancy and effectiveness. Admittedly, by early 1965 the United States had significantly expanded its military effort in Southeast Asia. No persuasive evidence exists, however, that the Johnson Administration was committed to this step at the time of the Gulf of Tonkin crisis or that it deliberately misled Congress and the American people during that period concerning the future steps it intended to take in Southeast Asia. The administration's announced goal was the same as the Kennedy Administration's goal: to preserve the region from Communist domination. After mid-1964, the strategy used for achieving it would be dictated as much by circumstances, and by the actions of Communist groups in Southeast Asia, as by the preconceived ideas and strategies of President Johnson and his advisers.

A third important question surrounding the Johnson Doctrine for Southeast Asia is posed by the contention of several critics that the Gulf of Tonkin Resolution became in effect a "blank check" giving the president unlimited authority to prosecute the war in any way he saw fit in Southeast Asia. In Chester L. Cooper's words, the resolution was "subsequently parlayed into a blank check to rationalize the President's unwillingness to have Congress play a meaningful role in his Vietnam policy." Armed with the Tonkin Gulf Resolution, President Johnson could, in the words of another study, "use the Armed Forces just about as he wished in the Vietnam War." Perhaps the most outstanding feature of the Tonkin Gulf Resolution was its ambiguity and flexibility. This quality of the resolution provided the White House

70. Goodwin, *Triumph or Tragedy*, 31; Graff, *The Tuesday Cabinet*, 41.

with all the power it required after mid-1964 to expand America's role in the Vietnam conflict.[71]

After the passage of the Tonkin Gulf Resolution, the president and other executive officials did cite it as an important source of presidential authority for increased American participation in the Vietnam War. Thus, a few days after congressional approval of the resolution, the State Department referred to it as granting the president authority to "oppose firmly, by all necessary means, DRV [Democratic Republic of Vietnam or North Vietnam] efforts to subvert and conquer South Vietnam and Laos."[72] Early in 1966, Secretary of State Dean Rusk told the Senate Foreign Relations Committee that the Tonkin Gulf Resolution provided the president with authority to deal with more than a single, isolated attack upon American naval forces off the coast of Vietnam. It constituted a more general grant of power to the chief executive, authorizing the steps taken by the Johnson Administration after mid-1964 to save Vietnam from Communist domination.[73]

More specifically, on several occasions after passage of the Tonkin Gulf Resolution, executive officials described it as constituting a de facto "declaration of war" by Congress. As Under Secretary of State Nicholas Katzenbach described it, the resolution served as the "functional equivalent" of a declaration of war by the House and Senate. Or, as a former State Department official expressed the idea, the Tonkin Gulf Resolution possessed the "same constitutional status" as a congressional declaration of war.[74]

By its emphasis upon the idea that the Tonkin Gulf Resolution was tantamount to or a "functional equivalent" of a declaration of war, the Johnson Administration was in effect making two points. First, Congress had formally recognized the fact that the United States was involved in an armed conflict in Southeast Asia. The logical extension of this idea was that (in contrast to the situation existing during the Korean War), after congressional passage of the resolution, the United

71. Berkowitz, et al., The Politics of American Foreign Policy, 222; Evans and Novak, Lyndon B. Johnson, 533; Wicker, JFK and LBJ, 223–24.
72. See the text of the State Department note delivered to the Canadian Embassy in Washington on August 8, 1964, in Sheehan, et al. (eds.), The Pentagon Papers, 291.
73. See Rusk's testimony in Senate Foreign Relations Committee, Hearings on Supplemental Foreign Assistance, 62. See also testimony of Gen. Maxwell D. Taylor, 465.
74. Katzenbach's testimony on August 17, 1967, Senate Foreign Relations Committee, National Commitments, 21; Eugene V. Rostow, Law, Power and the Pursuit of Peace (New York: Harper and Row, 1968), 64.

States was *not* involved in an "undeclared war" or conflict abroad without the approval of Congress. Second, by construing the Tonkin Gulf Resolution as the "functional equivalent" of a declaration of war, the Johnson Administration in essence was saying that Congress had been given ample opportunity to express its judgment about America's involvement in the Vietnam conflict. When it overwhelmingly approved the Tonkin Gulf Resolution, it thereby joined the executive branch in reasserting America's determination to resist the communization of Southeast Asia. In practice, this meant that thereafter, the president largely had a "free hand" to accomplish this common goal in any way he deemed necessary.[75]

By subsequently insisting upon repeal of the Tonkin Gulf Resolution, Congress indicated that it did not accept the Johnson Administration's interpretation of it, as giving the president unlimited authority to prosecute the war in Southeast Asia. More broadly—not only in that region, but in other foreign settings as well—by the late 1960s Congress began to assert its prerogatives in the foreign policy field and to reject claims of "executive supremacy" in external affairs.[76]

For their part, the president and his advisers simultaneously advanced the contradictory claim that the White House did not really "need" the Gulf of Tonkin Resolution to protect national security interests in Southeast Asia, and that the resolution was an important source of presidential authority to engage in armed conflict in that region. Whichever interpretation constitutional lawyers might judge the correct one (and, as always, eminent constitutional and legal authorities could be cited for either viewpoint), the White House was claiming maximum authority to achieve its proclaimed goals in Southeast Asia. The common denominator of both interpretations was that the president possessed the constitutional authority he needed in responding to the crisis in Southeast Asia. Under those conditions, officials of the Johnson Administration, therefore, hardly had grounds for complaint when the ultimate responsibility for the outcome of the war in Vietnam was assigned almost exclusively to the White House!

A fourth important aspect of the first Johnson Doctrine may be

75. Goldman, *The Tragedy of Lyndon Johnson*, 265; Wicker, *JFK and LBJ*, 222.
76. A detailed analysis of congressional assertiveness in foreign relations, focusing on the period during and after the Vietnam War, is Cecil V. Crabb, Jr., and Pat Holt, *Invitation to Struggle: Congress, the President and Foreign Policy* (Washington, D.C.: Congressional Quarterly Press, 1980).

highlighted by calling attention to one of its most paradoxical results. Formulated and presented to Congress as a measure which would create a new sense of "national unity" toward the Vietnam War, the resolution ultimately achieved exactly the opposite result. As time passed, it became a major source of national disunity and contention between the executive and legislative branches. After mid-1964, the ensuing controversy over the scope of the president's powers to wage the Vietnam War—and of the related issue of congressional noninvolvement in key decisions related to the conflict—contributed significantly to internal divisiveness, leading ultimately to President Johnson's decision not to seek reelection in 1968.

Initially, a few congressional dissenters—like Senator Morse—expressed their dissatisfaction with the Tonkin Gulf Resolution. Gradually, an ever widening circle of legislators began to complain that the resolution served to "entrap" Congress. If Congress had refused to approve the resolution, then it risked repudiating presidential leadership in the midst of a foreign crisis. Yet, as actually occurred, if Congress approved the resolution, then it risked relinquishing any meaningful legislative role thereafter in the formulation of national policy respecting the Vietnam War. Either way, the choice was unpalatable. Increasingly, legislators became disaffected because the president had placed them in this dilemma, and some legislators accused the president of distorting the facts in order to get his way with Congress. As the American military involvement in Southeast Asia grew (with no evidence of an impending Communist defeat), a deep feeling of ill-will toward the White House pervaded Capitol Hill. As Goldman has expressed it, an "ensnared Senate flailed about in frustration and rage." Designed as a measure to promote national unity on the Vietnam question, the Tonkin Gulf Resolution instead produced "serious friction" between the president and Congress. A noteworthy effect of the resolution, Tom Wicker has concluded, lay in planting the seeds of "distrust and suspicion" between the president and Congress. In time, many legislators interpreted the resolution as a "ruthless power play and a betrayal of the Congressional-Executive trust." [77]

From the perspective of constructive executive-legislative relations, the principal difficulty with the Gulf of Tonkin Resolution was that

77. Goldman, *The Tragedy of Lyndon Johnson*, 180; Wicker, *JFK and LBJ*, 227.

the White House arrived at, and adhered to, its own unilateral interpretation of its terms. The administration's "consultations" with Congress after early August, 1964, were designed primarily to enlist legislative cooperation in carrying out the Johnson Doctrine for Southeast Asia, as the White House defined that objective. Executive policymakers took little heed of legislative dissatisfaction with the doctrine—except to explain from time to time that congressional viewpoints were unjustified. Down to the time he left the White House, President Johnson insisted upon his interpretation of the doctrine, in the face of mounting legislative discontent with it. This fact contributed significantly to the loss of "credibility" which the administration encountered in its approach to the Vietnam conflict.

At the same time, undue weight must not be attributed to the first Johnson Doctrine in accounting for the fundamental disagreement which developed between the administration and its critics regarding the Vietnam War. In all likelihood, the main factor responsible for this phenomenon was the failure of the United States to achieve its goals in Southeast Asia. This fact was per se a profoundly traumatic event for the American society, which (since the War of 1812) had never "lost a war." No evidence exists that the Johnson Administration's critics inside and outside Congress had formulated a more successful strategy for attaining American objectives in Asia. Indeed, among the administration's detractors, wide disagreement existed both concerning the goals themselves and the most effective methods for achieving them. It is difficult to resist the conclusion that, if the administration's strategies in Southeast Asia had succeeded, much of the expressed discontent with the first Johnson Doctrine would never have occurred or would have remained muted and largely uninfluential.

Yet when examined in more general terms, instruments like the Tonkin Gulf Resolution perhaps inherently produce greater or lesser ill-will between the president and Congress. (The Formosa and Middle East resolutions earlier had also produced executive-legislative tensions, though less acute ones.) The reason is that a resolution of this kind is likely to embody a political "trap" for Congress, particularly for those members belonging to the political opposition party vis-à-vis the president's party. If the first Johnson Doctrine had succeeded in enabling America to realize its objectives in Southeast Asia, then this success would largely have accrued to the White House. It was, after all, the *Johnson* Doctrine: the president and his advisers formulated it, recommended it to Congress, and used their influence to gain legislative approval of it. Ultimately, Congress gave its support for a policy originating in the executive branch. As with all diplomatic doctrines in American history, the first Johnson Doctrine was a presidential policy statement, reflecting the chief executive's dominant position in the foreign policy process.

By contrast, as proved to be the case, if the doctrine failed to achieve its purposes, this fact placed critics of the administration's policies in Southeast Asia in a difficult and frustrating position. As the administration correctly asserted, Congress had approved the Tonkin Gulf Resolution by overwhelming majorities in the House and Senate. Legislators also gave de facto approval for efforts to implement the doctrine when they voted for Defense Department appropriations annually, when they continued the draft, and when they took other steps required to expand America's role in Southeast Asia. Moreover, critics were also inhibited by the realization that refusal to cooperate with the administration might be interpreted as failure to "support the president" during times of foreign crisis.

It is significant that, for these reasons primarily, there has been no congressional resolution comparable to the Gulf of Tonkin Resolution since 1964. (Perhaps recalling the contention that ultimately developed over that measure, as we shall see in Chapter 8, President Jimmy Carter did *not* resort to this mechanism in responding to the Soviet threat to the Persian Gulf area.) On the basis of experience with the Johnson Doctrine for Southeast Asia, executive and legislative policy-makers alike have apparently concluded that such resolutions really do little in the long run to produce a lasting national consensus on foreign policy goals.

6 / The Second Johnson Doctrine
Communism in the Americas

When a political structure collapses, nothing can replace it but fratricidal warfare, the most terrible of all. What happened in the Dominican Republic was the Spanish Civil War—but without content or ideas.
—Former U.S. Ambassador John B. Martin

The conclusion is inescapable that there are situations in which the President of the United States is damned if he does and damned if he doesn't— and this was a classic example [in the Dominican Republic].
—Charles Roberts

In fairness, it must be conceded there were no easy choices available to the United States in the Dominican Republic. . . . The United States engaged in a unilateral military intervention in violation of inter-American law, the 'good neighbor' policy of thirty years' standing, and the spirit of the Charter of Punta del Este [adopted by the Organization of American States].
—Sen. J. William Fulbright

"The American nations cannot, must not, and will not permit the establishment of another Communist government in the Western Hemisphere." This statement by President Lyndon B. Johnson to the American people on May 2, 1965, constituted the Johnson Doctrine for Latin America, issued after the president had ordered American armed forces to intervene in the Dominican Republic.

In his first speech to the nation on the Dominican crisis, on April 28, President Johnson justified the need for American military intervention by reference to a Communist effort to seize power in that country. Referring to Marxist efforts to impose a revolutionary regime upon the country, LBJ declared that "people trained outside the Dominican Republic are seeking to gain control" of this Caribbean nation. President Johnson pledged the United States to resist that threat to hemispheric security.[1] To use a phrase Johnson and later chief executives

1. The Johnson Doctrine for Latin America was stated and reiterated in President Johnson's speeches dealing with the political crisis in the Dominican Republic in late April, 1965, the text of which may be found in *Public Papers of the Presidents of the*

frequently employed, the United States did not propose to allow "another Cuba" to become established in the Western Hemisphere.

Context and Circumstances

In common with every other diplomatic doctrine we have considered so far, the second Johnson Doctrine was issued in response to a foreign crisis, to which the United States was compelled to respond. On April 2, 1965, political upheaval erupted in Santo Domingo, and within a few days it engulfed the country. In turn, this revolutionary ferment had its origins in long-term influences which had perhaps made some kind of violent eruption in the Dominican Republic inevitable.

From August 16, 1930, until May 30, 1961, the Dominican Republic was governed by one of the most ruthless and exploitive dictatorships in Latin America, headed by Rafael Trujillo. A generation of political oppression, exploitation, and *personalismo* under the Trujillo regime produced deep and growing popular discontents, culminating in his assassination. On December 20, 1962, Juan Bosch was elected president of the country. Bosch—described by one study as a "leftist, non-Communist visionary and writer"—was a popular figure throughout Latin America, especially among reformist and left-of-center political groups. Although he was not a Communist, Bosch had many Communist supporters, some of whom unquestionably believed they could manipulate him.

Yet following Bosch's election, officials in Washington did not conceal their pleasure at developments in the Dominican Republic. A threatened "return" of the Trujillo family to rule, for example, was thwarted by an American naval display off the coast. Vice President Lyndon B. Johnson represented the United States at Juan Bosch's presidential inauguration. Under the Bosch regime, American aid to the Dominican Republic was substantially increased, and the Kennedy Administration envisioned converting the Dominican Republic into a "showcase for democracy" in Latin America.[2]

United States: Lyndon B. Johnson, 1965 (Washington, D.C.: Government Printing Office, 1966), II, 461–74.

2. For background on events leading up to the Dominican crisis of 1965, see Abraham F. Lowenthal, *The Dominican Intervention* (Cambridge, Mass.: Harvard University Press, 1972), 33–63; Theodore C. Sorensen, *Kennedy* (New York: Harper and Row, 1965), 536.

Begun with high hopes, the administration of Juan Bosch quickly disappointed its supporters at home and abroad. Bosch proved to be a very poor administrator; his cabinet appointments were inferior; his relations with the Dominican military rapidly deteriorated; and he became closely linked with Marxist and crypto-Marxist elements that sought to subvert his democratically elected regime. Juan Bosch, said a former president of Venezuela, was "the best short-story writer and the worst politician in the hemisphere."[3]

The Bosch Administration lasted less than a year in the adverse Dominican political environment. On September 25, 1963, a military junta led by Gen. Wessin y Wessin seized power; President Bosch immediately left the country (a move his critics labeled a serious political mistake). In Washington, President Kennedy strongly denounced this seizure of power by the country's military elite. As a graphic sign of his displeasure, Kennedy recalled the American ambassador to Santo Domingo. In this period, the Kennedy Administration had launched the ambitious Alliance for Progress to promote Latin American modernization and development, as well as to cement more cordial inter-American relations. A dominant objective of this new program was the promotion of "democracy" throughout the Western Hemisphere, and the successful military coup in the Dominican Republic collided directly with that goal.[4]

Yet in this and other Latin American settings, it soon became evident that Washington's disapproval would not deter military elements from playing an active political role in the Dominican Republic. Ultimately, the Kennedy Administration accepted the political outcome in the country; and Washington provided a modest program of some $4 million in economic assistance in an effort to solve the Dominican Republic's acute social and economic problems. Late in 1963, Washington also extended formal recognition to the nominally civilian government, led by former Foreign Minister Donald Reid y Cabral (viewed by the Kennedy White House as a "moderate" regime in the Domin-

3. Tad Szulc, *Dominican Diary* (New York: Delacorte Press, 1965), 14; and see the judgment of Venezuelan President Romula Betancourt, as quoted in Rowland Evans and Robert Novak, *Lyndon B. Johnson: The Exercise of Power* (New York: New American Library, 1966), 537–38.

4. Arthur M. Schlesinger, Jr., *A Thousand Days: John F. Kennedy in the White House* (Boston: Houghton Mifflin, 1965), 1001.

ican setting).[5] Increasingly, however, the Reid government experienced difficulty preserving a moderate course in a country where political extremism was rampant and where no government could satisfy the demands of the society's poverty-stricken masses.

Then, to the surprise of American and other foreign officials within the country, to representatives of the news media, and to officials in foreign capitals, on April 24, 1965, rebellion broke out in Santo Domingo against the Reid government. Within a few days, a wave of what one study described as "uncontrolled fury" engulfed the country.[6] A group of pro-Bosch military officers toppled the Reid regime, plunging the Dominican Republic into a condition of rampant anarchy and violence. When this political upheaval occurred, United States Ambassador W. Tapley Bennett had left the country to visit his family in Georgia; he was of course immediately called to Washington to confer with the president about developments within the Dominican Republic. (During Bennett's absence, the American embassy was headed by his subordinate, William B. Connett, Jr.) After conferring with President Johnson, Bennett returned to his post in Santo Domingo, where he remained throughout the political crisis.

An informed observer has said that for some six months after April, 1965, United States policy toward the Dominican Republic was "a kind of political phantasmagoria, dizzying to actors and onlookers alike."[7] Within the Dominican Republic, events unfolded rapidly and confusingly. Even today, fundamental differences of opinion exist concerning both what occurred and the significance of major developments. In Washington, the statements and behavior of American officials during the crisis often appeared hardly less mystifying, as President Johnson and his advisers attempted to respond to poorly understood events in the Caribbean.

On the scene, Ambassador Bennett and his advisers confronted a chaotic and rapidly changing political milieu, in which it was difficult to separate rumor from fact. Anarchy and violence threatened the lives of Dominican citizens and foreigners alike—and this condition appeared to be becoming more ominous daily. In language which was

5. Evans and Novak, *Lyndon B. Johnson*, 536–37.
6. *Ibid.*, 536.
7. Theodore Draper, *The Dominican Revolt: A Case Study in American Policy* (New York: Commentary Reports, 1968), 198.

later to haunt the Johnson Administration, Ambassador Bennett graphically reported that "blood was flowing in the streets" and that the United States embassy (along with other foreign embassies) was coming under the fire of rival groups. Yet initially, Ambassador Bennett and his staff did not believe military intervention was required to protect American lives and property. As late as April 27, President Johnson publicly concurred in this view.[8]

Yet daily, the tempo of violence within the Dominican Republic increased, while the ability of Dominican authorities to preserve order steadily deteriorated. As a precautionary measure, on April 27 the embassy ordered the evacuation of Americans from the troubled country; but within hours, embassy officials became concerned about whether this evacuation could be carried out safely. On April 28, Ambassador Bennett warned Washington that a complete breakdown of public order within the country seemed imminent and that American lives were endangered. On the same day, for the first time the ambassador emphasized another danger: that Communist groups and their sympathizers were making an evident attempt to seize control of the Dominican revolution. Officials in Washington were now confronted with the prospect that "another Cuba" could become a reality in the Western Hemisphere.[9]

On April 28 also, a faction within the Dominican military—led by air force Col. Pedro Benoit—formed a new junta and proclaimed itself the new government. The Benoit regime immediately asked Ambassador Bennett to request the landing of 1,200 American marines on the island to preserve order. Similarly, the chief of the Dominican National Police informed the American embassy that he could not guarantee the safety of Americans and other foreigners being evacuated from the country.[10] Urgent requests for American intervention were also expressed by a number of foreign embassies in the Dominican Republic, the safety of whose citizens was being jeopardized by the spreading violence.[11]

8. Evans and Novak, *Lyndon B. Johnson*, 538; Lowenthal, *The Dominican Intervention*, 96.
9. Lyndon B. Johnson, *The Vantage Point: Perspectives of the Presidency, 1963–1969* (New York: Holt, Rinehart and Winston, 1971), 197–98.
10. *Ibid.*, 194–95.
11. See the statement by Sen. Russell Long (Democrat of Louisiana), in defense of the

Hour by hour, however, the Dominican crisis intensified. The cables from the American embassy in Santo Domingo to the State Department became more urgent and alarmist in tone. Finally, in a cable arriving at the White House late in the afternoon on April 28, Ambassador Bennett asked the president to order a landing by the marines (already close by, on the aircraft carrier U.S.S. *Boxer*). After brief consultation with his principal aides, President Johnson issued the first of a series of orders which ultimately involved some thirty thousand American troops and support personnel in the Dominican operation.

Almost immediately, the presence of American troops became decisive in the gradual restoration of public order and the protection of lives in the Dominican Republic. Altogether, under the protection of U.S. armed forces, some 4,000 people—including 2,300 foreigners, from 46 different countries—were evacuated from the country.[12] For a little less than a month, American troops preserved order on the island. On May 23, 1965, the Organization of American States created an Inter-American Peace Force (IAPF). When it became operational, the IAPF contained military contingents from the United States, as well as from several Latin American states. The presence of IAPF enabled the United States to evacuate most of its forces. On June 1, 1966, new national elections—closely supervised by several groups from outside the country—were held, and Joaquin Balaguer was elected president. With the installation of the Balaguer regime, and the departure of the IAPF on September 22, the Dominican crisis passed into history.

Formulation of Johnson's Latin American Doctrine

The Johnson Doctrine for Latin America is the second included in our study dealing with the security of the Western Hemisphere. The first was of course the Monroe Doctrine, which served as a highly influential precedent for the second Johnson Doctrine. A basic premise of the Monroe Doctrine—that a "special relationship" linked the American republics—was also implicit in the second Johnson Doctrine. In its not altogether successful efforts to "multilateralize" the Monroe Doctrine,

---

Dominican intervention, in *Congressional Record*, 89th Cong., 1st Sess., III, 23863; Johnson, *The Vantage Point*, 191.

12. U.S. Congress, Senate, Committee on Foreign Relations, *Background Information Relating to the Dominican Republic*, 89th Cong., 1st Sess., 1965, pp. 76–84.

Washington had persuaded the Organization of American States (OAS) to declare Communist attempts to gain a foothold in the Western Hemisphere in conflict with the principles of the Inter-American System.[13] Aware that "Monroeism" was an unpopular concept south of the border, the Johnson Administration did not directly invoke the Monroe Doctrine during the Dominican crisis. Yet a number of prominent citizens and news outlets did cite Communist machinations in the Dominican Republic as a violation of the Monroe Doctrine.[14]

America's post–World War II strategy of containment (as analyzed in Chapter 3) also of course influenced the Johnson Administration's diplomacy in the Caribbean. Communist political activities in the Dominican Republic could be viewed as posing the kind of threat against which the Truman Doctrine earlier had been issued. A few years later, in 1954, the Eisenhower Administration had overtly intervened to prevent the establishment of a Communist regime in Guatemala.[15] Some commentators believe that the second Johnson Doctrine was merely part of a long-standing American policy designed to contain communism globally. Several months after the Dominican crisis, Under Secretary of State Thomas Mann linked Communist strategies within the Western Hemisphere to Moscow's global objective of imposing its hegemony upon vulnerable societies. The Kremlin, said Mann, sought to achieve its goals "piece by piece"—in the kind of opportune situation presented by the Dominican revolution.[16]

Precedent for the second Johnson Doctrine could also be found in

13. At its Eighth Meeting of Consultation, at Punta del Este, Uruguay, on January 31, 1962, the Organization of American States adopted a resolution on Communist activities in the Western Hemisphere. This resolution stated: "The principles of communism are incompatible with the principles of the inter-American system." The text of the resolution may be found in U.S. Congress, House, Committee on Foreign Affairs, *Regional and Other Documents Concerning United States Relations with Latin America*, 89th Cong., 2nd Sess., 1966, p. 116.

14. See, for example, Herbert L. Matthews, "Diplomatic Relations," in Herbert L. Matthews (ed.), *The United States and Latin America* (2nd ed.; Englewood Cliffs, N.J.: Prentice-Hall, 1963), 145. This continuity is also emphasized in Jerome Slater, *Intervention and Negotiation: The United States and The Dominican Revolution* (New York: Harper and Row, 1970), 201. The *Congressional Record* for this period, 89th Cong., 1st Sess., contains numerous excerpts from American news media on the Dominican intervention, several of which refer to the Monroe Doctrine. See, for example, III, 13294.

15. For a discussion of American intervention in the Guatemalan crisis, see Dwight D. Eisenhower, *Mandate for Change: 1953–1956* (Garden City, N.Y.: Doubleday, 1963), 420–27.

16. Walter LaFeber, *America, Russia, and the Cold War, 1945–1966* (New York:

the more recent case of communism in Cuba and the American response to it. For a brief interval after Fidel Castro's revolutionary movement seized power in Cuba in 1959, Cuban-American relations were reasonably harmonious. Soon and perhaps inevitably, however, discord—followed in time by extreme tensions—characterized Cuban-American relations. Eventually, Castro openly proclaimed his devotion to Marxism, a fact that engendered mounting suspicion in Washington. The ill-fated Bay of Pigs episode late in 1961—in which the Kennedy Administration unsuccessfully supported efforts by Cuban exiles to topple Castro's regime—added new tensions to relations between the two countries. A few months later, the administration discovered evidence that Castro's government was making offensive missile sites available to the Soviet Union. For officials of the Kennedy Administration, this posed an intolerable threat to national and hemispheric security. Although it was resolved without war, the Cuban Missile Crisis was the most serious Soviet-American encounter in the postwar era, and it further embittered Cuban-American relations. After this crisis, policy-makers in the United States were more determined than ever to prevent the emergence of "another Cuba" in the Inter-American System.

Even before the missile crisis, Fidel Castro and his agents intervened in the Dominican Republic for the purpose of subverting the Trujillo dictatorship. Although at the time this effort was unsuccessful, the Dominican Republic—along with several other Latin American nations in the years ahead—remained the target of Cuban-sponsored revolutionary activities. According to Abraham F. Lowenthal, the "primary emphasis" in the Kennedy Administration's Dominican diplomacy was, therefore, to prevent the appearance of a "second Cuba" in the hemisphere. Contingency plans for the possible use of American military intervention in the Dominican Republic had been prepared by the Kennedy Administration; and these served as a basis for the intervention actually carried out by the Johnson White House in 1965.[17]

John Wiley and Sons, 1968), 244; Thomas C. Mann, "The Dominican Crisis: Correcting Some Misconceptions," *Department of State Bulletin*, LIII (November 8, 1965), 731–32.

17. Andres Suarez, *Cuba: Castroism and Communism, 1959–1966* (Cambridge, Mass.: Massachusetts Institute of Technology Press, 1967), 63–70; Lowenthal, *The Dominican Intervention*, 25–26; Johnson, *The Vantage Point*, 197.

In his personal account of the Dominican crisis, President Johnson observed: "The last thing I wanted—the last thing the American people wanted—was another Cuba on our doorstep." He reiterated this idea on April 26, 1965, to Ambassador Bennett on the eve of the latter's return to the Dominican Republic. The United States, LBJ instructed the ambassador, would not accept "another Cuba" in this hemisphere.[18]

American policy-makers also assessed developments and prospects within the Dominican Republic during 1965 within a larger context of recent political tendencies in Latin America. A leading goal of the Alliance for Progress was "to improve and strengthen democratic institutions" among the American republics. Washington's commitment to achieving this goal was illustrated by the support which the Kennedy Administration gave to the government of President Juan Bosch in the Dominican Republic after the overthrow of the Trujillo dictatorship in 1961.[19]

Yet on the basis of experience and of prevailing political tendencies in the region, American officials were aware that the democratization of Latin America would be a painfully slow process, interrupted by many setbacks. In the recent period, in one Latin American society after another military elites had emerged as the dominant political force. Some commentators spoke of the "new military" in Latin America.[20] In contrast to earlier military-supported regimes, military juntas throughout Latin America today are often devoted to modernization and fundamental change in at least some aspects of their society. In many cases, military elites are the only group within the society possessing sufficient power to effect needed changes. The risk was always present of course (as happened when Juan Bosch was ousted from the presidency of the Dominican Republic in 1963) that military elements would seize power and subsequently prove as incapable as civilian leaders of solving the country's underlying problems. Moreover, although often viewed as a monolithic force, in reality military elements

18. Johnson, *The Vantage Point*, 198; Lowenthal, *The Dominican Intervention*, 86.
19. J. Warren Nystrom and Nathan A. Haverstock, *The Alliance for Progress: Key to Latin America's Development* (Princeton, N.J.: D. Van Nostrand, 1966), 23; Schlesinger, *A Thousand Days*, 773.
20. For a detailed discussion of this point see *The Rockefeller Report on the Americas* (Chicago: Quadrangle Books, 1969), 24–37.

in Latin America were usually as politically divided as the societies they represented. Just as political fragmentation appeared to be increasing throughout Latin America as a whole, so too could divergences be detected in the ideologies and programs advocated by military elites. The rebellion which led to American military intervention in the Dominican Republic, for example, was precipitated by a faction within the Dominican armed forces.

As was also true of those doctrines that came before and after it, the Johnson Doctrine for Latin America bore the chief executive's imprint. Constitutionally of course, the president bears ultimate responsibility for important foreign policy declarations. LBJ's policy statements on the Dominican crisis appropriately bore the name of the *Johnson* Doctrine, since he personally made the decision to intervene in the country militarily. (In the sense that its goal was the prevention of "another Cuba" in the hemisphere, it might equally well have been designated the Kennedy-Johnson Doctrine.)[21]

President Johnson made another crucial judgment in the Dominican case: he determined the *timing* of the American intervention. As we have noted, the president deferred such action until an advanced stage of the Dominican revolution; he wanted convincing evidence that American and other foreign lives were endangered by the political upheaval sweeping the country. Our later treatment will call attention to a number of other influences affecting LBJ's decision. Yet in the end, his decision to use the armed forces in the Dominican Republic stemmed from a conviction that conditions in the country posed a danger to national and regional security. The situation in this strifetorn country, LBJ said after receiving an urgent call for intervention from Ambassador Bennett in Santo Domingo, was "just like the Alamo!" To Johnson's mind, the danger was twofold: that Americans and other foreign citizens would be killed or injured in the Dominican violence; and that, in the longer run, the breakdown of public order in the Dominican Republic would provide a highly favorable environment for the emergence of a Marxist regime closely tied to Cuba and the Soviet Union. Increasingly, in his public statements LBJ emphasized the latter danger, and it was the primary risk toward which the second Johnson Doctrine was directed.[22]

21. Lowenthal, *The Dominican Intervention*, 86.
22. Eric F. Goldman, *The Tragedy of Lyndon Johnson* (New York: Dell, 1969), 466–68.

It would be difficult to cite a case of recent American foreign policy decision-making in which presidential advisers were more actively and continuously involved than in the Dominican crisis of 1965. As always, in reaching his decisions the president was heavily dependent upon information and recommendations provided to him by subordinates in Washington and overseas. Although LBJ made the ultimate decisions determining America's response to the Dominican upheaval, he did so of course in close consultation with his advisers. In the aftermath of the Dominican affair, a number of critics of the administration's diplomacy were convinced that the responsibility for sending the armed forces to the country should rightfully be placed (in Senator Fulbright's words) on "those who advised the President"—especially the State Department and other diplomatic officials in the Dominican Republic.[23]

In whatever degree this criticism was warranted, two facts about the role of presidential advisers in the Dominican episode are incontestable: the president's advisers were massively and continuously involved in decision-making; and, with rare exceptions, they were in fundamental agreement concerning the response the United States ought to make to developments in the Caribbean. During the crisis, one study has concluded, President Johnson "consulted for days with his top advisers" in formulating American policy.[24] According to LBJ's own account, over a nine-day period, the president consulted eighty-six times with his special assistant for national security affairs (McGeorge Bundy); thirty-one times with Secretary of Defense Robert McNamara; and fifteen times with Secretary of State Dean Rusk. In addition, he had some fifty-two meetings on the Dominican crisis with groups of his principal subordinates.[25] This is a rather remarkable record, considering that the administration was responding to a crisis which caught American officials in Washington and in the Dominican Republic alike by surprise.[26]

23. See Senator Fulbright's speech on the Dominican crisis, in *Congressional Record*, 89th Cong., 1st Sess., III, 23859. The same criticism was made by Charles Yost, a former State Department official, in *The Conduct and Misconduct of Foreign Affairs: Reflections on U.S. Foreign Policy Since World War II* (New York: Random House, 1972), 75–76.

24. Charles Roberts, *LBJ's Inner Circle* (New York: Delacorte Press, 1965), 198.

25. *Ibid.*, 211. Roberts bases his statement upon the evidence of LBJ's conferences as revealed by the presidential appointments log.

26. Lowenthal, *The Dominican Intervention*, 64.

State Department officials in Washington and in Santo Domingo of course played a key role in decision-making during the Dominican affair. Cablegrams from officials on the scene kept policy-makers fully and currently apprised of developments. In the early phase, embassy officials informed Washington that the incumbent Reid regime was in danger of collapsing, that disorder was rapidly spreading throughout the country, that the identity of the major rebel groups was initially unclear, but that there was no immediate danger to American lives. Hour by hour, as the crisis intensified, the dispatches from Santo Domingo to the State Department became more urgent and ominous in tone.

Within the first twenty-four hours of the revolutionary upheaval, in Washington the State Department created a "Dominican Task Force" to follow developments closely and to make recommendations to the secretary of state and the president for responding to them. Early on the morning of April 25, President Johnson was informed of events in the Dominican Republic and Ambassador Bennett (who was visiting his family in Georgia) was recalled to Washington for consultations. During this early stage, American officials on the scene advised Washington to use diplomatic methods for resolving the crisis, rather than military force.[27]

Yet the rapid disintegration of the Dominican government, accompanied by the spread of anarchy and violence within the capital city, ultimately convinced American officials on the scene that military intervention was imperative to protect the lives of United States citizens and other foreigners. A recurrent criticism directed at the Johnson Administration's Dominican diplomacy was the alleged "panic" exhibited by Ambassador Bennett and his "overreaction" to developments within the country. A salient point missed by critics, however, is the fact that the ambassador's urgent plea that the president send armed forces was supported *unanimously* by the American embassy staff in Santo Domingo, including the ambassador's chief deputy, three military attachés, the economic attaché, and other American officials in the country. President Johnson—who valued "consensus" among his advisers—was unquestionably influenced by this fact.[28]

27. *Ibid.*, 65–85.
28. Evans and Novak, *Lyndon B. Johnson*, 534.

Within Washington, State Department officials had become progressively concerned about Communist influence within Juan Bosch's government. While few informed American officials believed that Bosch himself was a Marxist, he appeared to be indifferent toward Communist efforts to infiltrate his regime and perhaps ultimately dominate it. These apprehensions were reinforced by reports from officials in the American embassy in Santo Domingo, who discerned growing Communist militancy within the beleaguered country and who urged the Dominican military elite to unite in the face of this Communist challenge.[29]

Among President Johnson's principal advisers, only one—UN Ambassador Adlai E. Stevenson—had genuine misgivings at the time about United States military intervention in the Dominican Republic. A recent biographer has said that Stevenson (who was present at the White House when LBJ decided to send the marines to the country) was deeply "troubled" by the decision; he believed America's behavior contradicted long-standing pledges given to Latin America against "intervention" in their internal affairs. Nevertheless, in the weeks which followed, Stevenson eloquently and ably defended the Johnson Administration's action before the United Nations. Owing in no small measure to his efforts, the UN left primary responsibility for preserving order in the Dominican Republic to the Organization of American States (OAS).[30]

Another executive organization playing a role in the Dominican intervention was the Central Intelligence Agency (CIA). Somewhat to its embarrassment, the CIA was also "caught by surprise" by the political upheaval in the Dominican Republic and had given the White House no advance warning of it. (Yet during this period, the CIA was undergoing major personnel changes, including the selection of a new director, Adm. William F. Raborn.) Despite allegations that the CIA instigated the intervention, in fact the agency was informed of President Johnson's decision to land the marines only after the order had been issued to the Pentagon. No reliable evidence has been produced to show that the CIA (or any other agency of the United States government) instigated the Dominican revolution; nor did the CIA play a sig-

29. Lowenthal, *The Dominican Intervention,* 84–85.
30. John Bartlow Martin, *Adlai Stevenson and the World: The Life of Adlai E. Stevenson* (Garden City, N.Y.: Doubleday, 1977), 843–44.

nificant role in LBJ's decision to employ the armed forces in responding to the crisis.[31] After the landing of American forces in the country, however, the CIA did supply lists of known or suspected Communists among the Dominican revolutionaries to the president and his advisers. The accuracy of such lists became another highly contentious issue among defenders and critics of the Johnson Administration's diplomacy.[32]

Not unexpectedly, President Johnson's military advisers also participated in decision-making on the Dominican crisis. For several years before revolution erupted in the country, the Dominican and American governments had maintained close military ties. After Trujillo's ouster, Dominican military officers (along with those from many other Latin American nations) received extensive training in the United States. Law enforcement training was also made available to members of the Dominican National Police. In addition, the United States supplied modern weapons for the Dominican armed forces. These facts led some critics to believe that the military-led coup against Juan Bosch and the later military revolt against the administration of President Reid were directly sanctioned and encouraged by the United States. In more general terms, in Latin America and elsewhere, such evidence has been cited in behalf of the contention that Washington "preferred" military regimes to democratically elected governments.[33]

Throughout the Dominican crisis, Secretary of Defense Robert McNamara served as one of President Johnson's closest advisers. After the presidential order had been given to send the marines ashore in the Dominican Republic, implementation of the directive of course became the responsibility of the Defense Department. Yet Secretary McNamara was but one among several presidential advisers whose viewpoints were solicited by the president. No evidence can be cited to show that his influence was in any way disproportionate or improper

31. Roberts, *LBJ's Inner Circle*, 206; Lowenthal, *The Dominican Intervention*, 64.

32. For more detailed criticisms of these CIA-supplied lists of Communists within the Dominican revolutionary movement, see Martin C. Needler, *The United States and the Latin American Revolution* (Boston: Allyn and Bacon, 1972), 86–92; Fulbright's speech criticizing the Dominican intervention, in *Congressional Record*, 89th Cong., 1st Sess., III, 23855.

33. For expressions of this viewpoint, see Draper, *The Dominican Revolt*, 7, 77; and Juan de Onis, "The Hispanic Caribbean," in Tad Szulc (ed.), *The United States and the Caribbean* (Englewood Cliffs, N.J.: Prentice-Hall, 1971), 169.

vis-à-vis the role of other advisers. In brief, the traditional constitutional principle of civilian supremacy in decision-making was followed in the Dominican case. In fact, some studies of the Dominican episode have concluded that "military influence" upon national policy was less important in this instance than in other cases of postwar American diplomacy which might be cited.[34]

The transcendent fact emerging from an analysis of the role of the president's advisers in the issuance of the Johnson Doctrine for Latin America is the high degree of unity exhibited by them toward the Dominican crisis. Seeing no alternative, a united embassy staff in Santo Domingo finally urged the White House to order the marines ashore in the strife-torn country. Within Washington, President Johnson's highest-level advisers saw no feasible alternative to complying with this urgent request. Almost without a dissenting voice, the president's aides urged him to act decisively to protect American lives and to prevent a threatened Communist takeover of the Dominican Republic.[35]

Congressional Involvement and Public Opinion

As was the case with other diplomatic doctrines in American history, Congress also contributed to the issuance and implementation of the second Johnson Doctrine. Within a few hours after the president received the urgent message from Ambassador Bennett requesting military intervention, a group of influential congressional leaders was summoned to the White House to discuss the Dominican problem. Eight senators and seven representatives met with President Johnson and his chief executive advisers. The atmosphere of the White House session has been described as "disturbing" and "somber." Awareness existed among those present that the United States would now be involved in two simultaneous military interventions—in the Caribbean and in Southeast Asia.[36]

Legislators attending this meeting were briefed by executive officials concerning the deteriorating situation in the Dominican Republic. President Johnson showed them his proposed public speech informing

34. Slater, *Intervention and Negotiation*, 24–26.
35. The unanimity among President Johnson's advisers is emphasized in Johnson, *The Vantage Point*, 195; and in Philip Geyelin, *Lyndon B. Johnson and the World* (New York: Praeger, 1966), 245–46.
36. Evans and Novak, *Lyndon B. Johnson*, 540–41.

the American people that the marines had been ordered ashore on the island. At the suggestion of Sen. Mike Mansfield (Democrat of Montana), the president's speech was revised to include a reference to the future role of the Organization of American States in resolving the crisis. Otherwise, in company with the principal executive officials involved, congressional leaders were similarly united in approving the president's proposed action. As one legislator present, Sen. Russell Long (Democrat of Louisiana), later recalled the White House session, there was "not one dissenting voice" among the members of Congress consulted by the president (and this included a later critic, Sen. J. William Fulbright, chairman of the Senate Foreign Relations Committee). Sen. George Smathers (Democrat of Florida), who also attended this meeting, later referred to the "overwhelming consensus" characterizing legislative viewpoints toward LBJ's proposed actions in the Dominican crisis. This consensus included the conviction that the United States must take steps to prevent "another Cuba" from emerging in the Western Hemisphere.[37]

A more controversial aspect of the congressional role in the issuance of the second Johnson Doctrine relates to the *timing* of President Johnson's consultation with legislative leaders vis-à-vis his order for the marines to land on the Dominican coast. Did the president "consult" legislative representatives before or after he issued this crucial order? Did he seek prior congressional approval for the idea, or did he merely inform a selected group of congressmen of a decision to use armed force in the Dominican crisis?

Evidence on this question is not conclusive. Several commentators on the Dominican affair, along with some of the participants in the decision-making process, are persuaded that President Johnson merely informed legislators of a presidential decision already made and they overwhelmingly approved that decision. Thus, one study asserts that legislative leaders arrived at the White House "an hour" after LBJ had ordered the marines to go ashore in the Dominican Republic.[38] Yet two senators present at the meeting (Long and Smathers) subsequently

37. See Long's views on this White House meeting, in *Congressional Record*, 89th Cong., 1st Sess., III, 23861–62; Smathers' judgments are contained in the same source, p. 23862.

38. Evans and Novak, *Lyndon B. Johnson*, 540–41. In *The Vantage Point* (p. 196), President Johnson's treatment is unclear on this point.

asserted that the president requested the views of legislators before he made the decision to land the marines; their approval of this proposed action was thus an important element in the president's final decision to use force in the Dominican crisis. Another influential legislative leader, the longtime chairman of the Senate Armed Services Committee, Sen. Richard Russell (Democrat of Georgia), was also consulted independently by President Johnson before the decision to intervene. Senator Russell joined his colleagues in urging the president to use force if necessary, to prevent "another Cuba" in the hemisphere.[39]

The weight of the evidence—along with the nature of the crisis in the Dominican Republic, as depicted by American officials on the scene—favors the view that the meeting with legislative leaders occurred after the decision had been made. After receiving Ambassador Bennett's impassioned plea for military intervention, President Johnson and his advisers concluded that the marines must be dispatched *promptly* to the country. Accordingly, orders were immediately issued by the Pentagon to carry out the president's directive. Shortly thereafter, legislative leaders met with the president. He informed them of his decision and the reasons for it. The legislators present overwhelmingly endorsed the president's action.

In contrast to the Johnson Doctrine for Southeast Asia, LBJ's pronouncement for Latin America called for no congressional resolution or other direct action by the House and Senate. Although legislators were consulted in its formulation, the second Johnson Doctrine emerged as an exclusively executive undertaking. Yet President Johnson and the supporters of his Latin American doctrine believed that it had the support of a majority of members of Congress—a conclusion also shared by even certain critics of the administration's diplomacy in the Caribbean.[40]

Although Congress bore no formal responsibility for the implementation of the second Johnson Doctrine, in the months following its

39. *Congressional Record*, 89th Cong., 1st Sess., III, 23861–62; Herbert K. Tillema, *Appeal to Force: American Military Intervention in the Era of Containment* (New York: Thomas Y. Crowell, 1973), 107–108.
40. Goldman, *The Tragedy of Lyndon Johnson*, 470; and see Smathers' views, in *Congressional Record*, 89th Cong., 1st Sess., III, 23864. One of the sharpest critics of the Dominican intervention also believes that a majority of congressmen supported it. Melvin Gurtov, *The United States Against the Third World: Antinationalism and Intervention* (New York: Praeger, 1974), 124.

promulgation two actions—one by the House, and the other by the Senate—were significant. On September 20, 1965, by a roll-call vote of 312–52, the House of Representatives adopted a resolution which was tantamount to endorsement of the doctrine. This resolution reaffirmed the conviction of a substantial majority in the lower chamber that the activities of "international Communism" in the Western Hemisphere were incompatible with the principles of the Inter-American System. It sanctioned the use of armed force to prevent Communist control of an American state. In effect, the House resolution reiterated the second Johnson Doctrine. (Ironically, this action by the House occurred at a time when the State Department had become conscious of some of the adverse effects of the doctrine, particularly with regard to its negative impact upon Latin American opinion.) We should note that this House resolution was not adopted by the Senate, nor was it signed by the president. Accordingly, it was merely a statement of preponderant opinion within the House of Representatives and did not, therefore, have the force of law.[41]

A contrary development affecting the second Johnson Doctrine occurred in the Senate. On September 15, 1965, the chairman of the Senate Foreign Relations Committee, Sen. J. William Fulbright, made a dramatic and widely publicized speech on the Dominican crisis. Fulbright was highly critical of the Johnson Administration's handling of the affair; the speech marked his public break with President Johnson's diplomacy, not only in Latin America but in other regions as well. Although no public report of the committee's hearings on the Dominican question was ever released, Fulbright was convinced that President Johnson and his advisers had misled the American people concerning the facts about the Dominican revolution and America's response to it. In his view, neither the alleged danger to American lives, nor the administration's assertion that communism threatened the country, justified a policy of military intervention. Sending American troops to the country had alienated Latin America. More generally, to Fulbright's mind it exemplified an approach to the outside world motivated by the "arrogance of power" and other extraneous factors rather than by a desire to promote human welfare. With other

41. For the text of House Resolution 560 (1965) and commentary on it, see *National Diplomacy, 1965–1970* (Washington, D.C.: Congressional Quarterly, 1970), 67.

critics, Fulbright believed that the administration's Dominican moves arose from and reflected an official bias against revolutionary change throughout the Third World. Senator Fulbright's speech was a highly significant development. Its impact upon liberal opinion within the United States was especially profound. Increasingly, a number of influential Americans came to believe that Fulbright had supplied a persuasive indictment of the Johnson Administration's mismanagement of foreign affairs.[42]

A noteworthy, and in many respects unique, dimension of the Johnson Doctrine for Latin America was the role of public opinion in its formulation and application. Indeed, it would be difficult to cite other major developments in postwar United States foreign policy in which the public opinion implications were more significant and far-reaching.

From the beginning of the Dominican crisis, executive policymakers were concerned about the impact of their actions upon public attitudes. To some degree, they anticipated the negative response which military intervention in the Dominican Republic evoked throughout Latin America. (Yet it is doubtful that they were prepared for the intensity of the opposition expressed toward the doctrine by the other American republics.) President Johnson and his advisers knew that reliance upon armed force to stabilize the Dominican Republic would inescapably revive memories of "big stick diplomacy" and the Roosevelt Corollary to the Monroe Doctrine among Latin Americans. Contrary to what many critics of the second Johnson Doctrine asserted, the administration did consult Latin American governments in the early stages of the Dominican affair, prior to the president's decision to intervene with armed force. These governments were alerted to the possibility that military intervention in the country might ultimately be required. At the same time, executive policymakers also concluded that the predictably adverse reaction to this step throughout the hemisphere could not be a deterrent to military intervention, if circumstances in the Dominican Republic dictated this course.[43]

Before and after the Dominican crisis, a key characteristic of Ameri-

42. For the complete text of Fulbright's speech, see *Congressional Record*, 89th Cong., 1st Sess., III, 23855–65.
43. Roberts, *LBJ's Inner Circle*, 201, 208; Johnson, *The Vantage Point*, 204.

can public opinion was its overwhelmingly anti-Communist orientation. As had been true since the end of World War II, the American people remained deeply concerned about Communist expansionism abroad, and policy-makers in Washington were expected to take a firm stand in opposition to it. For reasons identified more fully in Chapter 1, historically Americans have been especially sensitive about foreign threats to the security of the Western Hemisphere. Communist political activities in the Dominican Republic must be understood against this background. Fully as much as the Johnson Administration, the American people were opposed to the emergence of "another Cuba" in the Inter-American System. Public apprehensions on this score were repeatedly communicated to the White House, the State Department, and Congress. American public sentiment, said the former ambassador to the Dominican Republic, John B. Martin, "would not have tolerated a second Cuba in the Caribbean." [44] Another study has alluded to the Johnson Administration's "fear of public opinion." Memories of the Cuban Missile Crisis—followed by Castro's growing ties with the Soviet Union—were at the forefront of public consciousness. After the recently concluded national elections of 1964, no one was better aware than President Johnson that his foreign policies were generating growing popular discontent and anxiety, in part because of Communist gains overseas.[45]

Even certain critics of the Johnson Administration's behavior during the Dominican crisis have conceded that it was largely dictated by "the historical and political conditions" affecting the decision-making process, which any incumbent president must accept as a "given." In this instance, a controlling reality was the deeply ingrained anti-Communist propensity of the American people.[46]

Insofar as mass opinion in the United States was concerned, the evi-

44. John Bartlow Martin, *Overtaken by Events* (Garden City, N.Y.: Doubleday, 1966), 739.

45. See the views of Hans J. Morgenthau in the "Foreword" to Slater, *Intervention and Negotiation*, x; and Slater's own conclusions on prevailing public attitudes in the same source, pp. 199–200. A year before the Dominican crisis, a Gallup Poll among Republican county political leaders showed that a "weak and indecisive" foreign policy was the strongest argument which the Republican party could use in the forthcoming political campaign against Democratic candidates. George Gallup, *The Gallup Polls: Public Opinion, 1935–1971* (New York: Random House, 1972), III, 1874.

46. Gar Alperowitz, *Cold War Essays* (Garden City, N.Y.: Doubleday, 1970), 76–77.

dence indicates overwhelming approval of the Johnson Administration's response to the Dominican problem. Late in 1964, for example, almost half of the respondents to one public opinion poll identified international problems (specifically, the Cold War) as the major issue confronting the American society. Both before and after the Dominican intervention, public opinion consistently approved the way President Johnson was doing his job. On the specific issue of LBJ's Dominican diplomacy, public opinion was also substantially favorable. During the crisis, upwards of 85 percent of the American people indicated their support for the Johnson Administration's response to it. President Johnson's contention—that his Dominican policy had the overall support of the American people—represented an accurate assessment of public sentiment.[47]

Despite the solid foundation of favorable public opinion supporting the Johnson Administration's Dominican diplomacy, LBJ and his advisers anticipated two problems in the public opinion realm: the predictably negative reaction to his Dominican policy by groups identified with liberal and left-of-center causes; and the adverse reception expected throughout Latin America. Events proved that these apprehensions were amply justified.

Following President Johnson's first speech to the nation on the Dominican crisis on April 28, the White House made an intensive effort to gain the understanding and support of possible liberal critics within the United States. The administration endeavored to "disarm" this group by such moves as assigning liberal defenders of its policies—notably, Arthur Schlesinger, Jr., and Teodoro Moscoso—to explain its Caribbean diplomacy. Another prominent liberal figure, John Bartlow Martin (former ambassador to the Dominican Republic), was dispatched to the Dominican scene; Martin was accompanied by Under Secretary of State Averell Harriman, who was also a widely respected advocate of liberal causes. In the words of one study, Martin's principal mission "was to prove to skeptical critics of the Dominican intervention that a trained observer with impeccable liberal credentials would uphold the President's decision. Martin did exactly that."[48]

47. See the results of the public opinion polls reproduced in Gallup, *The Gallup Polls*, III, 1909–76; and the poll data cited in the *Congressional Record*, 89th Cong., 1st Sess., III, 23864.
48. Evans and Novak, *Lyndon B. Johnson*, 543.

These efforts by the administration to win the support of liberal critics, however, not only failed. The campaign backfired—ultimately compounding the criticism directed at the president and his advisers. To many of his detractors, LBJ had employed a variety of techniques— "news management," deception, and efforts to "co-opt" liberal spokesmen who would support his position—in an effort to gain converts for his Dominican moves. As a result, the credibility of the Johnson Administration was more widely questioned than before.

As reflected in the response of the news media, criticisms of President Johnson's intervention in the Dominican Republic were sharp and prolonged. The New York *Times*, for example, condemned both the intervention itself and the reasons advanced by the administration to justify it. The Dominican rebels, this influential journal contended, were merely fighting for "social justice and constitutionalism"; the idea that communism posed a serious danger for the Dominican society was rejected. Other influential newspapers—including the Washington *Post*, the New York *Herald Tribune*, the St. Louis *Post-Dispatch*, the *Christian Science Monitor*, and the *Wall Street Journal*—expressed varying degrees of opposition to the administration's Dominican moves. A number of prominent Americans—among whom were Senator Fulbright, Sen. Robert Kennedy (Democrat of New York), Walter Lippmann, Archibald MacLeish, and Lewis Mumford—joined the chorus of protest. Mumford, for example, expressed "shame" and "anger" at the "high-handed power" displayed by the administration in its response to the Dominican revolution. For several months after the landing of American troops, a number of artistic, cultural, and academic groups conducted protest meetings and demonstrations against LBJ's Caribbean policies.[49]

As "unrepresentative" of overall American public sentiment as such criticisms might be, they were highly significant in one crucial respect: adverse public reaction to the administration's Caribbean diplomacy largely destroyed any national policy consensus the Johnson White House enjoyed on foreign policy issues. According to one study, liberal disaffection with the administration's Caribbean moves "sheared away the left wing of Lyndon Johnson's Great Society consensus" and

49. *Ibid.*, 543–44; Slater, *Intervention and Negotiation*, 86; Goldman, *The Tragedy of Lyndon Johnson*, 510–11; Martin, *Adlai Stevenson and the World*, 854–59.

led to growing opposition toward the administration's foreign policy generally.[50]

As policy-makers had anticipated, the prevailing reaction throughout Latin America to the administration's Dominican diplomacy was predominantly negative. Informed students of Latin American affairs have used terms like "consternation," "deeply disturbed," and "profoundly shocked" to describe official and public attitudes in other American republics. One commentator noted that the administration's response to the Dominican revolution—including the issuance of the second Johnson Doctrine—"raised a storm of reaction" throughout the Inter-American System. It revived painful memories of earlier U.S. intervention under the Monroe Doctrine, and it triggered a new wave of "Yankeephobia" south of the border. Even Latin American political figures who were usually sympathetic toward the United States, like Alberto L. Camargo (former president of Colombia), castigated Washington's handling of the Dominican crisis, likening it to the kind of "big stick" American behavior witnessed during the era of President Theodore Roosevelt. The Uruguayan delegate to the UN Security Council denounced the second Johnson Doctrine as a "new corollary" of the Monroe Doctrine. He emphasized that President Johnson's new doctrine had been issued unilaterally by the United States and was not binding upon any other American nation. The administration's own analysis of press opinion throughout Latin America showed editorial reactions running ten to one against Washington's diplomacy toward the Dominican Republic.[51]

Yet the administration's spokesmen also called attention to certain developments which placed the Latin American response to its Dominican moves in a different perspective. There was, for example, the discrepancy between the public attitudes expressed by Latin American officials and their private reactions as conveyed to American officials. At the United Nations, for example, public statements by Latin Ameri-

---

50. Evans and Novak, *Lyndon B. Johnson*, 535.

51. John N. Plank, "The Caribbean: Intervention, When and How," *Foreign Affairs*, XLIV (October, 1965), 37; Federico G. Gil, *Latin American-United States Relations* (New York: Harcourt Brace Jovanovich, 1971), 252; Goldman, *The Tragedy of Lyndon Johnson*, 470; Senate Foreign Relations Committee, *Background Information Relating to the Dominican Republic*, 22, 26.

can delegates tended to be uniformly negative toward American intervention. Privately, however, several Latin American spokesmen informed Ambassador Stevenson that they were in fact "relieved" when
the marines landed in the Dominican Republic and that they supported Washington's efforts to frustrate Communist gains in the
region.[52]

The negative response by Latin American governments could also
be attributed in part to domestic political considerations. In several
Latin American states, incumbent political leaders felt compelled to
undercut the appeal of Marxist and other left-wing groups, by engaging in dramatic gestures of Yankeephobia or otherwise condemning
the United States.[53] Another commentator has also called attention to
the fact that a number of prominent Latin American liberals did *not*
criticize the Johnson Administration's Dominican policies. Among
this group the belief existed that, in the light of existing conditions,
President Johnson had "no choice" except to order the marines
ashore; that the United States failed earlier (in the ill-fated Bay of Pigs
intervention in Cuba in 1961) to intervene decisively against communism, and it could not afford to make that same mistake again; and
that other Latin American states were as concerned about Communist
inroads in the region as was the United States. With regard to the general principle involved—Washington's reliance upon military force
and other "interventionist" measures to achieve its hemispheric
goals—Latin American liberals were not opposed to such behavior
when it was directed against their political enemies (as when the
United States intervened to prevent a return of rule by the Trujillo family in the Dominican Republic in 1961).[54]

Officials of the Johnson Administration also pointed out that several
Latin American diplomatic officials stationed in the Dominican Republic had urgently requested United States military intervention as
the only feasible means of protecting lives and property endangered by
the existing political turmoil. However adverse Latin American opin-

52. Martin, *Adlai Stevenson and the World*, 845.
53. Senate Foreign Relations Committee, *Background Information Relating to the Dominican Republic*, 26.
54. See the article by Charles Bartlett in the Washington *Evening Star*, May 4, 1965, as reprinted in *Congressional Record*, 89th Cong., 1st Sess., III, 9614.

ion about Washington's behavior might have been in the short run, in time a number of Latin American officials informed Washington that under the prevailing circumstances, the Johnson Administration could have taken no other course of action in the Dominican Republic.[55]

Outside Latin America, foreign opinion was also largely unfavorable to the issuance and implementation of the second Johnson Doctrine. During two days of UN Security Council debate early in May, for example, no delegate expressed approval of Washington's conduct. The most charitable judgment (expressed by two of America's closest allies—Britain and France) was "understanding" of the humanitarian considerations inducing President Johnson to order the marines ashore in the Dominican Republic. The official French verdict (said to have been personally prepared by French President Charles de Gaulle) was severely critical of America's conduct in the Dominican affair. (Yet, as President Johnson later observed, the French embassy in Santo Domingo had joined other foreign representatives in asking for the protection of American troops for their nationals!)[56]

A significant aspect of the Dominican episode was the involvement of the Organization of American States (OAS) in it. The administration's alleged "neglect" of the OAS—particularly during the early phase of the Dominican revolution—was a recurrent theme among critics of LBJ's diplomacy. We may conveniently divide the question of the relationship of the OAS to the Dominican issue into two stages: the initial phase of revolutionary upheaval, culminating in American military intervention in the country on April 28; and the period which followed beginning on May 23, when the OAS-sponsored Inter-American Peace Force assumed responsibility for maintaining law and order.

According to spokesmen for the Johnson Administration, in the initial stage of the Dominican revolt, policy-makers did consider and anticipate a role for the OAS in restoring stability to the country. On April 27 (a day before President Johnson ordered the marines ashore)

55. Johnson, *The Vantage Point*, 198, 204.
56. See the excerpts from debate in the UN Security Council, in Senate Foreign Relations Committee, *Background Information Relating to the Dominican Republic*, 22, 23; and the views of Sen. Russell Long (Democrat of Louisiana) in *Congressional Record*, 89th Cong., 1st Sess., III, 23863.

the State Department requested a meeting of the Inter-American Peace Committee of the OAS. The committee met that same day, discussed the Dominican situation, but rather typically took no action.[57] After President Johnson made the decision to intervene militarily in the Dominican crisis, he instructed Secretary of State Rusk to summon an "immediate meeting" of the OAS Council to deal with the Dominican question. The council meeting was held (more or less simultaneously with the landing of the marines). Characteristically, again the OAS took no action.[58] The effect of course was to leave American troops as the only stabilizing force within the country.

Two points about the initial involvement of the OAS in the Dominican crisis seem worth emphasizing. The first is that there was no inclination by officials in Washington to "turn over" the challenge of preserving order in the Dominican Republic to the OAS—an organization whose record in peace-keeping activities did not inspire confidence that it could meet the challenge effectively. The evidence does not indicate that the Johnson White House seriously considered immediate action by the OAS as a feasible alternative to unilateral American intervention in the country. The second point is—in the light of the OAS's record in dealing with hemispheric crises—that any delay by Washington in ordering the marines ashore in the Dominican Republic would have jeopardized the lives of American and other foreign nationals. As it was, once the Dominican question had been referred to the OAS, five days were required before the organization was prepared to send a "peace mission" to the strife-torn country.[59] Even Latin American political leaders themselves had recently expressed serious reservations about the ability or the willingness of the OAS to act decisively in dealing with hemispheric crises.[60]

By early May, however, the Organization of American States was prepared to assume the main responsibility for maintaining law and order within the Dominican Republic. On May 6, the OAS voted to establish an Inter-American Peace Force (IAPF), consisting of troops

---

57. See excerpts from transcript of news conference by Secretary of State Dean Rusk on May 26, 1965, in Senate Foreign Relations Committee, *Background Information Relating to the Dominican Republic*, 80.

58. Johnson, *The Vantage Point*, 195.

59. Roberts, *LBJ's Inner Circle*, 207–208.

60. See, for example, the views of President Frondizi of Argentina on the limitations confronting the OAS, in Schlesinger, *A Thousand Days*, 178.

from several American republics, including the United States. On May 19, it called upon all parties to the Dominican conflict to observe an immediate cease-fire (and it made the cease-fire permanent three days later). By late May, units of the IAPF began to be substituted for forces from the United States, gradually allowing most American troops to be withdrawn from the country. The IAPF remained in the Dominican Republic until September 22, 1966. Meanwhile, on June 1, 1966, new national elections, conducted under international supervision, were held throughout the country. In what was perhaps the most honestly conducted election in the history of the Dominican Republic, the people chose Joaquin Balaguer (who received 59 percent of the popular vote) as the new president, over his nearest rival—Juan Bosch.[61]

The United Nations also played a minor role in the Dominican episode. Urged by the Soviet Union, Cuba, and other Communist states to condemn American "aggression" against the Dominican Republic, the UN Security Council debated the issue for several days. In his detailed defense of American policy, on May 1 Ambassador Adlai Stevenson referred to earlier statements and actions by the Organization of American States directed against Communist inroads in the Western Hemisphere. He was convinced that—while most rebels within the Dominican Republic were *not* Communists—a small and dedicated group of Communists was seeking to subvert the revolution and to impose a Marxist regime on the country. President Johnson had acted to avert that danger. To Stevenson's mind, the doctrine enunciated by President Johnson stated a principle long accepted by the members of the Inter-American System. Stevenson declared: "The American nations will not permit the establishment of another Communist government in the Western Hemisphere." In effect, Ambassador Stevenson was trying to "multilateralize" the second Johnson Doctrine by associating it with policies adopted much earlier by the OAS. Stevenson's gambit did not win widespread acceptance—either within the UN or in the OAS. He was more successful in convincing the United Nations that, on the basis of precedents in dealing with regional disputes, the UN should leave primary responsibility for resolving the Dominican issue with the Organization of American States.[62]

61. Senate Foreign Relations Committee, *Background Information Relating to the Dominican Republic*, 69–70; *National Diplomacy*, 77.
62. Martin, *Adlai Stevenson and the World*, 846–47.

Johnson's Latin American Doctrine: An Assessment

The remainder of this chapter will be devoted to an assessment of the second Johnson Doctrine, in an attempt to answer the question: how well did it serve the diplomatic interests of the United States? Meanwhile, it is necessary to make three general observations about LBJ's Latin American policy dictum.

In the first place, the second Johnson Doctrine (even more, in some respects, than his earlier doctrine on Southeast Asia) became one of the most controversial developments in modern American diplomacy. Criticisms of the Johnson Administration's Caribbean diplomacy were intense and prolonged. Even defenders of it have often conceded that the Dominican episode does not rank among Johnson's most notable diplomatic accomplishments.

In the second place, individual verdicts upon the Johnson Administration's behavior during the Dominican crisis are likely to be heavily colored—if not largely predetermined—by the answers which individual observers make to a number of key questions. In the mid-1960s, for example, did communism still present a security threat to the United States and, more broadly, to other non-Communist countries? (Critics of the administration's involvement in the Vietnam War were likely to be equally certain that communism posed no threat to the security of the Western Hemisphere.) And did conditions of political turmoil and political upheaval abroad jeopardize American security interests—in the Western Hemisphere, and perhaps in other regions as well? Another pivotal consideration in assessing the contribution of the second Johnson Doctrine was whether the American people, Congress, and the news media could rely upon the Johnson White House to present an accurate and objective account of the facts upon which American diplomatic behavior was based. In brief, had the Johnson Administration "manipulated" the Dominican crisis and "managed" the news about it, for its own (largely undisclosed) purposes? By 1965, many Americans were apprehensive about such possibilities; and some critics were convinced that the administration had largely manufactured a crisis in the Caribbean to promote its own self-serving interests. The Dominican crisis, according to this interpretation, was merely a graphic example of the deeply ingrained "anti-Communist bias" that had guided American foreign policy since 1947.

Third, considerably more time will almost certainly be required before many of the questions and long-term implications surrounding the Johnson Administration's behavior toward the Dominican crisis can be evaluated with assurance. What long-term impact did the intervention of the United States in the Dominican Republic have upon inter-American relations? How did the second Johnson Doctrine affect the president's role in the foreign policy process and executive-legislative relations? Even today, answers to these and comparable questions must be tentative and incomplete.

In the short run, the issuance and application of the second Johnson Doctrine achieved two objectives formulated by LBJ and his advisers. The lives of American citizens and other foreign nations were protected in the Dominican Republic. The action of the United States also averted a possible Communist takeover of that Caribbean country.

From a more long-range perspective, the second Johnson Doctrine entailed a number of diplomatic liabilities for the United States, some of which adversely affected American diplomacy for many years thereafter. Admittedly, for example, the Dominican crisis contributed to the Johnson Administration's poor diplomatic image and to its reputation for diplomatic ineptitude. Even defenders of the second Johnson Doctrine have acknowledged this result. As one study concluded, the doctrine was "ineptly" explained to American and foreign opinion. State Department efforts to inform Latin American governments, for example, were described as "woefully inadequate." Because of such failings, the doctrine had "damaging effects" upon American foreign policy. The former ambassador to the Dominican Republic, John B. Martin, concluded that the Johnson Administration's behavior appeared to be erratic. His judgment was that "what we did in Santo Domingo was better than what we said" in justification of what was done. A perceived hiatus characterized the administration's deeds and words in the Dominican crisis, producing widespread confusion at home and abroad. Still another generally favorable study of the Johnson Administration concluded that its response to the Dominican crisis encouraged the view that President Johnson preferred to employ "secretive and devious" methods, including "playing fast and loose with the facts."[63]

Less charitable critics have characterized President Johnson's diplo-

63. Center for Strategic Studies, *Dominican Action—1965* (Washington, D.C.: Georgetown University Center for Strategic Studies, 1966), ix, 39; Martin, *Overtaken by Events*, 707–708; Goldman, *The Tragedy of Lyndon Johnson*, 485.

macy in the Caribbean as "hysterical," as being dictated by a sense of "panic" which overcame officials in Washington and Santo Domingo, and as reflecting LBJ's "trigger-happy" impulses. The overall impression conveyed at home and abroad was that of "an impetuous, unsophisticated, hot-tempered President, quick to resort to force, hostile to all revolutionary forces that carried a taint of Communist influence."[64] Justifiably or not, the Dominican case (taken in conjunction with the administration's handling of the Vietnam War) convinced many critics that under Johnson's leadership, American diplomacy was characterized by blundering, heavy-handedness, and mismanagement.

Yet it must also be noted that many of the administration's critics— who were convinced that LBJ "managed" information about events during the crisis to support his policies—based their own information about developments there upon news sources originating outside the Dominican Republic. Since foreign news media were no less unprepared for the Dominican revolution than Washington, they had to depend in the main upon second- and third-hand accounts of events in the country. Inescapably, this meant, as one study emphasized, that news dispatches dealing with the Dominican crisis often tended to be "confused and in some cases misleading" for readers.[65] At a minimum, the problem of the reliability of data about the Dominican revolution beset critics of LBJ's diplomacy, no less than its defenders.

No aspect of the Dominican crisis perhaps evoked such widely divergent judgments as the question of Communist influence within the revolutionary movement and the likelihood that Marxist groups were on the verge of controlling the government. Some of LBJ's critics asserted that the administration largely invented the Communist danger in order to justify American military intervention in, and political control over, the country.[66] How "real" was the Communist menace?

64. Lincoln P. Bloomfield, *In Search of American Foreign Policy: The Humane Use of Power* (New York: Oxford University Press, 1974), 37–38; Center for Strategic Studies, *Dominican Action*, 80; Evans and Novak, *Lyndon B. Johnson*, 539–40; Geyelin, *Lyndon B. Johnson and the World*, 239.

65. Eleanor L. Dulles, *American Foreign Policy in the Making* (New York: Harper and Row, 1968), 338; Center for Strategic Studies, *Dominican Action*, 41.

66. For a representative selection of criticisms in this vein, see *National Diplomacy*, 66; Goldman, *The Tragedy of Lyndon Johnson*, 468; Edwin Lieuwen, *U.S. Policy in Latin America: A Short History* (New York: Praeger, 1965), 106.

What was the probability that, in the absence of American intervention, the Dominican Republic would have become "another Cuba"?
Defenders of the Johnson Administration's diplomatic record call
attention to several key facts that must be understood in answering
such questions. They do not deny that in the early stages of the Dominican revolution, possible American intervention was justified
mainly by reference to the danger posed to the lives of Americans and
other foreigners. Conversely, in the initial phase the risk of a Communist seizure of power appeared to be minimal, evoking little official
American concern. As the Dominican crisis intensified, however, anxiety in Washington about a possible Communist political victory became more pronounced and more conspicuous in official statements
dealing with the political struggle in the Dominican Republic. Far
from proving the existence of a "credibility gap" in White House statements dealing with the Dominican situation, this change could legitimately be accounted for by rapid and confusing changes within the
Dominican political context, by Communist tactics once the revolution began, and by the lack of success experienced by "moderate"
groups within the country to contain political extremism. Even one of
LBJ's severest critics—Sen. J. William Fulbright—acknowledged that
Communist elements within the Dominican Republic *had* attempted
to exploit the revolutionary upheaval in order to achieve Marxist
objectives.[67]

Spokesmen for the Johnson Administration also called attention to
the fact that Communist political machinations in the Dominican Republic did not begin with the revolutionary ferment in 1965. As we
have seen, during the early 1960s Castro's Cuba sponsored revolutionary activities directed against the Dominican Republic and other Latin
American states. These efforts were renewed in the mid-1960s, when
Dominican Communists received training in Cuba in revolutionary
and subversive techniques.[68]

67. Mann, "The Dominican Crisis," 730–38; excerpts from transcript of news conference by Secretary of State Dean Rusk on May 26, 1965, in Senate Foreign Relations
Committee, *Background Information Relating to the Dominican Republic*, 76–84;
J. William Fulbright, *The Arrogance of Power* (New York: Random House, 1966),
90–91.
68. See Ambassador Stevenson's detailed account of Communist activities in Latin

The numerical strength of Marxist elements within the Dominican Republic was another issue on which the Johnson Administration and its critics differed fundamentally. The latter believed that the White House had greatly exaggerated the size (and inferentially, the influence) of the Dominican Communist movement. During the crisis—and as part of its effort to justify American intervention in the country—the administration had released "lists" of known and suspected Dominican Communists. According to one official estimate, some four thousand Communists were active in the country. In turn, they were divided into pro-Castro, pro-Soviet, and pro-Chinese factions holding different viewpoints about the proper political tactics to be employed in the Dominican situation. A more conservative and impartial estimate, by the London *Economist*, placed the number of members of the Dominican Communist movement at some three hundred, along with some three thousand Marxist "adherents" and sympathizers.[69] Whatever the precise number of Communists active in the Dominican revolution, American officials (recalling the experience of the Soviet Union in 1917) were convinced that the Marxists were a sufficiently dedicated and determined minority to exploit the country's political upheaval to their advantage.

The question of the size and strength of the Dominican Communist movement could (and did) degenerate into a kind of meaningless "numbers game" engaged in by defenders and critics of the Johnson Administration's diplomacy alike. In the end, answers given to the question depended upon how a "Communist" is defined, along with related terms like "Communist agent" and "Communist sympathizer." Throughout the Dominican crisis, the administration adhered to its contention that the Communist threat to the independence of the Dominican Republic and the security of the Inter-American System was genuine and imminent. A number of well informed studies of Latin American political developments confirm this judgment. It was significant, for example, that—despite the opposition which the second Johnson Doctrine encountered south of the border—the five Latin

America, in "Security Council Authorizes U.S. Representative in Dominican Republic," *Department of State Bulletin*, LII (May 31, 1965), 869–75; and the views of Under Secretary of State Thomas Mann, in Szulc, *Dominican Diary*, 291.

69. London *Economist* on May 8, 1965, quoted in Senate Foreign Relations Committee, *Background Information Relating to the Dominican Republic*, 21.

American members of an OAS investigating team which visited the Dominican Republic during its political crisis were unanimous in finding that the threat of a Communist takeover existed and was only averted by the arrival of the American marines.[70]

Despite assertions to the contrary by its critics, the Johnson Administration did not contend that the Dominican Revolution had been initiated by Communist elements or that the Dominican government was already Communist-controlled. Officials in Washington realized that most of the rebels were reformers and groups who were disaffected by the long pattern of Dominican misrule. Again, however, the administration emphasized that the Bolshevik Revolution in Russia had been engineered by small minority led by Lenin; this group had not been satisfied with the moderate reforms carried out (or planned) by the Kerensky regime that was overthrown. Moreover, with each passing day, Washington believed that Dominican Communists were becoming more determined to gain power, and that American intervention must be directed against this prospect.[71]

A crucial consideration affecting the Johnson Administration's diplomacy in the Caribbean was the earlier experience of the Eisenhower Administration in dealing with the Cuban revolution. Fidel Castro and his followers had won a large following within Cuba and abroad by emphasizing the need to "reform" Cuba and by their public commitment to doing so within a democratic framework. Only after Castro became the Cuban leader—and after most of his political opponents had been executed, imprisoned, or exiled—had he openly proclaimed his devotion to communism. Officials of the Johnson Administration did not look forward to repeating that traumatic experience in the Dominican Republic.[72]

To the minds of several critics, the Johnson Administration's diplomacy was lamentable for another reason. According to this indictment, it provided incontrovertible evidence of America's opposition to

70. For studies corroborating the Johnson Administration's assessment of the Communist danger, see Tillema, *Appeal to Force*, 127; Evans and Novak, *Lyndon B. Johnson*, 544; Slater, *Intervention and Negotiation*, 37–38; and Szulc, *Dominican Diary*, 108. The finding of the OAS investigating team is cited in Slater, *Intervention and Negotiation*, 37–38.

71. Martin, *Overtaken by Events*, 356–58, 650.

72. Evans and Novak, *Lyndon B. Johnson*, 540; Slater, *Intervention and Negotiation*, 195.

revolutions abroad, particularly those that might be directed against American hegemony or political influence. As Richard J. Barnet has assessed it, for example, the Dominican intervention continued a pattern established by the Truman Doctrine in 1947: it symbolized America's "suppression of insurgent movements" throughout the world. Or, as David Horowitz and other commentators concluded, the nation's attempt to preserve "political stability" in the Dominican Republic and other settings was synonymous with Washington's efforts to maintain political oligarchies or military elites in power and to "stifle democracy" beyond America's own borders.[73]

An adequate refutation of the charge that postwar American foreign policy has reflected a consistent antirevolutionary bias would require more space than is available here.[74] As applied to the Dominican setting specifically, however, several of the pitfalls and deficiencies in such reasoning may be identified briefly. Globally, approximately one hundred new nations have emerged since the end of World War II— representing an increase of almost 200 percent in the membership of the United Nations. The vast majority of these nations belongs to what is widely known as the Third World (or the poorest category today, the Fourth World). In countless instances, the United States actively encouraged the acquisition of political independence by former colonial dependencies. During and after World War II, for example, Washington's anticolonial stance (directed specifically against the British, French, and Dutch empires) was a potent force in accelerating the acquisition of independence by societies under colonial jurisdiction. America's own ideological system—epitomized by President Woodrow Wilson's concept of self-determination—was in a quite literal sense a "subversive" force undermining colonialism.

After they became independent, nearly all of these new nations required external assistance to meet their pressing domestic needs. Beginning with President Truman's Point Four Program in 1949, America responded to these needs. Depending precisely upon how "foreign

73. Richard J. Barnet, *Intervention and Revolution: America's Confrontation with Insurgent Movements Around the World* (New York: World Publishing Co., 1968), 9; David Horowitz, *The Free World Colossus: A Critique of American Foreign Policy in the Cold War* (New York: Hill and Wang, 1971), 231–33. See also James Petras, "The Dominican Republic: Revolution and Restoration," in Michael Perenti (ed.), *Trends and Tragedies in American Foreign Policy* (Boston: Little, Brown, 1971), 143; and the views of Dan Kurzman as quoted in Center for Strategic Studies, *Dominican Action*, 81–82.

aid" is calculated, the United States has made available over $200 billion in external assistance since World War II—and after the mid-1950s, the bulk of these funds was allocated to nations in the Third World. With rare exceptions, American aid has been dispensed without political "strings." It has gone to Marxist countries (like Yugoslavia and Poland); to a wide variety of political regimes in Africa, the Middle East, and Asia; to nations that belong to American-sponsored alliance systems and those which do not; to "friends" of the United States abroad, along with nations that have criticized American diplomatic conduct consistently. Since the Kennedy Administration at least, American officials have accommodated themselves to a world of political diversity and to a "pluralistic" international system.

Many of these general observations apply to postwar American diplomacy toward Latin America. Confronted with the repeated accusation that Washington had too long "neglected" its sister American republics, early in 1961 the Kennedy Administration inaugurated the Alliance for Progress to promote the region's modernization and development. Initially, the United States pledged to provide $10 billion to achieve the goal, with the Latin American states furnishing most of the funds required for the program's successful implementation. The Alliance for Progress was sometimes described as a "revolution in freedom" (in contrast to a Marxist-sponsored revolution) south of the border. High on the list of the program's proclaimed goals was the promotion of "democracy" throughout the Western Hemisphere.[75]

To say that the Alliance for Progress experienced difficulty throughout the years that followed in achieving its goals would be to understate the matter. One formidable difficulty was that few of the Latin American states undertook the internal reforms necessary for it to accomplish its objectives. The relevant point for our discussion, however, is that the United States took the initiative in promulgating the program, and officials in Washington had high hopes that, as a result

74. An excellent analysis, refuting the allegation that postwar American foreign policy has exhibited an "antirevolutionary" bias, is Philip W. Quigg, *America the Dutiful: An Assessment of U.S. Foreign Policy* (New York: Simon and Schuster, 1971). A briefer treatment is Cecil V. Crabb, Jr., *Policy-Makers and Critics: Conflicting Theories of American Foreign Policy* (New York: Praeger, 1976), 275–93.

75. A more comprehensive treatment of the subject is Nystrom and Haverstock, *The Alliance for Progress*; a briefer and more up-to-date analysis is Needler, *The United States and the Latin American Revolution*, 47–55.

of the program, democratic institutions would be strengthened in the American community.

With a few exceptions, the high hopes associated with the Alliance for Progress have not been realized. Instead of greater democracy, in one Latin American nation after another, there has been growing political extremism—and in some cases (like contemporary Guatemala) pervasive anarchy. A discernible trend has been the emergence of military elites as the dominant political force; and in a number of cases, their rule has been violently contested by Communists, radicals, and other groups opposed to military rule. A major portion of Latin America, that is to say—and by the 1980s, Central America provided a graphic example—experienced conditions not totally dissimilar from those existing in the Dominican Republic in the mid-1960s. As much as any other single factor, the failure by civilian leaders to solve age-old social and economic problems in Latin America accounted for the decisive political role of military elites.

These political tendencies in the other American republics posed painful choices for officials in Washington. Should they accept the political reality—that in many Latin American countries, military leaders were politically dominant—and try to maintain reasonably cordial and cooperative relations with established governments? (If they did so, America's leaders would of course be accused of "supporting dictatorships" and of "opposing democracy" abroad.) Or should they use American power and influence to oppose nondemocratic governments in Latin America? (If they adopted this course, officials in Washington would once more face the charge that they were "dictating" to Latin America and were "intervening" in its political affairs.) The truth was that—whatever course Washington followed in this dilemma—it would almost certainly be criticized for violating some established principle of inter-American relations or its own professed ideological values.

In assessing the impact of the second Johnson Doctrine upon American diplomacy, it is also necessary to be clear about America's exact goals in the Dominican Republic and the actions taken to implement them. Our earlier treatment called attention to the fact that the Johnson Administration did not instigate the Dominican revolution and was unprepared for its outbreak. Spokesmen for the administration said—and there is no reason to doubt their *bona fides*—that the

United States did not seek to specify the nature of the new Dominican government; it sought merely to prevent the country from lapsing into anarchy or passing under Communist control. In this and other settings, Washington used its power to prevent Marxist groups from foreclosing political alternatives for the society concerned. Because of American intervention, the Dominican people were subsequently allowed to express their preferences in a free election. Neither during the revolution nor afterward did Washington seek to "install" a particular regime in power and to maintain it in the face of popular opposition.

While critics of the Johnson Doctrine for Latin America have castigated it as evidence of America's opposition to revolutionary movements abroad, one commentator has pointed out that in the Dominican context, this criticism is misdirected. In a fundamental sense, it is a misnomer to describe the Dominican political upheaval as a "revolution." In George C. Lodge's words, in its early stages at least, it was "more a chaotic than a revolutionary situation"; American intervention was aimed more at "protecting the independence of the revolution" than at its defeat. Prior to the landing of the American marines, the Dominican situation might more properly be called "anarchistic," rather than revolutionary—in the sense that *no* government was able to make its authority effective throughout the country. The reestablishment of governmental jurisdiction was an essential prerequisite to the selection of a new political regime.[76]

Another significant dimension of the second Johnson Doctrine was its implications for international law. The doctrine's detractors believed American intervention in the Dominican Republic violated international law; and some used the term "aggression" to describe America's conduct.[77] President Johnson and his advisers naturally denied that action taken under LBJ's Latin American doctrine conflicted with international law—and some supporters of the doctrine contended that, to the contrary, it enhanced the prospects that international law related to the problem of peace-keeping would ·become more effective in the future. The State Department's legal adviser be-

76. George C. Lodge, "Revolution in Latin America," *Foreign Affairs*, XLIV (January, 1966), 173–97.
77. Gil, *Latin American-United States Relations*, 252; Bloomfield, *In Search of American Foreign Policy*, 168.

lieved that the second Johnson Doctrine was harmonious with existing international legal principles. America's intervention in the Dominican Republic provided the Organization of American States "essential time" in which to act; it carried out the purposes of earlier OAS declarations against Communist inroads in the Americas; and in the end, it gave rise to new precedents and machinery (such as the Inter-American Peace Force that ultimately assumed responsibility for preserving order in the country) for resolving regional crises.[78]

The controversy over the legal aspects of the second Johnson Doctrine may simply underscore a reality that is evident to informed students of international relations. International law remains primitive and incomplete—especially as related to a nation's use of armed force to preserve its diplomatic and security interests. After a generation, for example, the United Nations has still been unable to produce an acceptable definition of "aggression" (not to mention the infinitely more difficult concept, "indirect aggression"). In the Dominican case, the Johnson Administration could find as many legal precedents to support its conduct as there were precedents on the other side.

A still different criticism of the Johnson Doctrine for Latin America is Ronald Steel's verdict, that the Dominican intervention was not so much illegal as it was "merely stupid." In his view, it failed to promote any legitimate foreign policy interest of the United States in Latin America, while creating new grounds for misunderstandings and tensions in inter-American relations.[79] Among its other adverse effects, the landing of American armed forces in the Dominican Republic revived Latin America's traditional fear of Yankee "interventionism" that has colored attitudes toward the United States since the administration of Theodore Roosevelt. Critics of the Johnson Administration's diplomacy contended that, in the Dominican case (as concurrently in South Vietnam), American power was being used to maintain the political status quo in the face of mounting popular discontent with it.

Defenders of the second Johnson Doctrine emphasized two points

78. See, for example, the detailed discussion of the international law aspects of the Johnson Doctrine for Latin America, in Leonard C. Meeker, "The Dominican Situation in the Perspective of International Law," *Department of State Bulletin*, LIII (July 12, 1965), 60–65.
79. Ronald Steel, *Pax Americana* (Rev. ed.; New York: Viking Press, 1970), 248.

in rebuttal. One was that Latin American opinion has always been ambivalent about intervention by the United States in their political affairs. While the idea of American "intervention" in the affairs of its weaker hemispheric neighbors is widely denounced as a general principle, in practice time and again governments and groups throughout Latin America have *encouraged* interventionist behavior by the United States in behalf of goals and purposes they advocated. Established governments (often irrespective of their political orientation) desire economic and financial assistance by the United States—provided of course that there are no "strings" attached to such aid. (By contrast, most Latin American nations in the recent period have strongly resisted efforts by Washington to initiate the internal reforms needed to make such American aid effective.) Countless Latin American political groups have sought American moral and material support against their political opponents, while denouncing as "interventionism" American assistance given to their rivals in the political arena. Nearly all political factions in Latin America approve intervention by the United States to "promote democracy" in the Western Hemisphere— a cause each group customarily identifies with its own political program.[80]

Paradoxically, the United States has sometimes been condemned for "intervening" in Latin American political life even when it does nothing overtly. Latin American complaints about Washington's "neglect" of their problems is one specific form of this lament. The general dilemma confronting officials in the United States in dealing with Latin America was graphically depicted by Edgar A. Mowrer, who said, "In foreign politics the passivity of a power constitutes action. To do nothing is to move. Not to intervene when one's intervention would prove decisive is a form of intervention."[81] The basic premise of the Johnson Administration's diplomacy toward the Caribbean republic was the idea that "to do nothing" under the circumstances would amount to a form of intervention by the United States—in the direction of encouraging the continuation of anarchy and violence, and the possible imposition of a Communist political system upon this tradi-

80. Paul Y. Hammond, *Cold War and Detente: The American Foreign Policy Process Since 1945* (New York: Harcourt Brace Jovanovich, 1975), 202.
81. Edgar A. Mowrer, *The Nightmare of American Foreign Policy* (New York: Alfred A. Knopf, 1948), 9.

tionally backward and misgoverned country. Neither spokesmen for the Johnson Administration nor most informed students of Latin American affairs believed that these possibilities reflected the desires of a majority of the Dominican people.

Another recurrent criticism of the second Johnson Doctrine is the assertion that in the long run, it did little or nothing to resolve the underlying social and economic problems engendering political instability in the Dominican Republic. Some fifteen years after American military intervention in the country, it remained poverty-stricken and economically backward, with little discernible progress toward the emergence of a democratic political order. Periodically, charges were made that, as in the past, Dominican elections were "rigged" in favor of the incumbent government; and military elements showed no inclination to relinquish their traditional political role. Yet in 1978— after it appeared that direct military intervention in the political system was imminent—the armed forces permitted the peaceful election of a businessman, Antonio Guzmán, to the presidency. For the first time in Dominican history, a change of regimes occurred without widespread violence and upheaval.[82]

American military intervention in the country under the second Johnson Doctrine had not of course fundamentally changed the fact that the Dominican Republic remained one of the poorest countries on the globe; its economic prospects were bleak; and what might be called its "revolutionary potential" was still high. In common with other Caribbean and Central American states, several bedrock problems—overpopulation, illiteracy, unemployment, and rampant inflation—provided incentives for ongoing violence and radical political change.[83]

Yet after acknowledging these realities, it may be questioned whether this is a justifiable indictment of the second Johnson Doctrine. President Johnson and his advisers at no point claimed that his new foreign policy pronouncement would correct the deep-seated and difficult

82. George W. Grayson, "The United States and Latin America: The Challenge of Human Rights," *Current History*, LXXVI (February, 1979), 53.
83. Conditions within the Dominican Republic after the revolution of 1965 are discussed more fully in *Area Handbook for the Dominican Republic* (2nd ed.; Washington, D.C.: Government Printing Office, 1973); and in John Paxton (ed.), *The Statesman's Year-Book, 1979–1980* (New York: St. Martin's Press, 1979), 408. Subsequent publications in the latter series provide up-to-date information on the country.

problems giving rise to antidemocratic tendencies, violence, and political instability within the Dominican Republic. LBJ's new doctrine, critics of the administration's Caribbean diplomacy were sometimes prone to forget, was merely one prong or instrument of Latin American policy. The Alliance for Progress, for example, had already been promulgated and was designed to overcome the region's social and economic backwardness; and as we have already observed, in time the Alliance was expected to enhance the prospects for the emergence of democratic institutions throughout Latin America. In turn, its success was vitally dependent upon the willingness of Latin American governments to undertake requisite internal reforms, permitting effective use of American assistance. Without pressing the analogy too far (because of course several fundamental differences also existed between the two situations) Washington's objective in the Dominican Republic was basically the same as it had been in 1947 when the Truman Doctrine was promulgated in response to the Greek crisis: to permit the people in these respective countries to choose their own political destiny, without external dictation or hegemony. In the case of Greece, after 1947 there clearly *was* an evolution toward greater democracy; in the Dominican Republic, minimal progress in this direction could be detected after 1965. But this much could be said: even if few of its underlying problems had been solved, the chances for a democratic evolution in the Dominican Republic seemed substantially better than they were in Castro's Cuba. There, the people also confronted deteriorating economic and social conditions, with little prospect that they would soon be rid of a totalitarian Communist regime that had become a kind of ward of the Soviet Union. Ironically, by the late 1970s, the Castro regime was endeavoring to improve relations with the United States, in the hope of reversing Cuba's record of economic decline.[84]

For all of its shortcomings, the second Johnson Doctrine expressed a basic principle of American foreign policy, initially enunciated in the Monroe Doctrine in 1823. As the administration of Ronald Reagan reiterated several times during the early 1980s, for approximately a century and a half the United States has opposed efforts by foreign powers to influence the political destiny of the Western Hemisphere. It

84. George Volsky, "Cuba Twenty Years Later," *Current History*, LXXVI (February, 1979), 54–58, 83–84; Sergio Roca, "Revolutionary Cuba," *Current History*, LXXX (February, 1981), 53–57, 84.

engaged in the most serious encounter with the Soviet Union since World War II—the Cuban Missile Crisis of 1962—to uphold that principle. No evidence existed that the United States was less devoted to the principle in the last half of the twentieth century than in earlier periods of American history.

This leads us to identify what may have been, in retrospect, the most serious defect of the second Johnson Doctrine and a source of ongoing contention in inter-American relations. Like the Truman Doctrine before it, the second Johnson Doctrine was directed against Communist political machinations and expansionism. In the Dominican setting, this meant one of two things (or possibly both): Soviet or Cuban hegemony over the Dominican Republic. The second Johnson Doctrine reflected little or no awareness that political fragmentation is the rule of modern Latin American political life—a tendency that has become more pronounced with the passage of time.[85] Schism has been particularly characteristic of Marxist and other left-wing political movements throughout the region. By the mid-1960s, "polycentric" forces had all but destroyed the unity of what had formerly been a fairly cohesive Communist bloc, directed from Moscow; the concept of "international communism" had largely been reduced to little more than a slogan or epithet. The diversity characteristic of Marxism was more than ordinarily evident within Latin America, where pro-Soviet, pro-Cuban, pro-Chinese, and various indigenous species of Marxism and radicalism vied for supremacy. Not infrequently, rivalry and enmity among these Marxist factions were sometimes as sharp as their antipathy toward the United States!

The second Johnson Doctrine took no account of these political realities. It made no attempt to distinguish between *externally imposed* Communist systems and those (like the later regime of Dr. Salvador Allende in Chile, or the Marxist-oriented government of Jamaica) that appeared to be largely *indigenous*. Nor did it attempt to distinguish between Marxist movements that sought to acquire power by violent and revolutionary means and those that were content to work through the democratic process to achieve their goals. It was not until the late 1970s—when the Carter Administration sought to arrive at minimally

85. Viron P. Vaky, "Hemispheric Relations: 'Everything is Part of Everything Else,' " *Foreign Affairs*, LIX (Special Issue, 1980), 619.

cooperative relations with the Sandinista-controlled government of Nicaragua—that officials in Washington were prepared to accept the concept of an independent Marxist regime, substantially independent of Soviet or Cuban hegemony.[86] In brief, the second Johnson Doctrine did not allow for the possibility that "another Yugoslavia"—a country with which the United States had long maintained harmonious relations—might emerge in the Western Hemisphere. Admittedly, that outcome did not seem likely in the political environment existing in the Dominican Republic in the mid-1960s. (Even by the early 1980s, it remained questionable whether the Sandinista regime in Nicaragua could satisfy Washington that it was substantially independent of Cuban or Soviet influence, and that it was not actively sponsoring revolutionary activities in neighboring countries—basic requirements for distinguishing Yugoslavia's "national communism" from expansionist versions found in the Soviet Union and more recently, North Vietnam.)

In the final analysis, the paramount achievement of the Johnson Doctrine for Latin America was that it bought time in which long-range solutions for the Dominican Republic's massive social, economic, and political problems could be found. In view of the magnitude of the country's problems, such solutions would of course require many years for their successful implementation. America's military intervention afforded those groups interested in Dominican well-being "another chance" to attack its underlying problems effectively. By the early 1980s—with revolutionary turmoil and violence sweeping several Central American states, and with most nations in the Caribbean still immersed in social and economic backwardness—little evidence could be cited to show that Dominican political elites, officials in Washington, and other groups interested in the country's destiny had used the time available to them wisely or constructively.

---

86. The causes and nature of the revolutionary ferment gripping several Central American countries by the late 1970s are analyzed more fully in Richard Millett, "The Politics of Violence: Guatemala and El Salvador," *Current History*, LXXX (February, 1981), 70–75, 88; Thomas W. Walker, "Nicaragua Consolidates Its Revolution," *Current History*, LXXX (February, 1981), 79–82, 89–90; and Vaky, "Hemispheric Relations," 617–47.

7 / The Nixon Doctrine: The Post-Vietnam Retrenchment in American Commitments

In the years ahead, the most profound challenge to American [foreign] policy will be philosophical: to develop some concept of order in a world which is bipolar militarily and multipolar politically. But a philosophical deepening will not come easily to those brought up in the American tradition of foreign policy.
                                                              —Henry A. Kissinger

On a long tour of Asia, I found no responsible figure, official or unofficial, who . . . divined the essential meaning of America's new policy [the Nixon Doctrine]. In that sense, the Nixon Doctrine is a hazy shadow, unsettling, uncertain; it is welcome to some, unnerving to others, unclear to all.
                                                              —Flora Lewis

President Nixon's maxi-statement on American foreign policy is a little like the brilliant maxi-coats one sees swinging along the sidewalks of London these days: it is long, it covers a lot of territory, and it conceals the most interesting parts.
                                                              —James Reston

The Nixon Doctrine was a highly significant, and in many respects unique, development in the American diplomatic tradition. By almost any applicable criteria, it was different from the other major foreign policy doctrines examined in our study. A notable difference lay of course in the dramatic fate of its promulgator: after more than a year of trying to extricate himself from the deepening Watergate scandal, on August 9, 1974, Richard M. Nixon became the first president of the United States to resign his office. Nixon's resignation was prompted by the virtually certain knowledge that, if he did not resign, he would be impeached (or indicted) and convicted for abuses of presidential power. The opprobrium attached to the Nixon presidency because of these traumatic events inescapably colored public attitudes toward his administration's performance in domestic and foreign affairs. The Nixon Doctrine soon followed its promulgator into oblivion. Yet the doctrine marked an important evolution in postwar American foreign relations and deserves greater attention than it customarily receives.

The "Elusive" Nixon Doctrine

For the student of modern American diplomacy, the Nixon Doctrine presents a number of unusual problems that differ (if only sometimes in degree) from the other doctrines included in our analysis. At the outset, a difficult one is: what *was* the Nixon Doctrine? What were its essential components?[1] For several reasons, the answers to such questions even today are far from clear.

To anticipate our later discussion, the Nixon Doctrine may be construed either very narrowly or very broadly. In the former case, it was synonymous with the strategic principles that would guide the application of American military force abroad in the post–Vietnam War era. In the latter case, it was equivalent to the entire diplomatic program of the Nixon Administration, covering such diverse elements as the new strategic principles mentioned above, détente with the Soviet Union, "normalization" in relations between the United States and Communist China, stronger "partnership" between the United States and its NATO allies, and many other major and minor elements. The problem is compounded because President Nixon and his advisers referred to the Nixon Doctrine in both senses; and their understanding of its essential meaning appeared to change from time to time. The Nixon Doctrine was sometimes viewed primarily as an *approach* to the range of America's external problems. In other instances, it seemed to denote a comprehensive diplomatic *program* enunciated by the Nixon White House.

Uncertainty about the meaning and implications of the Nixon Doctrine was perhaps inevitable, given the context in which it was issued. As the end of the traumatic Vietnam War approached, there was great public doubt and confusion about the future direction of American foreign policy. Diagnoses of what "went wrong" in Vietnam were rife; a wide variety of prescriptions for preventing "another Vietnam" was offered by groups of every political orientation; and even more than ordinarily, American public opinion exhibited contradictory and ambivalent viewpoints both about why the United States had lost the

---

1. The fullest exposition of the Nixon Doctrine is contained in President Nixon's "Second Annual Report to the Congress on United States Foreign Policy," submitted on February 25, 1971. For the text of this report, see *Public Papers of the Presidents of the United States: Richard Nixon, 1971* (Washington, D.C.: Government Printing Office, 1971), 219–345.

Vietnam War and about how it could prevent involvement in a comparable situation in the future. As one commentator noted, the Nixon Doctrine marked "the beginning of a probably lengthy, and difficult process of defining new patterns of America's relationship to the world and of a similarly lengthy process of building up a new domestic basis for that relationship."[2]

Throughout its life-span, the essential meaning of the Nixon Doctrine remained elusive—and that problem pervades our analysis of it. As explained by its proponents, the Nixon Doctrine possessed three primary meanings or connotations. First, it could be construed as a general regulative principle of American diplomacy in the post–Vietnam War era. As such, it was applicable to the entire range of American foreign relations. So construed, the key concept of the Nixon Doctrine was retrenchment in America's overseas obligations. In effect, the Nixon Doctrine attempted to incorporate "the lessons of Vietnam" into American diplomatic behavior. Viewed in this vein, the Nixon Doctrine had a twofold purpose: to reduce America's overseas commitments, and to enable the United States to fulfill those which were retained more effectively and at lower cost. As President Nixon stated in his report to Congress early in 1971, "We are not involved in the world because we have commitments; we have commitments because we are involved. Our interests must shape our commitments rather than the other way around."[3]

Implicitly, the Nixon Doctrine was designed to refute the idea that, because of the results in Vietnam, the United States no longer had global—or Asian—commitments. To Nixon's mind, the doctrine served as a corrective to what he often called the "new isolationism" that had gained adherents within the American society because of the war; and it was intended to counteract the notion that any future application of American power abroad was bound to fail. If (as even officials in Washington ultimately concluded) the defense of Southeast Asia was not a vital interest of the United States, this fact did not mean that America lacked vital interests abroad which could be jeopardized with impunity.

A second possible interpretation of the Nixon Doctrine is to view it

2. Zbigniew Brzezinski, "Half Past Nixon," *Foreign Policy*, III (Summer, 1971), 21.
3. Richard Nixon, *The Memoirs of Richard Nixon* (New York: Grosset and Dunlap, 1978), 395; *U.S. Foreign Policy for the 1970s: Building for Peace* (Washington, D.C.: Government Printing Office, 1971), 13.

more narrowly—as providing a set of strategic principles or maxims governing the use of American armed force in behalf of foreign policy ends. If America's involvement in the Vietnam imbroglio had ended in failure, how could the power of the United States be applied beyond its own borders more successfully in the future? The Nixon Doctrine attempted to provide at least tentative answers to this question.

President Nixon emphasized, for example, that "the United States will keep all of its treaty commitments." Undramatic and prosaic as this assertion might seem, after Vietnam the Nixon White House deemed it imperative to underscore this determination. The anticipated retrenchment of American power in Southeast Asia did not presage a comparable withdrawal from the NATO area or other regions in which the United States had a vital security interest.

Yet the Nixon Doctrine clearly anticipated certain changes in the American outlook toward military alliances and other forms of overseas commitments. The earlier impulse toward "pactitis" (reaching its apogee in the Eisenhower-Dulles period) had ended. Both the United States and the Soviet Union were experiencing continuing difficulties maintaining cohesion within their respective alliance systems. Accordingly, the Nixon Doctrine held that—while the United States would honor its existing alliance obligations—it would not endeavor to undertake new security commitments abroad.[4]

Under the Nixon Doctrine also, officials in Washington proposed to reexamine the nature and extent of America's obligations under existing security agreements abroad. Ultimately, the Nixon Administration proposed a significant reduction in the level of American military forces in South Korea (although the volume of military assistance to the country would be increased). While the administration called for no reduction in American armed forces levels in Western Europe, it did have limited success in obtaining an expanded contribution to the NATO defense effort by the Western allies.

Another strategic principle embodied in the Nixon Doctrine was addressed to the problem of global nuclear war. The United States, the doctrine affirmed, would "provide a shield if a nuclear power threatens the freedom of a nation allied with us or of a nation whose survival we consider vital to our security." This strategic maxim had a number

4. "Secretary Rogers Interviewed on National Educational Television," *Department of State Bulletin*, LXI (December 22, 1969), 580.

of significant implications. The Nixon Doctrine's reference to threats posed by "a nuclear power" was obviously directed at the Soviet Union and Communist China (by the end of the 1960s, the latter was actively acquiring a nuclear arsenal).

The doctrine recognized two categories of countries facing a potential nuclear threat: the formal treaty allies of the United States and those that were not. To allay the apprehensions of the former in the post–Vietnam War era, the Nixon Doctrine reiterated the familiar strategic principle of "massive retaliation": a nuclear threat to the United States and its allies would be "answered" in kind. By the early 1970s, this could hardly be called a new strategic principle; the concept of massive retaliation had been reiterated many times, since the Eisenhower-Dulles period in the 1950s. Since it could be assumed that, by the era of the Nixon Administration, policy-makers in Moscow and Peking thoroughly understood America's determination to resist Communist expansionism, this provision of the Nixon Doctrine had another important purpose: to inhibit the spread of nuclear weapons throughout the international system. With America's nuclear shield available to protect the allies from a nuclear threat, it was thus unnecessary for them to develop their own nuclear arsenal for this purpose.

Yet according to the Nixon Doctrine, the American nuclear arsenal also protected *any* "nation whose survival we consider vital to our security"—not merely those having formal security ties with the United States. Now this announcement by President Nixon constituted a significant innovation in American foreign policy. The Nixon Doctrine thus went far toward acknowledging what experience had shown to be a reality: in many cases, "informal" and de facto defense commitments (and a leading example was America's longtime commitment to the security of Israel) created no less important and binding obligations than treaties or alliance systems. (As we shall see more fully in Chapter 8, this reality also underlay the Carter Doctrine, pledging the United States to protect the security of the Persian Gulf area.)

At the same time, this provision of the Nixon Doctrine was also one of its most puzzling and ambiguous. If a certain unspecified category of nations could hereafter count upon the military protection of the United States, because they were viewed as vital to American security, which nations exactly were they? By what criteria did American policy-makers determine them? How would Moscow, Peking, or other possible adversaries know which nations they were vis-à-vis those (like South Vietnam) that were not regarded as vital to the security of the United States? Neither the initial Nixon Doctrine nor subsequent explanations of it provided overly clear guidance in answering such questions. Hence, in practice the Nixon Doctrine did little to discourage the proliferation of nuclear weapons throughout the international system. And (depending precisely upon how this strategic principle was subsequently interpreted) the Nixon Doctrine created at least the possibility for a potential *expansion* in the foreign defense commitments of the United States—a development which appeared counter to the overall theme of retrenchment in American foreign policy in the post–Vietnam War era.

The third strategic maxim enunciated by the Nixon Doctrine was intended to apply to nonnuclear or "conventional" threats to American security in the post–Vietnam War period. Toward this problem, the Nixon Doctrine provided: "In cases involving other types of aggression [*i.e.*, posed by nonnuclear or conventional forces] we shall furnish military and economic assistance when requested in accordance with our treaty commitments. But we shall look to the nation directly threatened to assume the primary responsibility of providing the manpower for its defense."

With a nuclear "balance of terror" existing between the two superpowers—and both devoted to the concept of détente (much as they might disagree over its requirements)—this provision of the Nixon Doctrine was directed to what appeared the most likely and predictable category of threats confronting the United States abroad. This included civil wars, insurrections, revolutionary movements, terroristic activities, what Moscow called "wars of national liberation," and other forms of local and regional violence creating global instability. By the late 1960s, the potential for such conflicts was high. Indeed, nuclear stalemate between the United States and the Soviet Union may have encouraged a rising incidence of subnuclear conflict.

The Nixon Doctrine sought to answer two fundamental questions about America's future response to limited or conventional military conflicts. When was American security involved in them? And what would be the nature of America's response if another Vietnam-type conflict erupted in the international system? Toward the former question, the Nixon Doctrine reaffirmed the basic continuity of American foreign policy, by asserting that the security of the United States was involved when "aggression" occurred within the international system. Yet a major weakness of the doctrine was that neither at the time of its issuance nor later did American officials provide a clear standard for defining "aggression" that was any more acceptable at home or abroad than had been the case during the Vietnam War. (After some twenty-five years of effort, it also had to be said, the United Nations had been unable to gain a global consensus on the meaning of aggression.)[5]

By implication, the Nixon Doctrine held that in other categories of limited war—when aggression had not occurred—the security of the United States was not directly affected by such conflicts. Given the lack of clarity about the meaning of aggression, the Nixon Doctrine thus left the American response to limited violence largely unspecified. Presumably, it would be determined unilaterally by the United States, on a case-by-case basis. If that were true, then it was difficult to see how President Nixon's pronouncement in foreign affairs qualified as a "doctrine" or regulative principle of American diplomacy that was understood either by citizens at home or by foreign governments!

What kind of assistance might a country experiencing aggression anticipate from the United States? The Nixon Doctrine pledged Washington to "furnish military and economic assistance" to an endangered country. In fact, the doctrine specified that the United States "shall" supply such aid to a country facing nonnuclear aggression. Taken literally, the Nixon Doctrine's terms expanded America's overseas commitments, leaving Washington little choice in responding to conflicts in this category. This proviso of the Nixon Doctrine was clearly at variance with the earlier principle enunciated by President Nixon, that America's "interests must shape our commitments, rather than the other way around."

Several qualifications were contained in the Nixon Doctrine upon the extension of American assistance to countries confronting nonnuclear conflicts. Washington's assistance had to be "requested" by the country whose security was jeopardized. (Admittedly, as was emphasized in our earlier discussion of the Greek and Lebanese crises, in

5. See, for example, the analysis of the problem in Philip E. Jacob, Alexine L. Atherton, and Arthur M. Wallenstein, *The Dynamics of International Organization* (Rev. ed.; Homewood, Ill.: Dorsey Press, 1972), 67–72.

Chapters 3 and 4, such "requests" were usually forthcoming, in a form acceptable to Washington.) American military aid also had to be furnished "in accordance with our treaty commitments." In addition to the military pacts to which the United States belonged, the United Nations Charter was also one of America's treaty commitments. A basic principle of the UN Charter, for example, permitted any nation to provide for its "self-defense." Accordingly, any member of the United Nations was presumably entitled to protection against aggression.

Perhaps the most significant qualification which the Nixon Doctrine imposed upon the provision of military aid to a threatened state was the stipulation that the recipient country was to bear "primary responsibility for providing the manpower for its defense." This tenet of the Nixon Doctrine quite clearly reflected what many Americans were convinced was the paramount lesson of the Vietnam War. The United States had violated the strategic axiom (identified particularly with the World War II and Korean War military leader, Gen. Douglas MacArthur) of avoiding a large-scale "ground war" on the Asian continent. A more recent precedent for this provision of the Nixon Doctrine was the concept of "Vietnamization," proposed during the war by Secretary of Defense Melvin Laird. Laird's strategic concept embodied two key principles: American troops would gradually be withdrawn from Vietnam; and as this process occurred, the United States would "train, equip, and inspire the South Vietnamese to fill the gap" left by the American military evacuation.[6]

In the future, when foreign countries faced a nonnuclear threat to their security, the American response would be governed by a kind of military division of labor. The endangered country would supply the troops—and even more crucially perhaps, it would provide convincing evidence of a determination and capacity to defend its own security; in turn, the United States would provide needed logistical support and war matériel. The willingness of the country concerned to make its assigned contribution would be a precondition for the provision of American aid.

As we have already emphasized, the Nixon Doctrine emerged as the result not of a single presidential policy statement, but of several policy declarations by President Nixon and his advisers during the early

6. The concept of "Vietnamization" is explained more fully in Nixon, *Memoirs*, 392.

1970s. One such comprehensive exposition was President Nixon's report to Congress on February 9, 1972, entitled, "The Emerging Structure of Peace."[7] The third broad meaning of the Nixon Doctrine was highlighted in this document—and it was the one which was perhaps most frequently intended when officials of the Nixon Administration referred to the president's new foreign policy guidelines. In this connotation, the Nixon Doctrine encompassed the totality of the administration's foreign policy program. In the language of the president's report to Congress, the Nixon Doctrine was designed to create a new "structure" of global power and, on the basis of it, to enhance the prospects for global peace and security. Nixon was a longtime admirer of French President Charles de Gaulle, who had proposed a "Grand Design" for European stability; and Nixon also wanted to accomplish what one commentator has called "something great" in the foreign policy field: the "new structure for peace" envisioned by the doctrine that bore his name. More so perhaps than any chief executive in American history, Nixon was conscious of promulgating a new foreign policy doctrine. Nixon had an obvious pride of authorship in his doctrine which he did not bother to disguise.

The fundamental diplomatic reorientation envisioned by the Nixon Doctrine also owed much to the ideas of the president's closest foreign policy aide, his adviser for national security affairs, Dr. Henry Kissinger. Kissinger was a longtime and respected student of modern diplomacy; and he was an avowed devotee of the approach to foreign affairs known as realpolitik, pivotal concepts of which are power, the balance of power, and national interest. Realpolitik emphasizes the central role of power as the crucial element determining political relationships. For all states, the national interest is the dominant motivating force determining foreign policy, and the concept of the balance of power is the main regulative principle for preserving global stability.[8]

7. *U.S. Foreign Policy for the 1970s: The Emerging Structure of Peace* (Washington, D.C.: Government Printing Office, 1972).
8. For a fuller discussion of realpolitik as it applies to American foreign policy, see Cecil V. Crabb, Jr., *Policy-Makers and Critics: Conflicting Theories of American Foreign Policy* (New York: Praeger, 1976), 165–214. Kissinger's version of realpolitik is set forth more fully in his *Nuclear Weapons and Foreign Policy* (New York: W. W. Norton, 1958); and his *American Foreign Policy* (2nd ed.; New York: W. W. Norton, 1974). Useful commentaries on his thought are David Landau, *Kissinger: The Uses of Power* (New York: Thomas Y. Crowell, 1974); Stephen R. Graubard, *Kissinger: Portrait of a Mind* (New York: W. W. Norton, 1973); and Harry M. Joiner, *American Foreign Policy: The Kissinger Era* (Huntsville, Ala.: Stronde Publishers, 1977).

In company with most disciples of realpolitik, Kissinger was an admirer of the political equilibrium achieved in Europe by the Congress
of Vienna following the defeat of Napoleon in 1815. For a century
thereafter, the Concert of Europe had relied upon regulative principles
like balance of power and "legitimacy" to prevent a general war (although a number of smaller or limited wars did erupt during this period). To Kissinger's mind, many guiding principles associated with realpolitik were equally applicable to the problem of maintaining global
stability in the post–Vietnam War era.

As a comprehensive blueprint for the reorientation of American foreign policy after the Vietnam War, the Nixon Doctrine had implications for virtually every phase of the nation's diplomacy. In the foreign
policy process, for example, the Nixon Doctrine called for a new sense
of unity in approaching foreign affairs and envisioned a new partnership between the executive and legislative branches in dealing with
diplomatic issues. Abroad, the Nixon Doctrine anticipated closer cooperation between the United States and its NATO allies; a renewed
effort to solve the Arab-Israeli dispute and other controversies threatening the stability of the Middle East; closer relations between the
United States and the nations of black Africa; a new and more limited
role for the United States in Asian affairs; and the emergence of a re-
vitalized sense of community in inter-American relations. One of its
most important goals—to some minds perhaps, the essential precondition for the president's new "structure of peace"—was the maintenance and extension of détente between the United States and the Soviet Union. The general principle of détente would be translated into
new agreements between the superpowers limiting strategic armaments and other accords reducing suspicions and tensions between
them.[9]

Viewed in this light, the Nixon Doctrine was not, strictly speaking,
a "doctrine" or guiding principle of American foreign policy. It was a
diplomatic package, containing the major and minor goals of the
Nixon Administration overseas—the "record" that the Nixon-Kissinger team hoped to achieve abroad. As such, it is not surprising that the
Nixon Doctrine was also a casualty of the Watergate scandal that destroyed the Nixon presidency.

9. The goals of the Nixon Doctrine toward specific regions and problems of American foreign policy are explained more fully in *U.S. Foreign Policy for the 1970s: The*

Doctrinal Sources and Influences

In common with those doctrines that came before and after it, the Nixon Doctrine was influenced by a number of factors at home and abroad. Among these, three categories of factors deserve brief attention.

In his *Memoirs*, President Nixon observed that a leading goal of his diplomatic doctrine was to assure that there would be "no more Vietnams in the future" for the United States.[10] That the Vietnam conflict—in some respects, the most traumatic and internally divisive foreign policy undertaking in American history—momentously affected the content of the Nixon Doctrine seems incontestable. It is not necessary for our purpose to review the record of America's growing involvement in the Vietnam conflict to the point that, by the period of the Nixon Administration, it had largely become "America's war," which the United States was clearly losing. In time, the conflict resulted in some 56,000 American casualties, and the financial cost to the United States was estimated at close to $150 billion. The war in Southeast Asia had already largely destroyed the political credibility of the Johnson Administration; as it continued, it drained the American people psychologically; and throughout the conflict, the diplomatic influence and prestige of the United States became seriously eroded. By the time of the national election of 1968, two somewhat contrary demands were reflected in public opinion about the Vietnam War. On the one hand, most Americans wanted the conflict brought to a rapid end; and on the other, they also desired an honorable and durable peace settlement, commensurate with the enormous sacrifices the United States had made in this contest. "Dovish" solutions—calling for the immediate and unconditional evacuation of American forces from the region—found very little favor with most Americans.[11]

Emerging Structure of Peace, passim; and in *U.S. Foreign Policy for the 1970s: Building for Peace, passim.*

10. Nixon, *Memoirs*, 394–95. The lessons of the Vietnam War experience were also identified by Under Secretary of State Elliot Richardson, in "Controlling Local Conflicts," *Department of State Bulletin*, LXII (May 18, 1970), 628–31.

11. For informative analyses of the nature and influence of American public opinion during the Vietnam War, see the three essays included in Robert J. Lifton (ed.), *America and the Asian Revolutions* (New Brunswick, N.J.: Transaction Books, 1970), 61–117; and Ralph B. Levering, *The Public and American Foreign Policy: 1918–1978* (New York: William Morrow, 1978), 120–49.

Against this background, the extrication of the United States from the Vietnam conflict—accompanied by steps to prevent "another Vietnam"—was a dominant goal of the Nixon Doctrine. After prolonged and frustrating negotiations, on January 27, 1973, the United States, South Vietnam, and North Vietnam finally reached an agreement ending the conflict in Southeast Asia. As Washington had long feared, its result was to leave Communist forces dominant in Vietnam; and they were in a position to extend their hegemony over neighboring Laos and Cambodia as well, after American forces were withdrawn from the area. The Vietnam War was an undisguised military defeat for the United States; because of Hanoi's close ties with the Soviet Union, it was widely viewed as a victory for Moscow over its American adversary.

For many years thereafter, the "lessons of Vietnam" affected the formulation and conduct of American foreign relations. Even before the war ended, the Nixon-Kissinger team believed that several of these lessons were applicable to future American foreign policy. Among these, seven clearly affected the Nixon Doctrine.

1. The Nixon Administration feared a resurgence of "isolationist" sentiment within the United States as a result of the Vietnam debacle. Under the Johnson Administration, Secretary of State Dean Rusk had publicly warned Americans about the danger of lapsing into a new form of isolationism (called "neoisolationism"), as a consequence of the Vietnam failure.[12] The admonition was not unwarranted. By the late 1960s, anti–Vietnam War groups not only called for the withdrawal of American power from Southeast Asia. More broadly, they demanded that the United States no longer serve as the "policeman of the world" and eschew policies motivated by "the arrogance of American power."[13] According to this viewpoint, national leaders should give highest priority to long-neglected domestic needs. As isolationists before World War II had contended, America's "example" to the world was viewed as the principal key to its influence and power abroad.

Another group of critics—sometimes called conservative neoisolationists—demanded changes in American foreign policy for different

---

12. Dispatch by Bernard Gwertzman, New York *Times*, December 1, 1968.
13. Elsewhere, the author has analyzed this version of "liberal neoisolationist" thought. See Crabb, *Policy-Makers and Critics*, 253–99.

reasons. In the future the United States must avoid "no-win" situations like the Vietnam conflict. It must use its power abroad selectively—committing it only on the basis of a clear definition of vital diplomatic and security interests. But once American power was committed overseas, it ought to be employed decisively. In the process, Washington should insist upon substantial support by its professed allies and friends in the international community, perhaps as a price for continued American aid to them.[14]

Such neoisolationist sentiments were of course well known to officials of the Nixon Administration. To neoisolationist groups, the Nixon Doctrine said in effect: after the Vietnam War, the United States will continue to be a superpower, with global responsibilities; yet it will no longer attempt to serve as the "policeman of the world"; its overseas commitments will be reexamined and will be reduced to those that are truly essential for the security and well-being of the United States. Far from signifying a reversion to isolationism in fact, in some respects the Nixon Doctrine did the opposite. For example, it extended the protection of America's nuclear shield to an unspecified list of nonaligned countries that might face a nuclear threat to their security.

2. In the light of the Vietnam War experience, President Nixon believed it essential to reaffirm the basic continuity of American foreign policy. By withdrawing from Southeast Asia, the United States had not abandoned the containment policy or other goals of post–World War II American diplomacy. Insofar as Vietnam represented a failure of American diplomacy, it signified Washington's failure or inability to apply the containment strategy *effectively.* As Earl C. Ravenal explained, the Nixon Doctrine could be construed as an effort "to enable the United States to do essentially as much in the world as before, but with an economy of means, a fairer distribution of burdens, and a more rational allocation of tasks among allies."[15]

After Vietnam, it was perhaps essential to underscore the continuity of American foreign policy in Asia. As explained at length in Chapter 2, America's ties with Asia were established in the eighteenth century; and the Open Door policy toward China served as one of America's

14. See the author's more extensive treatment in *ibid.,* 214–53.
15. Earl C. Ravenal, "Nixon's Challenge to Carter," *Foreign Policy,* XXIX (Winter, 1977–78), 37.

historic foreign policy principles. In essence, the Nixon Doctrine stated that, although the United States might withdraw its forces from Southeast Asia, it remained an "Asian power," with basic security and diplomatic interests in the region. Thus, Secretary of State William Rogers reaffirmed "the permanence of American foreign policy interests in the well-being and security of Asia and the Pacific. We are a Pacific power, and we intend to remain so. We have every intention of remaining constant to our commitments in Asia."[16] Indicative of Asia's importance for the United States was the fact that perhaps the Nixon Administration's most notable foreign policy achievement— the "normalization" of relations between the United States and the People's Republic of China (PRC)—took place in that region.

During the Nixon Administration and even earlier, some commentators distinguished between the role of the United States as an "Asian power" and as a "Pacific power." Except for General MacArthur's dictum that the United States should never fight a "land war" on the Asian continent, this distinction had never been very clearly delineated. (Even after the Vietnam conflict, for example, the United States was still prepared to defend the security of South Korea, using its own troops for that purpose.) To some minds, the notion of the United States as a "Pacific power" meant primarily that America should adopt a maritime strategy for Asian defense, based mainly upon naval and air supremacy in Asian waters. Endangered Asian countries would in turn furnish the bulk of the manpower required for regional security.[17] Yet as our discussion of the Carter Doctrine in Chapter 8 makes clear, naval and air power require bases and depots, which must be defended; and this defense can seldom be carried out successfully without ground forces.

The ensuing normalization in Sino-American relations signified that the United States remained deeply involved in Asian affairs. By the early 1980s (as the two countries were drawing closer to each other militarily and economically), the entente that was emerging between them had become a foundation stone of America's Asian and global policy.

16. See Rogers' "Address Before the National Press Club, Canberra, Australia," *Department of State Bulletin*, LXI (September 7, 1969), 178–81.

17. See, for example, the article by former Chief of Naval Operations Adm. Arleigh A. Burke, in New York *Times*, March 2, 1971. The idea that the Nixon Doctrine would

3. The United States, many Americans believed the Vietnam War taught, must assume international responsibilities in conformity with its own interests and commensurate with its resources. As the Nixon-Kissinger team evaluated the problem, too often in the recent past the United States had merely "reacted" to crises abroad, particularly those believed to be Communist-instigated. By a process of what one commentator called "creeping involvements"—and other students of postwar diplomacy labeled "incrementalism"—the United States found itself burdened with an ever growing list of overseas commitments, many of which seemed peripheral to its own interests.[18] One antidote for this kind of incremental inflation in the nation's diplomatic responsibilities was offered by the Nixon Doctrine—a key concept of which was that hereafter, the United States would scrutinize the nation's global commitments more carefully and would assume only those dictated by America's security and diplomatic interests.

4. The Vietnam War had demonstrated that America's power to achieve its external goals was limited, and any reformulation of American foreign policy had to reflect this reality. A transcendent reality of the Vietnam conflict was the fact that one of the world's superpowers—possessing a nuclear arsenal capable of devastating the planet—had been defeated by one of the smallest and weakest countries on the globe. Few facts more dramatically underscored the changing nature of the international system since World War II than this paradoxical event. To paraphrase an analysis of recent American diplomacy, Gulliver had been rendered immobile and impotent by the Communist Lilliputians of Southeast Asia. The United States, said Sen. J. William Fulbright, was now a "crippled giant," whose power was in eclipse throughout the world. President Nixon himself publicly speculated about whether the United States was becoming a "pitiful, helpless giant" abroad.[19] The Soviet Union had attained nuclear parity with the

---

make America mainly a "Pacific power" is also explained in Alastair Buchan, "The Indochina War and World Politics," *Foreign Affairs*, LIII (July, 1975), 638–50.

18. Roger Hilsman, *To Move a Nation: The Politics of Foreign Policy in the Administration of John F. Kennedy* (Garden City, N.Y.: Doubleday, 1967), 548–49. The term "creeping involvements" is employed by Max Frankel in New York *Times*, August 3, 1969.

19. Stanley Hoffmann, *Gulliver's Troubles, or the Setting of American Foreign Policy* (New York: McGraw-Hill, 1968); J. William Fulbright, *The Crippled Giant: American Foreign Policy and Its Domestic Consequences* (New York: Random House, 1972). This

United States, and it was in the process of acquiring naval superiority over America in some categories of seapower. In Europe, NATO military forces found themselves confronting a progressively more formidable Communist adversary. An awareness of such realities led President Nixon to declare in his 1971 report to Congress on American foreign policy: "No nation has the wisdom, and the understanding, and the energy required to act wisely on all problems, at all times, in every part of the world."

Implicit in the Nixon Doctrine was a crucial distinction which in the past Americans had too often overlooked: the difference between possessing vast power and possessing infinite power. In the post–Vietnam War era, Secretary of State Rogers declared, "the United States must play a large and active role in world affairs"; yet it should not seek "a predominant one."[20] If the United States remained a superpower, the Vietnam experience demonstrated convincingly that it was not omnipotent. The limitations surrounding the use of American power in the future are the common theme of the last three "lessons" of the Vietnam War to be considered.

5. The Vietnam experience compelled Americans to rethink the strategic principles guiding the application of American power overseas. The broad question raised anew by the Vietnam War was the relationship between military force and diplomacy. What contribution did America's growing nuclear arsenal make to achieving foreign policy objectives? What did the Vietnam episode teach Americans regarding the kinds and quantity of "conventional" forces needed by the United States to defend its security and diplomatic interests abroad? A paramount lesson of the Vietnam encounter, an experienced American diplomatic official observed, was that thereafter the United States must use its power with "caution and discrimination in engaging it."[21]

Adherence to this precept in turn dictated two necessary precondi-

---

was also the theme of James Dornan, "The Nixon Doctrine, Strategy and Tripolarity," unpublished paper delivered to the American Political Science Association, New Orleans, September 6, 1973.

20. See the "Introduction" by Secretary of State William Rogers to "United States Foreign Policy, 1969–1970: A Report of the Secretary of State," *Department of State Bulletin*, LXIV (April 5, 1971), 465–66.

21. George W. Ball, "Slogans and Realities," *Foreign Affairs*, XLVII (July, 1969), 634.

tions: the United States must possess a varied military arsenal, capable of serving its foreign policy objectives; and Americans must have a reasonably clear conception of the principles or criteria that would determine the application of national power abroad. Tentative as they might be, the strategic maxims embodied in the Nixon Doctrine were an attempt to supply that need.

6. In part, America's failure in Vietnam could be attributed to the lack of support for its policies among its friends and allies. The outcome in Vietnam, it could reasonably be contended, was the inevitable result of a diplomatic behavior trait highlighted by every doctrine examined in our study: unilateral decision-making by the United States. If isolationist currents were evident in America during and after the Vietnam experience, that fact was not surprising. America had become increasingly "isolated" during the Vietnam conflict. Despite the stated intention of every administration since the Eisenhower period, the conflict had become "America's war" against communism in Asia. With rare exceptions (and the government of South Korea was one), other countries not only were unwilling to contribute to the war effort in Southeast Asia. To the contrary, they became increasingly critical of America's involvement in it. In a word, both at home and abroad America's role in the war lacked "legitimacy": citizens had growing difficulty relating the massive commitment required in Southeast Asia to any worthwhile national purpose.

Understandably, therefore, a keynote of the Nixon Doctrine was the concept of "partnership" between the United States and its allies and friends overseas. In the future, the defense of an endangered country had to become a collective responsibility of the United States and those nations with which it shared common goals. This principle had two important corollaries. One was greater allied participation in decision-making in dealing with issues likely to jeopardize regional or global security. A leading objective of American diplomacy after Vietnam, said President Nixon, was encouraging other countries "to participate fully in the creation of plans and the designing of programs. They must define the nature of their own security and determine the path of their own progress." [22]

The second and related requirement was that America's friends and

22. U.S. Foreign Policy for the 1970s: Building for Peace, 12.

allies assume a larger share of the burden for promoting their own, and regional, security. As President Nixon explained, a central purpose of his doctrine was to create conditions "in which those lands to which we have obligations or in which we have interests, if they are ready to fight a fire, should be able to count on us to furnish the hose and water." [23]

This principle of the Nixon Doctrine received tangible expression in the third strategic maxim which we have already discussed. In the most likely cases of violence (nonnuclear or "limited" war), the nation directly threatened was expected to make a maximum effort to promote its own security, by furnishing the "firemen," or the bulk of the military manpower required for the defense effort. On the assumption that it did so, the United States would largely provide logistical and financial support. With this anticipated allocation of responsibilities, hopefully the United States could avoid another Vietnam-style crisis.

7. The Vietnam episode had impressed policy-makers with certain powerful domestic constraints limiting the application of American power abroad. A dominant purpose of the Nixon Doctrine, as one commentator viewed it, was to make America's foreign commitments consonant with its "domestic capacities." [24] Among its unique features—and no other doctrine of American foreign policy gave significant attention to the problem—was the Nixon Doctrine's emphasis upon the policy-making process in the United States. As the Vietnam conflict had graphically reminded officials of the Johnson and Nixon administrations almost daily, a vital element in American power was the willingness of public and congressional opinion to support the nation's diplomatic undertakings. Perhaps more than any other single cause, the absence of this factor accounted for the Nixon Administration's decision to terminate the Vietnam War.

In the diplomatic reorientation contemplated by the Nixon Doctrine, two specific steps were required to avert the kind of internal divisiveness that had undermined American policy in Southeast Asia. One of these (a subject to which we shall return at a later stage) was to create and maintain a durable public consensus, providing a foundation for American diplomacy after Vietnam. The other prerequisite

23. See Nixon's interview with C. L. Sulzberger, in New York *Times*, March 10, 1971.
24. Dispatch by Robert B. Semple, Jr., New York *Times*, February 28, 1971.

was to expand congressional involvement in foreign policy decision-making.

Antiwar sentiment in the United States of course had many sources, but one of them was a widespread conviction that Congress had largely been excluded from the process of decision-making that led to America's military involvement in Southeast Asia. Correctly or not, on Capitol Hill and among many segments of American opinion, the belief existed that the outcome in Vietnam would have been different if Congress had played a more decisive role in formulating and carrying out American commitments in Southeast Asia. (This viewpoint did not, however, always lead to the same conclusion. Left-wing and liberal critics, for example, believed that Congress would have liquidated the Vietnam War earlier than executive officials. Right-wing and conservative critics were persuaded that a more influential congressional voice would have enhanced the prospect for "victory" in the Vietnam War.)

Accordingly, the Nixon Doctrine placed great emphasis upon creating a new "partnership" between executive and legislative officials in behalf of a unified foreign policy. In the past, said Secretary of State William Rogers, the United States had been prone to "slide into commitments sort of willy-nilly and imperceptibly." Under the Nixon Doctrine, executive officials pledged "to do what we can to work with Congress to see that that doesn't happen." The Nixon Doctrine, therefore, gave encouragement to one of the most conspicuous tendencies in American foreign relations during the 1970s: congressional assertiveness in the foreign policy process. Indeed, it would not exaggerate to say in dealing with some diplomatic questions arising during this period, congressional *dominance* was the rule of American foreign relations.[25]

A second set of factors influencing the Nixon Doctrine arose from the changing nature of the international system. Although these changes were complex and far-reaching, they may be summarized by saying that the international system had evolved from a "bipolar" pattern to an infinitely more complex "multipolar" model.[26] By whatever

25. "Secretary Rogers Interviewed on National Educational Television," 580. For a more detailed analysis of congressional militancy in foreign affairs during the 1970s, see Cecil V. Crabb, Jr., and Pat Holt, *Invitation to Struggle: Congress, the President and Foreign Policy* (Washington, D.C.: Congressional Quarterly Press, 1980).

26. Among students of contemporary international politics, terminology varies

term the new international system was described, the dominant reality perhaps was the growing difficulty encountered by the United States (and often by the Soviet Union, as well) in achieving its foreign policy goals. The American failure in Vietnam symptomized this transition.

For some fifteen years or so after World War II, the United States and the Soviet Union had few rivals; and the Cold War contest between them was the central theme of international politics. The Soviet-American duopoly of world power, however, was eroded by a number of forces, producing a highly pluralistic global system, in which power was increasingly diffused. As time passed, both of the superpowers experienced difficulty imposing their will upon some one hundred "non-aligned" countries throughout the Third World. Within their respective alliance systems (NATO and the Warsaw Pact), the United States and the Soviet Union encountered mounting unwillingness by once compliant allies to accept dictation from the superpowers. Under President Charles de Gaulle, for example, France declared its de facto independence as a member of NATO; behind the Iron Curtain, following the precedent set by Yugoslavia during the late 1940s, Rumania and Poland exhibited growing resistance to Soviet hegemony.

While the term *multipolarity* was widely used to describe the nature of the existing international system, it might more accurately be called "anarchistic." Throughout the world, smaller states resisted efforts by the superpowers to impose a particular ideological system or diplomatic line upon them. Within many Third World societies, in one country after another established governments encountered formidable difficulties in imposing their authority upon their own citizens. Increasingly, international and regional issues defied attempts by any governing authority to solve them. The rising incidence of international terrorism provided a graphic example of this tendency. In the words of the Nixon Doctrine, the emerging international system lacked "order" and was progressively prone to instability and violence.

---

widely concerning the nature of the emerging international system. No single term perhaps accurately describes its complexity. Kissinger once designated it as "bipolar militarily and multipolar politically." This description highlights the fact that on the nuclear strategic level, the two superpowers still have no rivals; but in terms of political and economic influence their power has been severely eroded. Henry Kissinger, "Central Issues of American Foreign Policy," in Kermit Gordon (ed.), *Agenda for the Nation* (Washington, D.C.: Brookings Institution, 1968), 602.

Some elements of order and instability could be identified in an otherwise turbulent international environment. Despite the Vietnam War, the superpowers, for example, were still dedicated to détente and were endeavoring to strengthen it. In general, however, by the early 1970s the international system appeared to be highly unstable—and it was becoming more so with each passing year. The decade of the 1970s, one State Department official predicted, was "not likely to be a placid one." Instead, it would witness "continuing disputes and unforeseen crises in world affairs." The United States must be prepared for "violent upheaval," rather than for "orderly and peaceful change" in many regions of the world.[27] The Nixon Administration, said Secretary of State Rogers, possessed "no panaceas" for the creation of a stable and benign international order.[28]

More specifically, the Nixon Doctrine took account of several destabilizing tendencies in the international system that would likely confront American policy-makers with difficult choices in the years ahead. Despite the existence of détente, Soviet-American arms competition remained intense. New arms limitations were needed between Washington and Moscow, therefore, to curb the arms race. A troublesome issue associated with détente also was the Soviet insistence upon sponsoring and encouraging what the Kremlin called "wars of national liberation," versus the American conviction that such conduct inflamed Soviet-American tensions and jeopardized the preservation of global peace. For American officials, a key requirement of lasting détente was the concept of "linkage"—or the expectation that Moscow's devotion to peace would be demonstrated by its actions in diverse settings, like sub-Saharan Africa, the Middle East, and Southeast Asia. In turn, the Kremlin consistently rejected the concept of linkage as a necessary ingredient of détente.[29]

Growing schisms within the once cohesive Soviet-controlled Com-

27. See the views of Under Secretary of State Richardson, in "Controlling Local Conflicts," 629. Similarly, at a conference of Asian experts early in 1971, the conclusion was reached that there would likely be greater upheaval in many parts of Asia during the 1970s than in the previous decade. New York *Times*, January 13, 1971.

28. See Rogers' "Introduction" to "United States Foreign Policy, 1969–1970," 477; and Under Secretary of State Elliot L. Richardson, "Differing Perceptions of U.S. Foreign Policy," *Department of State Bulletin*, LXII (June 29, 1970), 800–801.

29. "Under Secretary Johnson Interviewed for the Voice of America," *Department of State Bulletin*, LXIII (August 17, 1979), 190; Richardson, "Controlling Local Con-

munist system created possibilities for new patterns of international relationships—most notably, in Sino-American relations. As our discussion in Chapter 2 indicated, for some twenty years after the Communist victory in China, Sino-American relations remained tense and hostile. (The two countries had actually fought each other during the Korean War.) Within the United States, a vocal and politically influential "China Lobby," consisting of supporters of Chiang Kai-shek's regime (that fled to Formosa, or Taiwan) successfully prevented any significant change in American policy toward China. One of the singular features of the Nixon Doctrine, therefore, was its call for a new "dialogue" with the Communist government of China. Nixon's "opening" to China—highlighted by the president's visit to the Chinese mainland early in 1972—was a historic turning point in postwar American diplomacy. From a realpolitik perspective, the United States had finally accepted the outcome of the Chinese civil war; and it was now prepared to take advantage of the opportunities provided by the split between the Soviet Union and Red China. The "normalization" of Sino-American relations was a crucial step in creating a new power balance or "structure for peace" in Asia and perhaps for the world. Implicitly, the Nixon Doctrine recognized the emergence of an independent Communist China—a leading example of what was called "national communism"—and it laid the basis for growing collaboration between Peking and Washington toward a variety of regional and global issues.[30]

The Nixon Doctrine also anticipated an increasingly influential role in Asian affairs by an economically powerful Japan. Next to the United States and the Soviet Union, Japan had emerged as the strongest financial nexus on the globe. For several reasons—the desires of the Japanese people, their vivid memories of the destruction caused by World War II, the provisions of the Japanese constitution prohibiting

flicts," 629; Donald L. Clark, "Soviet Strategy for the Seventies," *Air University Review*, XXII (January–February, 1971), 2–19; New York *Times*, October 20, 1971, February 16, 1972. An informative analysis of détente, focusing upon differing Soviet and American conceptions of it, is Coral Bell, *The Diplomacy of Détente* (New York: St. Martin's Press, 1977).

30. *U.S. Foreign Policy for the 1970s: Building for Peace*, 105–10; *U.S. Foreign Policy for the 1970s: The Emerging Structure of Peace*, 26–38; Henry Kissinger, *White House Years* (Boston: Little, Brown, 1979), 163–95, 684–788, 1049–97.

rearmament—Japan had thus far not played a political and diplomatic role consonant with its growing economic power. Yet by the early 1970s, Tokyo was beginning to exercise greater leadership in Asian affairs—particularly in the direction of encouraging regional organizations and providing assistance to less developed societies. In some measure, the anticipated retrenchment of American power on the Asian scene would be counterbalanced by the assumption of new responsibilities by Japan.[31]

As the Nixon-Kissinger team viewed it, the existing international system exhibited another source of stability and enhanced global security: the steady emergence of regional organizations and institutions. The most prominent example of course was the European Economic Community, or European Community as it came to be called. This organization had contributed significantly to Western Europe's economic prosperity and vitality. Although its regional mechanisms were less advanced, prospects for regional collaboration also appeared favorable in Asia and perhaps in other regions like black Africa. Effective regional organizations, American officials believed, could also relieve the United States of some of its responsibilities for preserving global peace and stability.[32]

Another dimension of the Nixon Doctrine dealt with the problem of the "disarray" and disunity existing within the Western alliance system. Several of the European allies had been highly critical of America's role in the Vietnam War—in part because of this "diversion" of American military forces to Southeast Asia. The Nixon Administration was cognizant that the cohesion of NATO was being tested. On the one hand, under the Nixon Doctrine Washington once more called upon the European allies to assume a larger part of the responsibility for the security of the NATO area. On the other hand, the doctrine also committed American officials to consult the allies more frequently—and at an earlier stage—in the formulation of common Western policies.[33]

31. *U.S. Foreign Policy for the 1970s: Building for Peace*, 103–104.
32. *Ibid.*, 49–55, 98–102; Marshall Green, "A Look at Asian Regionalism," *Department of State Bulletin*, LXI (November 24, 1969), 445–48.
33. For a detailed study of the problems confronting NATO in the late 1960s, see Francis M. Bator, "The Politics of Alliance: The United States and Western Europe," in Gordon (ed.), *Agenda for the Nation*, 335–72.

A third important source of ideas embodied in the Nixon Doctrine consisted of policy antecedents and statements from the diplomatic experience of earlier administrations. As has been true of other diplomatic doctrines in American history (and a prominent example was the Monroe Doctrine), the Nixon Doctrine expressed ideas that had long been familiar to Americans. An outstanding example was the concept of American unilateralism (or what, in the nineteenth century, was sometimes called the "free hand"), reflected in the Nixon Doctrine no less than the others encompassed by our study. Several provisions of the Nixon Doctrine exemplified this idea—such as the notion that, in assuming new global commitments, the United States would be guided by its own national interests. In its strategic aspects also, the Nixon Doctrine stated that Washington would determine whether the survival of a given nation coincided with American interests.[34] (Admittedly, the Nixon Doctrine's simultaneous plea for "partnership" with the allies, and for greater "community" within the Western Hemisphere, collided with the theme of unilateralism. This fact added to prevailing confusion about the essential meaning of the Nixon Doctrine.)

Another evident motif in the Nixon Doctrine was the idea of maximum "self-help" by countries facing external threats. This idea had been foreshadowed as early as 1954 when, in a letter to the government of South Vietnam on October 25, President Dwight D. Eisenhower had predicated American assistance upon the "performance" of the government of South Vietnam in meeting the country's internal and external needs.[35] Theoretically, throughout the Vietnam War, the United States was merely "assisting" South Vietnam to maintain its independence. Concerning the threat to South Vietnam, President John F. Kennedy had said, "It is their war. They are the ones who have to win it or lose it. We can help them, we can give them equipment, we can send our men out there as advisers, but they have to win it, the people of Vietnam."

34. For a more complete discussion of unilateralism as a conspicuous element in traditional American isolationist thought, see Crabb, *Policy-Makers and Critics*, 1–34. For a critique of the idea as it relates to the Nixon Doctrine, see George Ball, *Diplomacy for a Crowded World: An American Foreign Policy* (Boston: Atlantic-Little, Brown, 1976), 14.

35. *Public Papers of the Presidents of the United States: Dwight D. Eisenhower* (Washington, D.C.: Government Printing Office, 1960), 305–306.

On several occasions also, Kennedy had cautioned the people about what was sometimes called "the illusion of American omnipotence." Late in 1961, for example, Kennedy declared, "We must face the fact that the United States is neither omnipotent nor omniscient . . . that we cannot impose our will upon the other 94 percent of mankind— that we cannot right every wrong or reverse each adversity—and that therefore there cannot be an American solution to every world problem." [36]

Kennedy's successor, President Lyndon B. Johnson, also contributed ideas that were reflected in the Nixon Doctrine. Following a tour of Asia in the spring of 1961, Johnson stated his conclusions on the problem of Asian security by saying, "These [Asian] nations cannot be saved by United States help alone. To the extent the Southeast Asian nations are prepared to take the necessary measures to make our aid effective, we can be—and must be—unstinting in our assistance." [37]

The Nixon Doctrine also owed much to the thinking of Sen. Mike Mansfield (Democrat from Montana). Mansfield was Democratic Majority Leader and a member of the Senate Foreign Relations Committee, who had long been active in dealing with foreign policy issues. Following a trip through Asia in August, 1969, Mansfield submitted a report to the committee containing a number of ideas and policy recommendations later embodied in the Nixon Doctrine. Mansfield was genuinely troubled about large-scale American military buildups in Asia and other regions. To his mind, these forces constituted an "indigestible alien presence" resented by, and disruptive for, indigenous societies. Within Asia, Mansfield believed that the principal danger facing most governments was insurgency, rather than external aggression, and he believed this challenge had to be met mainly by the countries most directly affected. Mansfield doubted that the United States had ever been "an Asian power"; but it was a "Pacific power," with vital

36. Theodore C. Sorensen, *Kennedy* (New York: Harper and Row, 1965), 511, 653–54, 658–59. For an even earlier critical analysis of American foreign policy in this vein, see D. W. Brogan, "The Illusion of American Omnipotence," *Harper's*, CCV (December, 1952), 21–28.

37. John W. Dower, "Asia and the Nixon Doctrine: The New Face of Empire," in Virginia Brodline and Mark Selden (eds.), *Open Secret: The Kissinger-Nixon Doctrine in Asia* (New York: Harper and Row, 1972), 140. President Johnson's ideas on Asian regionalism are cited in Bernard K. Gordon, *Toward Disengagement in Asia: A Strategy for American Foreign Policy* (Englewood Cliffs, N.J.: Prentice-Hall, 1969), 68.

interests in such locales as Hawaii, the Aleutian Islands, and many other islands and bases in the Pacific Ocean area. In the future, America should practice "restrained and judicious participation, as one Pacific nation among several" in the region's peaceful development.[38]

Not unexpectedly, President Nixon's diplomatic doctrine also reflected numerous ideas which he had expressed on the subject of American foreign and defense policy before entering the White House. As early as 1953, Nixon had called upon Japan, for example, to assume a larger proportionate share of the burden for Asian security. In an article in *Foreign Affairs* late in 1967, Nixon propounded several ideas that were subsequently incorporated into his doctrine.[39] There, he cautioned Americans about again lapsing into isolationist attitudes as a reaction to the nation's involvement in the Vietnam War; he called for a "collective effort" to deal with Communist expansionism and other external threats to global peace and security; he observed that a country's ability to preserve its independence ultimately rested upon a foundation of "economic and political stability"; and he asserted that governments throughout the world must "keep pace with change," thereby demonstrating that evolutionary, rather than revolutionary, methods were capable of solving their problems.

In this article, Nixon plainly foreshadowed perhaps his major diplomatic accomplishment: the "normalization" of relations between the United States and Communist China. Although Nixon continued to believe that a powerful and heavily armed China posed a danger to the security of certain Asian countries, he called upon Americans to accept "the reality" of a Communist regime in China. The objective of American policy should be to end the country's "angry isolation" and to restore China to "the world community," provided it does not serve "as the epicenter of world revolution."

The Issuance of the Nixon Doctrine

A distinctive feature of the Nixon Doctrine was the circumstances surrounding its issuance. A fact setting it apart from the other doctrines

38. The text of Mansfield's report is contained in U.S. Congress, Senate, Committee on Foreign Relations, Report by Senator Mike Mansfield on *Perspective on Asia: The New U.S. Doctrine and Southeast Asia*, 91st Cong., 1st Sess., 1969.

39. Dower, "Asia and the Nixon Doctrine: The New Face of Empire," 144–45; Richard M. Nixon, "Asia After Viet Nam," *Foreign Affairs*, XLVI (October, 1967), 111–26.

analyzed in our study is that it was not issued in response to a foreign crisis. Nor was it presented to the nation in the form of a television address or speech by the president to the assembled Congress. Instead, as one report expressed it, Nixon "announced the [Nixon Doctrine] in a discursive news conference on an island in the Pacific and under the noncommittal terms that his statements could not be quoted directly."[40]

At the time, Nixon's "off-the-record" statements on the island of Guam, on July 25, 1969, appeared to be an insignificant interlude in his trip to Rumania and Asia.[41] Over the months that followed, however, Nixon's "Guam Doctrine" was refined and elaborated—receiving its most comprehensive expression in President Nixon's two reports to Congress on American foreign policy in 1971 and 1972. On Guam, Nixon had said that in responding to future Asian crises, "the United States is going to encourage and has a right to expect that this problem will be increasingly handled by, and the responsibility for it taken by, the Asian nations themselves." Adherence to this principle would enable the United States to avoid "another Vietnam." A few months later, Nixon indicated that while his Guam Doctrine was intended to apply to Asian affairs, its principle had global application for American foreign policy.[42]

In contrast to President James Monroe (who was not conscious of having promulgated a major doctrine of American foreign policy), President Nixon himself designated his guidelines a *doctrine* of American diplomacy; he viewed it as a kind of monument to his diplomatic endeavors; he alluded to it repeatedly in his public statements; and the Nixon foreign policy team diligently publicized the president's new set of diplomatic principles. At the same time, the president and his advisers acknowledged that the Nixon Doctrine was in some respects formative, vague, and ambiguous. Nixon described it as exemplifying more of a "philosophic attitude" toward foreign relations, than a

40. Dispatch by John W. Finney, New York *Times*, January 11, 1970.
41. For the text of Nixon's remarks to the press on Guam, see *Public Papers of the Presidents of the United States: Richard Nixon, 1969* (Washington, D.C.: Government Printing Office, 1971), 544–56.
42. The idea that the Nixon Doctrine was meant to have global application was announced publicly by Sen. James B. Pearson (Republican of Kansas), following his meeting with President Nixon late in 1969. Dispatch by John W. Finney, New York *Times*, January 11, 1970.

finished and detailed "design" for American foreign policy. Or, as one official explained to the House Foreign Affairs Committee, the doctrine would be "applied in different forms to different countries and different areas of the world."[43] Even if Richard M. Nixon had completed a normal presidential term, it seems safe to predict, much of the vagueness and imprecision surrounding his foreign policy declaration would have been left unresolved.

The Formulation of the Nixon Doctrine

The Nixon Doctrine was appropriately named. As our treatment has indicated, President Nixon himself played a crucial role in its formulation and issuance. Nixon was keenly interested in foreign affairs—and he left no doubt that he would be actively involved in the foreign policy process. One of his first acts as chief executive was to direct that his national security adviser undertake a complete "inventory" of American policy overseas, focusing upon its strengths and weaknesses; and Kissinger was expected to submit recommendations for its improvement. Nixon's statement on Guam on July 25, 1969—followed by the more detailed reports to Congress early in 1971 and 1972—stemmed from Kissinger's analysis and recommendations. The idea for these reports apparently originated in the State Department. Kissinger's staff, however, "preempted" the idea and prepared a lengthy draft version for the president's approval. It was Nixon's practice personally to edit and revise the reports before they were submitted to the House and Senate.[44]

Under the Nixon Administration, the "decline of the State Department"—a process that began with the Franklin Roosevelt Administration—reached its nadir. This tendency was epitomized by the crucial role in foreign policy decision-making played by Henry Kissinger, who headed the president's White House staff for foreign policy and defense questions. Kissinger's influence upon the diplomacy of the Nixon Administration could hardly be exaggerated. On foreign policy

43. Brzezinski, "Half Past Nixon," 4; *U.S. Foreign Policy for the 1970s: Building for Peace*, 20; U.S. Congress, House, Committee on Foreign Affairs, *To Amend the Foreign Assistance Act of 1961*, 91st Cong., 2nd Sess., 1970, p. 109.

44. Rowland Evans, Jr., and Robert D. Novak, *Nixon in the White House: The Frustration of Power* (New York: Random House, 1971), 77–78; Graubard, *Kissinger: Portrait of a Mind*, 271; dispatch by Terence Smith, New York *Times*, January 18, 1971; dispatch by Robert B. Semple, Jr., New York *Times*, February 28, 1971.

issues, Kissinger's role was pervasive and unrivaled—an outcome assured in part by the fact that he spent more time in consultation with the president than any other official in the executive branch.

Before entering the White House, Nixon had known and respected Kissinger's approach to foreign affairs. While the two men sometimes differed, particularly in the manner in which they verbalized and explained diplomatic issues, their thought converged at many key points. Little evidence exists that Kissinger "imposed" his viewpoints upon an unwilling superior. Instead, Nixon accepted Kissinger's policy proposals mainly because he agreed with them and because Kissinger's thinking coincided with his own.[45] Among his other innovations, Nixon directed that new institutional mechanisms be established to furnish the president with a clear set of foreign policy "options." The elaborate National Security Council staff, headed by Kissinger, was designed to supply that need. From 8 to 12 members during the Truman Administration, the NSC staff was expanded to some 150 advisers in the Nixon-Kissinger era.[46]

Ironically, some of the provisions of the Nixon Doctrine reflected mounting public and congressional dissatisfaction with certain practices identified with the Nixon-Kissinger foreign policy team. One of Kissinger's administrative principles, for example, was "management of information"—a concept that many critics believed was tantamount to monopoly of information. Kissinger also advocated (and often practiced) maximum secrecy in the decision-making process, in order to prevent "sabotage" of forthcoming policies by an unsympathetic bureaucracy in the State Department or other executive agencies. Moreover, the Nixon White House frequently invoked the claim of "executive privilege" to preserve the confidential nature of its deliberations from scrutiny by Congress and the news media.[47] Kissinger also distinguished between the stages of policy *formulation* and *implementation*. To his mind, the former was a highly creative undertak-

45. The coincidence between his views and Kissinger's is emphasized by Nixon in his *Memoirs*, 340–42.
46. John P. Leacacos, "Kissinger's Apparat," *Foreign Policy*, V (Winter, 1971–72), 3–28.
47. The constitutional principle of "executive privilege," first invoked by President Washington in 1794, has repeatedly been relied upon by chief executives to protect the confidentiality of information and documents, disclosure of which would damage the nation's diplomatic interests. While Congress has from time to time challenged the

ing, requiring the kind of historical insight, keen intelligence, and training his own background exemplified. The latter, however, was the province of "bureaucrats"—and Kissinger's disdain for those in the State Department and elsewhere was legendary. Their impact upon the policy process tended to be stultifying and "smothering" and generally inimical to the emergence of effective diplomatic decisions. Such diplomatic creativity, in Kissinger's view, was confined to the White House under the Nixon Administration, while the State Department was left to serve in the role of policy "technician" which carried out diplomatic designs given to it.[48]

As a normal operating procedure, under the Nixon Administration foreign policy decisions were arrived at after a complex series of steps, in which Kissinger supervised preliminary discussions and the formulation of diplomatic options. These were considered by the National Security Council, where they were further refined and identified for the president. After he received this report, President Nixon frequently asked Kissinger for his own recommendations. In the end of course, as influential as Kissinger's role may have been, the resulting policy decision was President Nixon's.[49]

As our treatment has suggested, the influence of the secretary of state and of the State Department bureaucracy upon policy formulation during the Nixon-Kissinger era was limited—reaching perhaps its lowest point in recent history. Nixon was not the first modern chief executive to distrust the State Department and to bypass it in making key diplomatic decisions. President Kennedy had become disillusioned with State Department advice; and President Johnson had relied more

---

validity of this idea, in practice it recognized the president's unique prerogatives in the foreign policy field and the necessity to preserve the confidentiality of the decision-making process. For more detailed discussion, see Louis Henkin, *Foreign Affairs and the Constitution* (Mineola, N.Y.: Foundation Press, 1972), 112 and supporting documentation.

48. For more detailed analysis of Kissinger's administrative principles and procedures, see Leacacos, "Kissinger's Apparat," 3–28; Vincent Davis, "Henry Kissinger and Bureaucratic Politics: Some Disconnected Observations," unpublished paper presented to the Southern Regional Division of the International Studies Association, Columbia, S.C., October 28, 1977; John G. Stoessinger, *Henry Kissinger: The Anguish of Power* (New York: W. W. Norton, 1976), 211; and C. Y. Lin (ed.), *Kissinger's Diplomacy* (Brunswick, Ohio: King's Court Communications, 1975), 7.

49. Dispatch by James Reston, New York *Times*, March 3, 1971.

heavily upon the advice of Secretary of Defense Robert McNamara than upon the views of Secretary of State Dean Rusk in prosecuting the Vietnam War. The reasons for what is sometimes called the "decline" of the State Department are too numerous and complex to examine here. It must suffice to say that most of them were still present—and some of them had become even more acute—when Richard M. Nixon entered the White House.[50] The elaborate White House mechanism headed by Henry Kissinger that largely dominated the foreign policy process during the Nixon years stemmed in no small measure from the president's lack of confidence in the State Department (many of whose members were believed by pro-Nixon groups to represent the "liberal" eastern establishment).

The State Department's influence in policy formulation was not enhanced by Nixon's appointment of William P. Rogers—whose experience had been primarily in the legal field—as secretary of state. With rare exceptions, Rogers was unable to make the State Department's voice decisive. President Nixon observed that (to Rogers' "credit") in many cases, "his primary concern was simply to be kept informed of what was going on" in foreign affairs![51] Under Rogers, the State Department largely performed the role of policy "technician" envisioned by Kissinger. Some commentators believed that Nixon had deliberately chosen a "weak" secretary of state—in order to leave the Nixon-Kissinger White House team in a largely unchallenged position in managing foreign relations.

Under these conditions, it is not surprising that the State Department's role in the formulation and issuance of the Nixon Doctrine was minimal. State Department officials, for example, did not learn of President Nixon's forthcoming trip to Asia (where the initial "Guam Doctrine" was enunciated) until an hour before the White House announced the trip publicly. The State Department, therefore, presumably had no advanced knowledge that a major statement on American foreign policy—laying the basis for the later issuance of the more comprehensive Nixon Doctrine—was forthcoming. Similarly, although State Department officials were subsequently asked to contrib-

50. Many of the problems weakening the influence of the State Department in the modern period are discussed more fully in Cecil V. Crabb, Jr., *American Foreign Policy in the Nuclear Age* (3rd ed.; New York: Harper and Row, 1972), 65–73.
51. Nixon, *Memoirs*, 433.

ute ideas and recommendations for inclusion in the president's annual reports to Congress on American foreign policy, the preparation of the document was the responsibility of Henry Kissinger's office. When President Nixon signed the first report, Kissinger alone represented the foreign policy establishment; State Department officials were conspicuously absent.[52]

The contribution of the Department of Defense to the Nixon Doctrine was also limited. Some ideas embodied in the doctrine—such as the concept of "Vietnamization," associated with Secretary of Defense Melvin Laird—reflected the viewpoints of the Pentagon. As we have seen, the Nixon Doctrine could be interpreted as an effort to make Vietnamization a global principle of American foreign policy.

Terms like "partnership" and "new directions" in American diplomacy were employed frequently in the Nixon Doctrine—in part perhaps out of realization by the Nixon White House that they were urgently needed in a vital dimension of foreign policy. This was the sphere of executive-legislative relations, which had deteriorated badly during the Johnson Administration and (in the foreign policy field, which is our primary concern) became marked by even more tension and lack of cooperation during the Nixon-Kissinger era. Almost plaintively, the Nixon Doctrine thus called for a new "partnership" between the White House and Capitol Hill in dealing with external problems: "This partnership at home must include the advice and support of the Congress. Charged with constitutional responsibilities in foreign policy, the Congress can give perspective to the national debate and serve as a bridge between the Executive and the people."[53]

The Nixon Administration not only inherited a legacy of acrimonious executive-legislative relations from its predecessor. In addition, Richard M. Nixon was the first chief executive since 1848 who had to deal with a Congress controlled by the opposition party (in 1969, there were 242 Democrats and 190 Republicans in the House, and 57 Democrats and 43 Republicans in the Senate). Moreover, most of President Nixon's aides were new, inexperienced in dealing with Congress, and for the most part unknown to the members of the

52. Evans and Novak, *Nixon in the White House*, 97; dispatch by Terence Smith, New York *Times*, January 18, 1971; dispatch by Robert B. Semple, Jr., New York *Times*, February 28, 1971.
53. *U.S. Foreign Policy for the 1970s: Building for Peace*, 234.

House and Senate.[54] On Capitol Hill, legislators were in an increasingly militant mood. They were disaffected with the kind of executive leadership that had produced the Vietnam War; they were vocally apprehensive about the emergence of the "imperial presidency"; and they were determined to assert Congress' prerogatives forcefully in the foreign policy field.

After the usual honeymoon period most new presidents enjoy in their relations with Congress, the Nixon Administration soon encountered outspoken opposition to its diplomatic behavior from the House and Senate. As time passed, legislators complained that the White House was "withholding" information from them (which in a number of instances was true); that Henry Kissinger and other influential foreign policy officials were too often "unavailable" for questioning by congressional committee, and when they did appear, their answers to questions by members of the House and Senate were evasive and uninformative.[55] (Secretary of State William Rogers was more overtly interested in maintaining harmonious executive-legislative relations on foreign policy questions. But legislators lamented that Rogers was often uninformed about the administration's external policies himself and was in no position, therefore, to enlighten Congress about them.)

To no insignificant degree, the Nixon Administration's efforts to create and maintain "bipartisan" cooperation in foreign affairs were impeded by adverse developments within the legislative branch. Congress itself was becoming increasingly disunified and fragmented—both as regards relations between the House and Senate, and as regards the internal deliberations of each chamber. As experience during and after the Nixon Administration demonstrated, at the very time Congress was demanding an "equal voice" in the foreign policy process, its ability to engage in unified and effective decision-making was rapidly declining. By the early 1970s, for example, nearly all major committees within the House and Senate had some jurisdiction over one or more foreign policy issues; and neither during the Nixon period nor afterward were they able to concert their activities in behalf of carefully considered, coordinated measures serving the diplomatic interests of the United States.[56]

54. Evans and Novak, *Nixon in the White House*, 104.
55. John Lehman, *The Executive, Congress, and Foreign Policy: Studies of the Nixon Administration* (New York: Praeger, 1976), 162–64.
56. Crabb and Holt, *Invitation to Struggle*, 191–99.

This combination of factors—the Nixon White House's "fear" of Congress, and its natural tendency to maintain secrecy about its foreign policy decisions, in conjunction with Congress' determination to play a more decisive role in the foreign policy process—usually produced the opposite of "partnership" in executive-legislative relations. No legislator, for example, was invited to accompany President Nixon on his trip to Asia, where the Nixon Doctrine was initially issued. After this trip, upon his return to the United States Nixon briefed a group of some twenty-two legislators on the main points included in his new doctrine. Statements during and after this meeting indicated widespread legislative approval of its basic ideas, and this fact encouraged Nixon to amplify its meaning and to invoke it publicly.[57]

Some elements in the Nixon-Kissinger foreign policy blueprint for the post–Vietnam War era elicited evident legislative approval. Senator Fulbright, for example, commended the Nixon White House for its nonintervention in a crisis between Jordan and Syria in September, 1970. On August 2, 1971, the Senate also passed a resolution praising President Nixon for his "Journey for Peace" to Communist China, inaugurating a new era in Sino-American relations. Congress was also receptive to providing funds for the Asian Development Bank, thereby supporting the Nixon Doctrine's goal of encouraging regional institutions. In addition, Congress on more than one occasion defeated efforts by Democratic critics of Nixon's diplomacy to reduce American armed forces stationed in Western Europe. Even on the question of the Vietnam War—in the face of mounting legislative and popular disaffection with America's involvement in it—Congress repeatedly refused to require the evacuation of American forces from the area before the deadline (August 15, 1973) set by the White House for their evacuation.[58] As always, legislators hesitated to substitute their judgments for those of the commander-in-chief in making decisions affecting the safety of American forces in a combat situation.

Despite such examples, on balance the Nixon-Kissinger team failed to develop the kind of "partnership" with Congress envisioned by the

57. Dispatch by Richard Halloran, New York *Times*, August 5, 1969; dispatch by John W. Finney, New York *Times*, January 11, 1970.
58. Evans and Novak, *Nixon in the White House*, 265–66; U.S. Congress, House, Committee on Foreign Affairs, *U.S. Foreign Policy for the 1970s: A Comparative Analysis of the President's 1972 Foreign Policy Report to Congress*, 92nd Cong., 2nd Sess., 1972, pp. 15, 34; *Congressional Quarterly Almanac: 1973*, pp. 793–94, 803–11.

Nixon Doctrine—a result that was guaranteed by the Watergate scandal that discredited the Nixon Administration. On foreign policy issues, legislators complained about the "unavailability" of key Nixon advisers; about the lack of information supplied to Congress on major decisions; and about the tendency of the White House to rely upon "executive privilege" to keep legislators in the dark about significant diplomatic questions. On substantive issues, sentiment in the House and Senate was hostile to the proposed renegotiation of a new Panama Canal Treaty (eventually concluded under the Carter Administration). The House of Representatives refused to approve a White House proposal calling for American military and economic assistance to Greece and Pakistan; nor would the Senate accept an executive agreement providing for American military bases in Portugal and Bahrain. On July 29, 1971, the Senate took the unprecedented step of suspending all American overseas military aid, as a graphic protest against the administration's refusal to provide information desired by Congress.[59]

Other examples of congressional dissatisfaction with the Nixon Administration's handling of foreign affairs might be cited. The most graphic symbol of legislative disaffection, however, was the War Powers Resolution. The War Powers Resolution (or "War Powers Act," as it was often called) was the culmination of several years of efforts by Congress to limit the president's power to commit American armed forces abroad. After lengthy investigation and debate, it was initially passed by the House on July 18, 1973, by a vote of 244–170, and by the Senate two days later, by a vote of 72–18. After it was vetoed by President Nixon, the House and Senate voted on November 7, 1973, to override the president's veto, and it thus became law on that date. The War Powers Resolution was one of the most far-reaching developments in American postwar foreign policy, a forceful assertion of congressional influence in the diplomatic field. Its passage (by a two-thirds vote of the House and Senate) over the Nixon White House's outspoken opposition testified to the pervasive determination of legislators to become a potent force in foreign policy decision-making.[60]

59. *Congressional Quarterly Almanac: 1973*, p. 793; House Foreign Affairs Committee, *U.S. Foreign Policy for the 1970s*, 20, 38–41; dispatch by John W. Finney, New York *Times*, August 1, 1970; dispatch by Marjorie Hunter, New York *Times*, September 1, 1971.

60. For a detailed analysis of the resolution (PL 93-148), see the *Congressional Quarterly Almanac: 1973*, pp. 2024–25, 2740–43, 2855–56, 2985–86. Its text may

Space is not available to undertake a detailed analysis of the provisions and implications of the War Powers Resolution. It suffices to make a few brief observations about the measure. The resolution's basic intent was to limit the powers of the president to employ the armed forces abroad without explicit legislative authority. Its overriding purpose was to prevent "another Vietnam," whereby an incumbent chief executive relied upon his own "inherent" powers to commit American troops to combat overseas and discovered legislative approval for this action in what President Lyndon B. Johnson called "functional equivalents" for a declaration of war (such as Congress' approval of the national defense budget). According to this resolution, while the president might use the armed forces to meet temporary emergencies abroad, in any long-term commitment of American forces overseas, the White House was required to have congressional authorization; without it, American forces would have to be withdrawn from an area of existing or potential hostilities.[61]

As an unprecedented measure in American constitutional history, the War Powers Resolution encountered a mixed reception from authorities on the American Constitution. Some believed it was a lawful exercise of congressional power and was long overdue; others were skeptical of it, believing that (as President Nixon contended) it invaded the president's constitutional and inherent powers, inhibiting him from responding decisively to threats to national security. Nixon and later presidents cited the War Powers Resolution as one of a number of steps Congress took during the 1970s to cripple the chief executive's influence in the foreign policy process—to the detriment of America's diplomatic and security interests.

Insufficient time has elapsed for the full significance of the resolution to be determined in the light of experience. For our purposes, the primary meaning of the measure seems to have been that the Nixon Administration had failed to achieve its proclaimed goal of "partnership" with Congress in the foreign policy field. In retrospect, passage of the War Powers Resolution may have marked the high tide of con-

---

be found in *U.S. Statutes at Large* (Washington, D.C.: Government Printing Office, 1974), LXXXVII, 555–59.

61. The rationale and provisions of the War Powers Resolution are analyzed more fully in Crabb and Holt, *Invitation to Struggle*, 46–47, 123–28.

gressional assertiveness in the foreign policy process in recent years. As we shall see more fully in Chapter 8, for example, little or no attention was devoted to the War Powers Resolution in efforts by the Carter and Reagan administrations to augment American military power in the Persian Gulf area.

A detailed study of executive-legislative relations during the Nixon Administration concluded that little or no consensus existed between the two branches of government in dealing with foreign policy questions. Similarly, an analysis of the Nixon Doctrine prepared for the House Foreign Affairs Committee in 1972 found that the Nixon Administration had not "seriously addressed" the problem of what had to be done to create and maintain a durable "partnership" between executive and legislative officials in foreign affairs.[62]

Before becoming President Nixon's chief foreign policy adviser, Kissinger had observed, "The acid test of a [foreign] policy is its ability to obtain domestic support." On several occasions, Nixon stated that a successful foreign policy had to be in the "mainstream" of American public opinion.[63] The prevailing context of American public opinion during the late 1960s and early 1970s unquestionably influenced the issuance and content of the Nixon Doctrine. On more than one occasion, President Nixon asserted—and the evidence supported his contention—that the American people demanded retrenchment in the nation's overseas activities. Nixon and his advisers recognized that public support for national policies is indispensable for their success and the dominant public mood of Americans favored contraction in the nation's overseas obligations.

Evidence that the Nixon Doctrine enjoyed broad public support was available on all sides. During the period 1969–1972, for example, several public opinion polls confirmed the fact that upwards of three-fourths of the American people wanted their leaders to concentrate on domestic, rather than external, problems. During the period 1964–1975, there was a sharp drop—from 65 to 45 percent—in the number of Americans categorizing themselves as "internationalists"; conversely, the number describing themselves as "isolationists" rose from

62. Lehman, The Executive, Congress, and Foreign Policy, 228–35; House Foreign Affairs Committee, U.S. Foreign Policy for the 1970s, 96.

63. Lin (ed.), Kissinger's Diplomacy, 37; Louis Harris, The Anguish of Change (New York: W. W. Norton, 1973), 17–18, 30.

8 to 20 percent.[64] Among the nation's youth especially, neoisolationist sentiments were strong. The idea that America had a "world mission" to challenge communism globally was widely being questioned. Moreover, a majority of Americans was persuaded that the influence and prestige of the United States abroad was declining rapidly, whereas Soviet and Chinese influence was perceived as increasing.[65]

Polls also showed that the dominant concerns of the American people related overwhelmingly to internal problems. The general pattern in such poll findings was that Americans favored increased spending to meet internal needs and decreased spending on programs related to foreign affairs and national security.[66] Popular support for foreign aid was also dropping: by 1972, only 40 percent of the people advocated American assistance to other countries, while 55 percent opposed the idea.[67] Studies of public opinion also found declining popular support for American military interventionism abroad. It came as no surprise perhaps to discover that citizens were unwilling to use American armed forces to defend countries like Thailand, India, and Yugoslavia. But in the light of the Vietnam War experience, polls found that a majority of Americans now had reservations about defense commitments to Japan, Israel, Brazil—and even the NATO allies.[68]

Such evidence should not be interpreted to mean, however, that in the post–Vietnam War era the American people were reverting to the historic position of isolationism in foreign affairs. In the words of one

64. William Watts and Lloyd A. Free (eds.), *State of the Nation* (New York: Universe Books, 1973), 20; dispatch by William Watts, New York *Times*, September 19, 1975.

65. Our discussion of prevailing public attitudes toward foreign affairs draws heavily upon the evidence presented in Watts and Free (eds.), *State of the Nation*, 137–39, 202–204, and their *State of the Nation—1974* (Washington, D.C.: Universe Books, 1974), 211–14; and James A. Johnson, "The New Generation of Isolationists," *Foreign Affairs*, XLIX (October, 1970), 136–47.

66. *Newsweek*, October 6, 1969, p. 46.

67. Barry B. Hughes, *The Domestic Context of American Foreign Policy* (San Francisco: W. H. Freeman, 1978), 33; Richard E. Dawson, *Public Opinion and Contemporary Disarray* (New York: Harper and Row, 1973), 32; Lawrence I. Radway, "Domestic Attitudes as Constraints on American Foreign Policy Leaders," in David A. Baldwin (ed.), *Problems of United States Foreign Policy* (Hanover, N.H.: University Press of New England, 1976), 307.

68. Poll data on popular attitudes toward American military commitments abroad are contained in Radway, "Domestic Attitudes as Constraints on American Foreign Policy Leaders," 304–305; and Hughes, *The Domestic Context of American Foreign Policy*, 40.

informed student of public opinion in the United States, the American people believed "that the only foreign policy more dangerous than Hawk is Ostrich." Frustrated as they were by the Vietnam encounter, most Americans still rejected extreme dovish proposals for ending the war in Southeast Asia; nor did they favor a radical reorientation in America's global policies. A majority of the people believed that (although its global influence was declining) the United States was still the most powerful nation in the international system and that it was likely to remain so for an indefinite period in the future. Majority sentiment no less rejected the idea that in recent years American diplomatic behavior had been motivated by "the arrogance of power" or hegemonial impulses in Washington. On balance, American power was viewed as a force for "good" in the world, rather than a malevolent influence, and the United States was seen as having been reasonably successful in achieving its foreign policy objectives in diverse settings abroad. Although citizens might favor some reductions in military spending, they by no means advocated the drastic cuts in the Pentagon's budget called for by dovish critics of American policy in Vietnam and other locales. A poll taken on the eve of the national election of 1972, for example, showed that the American people preferred President Nixon's national defense policies by a margin of 55 to 30 percent over his Democratic opponent's.[69]

Other specific provisions of the Nixon Doctrine commanded widespread public approval, such as new efforts to strengthen détente between the United States and the Soviet Union and the attempt to normalize relations with Communist China. While public sentiment favored ending the Vietnam War, as noted before, the people also desired a just and durable peace settlement; the "unconditional" evacuation of American forces from Southeast Asia had very little support among the people. In fact, as a rule American public sentiment conformed to the usual pattern of supporting the president in steps taken by the White House to preserve national security.

The basically favorable public opinion environment in which the Nixon Doctrine was issued highlights a supreme irony about the dip-

69. Ben J. Wattenberg, *The Real America: A Surprising Examination of the State of the Union* (Garden City, N.Y.: Doubleday, 1974), 211; Watts and Free (eds.), *State of the Nation*, 203–22; Watts and Free (eds.), *State of the Nation—1974*, p. 211; Dawson, *Public Opinion and Contemporary Disarray*, 31–32.

lomatic behavior of the Nixon Administration. The Nixon White House was subject to mounting public and congressional criticisms directed against the "wall of secrecy" surrounding its decisions and the degree to which President Nixon and his principal advisers "ignored" public opinion in formulating external policy. Ultimately of course, the Watergate scandal thoroughly discredited the Nixon Administration and prevented many Americans from viewing its record objectively. The irony is that most of the foreign policy undertakings of the Nixon-Kissinger team enjoyed substantial public approval. President Nixon and his aides did not need to resort to secrecy, the manipulation of the news media, and other tactics that eventually destroyed their public image and eroded public confidence in their leadership. No administration in American history perhaps had devoted such time and effort to communicating its foreign policy objectives to the American people and, as one commentator expressed it, "yet been so little understood." [70]

The Nixon Doctrine: A Balance Sheet

With the departure of Richard M. Nixon from the White House, the Nixon Doctrine rapidly faded into diplomatic obscurity. Among the other failures of his administration must be listed the fact that Nixon was unsuccessful in his evident desire to bequeath the nation an enduring diplomatic doctrine bearing his name. After the painful events of Watergate, the tendency of most Americans was to "forget" the Nixon incumbency—including the diplomatic pronouncement with which Nixon's name was associated. Following the demise of President Nixon, references to his diplomatic doctrine became extremely rare.

A persuasive case can be made for the contention that the Nixon Doctrine fully deserved the fate it received. More than any diplomatic doctrine encompassed in our study, the Nixon Doctrine was vague, ambiguous, and contradictory. Its precise meaning was never very clear—even perhaps to its promulgator. One commentator has described the doctrine as a kind of "political accordian"; President Nixon and his advisers were skillful in "playing by ear"; they could "stretch it out or squeeze it tight depending on their particular audience." [71]

70. Brzezinski, "Half Past Nixon," 3.
71. Dower, "Asia and the Nixon Doctrine: The New Face of Empire," 129.

In contrast to the other doctrines analyzed here, the Nixon Doctrine did not state a single principle of American foreign policy, applicable to a rather narrow range of circumstances abroad. As we have noted, it was a kind of diplomatic package or grabbag containing a multitude of major and minor concepts that applied to the entire range of American foreign relations. Accordingly, it was difficult for even informed students of American diplomacy to distinguish between those ideas which were essential to the meaning of the Nixon Doctrine and those that were peripheral (or in some cases irrelevant) to it. Stated differently, the Nixon Doctrine lacked an integrating idea that would presumably impart more consistency and effectiveness to American diplomatic behavior in the post–Vietnam War period.

A leading purpose of the Nixon Doctrine was to remedy those defects in American foreign policy that had contributed to America's agonizing involvement in the Vietnam War. Yet in some respects, the Nixon Doctrine itself reflected many of these same deficiencies. It too suffered from "incrementalism," or the tendency to define American foreign policy piecemeal and in response to particular challenges facing the United States abroad. Other than vague assurances that they all somehow contributed to peace and global stability, it was difficult to discover any common theme in extending détente with the Soviet Union, normalizing relations with Communist China, trying to create a stronger sense of "community" within the Western Hemisphere, and promoting regionalism abroad. Some critics alleged, and with considerable justification, that in reality the Nixon Doctrine was merely synonymous with the entire foreign policy program of the Nixon-Kissinger team and was indistinguishable from it. By calling it a *doctrine*, President Nixon was somehow trying to endow this program with a mystique that would enhance its public and congressional acceptability, without encouraging public discussion of it. In that sense, the Nixon Doctrine could be regarded as merely another effort by the Nixon Administration to shield its policies from public scrutiny and accountability.

The Nixon Doctrine was seriously flawed for another reason. Widely advertised as a "new" foreign policy for the United States—as a diplomatic blueprint that would enable the nation to avoid "another Vietnam" and other diplomatic misadventures—the Nixon Doctrine was actually based upon very old and traditional diplomatic principles, associated with the approach to foreign policy known as realpolitik. Such key ideas as national interest, national power, and balance of power were pillars of the Nixon Doctrine. At the same time, as the Nixon-Kissinger team frequently reminded citizens at home and abroad, the international system that had emerged by the early 1970s was in many respects quite different from any system witnessed in earlier eras—and fundamentally different from the one existing during the heyday of realpolitik in the eighteenth and nineteenth centuries. Yet it was difficult to discern how this awareness affected the Nixon Administration's supposedly new set of foreign policy guidelines.

To cite but one example of this anomaly: a keynote of the Nixon Doctrine was the growing "interdependence" of the contemporary international system. Yet another implicit idea prominent in the doctrine was the old concept of American unilateralism. In the strategic principles that would guide the United States after the Vietnam War, Washington would continue to decide when and where to employ the American nuclear arsenal abroad, and it would determine the countries whose continued security was vital to the well-being of the United States. It is, therefore, no mystery why the Nixon Doctrine failed to deter countries like Israel, Iraq, India, Pakistan, and Brazil from acquiring their own nuclear arsenals.

Another crucial weakness of the Nixon Doctrine was the concept of "Vietnamization," which it endeavored to convert into a global principle of American foreign policy. In the Nixon Doctrine, this translated into the requirement of maximum "self-help" by countries facing a threat to their security as a precondition for American assistance. Yet the transcendent fact about "Vietnamization" (ignored by the Nixon Doctrine) is that it failed to work in Southeast Asia. Beyond stating a truism—it is virtually impossible for the United States to defend a country which is unwilling or unable to defend itself—the Nixon Doctrine provided little or no guidance in solving the difficult problem of *how* other countries can be induced to elect able national leaders, to eliminate corruption, to promulgate effective internal reform programs, to maintain popular support—in short, to do those things that the government of South Vietnam had failed to do in its struggle against the Communist enemy.

These and other shortcomings of the Nixon Doctrine should not, however, obscure the fact that it made certain positive and useful contributions to the conduct of American diplomacy in the post–Vietnam War era. If the Nixon Doctrine clearly is not on a par with the Monroe and Truman doctrines as landmarks in the American diplomatic record, it should not be totally dismissed or ignored as an insignificant development in American foreign relations. As the old adage has it, in diplomacy, as in other realms, it is sometimes less imperative to learn new truths than to relearn old ones—and to apply them anew to conditions arising in the future. Much of the value of the Nixon Doctrine lay in reasserting diplomatic axioms which have too long been ignored by the American people and their leaders.

One of these is the precept that a nation's foreign policy commitments must be brought into an approximate balance with its capabilities or power. Axiomatic as this idea is, America's "overcommitment" abroad could largely be explained by the fact that successive administrations in Washington had forgotten that maxim. In the phrase coined by D. W. Brogan early in the postwar period, the diplomatic behavior of the United States had too often reflected "the illusion of American omnipotence"—or the belief that there was literally no problem beyond the borders of the United States that could not be solved by massive applications of American power, energy, and ingenuity![72] The United States, successive administrations in Washington appeared to believe, could simultaneously "contain" Communist (during some periods, both Soviet and Chinese) influence around the world; successfully engage in "nation-building" and modernization throughout the Third World, thereby presumably assuring political stability and eventual democracy throughout this zone; eliminate poverty and raise standards of living among the less developed societies—while concurrently solving a host of problems, like poverty, crime, the drug problem, the promotion of racial equality in education and other spheres, inflation, and other issues confronting Americans at home. Imperfect as it was, the Nixon Doctrine did endeavor to remind the American people and their leaders that vast national power is not synonymous with infinite power. For America to pretend that its power was unlimited was to invite certain diplomatic defeats.

The Nixon Doctrine was a needed corrective to the almost limitless diplomatic ambitions of the United States from the end of World War

72. Brogan, "The Illusion of American Omnipotence," 21–28.

II until the Vietnam War. As we have emphasized, the Nixon Doctrine reiterated the idea that it was impossible for the United States to return to the comfortable seclusion of an isolationist existence. After Vietnam, the United States remained a superpower, with global commitments and responsibilities. But if the Vietnam experience had not left the American nation a "crippled giant," neither was it Atlas: it could not bear every burden, or meet every challenge to the stability of the international system, alone. In an era when the traditional distinction between "foreign" and "domestic" affairs had become severely eroded and almost meaningless, the Nixon Doctrine was a pointed reminder that the power of the United States had to be apportioned among a long list of competing internal and external demands. Failure to do so in the future would make "another Vietnam" well nigh inevitable.

In the light of this reality, the Nixon Doctrine also underscored the idea that greater selectivity and discernment must govern the application of American power abroad. As the doctrine attempted to do, some kind of order of priority or hierarchy must be established and adhered to among the nation's goals overseas. All are not of equal importance—and what may be no less crucial, all are not equally susceptible of being accomplished within the limits of American power. The Nixon Doctrine (and its authors were aware that it was merely an initial and formative stage in the process) at least attempted to establish a crude order of priority among America's myriad external objectives. Implicitly, for example, in the strategic guidelines contained in the Nixon Doctrine, American officials recognized that the security of the United States was not at stake in all foreign crises. If the doctrine did little to define the elusive term *aggression*, it was at least a step in the direction of specifying some criteria by which Washington would judge the impact of foreign crises upon American security.

Much the same objection can be made with another standard employed by the Nixon Doctrine for evaluating America's involvement in crisis situations abroad: the concept of the "national interest" of the United States. In his doctrine, President Nixon stated explicitly that the United States has its own unique interests in foreign affairs, and after the Vietnam War, it would be guided by these interests in its response to crises overseas. Again, the concept of national interest is admittedly vague, ill-defined, and unsatisfactory. From one perspective, in a democracy the political process is a continuing exercise in defining the national interest at any given time, or in choosing one version of it over another as the basis for governmental policy. As often as not, the term *national interest* (when it has any clearly defined content at all) actually describes how policy is rationalized and explained, rather than how it is formulated. After recognizing this, the Nixon Doctrine's emphasis upon America's national interest does imply recognition in Washington that some situations overseas do affect the interests of the United States directly, while others do not. At a minimum, the national interest is better than no standard for ordering America's diplomatic priorities.

With all of its defects, the Nixon Doctrine acknowledged another prerequisite for diplomatic success that had become more imperative than ever in a rapidly evolving international system. This is the need to adapt American foreign policy to changing conditions abroad. If this idea also might be classified as a truism, it was another one that had been ignored in Washington for several years before the issuance of the Nixon Doctrine.

The outstanding example of rigidity in American policy was perhaps the nation's almost instinctive and largely emotional reaction to the communization of China—an event that was regarded at home and abroad as a serious diplomatic setback for the United States. By many criteria, that was not an unwarranted interpretation. For more than twenty years, Sino-American relations remained tense and unproductive. By the period of the Nixon Administration, however, American officials recognized two realities: irrespective of America's desires, a Communist regime existed in China and it appeared to be effectively governing the country; and in the light of the break between Soviet Russia and Communist China, opportunities now existed to improve Sino-American relations, in which the United States would realize certain real benefits. The Nixon Doctrine reflected these realizations. Ironically (as one who had repeatedly criticized earlier Democratic administrations for having "lost China" to communism), President Nixon had the courage and diplomatic acumen to modify American foreign policy and to inaugurate the era of normal Sino-American relations.

Finally, the Nixon Doctrine unquestionably did result in some benefit for the United States in the matter of encouraging greater "self-help" by America's friends and allies abroad. If the criteria by which

American assistance would be extended to endangered countries abroad remained unclear in the Nixon Doctrine, it could at least be said that the doctrine "sent a message" whose general import was unmistakable. To America's allies in Europe and Asia, for example, the doctrine forcefully conveyed the idea that the United States expected a larger proportionate contribution from them to the common defense effort. While this could hardly be called a new theme in recent American diplomacy, its embodiment in the form of the Nixon Doctrine communicated the seriousness with which the American people and their leaders viewed the issue. It was not altogether coincidental, therefore, that in the years that followed the Nixon Doctrine, the European allies did agree to increase their share of the NATO defense burden; and Japan began to play a somewhat more expanded role in preserving the security and stability of Asia.

In several fundamental respects, the Nixon Doctrine was the most ambitious, ambiguous, and unsatisfactory doctrinal pronouncement in American diplomatic history. Even today, its essential meaning and many of its implications remain elusive. To no inconsiderable degree, however, this fact can be accounted for by the context within which the Nixon Doctrine was promulgated. The Nixon Administration marked a major turning point in postwar American foreign relations. If, as many critics complained, President Nixon's doctrine was vague, incomplete, inconsistent, and contradictory, in some degree this phenomenon merely reflected the environment within which the doctrine was issued.

As the Vietnam War drew to a close, the American society's attitudes toward foreign affairs were more than ordinarily marked by feelings of guilt, self-doubt, anxiety, and deep-seated confusion about the role their nation should play in international affairs. If ordinary citizens could not articulate the parameters of American policy clearly, they sensed that America's diplomatic course had to be charted between two outer markers designating the channel. One of these was the realization that the United States could no longer serve as "the policeman of the world." With the end of the Vietnam War, the era of indiscriminate American interventionism abroad also drew to a close. The other parameter of American foreign policy after Vietnam was isolationism: Americans realized that, much as they might yearn for it, the period of isolationism had also ended for the United States. Somewhere between these two extremes lay America's proper diplomatic course. If the Nixon Doctrine did not answer all possible questions about it—and if it left a number of major problems unresolved—at least it began the process of redefining America's international role in this new era. It was a quest that was likely to occupy the American people and their leaders for many years to come.

8 / The Carter Doctrine: The United States in the Persian Gulf Vortex

A prudent President had to register America's alarm and new-found determination. . . . For whatever the Russians' purpose in Afghanistan, their invasion has become a new factor in an unstable region. . . . They need to know that defense of the Gulf and military preparedness will be priority projects of the West. . . . The Carter "doctrine" was a necessary response to an unexpected sign of . . . danger.
—Editorial in the New York *Times*, February 17, 1980

Preserve us, then, from tough-sounding "doctrines" from disillusioned doves whose empty threats are not believed. What we need is a substantive position on defense and foreign policy laid out by a candidate whose views will carry weight—and whose judgment of Soviet intentions is not subject to instant change.
—William Safire

Mr. Carter's doctrine appears to be consistent with a grand tradition in American foreign policy. . . . there is a persistent belief among Americans in the pre-eminent power of brave ideas, even when those ideas stand alone.
—Timothy Lovain

The closing months of 1979 marked a crucial turning point in the post–Vietnam era of American foreign policy. A combination of developments during that year severely challenged the prevailing approach to foreign policy, sometimes known as the "Vietnam War syndrome" in American diplomacy. This frame of mind was characterized by public and official doubt and uncertainty concerning the nation's foreign policy role. The election of the Republican candidate, Ronald Reagan, to the White House in 1980 presaged significant changes in the diplomatic behavior of the United States. In dealing with both internal and external problems, Reagan promised to "make America great again," and his electoral landslide indicated that a majority of the American people shared this goal.[1]

1. Ellis Sandoz and Cecil V. Crabb, Jr. (eds.), *A Tide of Discontent: The 1980 Elections and Their Meaning* (Washington, D.C.: Congressional Quarterly Press, 1981), especially Chapter 8.

In reality, American foreign policy had begun to undergo a significant reorientation even before President Jimmy Carter left office.
Three events at the end of his term were largely responsible for these
modifications. One of them was the belated discovery (finally confirmed by the Carter Administration in late August, 1979) of a large
Soviet military presence on the island of Cuba. Estimated to number
some three thousand men, these Russian forces had evidently been in
Cuba for several years—a fact that did not reassure Americans about
the effectiveness of the nation's intelligence establishment. After the
existence of these Russian units in Cuba had been verified, President Carter called their presence in the Caribbean "unacceptable" to
the United States. Yet in the end—when Moscow showed no disposition to remove its forces—Washington did in fact accept their presence in the Caribbean area. For many Americans, the outcome reinforced existing doubts about the Carter Administration's diplomatic
competence.[2]

The other crucial events occurred in the Middle East and are more
directly related to our subject. One was the overthrow of the pro-
American Iranian monarchy by a revolutionary movement early in
1979. On November 4, 1979, Iranian militants seized some fifty-three
Americans as hostages; their captors insisted that Washington meet a
long list of demands—such as the physical return of the Shah to Iran
and the restoration of the royal family's wealth to the Iranian people—
before the Americans were released. In the face of pervasive international censure, the Iranian revolutionaries refused to release the imprisoned Americans unless their terms were met. The Carter Administration no less adamantly refused to yield to "blackmail" to secure
their release. For over a year, the deadlock remained. Finally, using the
good offices of Algeria, Washington and Iran arrived at a negotiated
settlement of the hostage dispute; the captured Americans were finally
returned to the United States on January 20, 1981.[3] As a result of the
Iranian revolution and of the ensuing hostage controversy, American
influence in Iran was at the lowest ebb in recent memory. Meanwhile, a
new element of instability in the strife-torn Middle East was added late

2. Dispatch by David Broder, New York *Times*, September 13, 1979.
3. A detailed chronology of the hostage crisis is available in the *Congressional Quarterly* (Weekly Report), XXXVIII (January 5, 1980), 5–17, and XXXIX (January 24,
1981), 166–70.

in March, 1980, when open warfare erupted between Iraq and Iran. Oil shipments to the industrialized nations were curtailed for many months by this conflict.

The third development that led to a momentous change in American foreign policy was the Soviet military invasion of Afghanistan, beginning on December 27, 1979. Moscow's reliance upon military force to subjugate Afghanistan was the climax of a long and unsuccessful effort by the Kremlin to impose a Communist regime upon this predominately Moslem and fiercely independent society. On July 17, 1973, a revolutionary movement within Afghanistan overthrew the reformist monarchy of King Mohammad Zahir Shah. Throughout the years that followed, Afghanistan experienced greater or lesser political upheaval and growing internal repression.[4] In a new coup on April 27, 1978, the pro-Marxist People's Democratic Party, led by Nur Mohammad Taraki, seized power; and the Taraki regime became heavily dependent upon the Soviet Union. Yet as time passed, the population of Afghanistan exhibited growing resistance to Communist rule. A new pro-Marxist government that took office on September 16, 1979, had no better success than its predecessors in gaining popular support and restoring political stability.

By the end of the year, Soviet officials faced a difficult choice. They could replace the unpopular government in Kabul with another hand-picked Communist regime, with little assurance that it would win popular support. Or they could rely directly upon Soviet and progovernment troops to impose order upon the rebellious country. Moscow chose the latter course. On December 27, some fifty thousand Soviet forces crossed the frontier into Afghanistan. After gaining initial victories, however, the U.S.S.R. encountered as many difficulties subduing the Afghan insurgents as earlier alien forces. The Afghan tribesmen proclaimed a *jihad* (or holy war) against the "Communist infidels" and largely retained their control over the countryside. As the months passed, Moscow was compelled to send reinforcements to Afghanistan; and after a year, some eighty-five thousand Soviet troops were in the country. But even then, some foreign estimates held that Moscow

4. For background on political developments within Afghanistan after the ouster of the monarchy in 1973, see James Philips, "Afghanistan: Islam Versus Marxism," *Journal of Social and Political Studies,* IV (Winter, 1979), 305–21; and dispatch by Craig R. Whitney, New York *Times,* December 6, 1978.

would need upwards of half a million troops to subjugate Afghanistan and to enforce its hegemony upon an unwilling population. Yet a military commitment of this magnitude would seriously weaken the strength of the Warsaw Pact in Europe, impair Moscow's hold over the Eastern European satellite countries, and require a reduction in Russian forces along the Sino-Soviet frontier.[5]

Issuance and Connotations of the Carter Doctrine

Confronted by an overt Soviet attempt to dominate Afghanistan—and from that base, to threaten Western access to the Persian Gulf area—President Jimmy Carter made the volatile Middle East the focal point of his State of the Union Message to Congress on January 23, 1980. In his speech, Carter enunciated a new Persian Gulf strategy for the United States that came to be called thereafter the Carter Doctrine.[6]

President Carter referred to the deterioration in Iranian-American relations and to the seizure of American hostages in Tehran. Labeling this an act of "international terrorism," Carter pledged that the United States would meet the challenge and would never yield to "blackmail" by the Iranian militants.

The major portion of the president's address, however, was devoted to the crisis in Afghanistan and its implications for global peace and security. Carter's words constituted perhaps the most explicit denunciation of Soviet external behavior spoken by an American chief executive since the issuance of the Truman Doctrine early in 1947. Describing Moscow's intervention in Afghanistan as "military aggression," Carter related it to a broader pattern of global Soviet expansionism and adventurism, supported by the continuing buildup in Soviet military power. In the Carter Administration's view, Soviet-American relations remained the key factor in determining the future course of the international system. He called upon both superpowers, therefore, to "exercise restraint" in pursuing their foreign policy goals. To the Carter White House, the Soviet invasion of Afghanistan "could pose the most serious threat to the peace since the Second World War."

Then, in what was the crux of President Carter's new foreign policy

5. Dispatch by Anthony Lewis, New York *Times*, June 23, 1980.
6. President Carter's message is contained in *Weekly Compilation of Presidential Documents*, XVI (January 28, 1980), 194–200.

dictum, he stated candidly: "Let our position be absolutely clear: An attempt by any outside force to gain control of the Persian Gulf region will be regarded as an assault on the vital interests of the United States of America, and such an assault will be repelled by any means necessary, including military force."

To implement his new Persian Gulf doctrine, the president enumerated a long series of measures his administration had already taken, or would take in the near future, to bolster the security of the Persian Gulf area and to induce changes in Soviet behavior. These included: a variety of economic sanctions—such as denying Soviet ships the right to fish in American coastal waters, curtailing high technology and agricultural exports to the U.S.S.R., and persuading the European allies to restrict their trade with Communist countries; America's withdrawal from the Olympic Games scheduled to be held in Moscow (an affair the Kremlin had counted upon heavily to enhance its prestige abroad); a significant increase in American military spending; the creation of a new Rapid Deployment Force (RDF), designed to project American military power quickly to the Persian Gulf area and other endangered regions; improvement in the defenses of the North Atlantic area (NATO); a renewal of America's earlier pledge to defend the security of Pakistan; the inauguration of a system of national "registration" of young men, as a possible initial step in a reimposition of the Selective Service System (or draft); and, in what may have been the administration's most graphic expression of concern about Soviet behavior, President Carter's subsequent decision to withdraw the pending Soviet-American strategic arms-control agreement (SALT II) from further consideration by the Senate. The last step particularly was a "message" to the Kremlin intended to underscore Washington's apprehension about Soviet expansionist moves abroad and America's determination to resist them.[7]

The Carter Doctrine was a noteworthy development in the American diplomatic record for several reasons. In the first place, it reaffirmed the basic continuity of American postwar foreign policy generally and underscored the nation's growing stake in the stability of the Middle

7. The SALT II strategic arms-control agreements, which had been initiated by the Ford Administration, were withdrawn from further consideration by the Senate by the Carter White House on January 3, 1980.

East. The Truman Doctrine of 1947 had enunciated the strategy of containment that has guided American foreign policy toward the Soviet Union since World War II. A decade later, the Eisenhower Doctrine pledged the United States to preserve the security of the Middle East against threats posed by "international communism." Although the Carter Doctrine stated that the United States would defend the Persian Gulf region against "any outside force" seeking to dominate it, the context of Carter's message left no doubt that his warning was aimed primarily at the Soviet Union. In common with every other foreign policy doctrine enunciated after 1947, therefore, President Carter's dictum could legitimately be viewed as a regional application of the containment principle.

In the second place, the Carter Doctrine called attention to the fact that the United States had emerged as a Middle Eastern power and had acquired permanent diplomatic and security interests in the region. Although that idea may have been implicit in the earlier Eisenhower Doctrine, it was made explicit in the Carter Doctrine. Before 1980 (with the possible exception of America's long-standing ties with the State of Israel), the involvement of the United States in the affairs of the Middle East had largely been episodic and fragmentary. Yet according to the Carter Doctrine, the United States was now prepared to take the lead in preserving the security of the Persian Gulf area from an external threat.

Third, perhaps the most novel feature of the Carter Doctrine was that, within the Middle East, it publicly recognized America's strategic, military, and economic interests in the Persian Gulf area. In effect, the Carter Doctrine conceded that since the "Six-Day War" in the Middle East in 1967, the United States had become increasingly dependent upon uninterrupted oil shipments from the Persian Gulf region.

The countries bordering the Persian Gulf contained three-fourths of the world's oil reserves. When the Carter Doctrine was promulgated, the United States obtained some 25 percent of its oil imports from this source; and this increment was expected to increase in the years ahead. America's friends and allies, however, were even more dependent upon unimpeded oil shipments from the Middle East. Western Europe, for example, obtained almost 70 percent of its oil imports from the area; Japan (which lacked any significant domestic petroleum supply) was almost totally dependent upon external sources; some

75 percent of its foreign oil purchases were made from Persian Gulf suppliers. Issuance of the Carter Doctrine thus signified that the United States now ranked continued access to the Persian Gulf area as a diplomatic vital interest that Washington was determined to protect.

Fourth, the issuance of the Carter Doctrine was a major event in the evolution of American postwar diplomacy for another twofold reason: it signified awareness in Washington of a worldwide belief that American power and diplomatic credibility had declined seriously since the Vietnam War; and it indicated the Carter Administration's determination to reverse that process. On all sides—in Moscow, in the capitals of Western Europe and the Middle East, in Japan and other Asian nations—a perception existed that America's power vis-à-vis the Soviet Union was deteriorating; that, under the influence of the "Vietnam War syndrome," officials in Washington were incapable of either undertaking or protecting the nation's vital external interests; and that, as a result, America's diplomatic competence and credibility were being widely questioned. Some commentators described the president's speech as an "ultimatum" to the Soviet Union to desist from trying to dominate the Persian Gulf area, or to face the risk of war with the United States. In the post–Vietnam War era, it would be difficult to imagine a more pointed and serious reminder that the United States was, and was determined to remain, a superpower than the language of the Carter Doctrine.

Fifth, the issuance of the Carter Doctrine marked a dramatic reversal in the foreign policy of the United States on the issue of détente with the Soviet Union. The Carter Administration had made the concept of Soviet-American détente a foundation stone of its foreign policy. The Nixon and Ford administrations had sought to achieve détente before Carter's election in 1976; but no administration since World War II had emphasized its necessity as strongly or as frequently as the Carter foreign policy team. Early in his administration, for example, Jimmy Carter had accused the American people of having an "inordinate fear" of communism, implying that unwarranted American anxieties and suspicions about Soviet behavior had been the leading cause of the Cold War.[8] Among the president's advisers, Secretary

---

8. See, for example, the text of Carter's speech at Notre Dame University on May 22, 1977, in *Weekly Compilation of Presidential Documents*, XIII (May 28, 1977), 773–79.

of State Cyrus Vance was particularly identified with the concept of détente, believing it to be essential for the maintenance of global peace and stability.[9]

A few days before his State of the Union Message to Congress, President Carter stated, "My opinion of the Russians has changed more drastically in the last week than even the previous two and a half years before that. It's only now dawning on the world the magnitude of the action that the Soviets undertook in invading Afghanistan. This is a circumstance that I think is now causing even former friends and allies of the Soviet Union to reexamine their opinion of what the Soviets might have in mind." Soviet officials, Carter declared, must understand that they cannot "violate world peace" in Afghanistan and other locales "without paying severe political consequences." [10]

If the president's "ultimatum" to the Soviet Union, in the form of the Carter Doctrine, did not totally destroy détente, it clearly revived the concept of "linkage" that had been prominent in earlier American attitudes toward it. Time and again, for example, the Truman and Eisenhower administrations had called upon Soviet policy-makers to prove "by deeds, and not words" that they desired cooperative relations with the United States and other countries. During the early 1970s, the concept of linkage was particularly identified with Henry Kissinger, who held the position of national security adviser to President Nixon, and (while continuing to serve in that capacity) became secretary of state under the Ford Administration.[11] Kissinger's view was that for détente to be meaningful, the Soviet Union must demonstrate its professed devotion to "peaceful coexistence" with the United States *by its behavior* in the Middle East, in Africa, in Latin America, and in other settings. Although he did not use the term, President Jimmy Carter in effect revived the concept of linkage, making it once again a pivotal idea in American-Soviet relations. If the Soviet hierarchy genuinely desired peace with the United States, then it would

9. See the analysis of Vance's viewpoints in "Vance Resignation Leaves Future of Carter Foreign Policies Uncertain," *Congressional Quarterly* (Weekly Report), XXXVIII (May 3, 1980), 1160–63.

10. Carter's interview with ABC-TV reporter Frank Reynolds, New York *Times*, January 1, 1980.

11. Henry Kissinger's views on "linkage" are set forth in his *White House Years* (Boston: Little, Brown, 1979), 112–30. See also the discussion of Kissinger's views in Coral Bell, *The Diplomacy of Détente* (New York: St. Martin's Press, 1977), 20–54.

have to conduct itself peacefully in the Persian Gulf area and other regions where American security interests were at stake.

In the sixth place, along with the other doctrines included in our study, the Carter Doctrine was an important and dramatic diplomatic pronouncement made *by the president*. In the post–Vietnam War context of American foreign relations, this was an especially significant aspect of the Carter Doctrine. Throughout most of the 1970s, fears of the "imperial presidency" were at the forefront of public and congressional concern. Correctly or not, countless Americans believed that the nation's prolonged and unsuccessful involvement in the Vietnam conflict could be attributed to a series of unilateral decisions by presidents Kennedy, Johnson, and Nixon, with little effective involvement by public opinion or Congress. Then beginning in mid-1972, the Watergate episode—resulting ultimately in the resignation of President Richard M. Nixon, along with fines and jail terms imposed upon many of his advisers—provided new evidence to support the view that unrestrained presidential power endangered American liberties and values.

For these reasons, throughout most of the 1970s the president's authority in both foreign and domestic affairs was subject to numerous congressionally imposed limitations and to restraints posed by American public opinion. Two outstanding examples of this tendency were the War Powers Resolution of 1973 (considered more fully in Chapter 7) and Congress' refusal to permit the Ford Administration to become involved in the political crisis in the new African nation of Angola in 1975–1976. By the end of the decade, ex-President Ford observed, "The pendulum has swung so far that . . . we have moved from an imperial Presidency to an imperiled Presidency." Former advocates of forceful congressional leadership in foreign affairs, like Sen. J. William Fulbright (Democrat from Arkansas) joined Ford in deploring the decline of executive power and influence in the diplomatic field.[12]

During the latter part of his term, President Carter encountered mounting criticisms at home and abroad that his diplomatic leadership was weak and indecisive. Both within the Democratic party and

12. Gerald R. Ford, *A Time to Heal* (New York: Harper and Row, and Reader's Digest Association, 1979), 345–46, 358–59; *U.S. News and World Report*, January 15, 1979, p. 88; J. William Fulbright, "The Legislator as Educator," *Foreign Affairs*, LVII (Spring, 1979), 719–33.

from the Republican opposition Carter faced formidable political challenges and public discontent directed at his lack of dynamic diplomatic leadership.[13]

Following the tradition of other doctrines in American diplomatic experience, the Carter Doctrine was a forceful instrument of executive leadership in the foreign policy field. As had been true when the Truman Doctrine was issued in 1947, Congress found itself in a difficult position: it could approve and support this display of diplomatic firmness by the chief executive; or it could contest his leadership, thereby further weakening the nation's power globally and perhaps inviting some new Soviet move directed against America's national interests.

The Formulation of the Carter Doctrine

Almost from the beginning of his administration, President Jimmy Carter's management of foreign affairs was marked by sharp differences of opinion among his principal foreign policy advisers. In time, this fact engendered criticisms at home and abroad that his diplomacy was indecisive, unpredictable, and subject to numerous changes of course. The Carter foreign policy team, critics contended, lacked a "coherent strategy" for responding to a wide variety of major and minor developments abroad. As some commentators viewed it, this lack of coherence in the diplomacy of the Carter Administration was one factor motivating Moscow to embark upon adventurist moves in Afghanistan and other settings.[14]

As a chief executive who was lacking in firsthand diplomatic experience, Jimmy Carter was compelled to lean heavily upon his advisers. From them, he received increasingly diverse assessments and policy recommendations on relations with the Soviet Union, on America's proper response to the Iranian crisis, on the priority to be accorded

13. See, for example, the poll results dealing with Carter's job performance, in "Public Opinion Polls Play Key, but also Misunderstood, Role in American Political Arena," *Congressional Quarterly* (Weekly Report), XXXVIII (March 15, 1980), 723–27.

14. Disunity within the executive branch, focusing upon problems experienced by the Carter Administration, is discussed more fully in Cecil V. Crabb, Jr., and Pat Holt, *Invitation to Struggle: Congress, the President and Foreign Policy* (Washington, D.C.: Congressional Quarterly Press, 1980), 5–33. See also Stanley Hoffman, "A View from at Home: The Perils of Incoherence," *Foreign Affairs*, LVII (Special Issue, 1978), 463–92; and Leslie H. Gelb, "The Struggle over Foreign Policy," *New York Times Magazine*, July 20, 1980, pp. 26–27, 34–40.

human rights in American foreign relations, and on a variety of other issues. Under the American constitutional system, the resulting policies were of course ultimately the president's, who served as the nation's chief foreign policy spokesman.[15] The months immediately preceding the issuance of the Carter Doctrine were especially trying ones for President Jimmy Carter and his chief aides, as they endeavored to reassess and reformulate American foreign policy in response to a series of crises overseas. Disunity among his foreign policy advisers was more than ordinarily pronounced, as the president in time approved a series of measures amounting to "a virtually unparalleled reversal of U.S. foreign policy."[16]

Against this background, the Soviet invasion of Afghanistan inevitably evoked sharply differing viewpoints among President Carter's principal foreign policy advisers. As we have seen, Secretary of State Cyrus Vance was a leading advocate of détente with the Soviet Union and of negotiating differences between the United States and Iran. Within the State Department, the Soviet expert Marshall Shulman shared and supported Vance's viewpoints concerning the necessity for preserving détente. Ongoing Soviet adventurism, however, climaxed by the Russian invasion of Afghanistan, largely undermined the credibility of the Vance-Shulman approach.

In anticipation of his forthcoming State of the Union Message to Congress, Carter asked Secretary Vance to prepare a draft dealing with foreign policy issues. As directed, Vance submitted his version to the White House. But in the text of Carter's speech, Vance's broad and low-key references to the Soviet Union had largely been eliminated, in favor of a message to Moscow couched in ominous tones concerning the future of détente and world peace. On April 21, Secretary Vance resigned from the administration in protest against President Carter's decision to use military force in an unsuccessful attempt to rescue the American hostages in Tehran.[17]

As delivered to Congress, the president's speech reflected the "hardline" approach to the Soviet Union long identified with national se-

15. See the discussion of the viewpoints identified with Carter's most influential foreign policy advisers in *U.S. News and World Report*, January 28, 1980, pp. 21–25.
16. *Ibid.*, 23.
17. See the analysis of the formulation of the Carter Doctrine in *Newsweek*, February 4, 1980, pp. 22–23.

curity adviser Zbigniew Brzezinski, along with other executive officials who supported his point of view, such as Secretary of Defense
Harold Brown. This group called for an increasingly firm and decisive
American response to the Soviet Union's growing military power and
expansionist tendencies. As an experienced observer expressed it late
in 1979, Brzezinski and his colleagues were convinced that Soviet officials sought "to change the balance of power in their favor" and that
the Carter Administration must take steps counteracting this tendency. As Brzezinski assessed the matter, "The Soviets have been challenging vital United States interests from the Sea of Japan to the Mediterranean and . . . this challenge must be opposed much more directly
by the United States."[18]

The diplomatic change of course signified by the Carter Doctrine
had thus been under consideration by President Carter and his advisers several months before the State of the Union Message was delivered to Congress early in 1980. A few months after Carter entered the
White House, national security adviser Brzezinski received a memorandum from Professor Samuel P. Huntington of Harvard University
predicting that, in the years ahead, the Persian Gulf area would become the most likely zone of Soviet-American confrontation. Brzezinski's early preoccupation with the security of this region reflected the
even earlier concern of his predecessor Henry Kissinger. In the aftermath of the oil boycott imposed during the 1973 war, Kissinger publicly intimated that the United States might be required to intervene
militarily in order to maintain Western access to the Persian Gulf oil
fields. In response, some Arab spokesmen indicated they would destroy the oil facilities, rather than let them be seized by foreign troops.
(By contrast, the Carter Doctrine pledged the United States to preserve
the security of the Persian Gulf area from "any outside force," which
under existing conditions clearly meant a Soviet-sponsored effort to
dominate the Persian Gulf area.) Then in mid-1977, Brzezinski submitted a proposal calling for the creation of a special military force (later
called the Rapid Deployment Force, RDF) to defend American security interests in this volatile region. Brzezinski's plan, however, encountered opposition from the State Department and, at the time,
from the Defense Department; the latter feared that its implementa-

18. Dispatch by James Reston, New York *Times*, December 30, 1979.

tion would seriously weaken America's military commitment to the NATO area.[19]

After the collapse of the American position in Iran, followed by the Soviet Union's military incursion into Afghanistan, the prospects for presidential approval of Brzezinski's ideas improved dramatically. In the wake of Moscow's aggression against Afghanistan, Brzezinski presided over some twenty meetings of the National Security Council devoted to formulating an American response to the Kremlin's expansionist move. President Carter also asked Brzezinski to submit a draft of his scheduled State of the Union Message. After receiving it (along with another version from Secretary of State Vance), Carter next asked Brzezinski to prepare a new version combining the thoughts of the National Security Council and the State Department on American policy toward events in the Persian Gulf area. President Carter himself then refined his message, incorporating his own ideas and suggestions from other officials, such as Secretary of Defense Brown. By this stage, Brown had become deeply concerned about American military weakness vis-à-vis the Soviet Union; and he urged the president to call for a system of "national registration" as a possible first step in the reimposition of the draft. Carter also apparently decided to cast what was described as his ultimatum to the Kremlin in the form of a warning against "any outside force" threatening the security of the Persian Gulf area, rather than a more specific threat to the oil fields of the region, as recommended by some of his advisers.[20]

As ultimately presented to Congress, the Carter Doctrine commanded what one commentator described as a "surprising consensus" among President Carter and his principal foreign policy advisers. Yet irrespective of the contributions and support of his advisers, in accordance with the American constitutional tradition, President Jimmy Carter bore the ultimate responsibility for this major foreign policy declaration. And on the basis of precedent, the pronouncement quickly bore the name of the president who delivered it. Ironically, however, President Carter's foreign policy dictum did *not* deal with a theme

19. *The Middle East: U.S. Policy, Israel, Oil and the Arabs* (4th ed.; Washington, D.C.: Congressional Quarterly, 1979), 70; dispatch by Richard Burt, New York *Times*, January 25, 1980.
20. Dispatch by Hedrick Smith, New York *Times*, February 27, 1981; *Newsweek*, February 4, 1980, p. 23.

(such as respect for international human rights) that was conspicuously identified with his approach to foreign affairs. The dominant
motif of the Carter Doctrine was the same idea that had been prominent in every major diplomatic doctrine issued since World War II: the
contest between the United States and the Soviet Union. After the Carter Doctrine, as one White House official expressed it, the Soviet challenge had once again become "top priority in American [foreign]
policy." [21]

As in the other doctrines included in our study, the congressional
role in the Carter Doctrine had two significant dimensions. One of
these was the legislative contribution to the formulation and issuance
of the doctrine; the other was Congress' responsibility for its implementation. In his State of the Union Message, President Carter stated
that he had "consulted with leaders of Congress" before delivering it.
Yet nearly all the references within the speech to Congress' participation related to the role of the House and Senate in supporting a series
of measures needed to carry out the administration's new Middle Eastern strategy.

Indirectly, congressional sentiment was an influential factor in producing a sharp diplomatic change of course by the Carter Administration. By the end of the 1970s, the administration's diplomatic record
was being vocally attacked on Capitol Hill—even by members of the
president's own political party. The belated discovery of Soviet troops
in Cuba; the collapse of the American position in Iran and the subsequent seizure of the American hostages; the Soviet Union's growing
military power; and Moscow's decision to use force against Afghanistan—these events produced growing anxiety in the House and Senate
about external events and America's response to them. Many observers agreed with the former State Department official, George Ball, that
the "Vietnam War syndrome" in American foreign policy was rapidly
disappearing; the American people and their legislative representatives were abandoning the "post-Vietnam reticence" that had colored
their approach to foreign relations throughout the 1970s. Dwindling
enthusiasm in the Senate for the SALT II arms-control agreement with
the Soviet Union provided tangible evidence of this new attitude on

21. Hedrick Smith, "Russia's Power Strategy," New York Times Magazine, January
27, 1980, p. 27; dispatch by Richard Burt, New York Times, January 9, 1980.

Capitol Hill. By the period of the Carter Doctrine, a consensus was emerging among Republicans and Democrats alike that in recent years the United States had become dangerously vulnerable and that this tendency must be reversed.

After witnessing the deterioration of the American position in Iran, for example, the chairman of the Senate Foreign Relations Committee, Frank Church (Democrat of Idaho), underwent the same kind of transformation in his thinking about foreign policy issues that President Carter had experienced. In Church's view, the United States "must be prepared to take action to protect vital interests" in the Middle East and other regions. Church believed that if achieving that goal "required organization of [military] strike forces, there would be strong support for this on Capitol Hill." Other prominent Democratic legislators called upon the Carter White House to strengthen American naval forces in the Indian Ocean-Persian Gulf area; to improve the operation of the American intelligence establishment; and to increase overall defense spending.[22]

Against this background of changing congressional attitudes toward foreign affairs, it is not surprising that the Carter Doctrine found a receptive audience on Capitol Hill. One report referred to the "thunderclap of applause in Congress" that greeted President Carter's pointed warning to the Soviet Union against new aggressive moves in the Middle East. The congressional mood was described as exhibiting "nationalist fervor"; legislators were "angered, anxious, frustrated and feisty"; above all, they were determined to "react to the Soviet actions" against Afghanistan and to "punish the Russians" for their recent diplomatic record of adventurism. Accordingly, there were "only a few voices of dissent" in Congress toward President Carter's new Persian Gulf strategy. Legislators widely endorsed the president's firm stand toward the Soviet Union and indicated support for the measures needed to make his doctrine a reality.

Summarizing the congressional reaction to the Carter Doctrine, one study concluded that it met with "general applause" on Capitol Hill. Rep. Lee Hamilton (Democrat of Indiana), an influential member of the House Foreign Affairs Committee, said that it was essential that

22. See the discussion of changing legislative attitudes on foreign policy issues in New York *Times*, December 2, 1979, dispatch by Hedrick Smith, and January 1, 1980, dispatch by Richard Burt.

the United States defend its interests in the Persian Gulf region; he called upon the White House to step up arms aid to Pakistan and take other steps to deter Soviet expansionism. Republicans also commended President Carter's new stance toward the Soviet Union—even while they criticized him (in the words of Rep. Phillip Crane, Republican of Illinois) for being "a modern Rip Van Winkle," who had finally awakened to the Communist danger. Sen. Robert Dole (Republican of Kansas) said that the Carter Doctrine represented White House acceptance of long-standing Republican demands in foreign affairs. The former Republican governor of California, Ronald Reagan, also endorsed the Carter Doctrine and called for stationing American troops in Pakistan to enforce it.[23]

Legislative reservations about the Carter Doctrine centered mainly upon two questions about it. As we have seen, some legislators wondered why it had taken the Carter Administration so long to react forcefully to the Soviet challenge. The other doubt was whether the Carter Administration would now move energetically to *enforce* the president's new foreign policy dictum. Some legislators were skeptical about whether the Carter Doctrine would be a credible instrument of American diplomacy, rather than a merely verbal and symbolic gesture having little impact on the course of external events. Congress, said Sen. Edmund Muskie (Democrat of Maine), would be inclined "to put up money first" and to "worry about how to spend it later." Restraint in enforcing the president's declaration would be viewed as "unpatriotic."[24]

Throughout the weeks that followed, nearly all the steps called for in President Carter's message—the boycott of the Moscow summer Olympic games, the embargo on shipments of grain and high technology exports to the U.S.S.R., the suspension of Senate debate on the SALT II arms-limitation accord, the expansion of trade and other ties between the United States and Communist China—received congressional approval. Perhaps most significantly, the House and Senate were receptive to increases in the national defense budget—and some Democrats joined Republicans in calling for even larger defense out-

23. These and other reactions to President Carter's speech are cited in "Carter: America Will Meet Soviet Challenge," *Congressional Quarterly* (Weekly Report), XXXVIII (January 26, 1980), 171–76.

24. Dispatch by Hedrick Smith, New York *Times*, January 27, 1980.

lays than the White House recommended. Congress, said House Speaker Thomas P. ("Tip") O'Neill, was "following the will of America" in responding positively to the Carter Doctrine.[25]

An episode occurring a few weeks after the issuance of the Carter Doctrine graphically illustrated the existing congressional frame of mind and provided an interesting contrast to the legislative temper during the early 1970s. This was the Carter White House's reliance upon military force to rescue the American hostages in Iran on April 24, 1980. The rescue mission failed. Yet according to one study, "the overwhelming majority of members of Congress either supported Carter's decision to attempt the rescue, or refused to second guess the president." While there was "some grumbling" on Capitol Hill about White House failure to consult Congress before using the armed forces for diplomatic ends, most legislators believed that the need for surprise and secrecy concerning the mission justified this omission. Significantly, no substantial sentiment existed on Capitol Hill in favor of the view that President Carter had violated the provisions of the War Powers Resolution of 1973 by failing to consult Congress before the rescue effort was undertaken. One of the authors of that resolution, Sen. Jacob Javits (Republican of New York), subsequently declared that, in his view, President Carter had been amply justified in ignoring its provisions.[26]

Domestic and Foreign Reaction to the Carter Doctrine

The available evidence indicates that American public opinion was overwhelmingly favorable toward President Carter's new Persian Gulf strategy and that it was prepared to support those measures needed to make it a reality. The Carter Doctrine, one commentator has said, was "enthusiastically received, giving the American people a renewed sense of pride and purpose" in foreign affairs. President Carter, another report found, was "widely praised for his initial muscular response" to the Soviet incursion into Afghanistan. Still another com-

25. Dispatch by Associated Press reporter Tom Raum, Baton Rouge *Sunday Advocate*, January 27, 1980.

26. Dispatch by Washington *Post* reporter Joanne Omang, Baton Rouge *Morning Advocate*, April 27, 1980. See also the discussion of the applicability of the War Powers Resolution to the Iranian rescue mission in *Newsweek*, May 5, 1980, p. 41; and editorial in New York *Times*, May 2, 1980.

mentary found evidence of massive public approval for the Carter Administration's diplomatic change of course in Jimmy Carter's decisive victory early in January in the Iowa presidential primary election.[27]

Public opinion polls during the months after President Carter's speech to Congress confirmed the fact that the Carter Doctrine was approved by a substantial majority of the American people. A New York *Times*/CBS poll taken just before the president's address, for example, indicated that some 67 percent of the respondents favored a tougher American response to Soviet adventurism in the Middle East and other areas. After the president's speech, an Associated Press/NBC poll found that 64 percent of those questioned advocated using American military force if necessary to preserve Western access to the Persian Gulf area. Some 69 percent of the people also called for increased national defense spending in order to protect American interests abroad. On a related issue, a Gallup Poll taken a month after President Carter announced his new diplomatic doctrine showed a sharp decline in positive American attitudes toward the Soviet Union: only 13 percent of those interviewed now viewed the U.S.S.R. positively, in contrast to 34 percent who were favorably disposed toward it a year earlier.[28]

A Gallup Poll taken a few weeks after the issuance of the Carter Doctrine found that 60 percent of the respondents called for a "tougher" response by the United States to Soviet behavior abroad. In the same period, a *Newsweek* poll found that 64 percent of the American people favored a substantial increase in national defense spending; 78 percent of those interviewed expressed concern about the state of America's military preparedness; and 68 percent believed that America was falling seriously behind its Soviet rival in global power and influence. American military assistance to the nation's allies was approved by 74 percent of the people; and 62 percent called for restricting American trade with the Soviet Union, especially in goods (like computers) that might enhance Russian military strength. Over 80

27. Leslie Gelb, "Beyond the Carter Doctrine," *New York Times Magazine*, February 10, 1980, p. 19; *U.S. News and World Report*, March 17, 1980, p. 49; dispatch by Hedrick Smith, New York *Times*, January 27, 1980.

28. Dispatch by William K. Stevens, New York *Times*, February 3, 1980; dispatch by Associated Press reporter Evans Witt, Baton Rouge *Morning Advocate*, February 4, 1980; Baton Rouge *Morning Advocate*, February 21, 1980.

percent of the respondents believed that American officials would be justified in using armed force to prevent an interruption of Middle East oil shipments to the West. Majorities also favored an American commitment to defend Pakistan from possible Soviet aggrandizement and the provision of American military equipment to Communist China.[29]

This evidence supports three overall conclusions about American public opinion as it related to the Carter Doctrine. First, the Carter White House had unquestionably interpreted the temper of the American people correctly; and his new doctrine toward the Persian Gulf area elicited widespread public approbation. Second, as in the past when the United States had faced a foreign crisis, the people looked to the White House for dynamic leadership in meeting it. Almost instinctively, citizens expected the chief executive to take the initiative in protecting the nation's diplomatic and security interests. Conversely, little or no discernible public sentiment existed for Congress to exercise the necessary leadership. Despite recent fears about the "imperial presidency," little evidence existed that the people believed Congress capable of managing foreign relations successfully. Although public confidence in President Carter's leadership ability was eroding, it nevertheless remained higher than the public's esteem for Congress as an effective institution.[30] Third, the American people were prepared to give the president broad latitude in formulating an effective American policy in the Persian Gulf area. Jimmy Carter, and after him Ronald Reagan, possessed the kind of "permissive" public mandate to meet an external challenge that chief executives have normally possessed in responding to foreign crises.[31]

Another significant dimension of the Carter Doctrine was the reaction of foreign governments and commentators to it. We may more meaningfully discuss this question in greater detail in the context of analyzing problems associated with the doctrine's enforcement. Here,

29. Baton Rouge *Sunday Advocate*, March 23, 1980; *Newsweek*, March 3, 1980, pp. 27–28.

30. See, for example, the national poll results on public attitudes toward Congress cited in dispatch by Clayton Fritchey, Baton Rouge *Morning Advocate*, January 3, 1981.

31. The wide latitude possessed by an American president in managing foreign affairs without infringing upon constraints derived from public opinion is a major theme of Bernard C. Cohen, *The Public's Impact on Foreign Policy* (Boston: Little, Brown, 1973). See especially pp. 133–208.

we shall allude only briefly to the attitudes of the European allies, the countries of the Middle East, and the Soviet Union toward it.

Although the Europeans were outspoken in condemning the Soviet invasion of Afghanistan, the Conservative government of Great Britain was virtually alone in supporting the Carter Doctrine enthusiastically. Elsewhere within Europe, the reaction ranged from skepticism toward the doctrine to very limited support for it.[32] The response of former French Foreign Minister Michel Jobert was not untypical of prevailing European opinion toward President Carter's new Persian Gulf strategy. To Jobert's mind, the Carter Doctrine was but the most recent example of important "policies decided in Washington," with little or no participation by the European allies. As in the past, in issuing the doctrine Washington had apparently counted upon Europe's "docility" and willingness to support unilateral American policies, promulgated in the name of the NATO alliance. Consequently, the United States now faced "vague and reluctant allies" who questioned the Carter Doctrine's usefulness and who were reluctant to join the United States in its implementation.[33]

That this French reaction accurately reflected the dominant opinion on the continent was indicated in the behavior of the European governments in the period that followed President Carter's State of the Union speech. Only limited support could be found in Europe for coercive measures—like America's boycott of the Moscow Olympic games and an embargo on Soviet trade with the West—designed to liquidate the Russian military presence in Afghanistan. Officials particularly in Paris and Bonn believed that détente between the United States and the Soviet Union must be preserved; and in the face of evident disapproval in Washington, they took steps independently to strengthen it. European officials also differed with their counterparts across the Atlantic about the likelihood of a new Soviet thrust into the Persian Gulf area. As time passed, they believed that Moscow actually desired a negotiated settlement of the Afghanistan question, provided it could be achieved without producing an overt Soviet diplomatic "defeat."

32. A fuller discussion of European attitudes toward the Carter Doctrine may be found in Stephen Milligan, "Such Good Friends? Afghan Crisis Tests Atlantic Alliance," *Europe*, No. 218 (March–April, 1980), 6–10; and New York *Times*, May 23, 1980, dispatch by James Reston, and June 22, 1980, dispatch by Bernard Gwertzman.
33. New York *Times*, May 28, 1980.

Among the sources of tension jeopardizing the peace and stability of the Middle East, the French government especially believed that regional conflicts—like the Arab-Israeli controversy and the Iraqi-Iranian war—posed the most serious risks of impairing Western access to Persian Gulf oil. Again in defiance of Washington's evident desires, French officials strengthened their contacts with the Palestine Liberation Organization (PLO) and several Arab governments in an independent effort to break the deadlock in the Arab-Israeli conflict. With France, other European governments and business concerns sold modern military equipment, and provided nuclear technology, to countries in the Middle East.[34]

Outside Europe, the reaction to the Carter Doctrine was similarly mixed. Nearly all Moslem nations condemned Moscow's attempt to subjugate the Islamic population of Afghanistan, and some interpreted the Kremlin's behavior as reflecting a deep-seated hostility toward the Islamic religion. In time, some Moslem countries (notably, Saudi Arabia and Pakistan) provided moral and material support for the Afghan rebels. Yet few Moslem nations—particularly those within the Persian Gulf area—were enthusiastic about the proposed American military buildup in the region implied by the Carter Doctrine. Tiny Oman—along with the African states of Somalia and Kenya—subsequently offered to make airfields and other base facilities available to the United States to enforce the Carter Doctrine. In time also, President Sadat's government in Egypt agreed to limited cooperation with the United States in implementing the Carter Doctrine. Not unexpectedly, the government of Israel applauded this new sign of American firmness in resisting Soviet encroachments in the Middle East; and it also offered military base facilities to enforce the Carter Doctrine. Officials in Washington realized, however, that acceptance of Israel's offer would gravely damage prospects of Arab cooperation in preserving the security of the Persian Gulf area.[35]

34. Editorial in New York *Times*, March 15, 1980; *Newsweek*, December 1, 1980, p. 55. Efforts (thus far unsuccessful) to extend NATO cooperation outside Europe are assessed in Henry Stanhope, "NATO in a Wider World," *NATO Review*, XXVIII (December, 1980), 7–12, and, more briefly, by Christoph Bertram, Director of the International Institute for Strategic Studies, in *U.S. News and World Report*, June 30, 1980, p. 19.

35. See the text of the resolution adopted by the 39-nation Islamic Conference held in Islamabad, Pakistan, in New York *Times*, May 23, 1980. Late in January, the Islamic foreign ministers denounced the Soviet invasion of Afghanistan as a "flagrant violation" of international law and called for the immediate withdrawal of Soviet troops from the

The Soviet response to the Carter Doctrine was fully predictable. A few weeks after President Carter's speech to Congress, President Leonid Brezhnev told the Twenty-sixth Soviet Communist Party Congress, "Imperialism launched a real undeclared war against the Afghan revolution," thereby creating "a direct threat to the security of our southern frontier." Under these conditions, Moscow had been "compelled to render the military aid asked for by that friendly country." Brezhnev went on to say that Moscow would be prepared to withdraw its forces from the country after "the infiltration of counterrevolutionary gangs into Afghanistan" had ended. Once that occurred, the Soviet Union was ready to engage in an agreement providing for the recognized neutralization of Afghanistan. Meanwhile, in the Soviet leader's view, the "notorious Carter Doctrine" posed a new and dangerous threat to the peace and security of the Middle East and to the future of détente.[36]

Among the more intriguing aspects of the crisis in Afghanistan and America's response to it was the question: how had Soviet perceptions of American power and diplomatic credibility influenced Moscow's decision? Informed commentators tended to answer this question very differently. On the one hand, some Kremlinologists believed, Soviet officials had concluded relations with the United States were already deteriorating; that détente was in serious jeopardy; and that anticipated American opposition to the Russian thrust into Afghanistan would not basically change these realities. On the other hand, by the late 1970s, the Communist hierarchy apparently also believed that the diplomacy of the Carter Administration lacked credibility and that—while it was in the grip of the "Vietnam War syndrome"—the United States was incapable of an effective response to its adventuristic policies in the Persian Gulf area. In any case, the almost universal condemnation of Soviet behavior in Afghanistan—particularly by nations in the Third World—most likely surprised policy-makers in the Kremlin.[37]

country. New York *Times*, January 29, 1980. The attitudes of Oman, Somalia, and Kenya toward the Carter Doctrine are discussed more fully in New York *Times*, April 22, 1980, dispatch by Richard Burt, and July 16, 1980, unsigned dispatch. See also *U.S. News and World Report*, March 31, 1980, pp. 51–52, and *Newsweek*, December 1, 1980, pp. 46–47.

36. New York *Times*, February 24, 1981.

37. See the analysis from Moscow by Robert P. Martin, in *Newsweek*, January 14, 1980, p. 21; the report from Moscow in *U.S. News and World Report*, May 12, 1980, p.

Another interesting dimension of the Persian Gulf crisis also was that it could be interpreted as a collision between two diplomatic doctrines identified with the superpowers. The Soviet Union justified its intervention in Afghanistan under the Brezhnev Doctrine, according to which Moscow could legitimately rely upon armed force to maintain a Marxist regime in power. The Brezhnev Doctrine was issued by the Kremlin following the massive Soviet invasion of Czechoslovakia on August 20–21, 1968. The doctrine justified Soviet intervention to prevent "a deviation from socialism" or "restoration of the capitalist order" within a country having a Communist regime. The Kremlin's expansionist moves in the Persian Gulf area were being contested under the Carter Doctrine, pledging the United States to preserve the security of this vital region.[38]

One other significant factor influencing the formulation and issuance of the Carter Doctrine remains to be identified. In common with nearly all other doctrines analyzed in this study, the Carter Doctrine can only be intelligently understood by considering its *internal political context*. As our earlier discussion has emphasized, the Carter Doctrine was promulgated at a time when the diplomatic credibility of the Carter Administration was being widely questioned at home and abroad.

The Carter Doctrine must, therefore, be evaluated against the backdrop of the 1980 national elections, in which Jimmy Carter faced a twofold challenge. Initially, Carter had to defeat contenders for the nomination to the presidency by challengers within the Democratic Party (notably, Sen. Edward Kennedy, Democrat of Massachusetts). Then, after winning his party's nomination, Carter found himself in an increasingly tough political fight against the Republican candidate, Ronald Reagan—a contest which Carter eventually lost. To a degree unprecedented in recent American political experience, foreign policy became a prominent issue in the presidential and congressional elections. For many months, Jimmy Carter and his supporters faced a barrage of criticism directed at his administration's mismanagement of

---

23; and the more extended discussion by Richard F. Starr, "U.S.-Soviet Relations in the 1980s," *NATO Review*, XXVIII (December, 1980), 18–23. A detailed comparison of Soviet and American military and economic power may be found in *U.S. News and World Report*, December 22, 1980, pp. 27–32.

38. U.S. Senate, Committee on Government Operations, *Czechoslovakia and the Brezhnev Doctrine*, 91st Cong., 1st Sess., 1969, pp. 1–21.

foreign affairs. Like the Truman Administration in the late 1940s, Jimmy Carter and his fellow Democrats were denounced for being "soft on communism" and for failing to protect American security and diplomatic interests against repeated encroachments by the Soviet Union, Iran, Cuba, and other countries.[39]

Jimmy Carter and his supporters counted heavily upon the new Persian Gulf strategy to reverse the Democratic party's declining political fortunes. "Politically, as well as diplomatically," one commentator concluded, the Carter Doctrine was "a forceful stroke" that greatly strengthened prospects for political victory by the Democratic party. The effect of President Carter's new doctrine was "to shape the nation's political agenda, to pre-empt his political opponents and to alter the political landscape to cover perceived weaknesses." According to another experienced observer, Jimmy Carter had the extraordinary good fortune to be running against two highly visible foreign enemies: the Ayatollah Khomeini in Iran and Soviet Premier Brezhnev in Afghanistan! His response to them was to issue the Carter Doctrine, and in doing so, Carter "wrapped himself in the flag and rejoiced in his enemies."[40]

The Carter Doctrine of course did not save Jimmy Carter and many of his Democratic followers from political defeat in the 1980 national elections. What has been called a massive "tide of discontent" swept the Carter Administration out of power and gave control of the executive branch and the Senate to the Republican party, led by Ronald Reagan. The main political effect of the Carter Doctrine, therefore, may have been to focus the 1980 campaign largely upon the domestic record of the Carter Administration. In the end, that may have been more of a loss than a gain for the Democratic party in determining the electoral outcome.[41]

Implementing the Carter Doctrine

During a trip to the Middle East early in 1981, President Ronald Reagan's secretary of state, Alexander Haig, said that a major purpose of

39. Dispatches by James Reston, New York *Times*, February 29 and March 16, 1980; editorial in New York *Times*, February 3, 1980.
40. Dispatch by Hedrick Smith, New York *Times*, January 25, 1980; dispatch by James Reston, New York *Times*, February 29, 1980.
41. A more detailed analysis of the causes and implications of the Republican elec-

his visit was to forge "a consensus of strategic concerns" regarding the Soviet threat to the Middle East. According to one account, the "first priority" of the Reagan Administration toward the Middle East was "to safeguard the West's oil lifeline in the Persian Gulf area." Other goals—such as resolving the Arab-Israeli dispute—were subordinate to this objective. Haig's purpose was to enlist "pro-Western governments, Arab and Israeli alike, in a U.S.-coordinated security framework" designed to "fight off an expansion of Soviet influence in vital areas."[42]

Secretary Haig's visit to the Middle East signified three things which related directly to the Carter Doctrine. In the first place, the Reagan Administration had accepted the Carter Doctrine as an axiom of American diplomacy in the Middle East. In the second place, Republican policy-makers accorded the preservation of Middle Eastern security from Soviet hegemony an even higher priority than their Democratic predecessors, making it the centerpiece of their diplomatic efforts in the region. In the third place, as our discussion will show, achieving "a consensus of strategic concerns" as a foundation for the Carter Doctrine was proving to be a challenging and frustrating undertaking for officials in the United States.

We may conveniently discuss the challenge of implementing the Carter Doctrine by examining four significant problems associated with it. These are: (1) correctly identifying the threat (or threats) to Middle Eastern security; (2) gaining the cooperation and contribution of the Western allies (along with Japan) in enforcing the doctrine; (3) building a basis of support for the Carter Doctrine among the nations of the Middle East; and (4) projecting American military power into the Middle East.

A crucial step in the successful application of the Carter Doctrine was identifying the source and nature of the threat toward which the doctrine was directed. As the text of Carter's speech to Congress made clear, for the president and his advisers the most ominous and direct threat to the security of the Middle East was evident. It stemmed from Moscow's undisguised reliance upon military force to achieve its ex-

---

toral victory in 1980 is available in Sandoz and Crabb (eds.), *A Tide of Discontent*. See especially Chapter 7.
42. *Newsweek*, April 13, 1981, p. 66.

pansive foreign policy goals. Thus, Carter accused Moscow of engaging in "military aggression" and of exhibiting a behavior pattern involving the "steady growth and increased projection of Soviet military power beyond its own borders."

Officials of the Carter Administration refused to speculate about ultimate Soviet motivations in its attempt to dominate Afghanistan. On one occasion, for example, Secretary of State Cyrus Vance said that it accomplished no useful purpose to "psychoanalyze" the motives of the Soviet hierarchy. Vance acknowledged that "all kinds of theories" could be advanced to explain the Soviet Union's behavior. But to his mind, "the plain fact is that the Soviet Union committed aggression" against Afghanistan. Vance clearly implied that aggressive behavior might be expected in the future from the U.S.S.R., and he was convinced that "there must be a sharp and firm response" by the United States.[43]

The Carter Administration's evaluation of the problem of Persian Gulf security did not lack support outside the White House. Thus, Soviet specialist Richard Pipes (who became the leading State Department authority on Soviet affairs in the Reagan Administration) believed that by seeking to dominate Afghanistan, the U.S.S.R. had once again embarked upon a diplomatic offensive aimed directly at the United States. Moscow's move in Afghanistan illustrated that the "global objective of the Soviet Union . . . is a world which is Communist." To achieve that objective, the Soviet Union must "isolate" the United States and render it economically and militarily vulnerable by threatening Western access to Middle East oil.[44] Other students of Soviet behavior believed that Moscow's move against Afghanistan could be explained by reference to the Russian state's historic "urge to the sea" and its quest for warm-water ports, by Moscow's effort to gain control of the world's sealanes, or perhaps by the Kremlin's attempt to encircle and intimidate Iran. A high Israeli official was convinced that the Soviet thrust against Afghanistan meant that Moscow intended to "go for the oil in the Persian Gulf."[45] An alternative explanation was

43. Interview with Secretary of State Cyrus Vance on January 15, 1980, in "New York Times Interview," Department of State, Bureau of Public Affairs, Current Policy No. 127, January 15, 1980, p. 1.

44. U.S. News and World Report, March 10, 1980, pp. 33–34.

45. Philips, "Afghanistan: Islam Versus Marxism," 308–12; dispatch by Drew Middleton, New York Times, April 6, 1980; U.S. News and World Report, January 14, 1980,

that—as it faced an increasingly serious energy crisis behind the Iron Curtain in the years ahead—the Kremlin was seeking to gain access to at least a share of the oil output of the Persian Gulf area.[46]

Another school of thought about the meaning of Soviet expansionism in Afghanistan concluded that the underlying motivations for it were essentially opportunistic and eclectic, carrying no necessarily long-range connotations of a Soviet effort to embark upon regional or global hegemony. In military parlance, the Kremlin's move in Afghanistan had been directed against a "target of opportunity": the Soviet hierarchy believed that (with the deterioration of the American position in Iran) it was presented with a combination of circumstances favoring consolidation of its hold over Afghanistan and strengthening its position in the Persian Gulf area; and the Kremlin seized the opportunity available to it. Moscow may have been emboldened to embark upon this course because the Communist hierarchy had concluded that American power was at a low ebb and that the Carter Administration lacked both the capability and the will to resist a new wave of Soviet expansionism.[47]

A fundamentally different interpretation of the Soviet move against Afghanistan was offered by the distinguished Kremlinologist, George F. Kennan, who believed that Moscow's behavior was dictated chiefly by defensive considerations. Kennan attributed Soviet actions to deep concern in the Kremlin about the U.S.S.R.'s growing internal problems; and he believed that Moscow was gradually "sucked into" invading Afghanistan "rather involuntarily" after the internal political situation in the country proved increasingly adverse for a succession of pro-Marxist regimes. Kennan did not regard the Soviet thrust into Afghanistan as part of larger Communist designs for regional or global hegemony, and he urged officials in Washington not to misconstrue the Russian venture into Afghanistan or to overreact to it.[48]

Other students of Soviet behavior basically shared Kennan's evalua-

---

pp. 22–26. See the views of Israeli Agriculture Minister Ariel Sharon, in dispatch by Drew Midddleton, New York *Times*, March 14, 1980.

46. See editorial in New York *Times*, January 14, 1980; *U.S. News and World Report*, January 14, 1980, p. 20; and the views of officials in Saudi Arabia in dispatch by Youssef M. Ibrahim, New York *Times*, February 27, 1980.

47. Smith, "Russia's Power Strategy," 27.

48. Interview with George F. Kennan, *U.S. News and World Report*, March 10, 1980, p. 33.

tion of the crisis in Afghanistan. Some believed that a crucial element in the Soviet decision to invade Afghanistan was growing concern in the Kremlin about the Soviet Union's own Moslem minority (estimated to number as high as fifty million people). The recent emergence of Islamic-based regimes in Iran and Pakistan—together with the strength of Islamic opposition to Marxist rule in Afghanistan—perhaps engendered deep anxieties in the Kremlin. An alternative explanation was that the crisis in Afghanistan was intimately related to the increasingly tense Sino-Soviet quarrel. By 1979, relations between the United States and the People's Republic of China had improved significantly—a fact that caused evident apprehension to the Kremlin. As it affected China, the Soviet move against Afghanistan had both an offensive and a defensive dimension. It might signify a Soviet effort to increase its military potential along a crucial salient of the Sino-Soviet border. Viewed defensively, it might represent an attempt by Moscow to protect itself against expansionist moves by China (in concert with the United States).[49]

These were among the leading theories advanced to explain the origins of the crisis in Afghanistan and its long-term implications for the United States. If the Carter and Reagan administrations subsequently experienced difficulty in forging a "strategic consensus" in behalf of the Carter Doctrine, a major reason was that little unanimity existed among informed students of Middle Eastern affairs concerning the precise nature of the threat to the Persian Gulf area or the steps required to counter it. Among the European allies, for example, a belief existed that Moscow preferred a negotiated resolution of the Afghanistan crisis, provided a means could be found that did not entail an overt Soviet diplomatic defeat. By contrast, the kind of confrontational approach to the issue envisioned by the Carter Doctrine would inevitably aggravate Soviet-American tensions and make the crisis more difficult to resolve. Within the Middle East, the dominant view perhaps was that if the Soviet Union posed a threat to the security of the Persian Gulf area, it was largely because of two developments: America's continuing support of Israel, providing opportunities for

49. Dispatch by Bernard Gwertzman, New York Times, January 1, 1980; Helmut Sonnenfeldt, "Implications of the Soviet Invasion of Afghanistan for East-West Relations," NATO Review, XXVIII (April, 1980), 1–2; dispatch by Louis Wiznitzer, Christian Science Monitor, February 6, 1980.

Soviet intervention in the region; and ongoing revolutionary movements, some of which were instigated and supported by Moscow. The Carter Doctrine was not viewed as a relevant or effective response to either danger.

A second major problem encountered by the Carter and Reagan administrations in their efforts to implement the Carter Doctrine was endeavoring to obtain foreign support for it. As events demonstrated, this could prove to be the most difficult obstacle of all to surmount in America's effort to preserve the security of the Persian Gulf region.

This problem underscores one of the unique features of the Carter Doctrine vis-à-vis other doctrines in American diplomatic experience. In common with its predecessors, the Carter Doctrine was issued *unilaterally* by the United States. No evidence exists that the Western allies or other foreign governments participated in its formulation. Yet officials of the Carter and Reagan administrations were aware that, if it were to accomplish its objectives, the doctrine would have to be implemented *collectively*. President Carter and his advisers were mindful of America's frustrating experience during the recent Vietnam War, when the conflict in Southeast Asia largely became "America's war," with little or no tangible support by the nation's allies. (To the contrary, as often as not, opinion in friendly countries was highly adverse to America's role in the Vietnam conflict.) Several months after the issuance of the Carter Doctrine, former Secretary of Defense James Schlesinger told a group of European officials that the Persian Gulf was "the coronary artery of the West" that was in danger of being severed by growing Soviet military power. He informed the Europeans that they were enjoying the benefits of preserving this artery "without being willing to accept the risks involved in maintaining" its security.[50]

In his speech to Congress enunciating the Carter Doctrine, Jimmy Carter had underscored the necessity for a collective and coordinated response to Soviet adventurism in the Middle East. In Carter's view, Moscow's actions demanded "resolute action" by the United States and its allies and friends "for many years to come." It called for "collective efforts" to meet this new threat by "all of those who rely on oil from the Middle East and who are concerned with global peace and stability."

50. Dispatch by Drew Middleton, New York *Times*, April 20, 1981.

This viewpoint was echoed by officials of the Reagan Administration. Early in 1981, for example, a Defense Department spokesman declared, "The threat to vital Western interests in key areas, such as the Persian Gulf, can be met only if all concerned share the burden and find new ways to make greater contributions in support of our common interests."[51]

Despite the belief of American officials that implementation of the Carter Doctrine must be an obligation of the United States and its allies (including Japan), efforts by the Carter and Reagan administrations to achieve the goal met with very limited success. As in the past, American-led attempts to extend the compass of NATO beyond the European continent and the Mediterranean area encountered strong resistance among the Western allies. Following a meeting of NATO military planners some eighteen months after the issuance of the Carter Doctrine, one report summarized prevailing opinion by saying, "NATO's military leaders agreed that the alliance should not become involved in [the Persian Gulf area] through a multinational force, but that individual governments should conclude agreements with the United States to provide assistance [in defending the region]."[52]

For various reasons, the individual members of NATO were reluctant to endorse the Carter Doctrine and to share in the responsibility for implementing it. France, for example, maintained a substantial naval force in the Indian Ocean-Persian Gulf area. Yet for several years (while formally remaining a member of NATO), the French government had played no role in the NATO joint command structure and had kept French armed forces under its independent control. After the Carter Doctrine was promulgated, Paris engaged in its own diplomatic initiatives in the Middle East, sometimes in the face of evident misgivings by American officials. The election of a Socialist, Francois Mitterand, as the president of France in May, 1981, presaged even more independent diplomatic initiatives by Paris in the Middle East and other regions. Under Mitterand, as one observer expressed it, Washington "faces the prospect that a Gallic-socialist France will revive its taste for independence and resistance to American policies." To President Mitterand and his supporters, the French military establishment

51. See the excerpts from the speech by Deputy Secretary of Defense Frank C. Carlucci, in New York *Times*, February 22, 1981.
52. New York *Times*, May 13, 1981.

will be viewed "as a pillar of independence" from the United States, fully as much as a deterrent against Soviet expansionism. While Mitterand had vocally condemned the Soviet invasion of Afghanistan and other expressions of Soviet hegemony, he also believed that Soviet-American tensions should be resolved by negotiations, rather than by the kind of confrontational approach exemplified by the Carter Doctrine.[53]

For different reasons, the government of West Germany was not enthusiastic about the Carter Doctrine and was equally cautious about collaborating with the United States to enforce it. More than any country in Western Europe, the Federal Republic of Germany was a beneficiary of détente between the United States and the Soviet Union, and Bonn desired its continuation. Moreover, by the early 1980s the German government was experiencing financial problems. Bonn not only was reluctant to embark upon new military expenditures, but it was also hard-pressed to meet its promised contribution to the NATO defense budget. Most fundamentally perhaps, from a strategic viewpoint West German authorities were deeply concerned about the possible "diversion" of Western military strength to the Persian Gulf area (which might entail a weakening of American forces on the European continent), at a time when Communist military strength across the Iron Curtain was continuing to increase.[54]

As our previous discussion has emphasized, European doubts about the Carter Doctrine stemmed from another source: fundamental disagreement on both sides of the Atlantic concerning the meaning and implications of the Soviet incursion into Afghanistan. Few Europeans agreed with Washington that Moscow's move was part of a Soviet "global offensive" directed at Western interests; Europeans believed that regional disputes (like the Arab-Israeli conflict) jeopardized the security of the Middle East more than hegemonial Soviet moves; and they were convinced that diplomacy, rather than armed force, offered greater promise of preserving the security of the Persian Gulf.[55]

53. Dispatch by Michael M. Harrison, New York *Times*, May 13, 1981; dispatch by Flora Lewis, New York *Times*, May 11, 1981.
54. Dispatch by Drew Middleton, New York *Times*, May 12, 1981; Gerard Braunthal, "West Germany Moves into the 1980s," *Current History*, LXXX (May, 1981), 193–97, 223–24.
55. See the reports on European opinion in New York *Times*, March 4, 1980, dispatch by Fred Halliday, April 27, 1980, dispatch by Bernard Gwertzman, October 21,

From the American perspective, the disagreement within NATO over implementation of the Carter Doctrine highlighted a recurrent problem within the Western alliance. Time and again, the European allies had complained—most vocally perhaps under the Carter Administration—about the lack of "diplomatic leadership" in Washington and about the "unpredictability" of American diplomacy. Many Europeans had also expressed misgivings about the decline of American power since the Vietnam War. Yet when Washington did exhibit leadership in an effort to safeguard the security of the vulnerable Persian Gulf area—on whose oil supplies Europe and Japan were even more dependent than the United States—it found the allies extremely reluctant to join in a collaborative effort directed against a common danger. A major reason was that by the period of the Carter Doctrine, the nations of Western Europe were sharply divided among themselves on Middle Eastern and other international questions, and since the first Arab oil boycott of 1967, this disunity appeared to be growing. After the Reagan Administration took office early in 1981, American officials had substantially conceded that the prospects for a unified "NATO response" to the challenge of preserving the security of the Persian Gulf region were remote.[56]

In and around the Middle East, official responses to the Carter Doctrine were equally mixed and, on balance, unfavorable. Not surprisingly, the most enthusiastic response to it came from the government of Israel. For many years, Israeli officials had been concerned about growing Soviet influence and power within the region, and Israel offered to cooperate in strengthening the American military position in the Middle East. Yet Israel's enthusiastic support of the Carter Doctrine only heightened Arab opposition to it.[57]

Several other countries in, or adjacent to, the Middle East also offered limited support for implementing the Carter Doctrine. In East Africa, Somalia and Kenya offered air and naval base facilities to the

---

1980, dispatch by Flora Lewis, and April 20, 1981, dispatch by Drew Middleton. See also the views of Christoph Bertram, in *U.S. News and World Report*, June 30, 1980, pp. 19–20.

56. *Newsweek*, April 20, 1981, p. 48; dispatch by Robert Reinhold, New York *Times*, February 22, 1981.

57. See, for example, the Israeli reaction to Washington's proposed sale of modern aircraft to Saudi Arabia, in dispatches by Bernard Gwertzman, New York *Times*, April 22 and 23, 1981.

United States, in exchange for expanded American economic and military assistance. (American officials remained wary, however, about becoming drawn into the existing conflict between Soviet-supported Ethiopia and Somalia or about becoming a party to a possible future conflict between Somalia and Kenya.)[58] By early 1981, under its new military-led government, Turkey indicated a willingness to contribute to the defense of the Middle East against "any threat" to its security. Traditionally suspicious of Russian intentions, Turkish officials called upon other members of NATO to join in supporting American-led efforts to redress the regional balance of power. Within the Persian Gulf area, only the tiny—but strategically located—sultanate of Oman offered to make air base facilities available to the United States to defend the region. In return, Sultan Qaboos asked for substantial credits, permitting him to buy modern American weapons. Apprehensive about Communist ambitions in the Middle East (and particularly about the creation of a Communist base in South Yemen), Sultan Qaboos applauded America's attempt to bolster regional security.[59]

Alone among the influential Arab states, President Anwar Sadat's government in Cairo offered qualified assistance to Washington to enforce the Carter Doctrine. After the Egyptian-Israeli peace treaty on March 26, 1979, Sadat's regime became increasingly isolated from the other Arab states—many of whom belonged to the "Rejectionist Front" devoted to carrying on the struggle against Israel. In addition, by the end of the 1970s Egypt had become heavily dependent upon the United States for economic assistance in meeting its progressively more acute internal problems. Cairo denounced the Soviet attempt to subordinate Afghanistan, offered to aid the Afghan rebels, and signified a willingness to provide limited use of Egyptian air bases for the protection of the Persian Gulf area.

At the same time, Sadat emphasized two points about Egypt's association with the Carter Doctrine: American military forces would not be stationed on Egyptian soil permanently; nor, as a leading nonaligned nation, would Egypt join an American-sponsored alliance system in the Middle East. Even this qualified Egyptian endorsement of the Carter Doctrine, however, evoked sharp criticisms from other

58. New York *Times*, July 6, 1980; dispatch by Stephen J. Solarz, New York *Times*, July 16, 1980; *U.S. News and World Report*, March 31, 1980, pp. 51–52.

59. New York *Times*, February 19, 1981; *Newsweek*, December 1, 1980, p. 46; dispatch by Richard Burt, New York *Times*, April 22, 1980.

Arab spokesmen. "The United States doesn't want friends in the Middle East," said Syrian President Hafez al-Assad. It wants "lackeys and agents and satellites, like Anwar el-Sadat."[60]

Elsewhere in the Middle East, the response to the Carter Doctrine ranged from extremely skeptical to overtly negative. Even the American-oriented ruler of Jordan, King Hussein, reiterated his conviction that Israeli expansionism remained the principal threat to regional peace and security. Hussein openly expressed his opposition to American military bases in the Middle East. Nor did he believe that creation of the proposed Rapid Deployment Force for use against Communist expansionism in the area would contribute positively to Middle Eastern security.[61]

The Carter Doctrine elicited a no less negative official reaction from perhaps the most influential state in the Persian Gulf area—Saudi Arabia. The de facto ruler, Crown Prince Fahd, denied Washington permission to use Saudi airfields and bases to enforce the Carter Doctrine; and Saudi officials echoed the prevailing Arab view that other forces jeopardized the security of the Persian Gulf more than the prospect of Soviet hegemony.

Yet Saudi attitudes toward the Carter Doctrine also exhibited a dichotomy not entirely absent perhaps in other settings. As unenthusiastic as officials in Riyadh were about the Carter Doctrine, privately many of these same officials applauded America's growing naval presence in the region, and they sought to purchase advanced American aircraft and other military equipment to improve the country's defensive position against an external threat. In turn, Saudi Arabia's request engendered intense criticism from Israel and its supporters within the United States, who believed that it would jeopardize Israeli security and lead to a new round of fighting in the Arab-Israeli conflict.[62]

At the head of the Persian Gulf, opinion in oil-rich Kuwait was no less adverse toward the Carter Doctrine. In the Kuwaiti view, the doc-

60. New York *Times*, April 12, 1981. The Egyptian viewpoint toward the Carter Doctrine is discussed more fully in dispatch by Henry Tanner, New York *Times*, November 12, 1980, and *U.S. News and World Report*, December 1, 1980, p. 35.
61. Interview with King Hussein in *U.S. News and World Report*, August 11, 1980, pp. 50–51; dispatch by Henry Tanner, New York *Times*, January 15, 1980.
62. See New York *Times*, April 16, 1981, dispatch by Bernard Gwertzman, January 15, 1980, dispatch by Henry Tanner, January 25 and 26, 1980, dispatches by John Kifner.

trine was an ill-concealed effort by the United States to impose its own hegemony upon the Persian Gulf area. Late in May, 1980, the thirty-eight countries attending an Islamic conference condemned the Soviet effort to dominate Afghanistan. But the participants were no less critical of American support of Israel in violation of Arab rights and of attempts by the United States to expand its power in the Indian Ocean-Persian Gulf area.[63]

On the eastern edge of the Persian Gulf, the Carter Doctrine also encountered skepticism and overt opposition. Pakistan—the country whose vulnerability had been crucially affected by the Soviet invasion of Afghanistan—was understandably apprehensive about close military identification with the United States. The military junta that governed Pakistan, headed by Gen. Mohammed Zia ul-Haq, spurned the Carter Administration's offer of $400 million in military aid as "peanuts." As a price for joining with the United States in enforcing the Carter Doctrine, Pakistan demanded an American "guarantee" of its security against possible Soviet aggression. After the Vietnam experience, American officials were of course reluctant to undertake such a commitment; and they were also mindful that a massive military buildup by Pakistan would trigger new tensions with its traditional rival, the government of India. Pakistan's determination to acquire nuclear weapons also elicited outspoken opposition from Washington.

Yet during the months that followed the issuance of the Carter Doctrine, negotiations between American and Pakistani officials continued. Pakistan, said an official in Islamabad, sought "credible and durable assurance of U.S. support." It also wanted a substantial increase in American arms aid (in part to counterbalance a large Soviet military assistance program in India). By mid-1981 Pakistani and American officials were near agreement on a package totaling $500 million in American arms aid. At the same time, Pakistani spokesmen emphasized that no American military bases would be established in the country, nor would Pakistan serve as a conduit for large-scale military assistance to the Afghan rebels.[64]

Predictably, the Carter Doctrine elicited a highly critical response from the government of India, led by Prime Minister Indira Gandhi.

63. Dispatch by Marvin Howe, New York *Times*, May 22, 1980.
64. Dispatch by Michael T. Kaufman, New York *Times*, May 12, 1981; *U.S. News and World Report*, June 30, 1980, p. 31.

As a leading devotee of diplomatic nonalignment, New Delhi reiterated its belief that the Indian Ocean-Persian Gulf area must not be converted into an arena of conflict between the superpowers. India opposed both Soviet and American efforts to control the region and Indian officials were especially apprehensive about any proposed military buildup in Pakistan. As always (except in its own quarrels with Pakistan), Indian officials advocated reliance upon negotiations to resolve the crisis in Afghanistan.[65]

In the light of prevailing Middle Eastern reactions to the Carter Doctrine, it is understandable that the results of Secretary of State Haig's visit to the region were described as "mixed." For policymakers of the Reagan Administration, the Soviet danger to the Middle East—viewed in Washington as part of a larger Soviet offensive aimed at the Third World—was the paramount threat to its security.[66] While few states within the Middle East were oblivious to the risk of external Soviet intervention, they believed regional security was more acutely jeopardized by other threats—like Israeli expansionism and violation of Arab rights or revolutionary movements directed against established governments. In their view, the Carter Doctrine made little positive contribution to the elimination of these dangers.[67]

The Rapid Deployment Force: Problems and Prospects

A major underlying premise of the Carter Doctrine was that the security of the Persian Gulf region was endangered primarily by a *military* threat posed by the Soviet Union. On that assumption, the Carter and Reagan administrations depended heavily upon military countermeasures to meet it. Two steps in particular were viewed by officials in the White House as essential for implementing the Carter Doctrine.

65. New York *Times*, June 4 and October 22, 1980, and April 18, 1981, dispatch by Bernard Gwertzman.

66. By early 1981, some commentators had begun to refer to an emerging "Haig Doctrine," named for Secretary of State Alexander Haig. In effect, it was a corollary or global application of the Carter Doctrine. To Haig's mind, the Soviet attempt to dominate the Third World had to be countered by such steps as the buildup of American military power, a demonstrated willingness by the United States to use it for diplomatic ends, and the provision of arms aid and other forms of assistance to vulnerable Third World countries. *Newsweek*, April 6, 1981, pp. 32–37.

67. *Newsweek*, April 20, 1981, p. 53; dispatch by Bernard Gwertzman, New York *Times*, April 9, 1981.

One of these was an overall increase in American defense spending, leading to a significant improvement in the nation's military position. Even before the Soviet invasion of Afghanistan, the Carter White House called for a 5.6 percent increase in military spending, and before he left office, President Carter had recommended even larger increases in the defense budget, exceeding $190 billion for 1982. Less than two months after he entered the Oval Office, President Ronald Reagan proposed raising national defense spending to $222 billion for 1982; even larger increases in military outlays were expected to be proposed by the Reagan White House in the future.[68]

The proposed overall improvement in the American military establishment would take several specific forms. Both the Carter and Reagan administrations were committed to building the new MX missile system (although whether it would be land- or sea-based had not yet been determined). The aging B-52 bomber—perhaps the most reliable component of America's strategic deterrent force—would be replaced by a new bomber (the B-1, or perhaps a still-to-be-developed "stealth" bomber capable of eluding radar detection). The Reagan Administration revived plans to develop a neutron bomb for possible use against Soviet ground forces in Europe; a new generation of intermediate-range missiles was also planned for introduction within the NATO area. High on the defense priority list also was a significant expansion in naval forces (from 450 to 600 ships) to counteract the U.S.S.R.'s growing lead in sea power and to give the United States the capability of defending the Persian Gulf area. With the armed forces of the United States at the lowest level in recent years (some two million troops in 1980 versus three million in 1970), a serious question also existed about whether the United States could continue to rely upon volunteers to meet its military personnel needs. Although many informed observers were skeptical that it would succeed, the Reagan Ad-

68. More detailed discussion of the improvement in America's military position after the Carter Doctrine is contained in "Many Actions Taken, Studied in Response to Mideast Crisis," *Congressional Quarterly* (Weekly Report), XXXVIII (January 26, 1980), 180–81; "Reagan Facing Tough Defense Choices," *Congressional Quarterly* (Weekly Report), XXXIX (February 7, 1981), 251–56; "Reagan's Defense Budget Calls for Few New Programs," *Congressional Quarterly* (Weekly Report), XXXIX, (March 7, 1981), 425–26; and New York *Times*, March 5, 1981, dispatch by Richard Halloran, and May 9, 1981, dispatch by Ernest Holsendolph.

ministration hoped to solve the problem by improving military pay scales and fringe benefits, as well as by hiring more civilian workers.[69]

The second, and most novel, step taken by the Carter and Reagan administrations to implement the Carter Doctrine was the creation of a new military contingent called the Rapid Deployment Force (RDF). As conceived, the RDF exemplified the kind of "projectable power" that Secretary of State Haig believed the United States required to protect its vital interests abroad.

The creation of the RDF must be understood against a background of declining American power globally, but particularly in the Middle East. Down to around 1970, Great Britain exercised the responsibility of preserving peace and stability in the Persian Gulf area. The evacuation of British power was followed by the emergence of Iran under the Shah as the strongest power within the region. In turn, Iranian military power was dependent upon maintaining close ties with the United States. After the Iranian revolution, the Soviet invasion of Afghanistan, and the Iraqi-Iranian war, the Persian Gulf area became a classic "power vacuum" or zone of ongoing political turbulence and conflict, with no country in a position to preserve the regional balance of power. Creation of the RDF signified that the United States was prepared to assume this role.[70]

The strategic concept that was given tangible form in the Rapid Deployment Force antedated the issuance of the Carter Doctrine. Strengthening the American military position in the Persian Gulf-Indian Ocean area, for example, had been recommended by President Carter's National Security adviser Zbigniew Brzezinski shortly after the Carter Administration took office. But as long as détente was a leading goal of the Carter White House, the concept received little encouragement. After the president's State of the Union Message on January 23, 1980, however, the idea was revived and in time became the primary instrument for the enforcement of the Carter Doctrine.[71]

The Rapid Deployment Force was a novel and continually evolving concept in American military strategy. Officials in Washington envi-

69. *U.S. News and World Report*, August 4, 1980, pp. 24–25.

70. Dispatch by Drew Middleton, New York *Times*, December 27, 1979.

71. America's strategic ties in the Persian Gulf area are analyzed more fully in Emile A. Nakhleh, *Arab-American Relations in the Persian Gulf* (Washington, D.C.: American Enterprise Institute, 1975), 27–55.

sioned it, for example, as a strike force that would be available for use not only in the Persian Gulf area, but in other regions where the security interests of the United States were endangered.[72] As conceived, the RDF would comprise a military unit of some 150,000 to 200,000 troops, drawn from all branches of the armed services. Some $25 billion would be expended during the period 1980–1985 to bring the RDF into being. By the latter date, it was envisioned that the United States would be able to deploy a fully equipped force of 100,000 troops to the Persian Gulf area within 35 days. The units comprising the RDF would be stationed in the United States, in the NATO area, in and around the Persian Gulf, and as far away as Diego Garcia (in the Indian Ocean), Guam, and other Pacific bases. New "floating supply depots" would also be constructed to lessen the dependence of the RDF on foreign base facilities.[73]

The Rapid Deployment Force, it must be emphasized, is a new and untested concept. Several years will be required before the RDF becomes fully operational, and an even longer period will be needed before many of the problems associated with its use are fully (or in some cases, even partially) overcome. In limited space, we may focus upon the more important of these problems by posing a series of interrelated questions about the Rapid Deployment Force as an instrument for implementing the Carter Doctrine.

What is the principal threat against which the RDF would be used? In the context of events of the early 1980s, as our previous discussion has emphasized, the answer to that question seemed clear enough. The RDF was designed to counter overt Soviet aggression in the Persian Gulf area. In short, it was created to prevent "another Afghanistan" from cutting the oil lifelines from the Middle East to the West.

Yet officials of both the Carter and Reagan administrations recog-

72. Dispatch by Drew Middleton, New York *Times*, March 20, 1980.
73. As the RDF evolved, its core would be the 82nd and 101st Army Airborne divisions, along with the 24th Infantry Division (collectively, less than fifty thousand troops), supplemented by a marine brigade and other navy and air force units. More detailed discussion of the composition, mission, and problems of the Rapid Deployment Force may be found in "Carter Legislative Message to Congress," *Congressional Quarterly* (Weekly Report), XXXVIII (January 26, 1980), 224; "Budget Stresses Rapid Deployment Forces," *Congressional Quarterly* (Weekly Report), XXXVIII (February 2, 1980), 247–54; "Reagan Facing Tough Defense Choices," 251–56; and dispatch by Richard Halloran, New York *Times*, April 20, 1981.

nized that Soviet aggrandizement was not the only—and it might not be the most dangerous—threat to Persian Gulf security. Theoretically, one commentator declared, the RDF existed to counter *any* threats to regional security, "whether they come from the Soviet Union, from disputes among nations in the region, such as the current war between Iraq and Iran, or from internal instability." Governments within the Middle East were cognizant that, several years earlier, Secretary of State Henry Kissinger had threatened to use American military forces to preserve Western access to Middle East oil supplies—even against efforts by governments within the region to restrict shipments to the United States and its allies. Moreover, late in November, 1979, President Carter had seriously considered a seizure by the American armed forces of Iran's oil installations in retaliation against Tehran at a time when Iranian authorities were threatening to try the captured American hostages as spies.[74] While neither of these moves was actually carried out, the existence of the Rapid Deployment Force meant that comparable actions by the United States might be taken in the future.

Uncertainty about the nature of the enemy against which the RDF would be used was highlighted by the views of a former high-ranking American military official, who wrote, "In the Persian Gulf . . . we do not know exactly who the enemy may be or where he may attack. Perhaps we may face a massive Soviet attack to capture Iran's oil fields, or perhaps an internal rebellion in some key oil-producing area, or perhaps a thrust by one Arab country into another that would jeopardize our oil supplies."[75]

What precisely is the purpose or "mission" of the RDF? From the inception, that question has elicited widely varying answers from American military planners and informed students of American foreign policy. The RDF may in fact have one or more distinct missions. The primary mission of the RDF, for example, may be to serve mainly as a deterrent force, preventing new Soviet encroachments within the Persian Gulf region. Alternatively, the RDF may function mainly as a symbol of America's direct involvement in the security of the Persian Gulf area, with Western strategic missile and air power constituting the ultimate deterrent against Soviet aggression.

74. Dispatch by Richard Halloran, New York *Times*, March 10, 1981; "Reagan Facing Tough Defense Choices," 255; New York *Times*, May 13, 1981.
75. Adm. Stansfield Turner, "Toward a New Defense Strategy," *New York Times Magazine*, March 29, 1981, p. 16.

Another possibility is that the RDF may exist primarily to fight a kind of "holding action" against superior Soviet forces, making any contemplated Russian aggression very costly for Moscow and defending the endangered area long enough for large-scale reinforcements to be brought in from the United States, Western Europe, and other sites. (In turn, the military feasibility of this mission depends heavily upon another problem we shall consider at a later stage: the availability of adequate and highly mobile facilities for reinforcing the RDF in the Middle East.)

As other qualified commentators assess the matter, the RDF may have still another important mission: to engage in possible "preventive action" to forestall Soviet seizure of Persian Gulf oil fields, thereby keeping them out of Russian hands. If, for example, the Soviet Union threatened to invade Iran, America's countermove might be to seize the country's southern oil fields before they could be occupied by the Red Army. As one commander analyzed the problem, the goal would not only be to retain Western access to Persian Gulf oil, but also to convince Soviet officials that "it would be in their best interest to stop at some point short of the oil fields."[76]

If uncertainty surrounded the exact mission of the Rapid Deployment Force, a partial explanation was that, under the Reagan Administration, American officials were reexamining the larger problem of the nation's response to Soviet diplomatic and military adventurism. The Reagan White House hoped to provide the United States with a wider range of military options than had been available in the recent past. Toward the Middle East, one commentator found, Republican policy-makers sought to confront Moscow "with the possibility of a far larger conflict if Russian forces try to deny the United States access to oil." If a new Soviet-instigated threat to the security of the Persian Gulf area occurred, it "could turn into a long conventional war for which the United States must be prepared."[77]

Is the RDF a militarily feasible undertaking? The salience of this question was underscored by the observation of one commentator early in 1980: "It is 12,000 miles, or about 25 days' [sailing for the U.S. Navy], from the East Coast [of the United States] and around Af-

---

76. *Ibid.*
77. See the views of Defense Department officials, as summarized in dispatch by Richard Halloran, New York *Times*, April 19, 1981.

rica to the Arabian Sea [or Persian Gulf], and the same from [the] West Coast across the Pacific and Indian Oceans" to the Persian Gulf area.[78]

The military feasibility of the Rapid Deployment Force depends of course upon a host of circumstances and factors, many of which cannot be fully anticipated. These include the nature, locale, and timing of a new Soviet incursion into the Middle East; the response of the countries within the area to it; the availability and readiness of American forces to repel that attack; the reaction of the NATO countries, Communist China, and other nations outside the area; and many other imponderables.

Based upon the model of Afghanistan, for example, it is not unrealistic to suppose that if Moscow plans another aggressive move in the Persian Gulf area, it will launch a surprise attack, carried out by overwhelming military force, against a target (perhaps such as the northern provinces of Iran or Iraq) that is well adapted to Moscow's power and purposes. In that case, the RDF could be outnumbered by as much as ten to one by Soviet troops and armored forces. The RDF could do little more than wage a "delaying action" against a superior Soviet military machine.[79]

A few months after the issuance of the Carter Doctrine, a report prepared by the Library of Congress found that in attempting to defend the Persian Gulf area, the United States would assume very high, possibly unacceptable, military risks. While American forces could likely preserve the security of Middle East oil fields from local threats, it would face a difficult challenge in defending them against a determined Soviet drive to capture them. Another experienced military official is convinced that the United States cannot possibly "station enough forces permanently in the area" to defend against a Soviet military thrust against Iran or even against an attempt by indigenous military forces to seize the Persian Gulf oil fields in an effort to deny their use to the United States and its allies.[80]

Some American military strategists believe that in the face of a determined Soviet military drive to dominate the Persian Gulf area, the United States would sooner or later be compelled to use tactical nu-

78. Dispatch by Richard Halloran, New York *Times*, January 5, 1980.
79. *Newsweek*, February 4, 1980, p. 25.
80. Dispatch by Drew Middleton, New York *Times*, July 14, 1980; Turner, "Toward a New Defense Strategy," 16.

clear weapons against militarily superior Russian forces. In the process, extensive damage of course would be inflicted upon Middle East oil installations, perhaps rendering them inoperable for a prolonged period of time.[81]

Yet as our earlier discussion emphasized, undisguised Soviet aggression against one or more oil-producing states of the Middle East seems a relatively remote contingency. If the Kremlin seeks to block Western access to Persian Gulf oil, it is more likely to pursue this goal by relying upon pro-Communist groups and revolutionary movements in the area. Alternatively (as it had done for several years in Africa), the Kremlin may seek to wage a "proxy war," in which its client states threaten established governments and Western interests in the region.

From a different perspective, the creation of the RDF poses a unique and highly complex set of command and operational problems for the Defense Department. The RDF will be an "independent" command consisting of army, marine, navy, and air force elements merged into a single strike force capable of defending the nation's vital interests in the Middle East and other crisis zones. Its successful operation will require the utmost in coordinated military planning and cooperation among the separate service arms.[82]

Logistically, the RDF also faces innumerable and difficult problems—so many as to induce one study to say that in its effort to defend the Persian Gulf area, the RDF is in danger of "getting there firstest with the leastest"! Some units comprising the RDF will be based in the United States; others in Western Europe; others within the Middle East; others on the Indian Ocean island of Diego Garcia (2,500 miles distant); and still others many thousands of miles away on Pacific bases like Guam and Okinawa. Transporting the RDF to a Persian Gulf trouble spot calls for the existence of air and naval transport facilities that are still now on the drawing boards (such as the planned CX cargo plane). Even the problem of providing adequate supplies of drinking water for the RDF in some regions of the Middle East could prove an extremely difficult undertaking.[83]

Does the existence of the RDF enhance the stability and security of

81. Dispatch by Richard Burt, New York *Times*, February 2, 1980.
82. Dispatch by Fred S. Hoffman, Baton Rouge *Morning Advocate*, April 25, 1981.
83. *Newsweek*, July 14, 1980, pp. 30–36.

the Persian Gulf area? As with the other questions posed about the Rapid Deployment Force, this one also is highly debatable. For officials of the Carter and Reagan administrations, the issuance of the Carter Doctrine and the creation of the RDF have *already* contributed positively to the security of this vital region. Since its invasion of Afghanistan, the Kremlin has not similarly threatened the independence of other Persian Gulf states. For example, Moscow refrained from exploiting the internal political chaos in Iran, to jeopardize that strife-torn country's national integrity, nor did the Soviet Union overtly intervene in the Iraqi-Iranian war to pursue expansionist goals. Despite the country's vulnerability, Pakistan has thus far experienced no direct threat of Soviet aggrandizement. Such Soviet restraint in the Persian Gulf area might, therefore, be attributed to caution displayed by Russian policy-makers in the light of the Carter Doctrine and the creation of the RDF. (It could, of course, equally well be explained by a variety of other factors, such as Soviet difficulties in Poland, continuing tensions with Communist China, and ongoing Soviet internal problems. Soviet restraint might also prove, as some commentators have asserted, that Moscow's objectives in Afghanistan were always limited and dictated by the unique circumstances existing in that country.)

As our earlier discussion has indicated, the prospect of a substantial American military buildup in the Middle East has also proved a destabilizing development in several respects. Although officials in Washington may view the RDF as a force whose dominant purpose is to deter Soviet ambitions in the area, most governments within the region do not view it in that light. Inescapably, the RDF has become enmeshed in existing regional disputes, and its presence has unquestionably aggravated regional tensions. Thus far, American officials have discovered no way of disentangling efforts to enforce the Carter Doctrine from Middle Eastern political controversies having no direct relation to the prospect of Soviet military intervention in the Persian Gulf area.

This problem was highlighted in 1981 by Saudi Arabia's urgent request that the Reagan Administration sell that nation airborne radar planes (AWAKs) and other modern aircraft. In submitting this request to Congress, the Reagan White House emphasized that this step was necessary in order to preserve Saudi Arabia's security from external aggression. Traditionally, Saudi Arabia has maintained close ties with the United States; and the Saudi government's influence in the deliberations of the Organization of Petroleum Exporting Countries (OPEC) has often been decisive. During a visit to the United States, in 1981, the Saudi oil minister, Sheik Ahmed Yamani, told an American audience that these modern weapons were essential to his country's defense needs. Yamani declared, "We are surrounded by all types of countries who are focusing on the oil fields, on your own interests, and we think Saudi Arabia has to be strong." Predictably, Saudi Arabia's request elicited a highly negative reaction from the government of Israel and its supporters within the United States, who believed it would gravely jeopardize Israel's security.

Yet even while Riyadh was pressing Washington to provide modern aircraft, Saudi officials continued to express their opposition to a large American military presence in the area. Saudi Arabia still refused to make base facilities available to the RDF, on the grounds that doing so would produce a new source of instability in the region. "We don't think that the American [military] presence will help," said Sheik Yamani. "We think it will invite a Russian presence somewhere in the area." [84]

Insofar as the Rapid Deployment Force became a graphic symbol of the Carter Doctrine, its creation marked a significant change from the principles enunciated by the Nixon Doctrine. Issued while memories of the Vietnam experience were still fresh in the American mind, the keynote of the Nixon Doctrine was the idea that vulnerable countries must assume the primary responsibility for their own defense against external aggression. The Nixon Doctrine thus expressed a military reality derived from the Vietnam conflict: it is virtually impossible for the United States to defend another country against an external threat when it is unable or unwilling to defend itself. With some measure of justification, critics asserted that this lesson was largely being ignored in the creation and use of the Rapid Deployment Force. A Pakistani

84. See the excerpts from the speech by Sheik Ahmed Yamani, in dispatch by Steven Rattner, New York *Times*, April 20, 1981. For congressional attitudes on the question of military sales to Saudi Arabia, see "Fight Likely in Congress This Year over Proposed Weapons Sales to Saudi Arabia," *Congressional Quarterly* (Weekly Report), XXXVIII (January 12, 1980), 59–62. Israeli attitudes are described in UPI dispatch, Baton Rouge *Morning Advocate*, April 23, 1981.

official reminded Washington of this fact when he observed, "The Carter Doctrine brings us no solace. . . . If the U.S. wants to stop Soviet aggression, it must strengthen the frontline countries to defend themselves." [85]

Another problem inherent in the creation and deployment of the RDF within the Middle East is the question of what would happen if supplies of modern American weapons fell into the hands of Communist or other anti-American groups. Generalizing about earlier American attempts to establish a strong military position in the Persian Gulf area, a member of the Senate Foreign Relations Committee warned: "We should have learned from the fall of the Shah [of Iran] that our sophisticated military equipment should not be entrusted to unstable regimes. . . . A change in government or the outbreak of another regional war could entrap both our personnel and our policies." [86]

With all the problems surrounding its creation and deployment, the RDF has become part of the American military establishment and an important instrument of its Middle Eastern diplomacy. For reasons we have indicated, its effectiveness remains to be tested by experience. Whatever else may be said about it, the RDF marks a crucial development in American foreign policy toward the Middle East. Making it an effective instrument of American diplomacy in the vital Persian Gulf area will likely test the ingenuity and resourcefulness of policymakers in Washington for many years to come. [87]

85. *Newsweek,* July 14, 1980, p. 31.

86. See the views of Sen. Joseph R. Biden, Jr. (Democrat of Delaware), in New York *Times,* April 15, 1981.

87. The discussion of the nature and problems of the Rapid Deployment Force draws upon more extended treatment in New York *Times,* February 29, 1980, dispatch by Richard Burt, March 20, July 14, and September 28, 1980, dispatches by Drew Middleton, March 30, 1980, dispatch by Roger Fisher, and June 13, 1980, and March 10, 1981, dispatches by Richard Halloran. See also the discussions of the RDF in *U.S. News and World Report,* February 25, 1980, pp. 33–34, November 3, 1980, pp. 39–41; and *Newsweek,* July 14, 1980, pp. 30–36.

9 / Conclusion: Doctrines in the American Diplomatic Tradition

There is no Carter Doctrine, or Vance Doctrine . . . because of a belief that the [international] environment we are looking at is far too complex to be reduced to a doctrine in the tradition of post–World War II American foreign policy. Indeed, the Carter approach to foreign policy rests on a belief that not only is the world too complex to be reduced to a doctrine, but there is something inherently wrong with having a doctrine at all.
—Leslie Gelb

I have been struck by the congenital aversions of Americans to taking specific decisions on specific problems, and by their persistent urge to seek universal formulae or doctrines in which to clothe and justify particular actions. —George F. Kennan

Most American statesmen, so it seems, have cherished during their careers the possibility that they may become authors of [diplomatic] Doctrines.
—Robert H. Ferrell

Our concluding chapter on the role of doctrines in American foreign policy begins by once more calling attention to an intriguing paradox about the American society. In their internal political affairs, Americans are among the least "doctrinal" peoples known to modern history. The American people tend to shun rigidly doctrinal political movements, and they have traditionally exhibited very little interest in political ideologies (except perhaps to be suspicious of them). Politically, the preference of most Americans is for middle-of-the-road positions. A typically American approach to public issues was the New Deal—a highly eclectic combination of programs, with little ideological coherence. For most citizens, the proper standard for judging the success of the New Deal was essentially pragmatic: how well did it work in solving the country's domestic problems? Not one American in ten thousand knew or cared about its ideological origins or its philosophical consistency. Referring to this historic American propensity, a European observer said, "If America ever dies it will be from a sur-

feit of pragmatism." Or as a study of American public opinion toward
foreign policy issues in the mid-1970s found: "Faced with some different ideas and a changing world, Americans chose eclectically what
they thought made sense and rejected what they thought didn't."[1]

Indeed, it is not amiss to say that in their outlook toward foreign
affairs, Americans have often displayed a strong antidoctrinal bias.
This was clearly exemplified by the American attitude toward communism during and after World War II. As much as any other feature of
the Soviet system, it was Communist doctrine—particularly such specific tenets as the concept of a "world revolution" led by Moscow—
which repelled and alarmed Americans. As one study of the Cold War
found, the United States perceived a grave threat to its security from
"the real or apparent nature of Soviet doctrine, expectations, and intentions."[2] Or, as another analysis of recent American diplomacy expressed it, since 1917 the Kremlin's diplomatic behavior has endangered the security of other countries because Soviet policy has been
made by "doctrinal universalists in accordance with their own lay religion." Insofar as they conceived of the Cold War as an ideological
clash, many Americans tended to regard it as a contest between democratic pragmatism and Communist doctrinal orthodoxy and rigidity.[3]

Yet pragmatic as American attitudes have been historically, the United States has also exhibited an affinity for diplomatic "doctrines"—
and this process has been greatly accelerated in the postwar period.
With regard to their role as diplomatic instruments, most commentators would agree that this reliance upon doctrines is a distinctively
American phenomenon. Other countries may from time to time promulgate diplomatic doctrines, but such pronouncements have been exceptional and of relatively minor importance vis-à-vis the conspicuous

1. Quoted in George W. Ball, *The Discipline of Power: Essentials of a Modern World
Structure* (Boston: Little, Brown, 1968), 27; Ben J. Wattenberg, *The Real America: A
Surprising Examination of the State of the Union* (Garden City, N.Y.: Doubleday, 1974),
211.

2. Paul Seabury, *Power, Freedom, and Diplomacy: The Foreign Policy of the United
States of America* (New York: Random House, 1963), 388. See also the view of Marshall Shulman that the most striking characteristic of Soviet foreign policy has been the
"way in which policies undertaken for short-term, expediential purposes have tended
to . . . become embedded in doctrine and political strategy." J. W. Fulbright, *Old Myths
and New Realities* (New York: Random House, 1964), 66.

3. George W. Ball, *Diplomacy for a Crowded World: An American Foreign Policy*
(Boston: Little, Brown, 1976), 43–44; Seabury, *Power, Freedom, and Diplomacy*, 388.

place held by such doctrines in the diplomatic tradition of the United States.

How is this interesting dichotomy to be explained? Why should a nondoctrinal society exhibit such a preference for doctrinal pronouncements in foreign affairs? What role do such doctrines play in American diplomacy? How do they contribute to—and how do they impair—the achievement of important external goals? What is the future of foreign policy doctrines for the United States? Such questions will provide the focus of our final chapter. At the outset, attention needs to be devoted to a problem that is common to each of the individual doctrines analyzed thus far: what have been the meaning and connotations of foreign policy "doctrines" in the American experience?

Significant Doctrinal Connotations

An eminent diplomatic historian has relayed this anecdote about two "patriotic Americans" who were discussing the Monroe Doctrine. "What is this I hear," one asked the other, "that you do not believe in the Monroe Doctrine?" The other replied indignantly: "It's a lie. I never said I did not believe in the Monroe Doctrine. I do believe in it. It is the palladium of our liberties. I would die for the Monroe Doctrine. All I said was that I do not know what it means." Another commentator has observed that the Monroe Doctrine "has been invoked by isolationists on the one hand and internationalists on the other." Still another historian has described the doctrine by saying: "Whatever our foreign policy happens to be for the moment, it is called the 'Monroe Doctrine.'"[4]

From President Monroe's pronouncement in 1823 to President Carter's in 1980, the problem of the "meaning" of the nation's diplomatic doctrines has been a recurrent question, eliciting a wide variety of answers. At the risk of some oversimplification, the problem may be viewed as involving two rather distinct questions. In what sense did these important policy statements constitute diplomatic doctrines? And what did their particular provisions mean under any given set of

4. Thomas A. Bailey, *The Man in the Street: The Impact of American Public Opinion on Foreign Policy* (New York: Macmillan, 1948), 256; Julius W. Pratt, *A History of United States Foreign Policy* (Englewood Cliffs, N.J.: Prentice-Hall, 1955), 167; Albert B. Hart, *The Monroe Doctrine: An Interpretation* (Boston: Little, Brown, 1916), 350.

external circumstances? We shall reserve treatment of the latter problem for a later stage. At this point, we are interested primarily in why these declarations were viewed as *doctrines* of American foreign policy.

Collectively, the major foreign policy doctrines of the United States may be said to possess three important and reasonably distinct connotations. First, they have nearly always had a legal dimension. Most have stated (or attempted to state) a legal principle. The Monroe Doctrine survived, it has been said, because it symbolized "the highest and finest contribution of the Americas to international law."[5] A French student of Monroe's message noted that American diplomatic behavior under the Monroe Doctrine had "a judicial look" highly appealing to a society in which terms like "law" and "legality" were venerated.[6]

According to George F. Kennan, the Open Door policy, and its offshoot the Stimson Doctrine, stemmed from America's tendency "to transplant legal concepts from the domestic to the international field." Traditionally, the United States has conceived of diplomatic problems in terms of "general contractual obligations and verbal understandings." In the same vein, Secretary of State Stimson believed that his doctrine affirmed a fundamental and indispensable principle of international law condemning aggression by one state against another, and it attempted to prevent "a return to the jungle law of international diplomacy."[7]

To the assertion by Soviet Premier Khrushchev in 1960 that the Monroe Doctrine was now moribund, the State Department replied with a detailed rejoinder, emphasizing that the doctrine was still operative, since it enunciated established principles of international law.[8] Regarding the Truman Doctrine, several commentators have made the point that it was a vital step in the emergence of a set of "ground rules" or tacit set of international law principles recognized by Wash-

5. Donald M. Dozer (ed.), *The Monroe Doctrine: Its Modern Significance* (New York: Alfred A. Knopf, 1965), 177.
6. See the views of the French writer De Beaumarchais in 1898, as quoted in Hart, *The Monroe Doctrine*, 352–53.
7. George F. Kennan, *American Diplomacy: 1900–1950* (New York: New American Library, 1952), 49, 93–94; Norman A. Graebner (ed.), *Ideas and Diplomacy: Readings in the Intellectual Tradition of American Foreign Policy* (New York: Oxford University Press, 1964), 497.
8. *Department of State Bulletin*, XLIII (August 1, 1960), 170–71.

ington and Moscow for waging the Cold War. The acceptance of rules was in turn essential for progress toward détente.[9]

America, innumerable observers of the culture at home and abroad have concluded, is a "law-oriented" (not of course necessarily a "law-abiding") society. The perceptive Frenchman Alexis de Tocqueville observed that most questions of American public policy were sooner or later converted into legal controversies, which the courts are called upon to resolve—a tendency that is even more pronounced today than in the early nineteenth century.[10] The American preference for a "government of laws and not of men" finds its reflection in the nation's diplomatic conduct. Ideas embodied in legal precepts are entitled to respect and to obedience. America's influence abroad, Stanley Hoffmann believes, is in part conveyed by "the civilizing and refining power through law and legal institutions."[11]

For a season (and there are perhaps cycles in such intellectual fads), it was fashionable among the realpolitik school of international politics to derogate international law and to contend that its influence upon the diplomatic behavior of states was nil vis-à-vis the pursuit of "national interest" or attempts to maintain the balance of power. Few well informed students of international relations in the nuclear age are prepared to accept such reasoning. Throughout its diplomatic experience, the United States has been identified with the concept of "global community" or what is sometimes called "the rule of law" in global political relationships. The diplomatic doctrines of the United States testify to the durability of this ideal in the American consciousness.

Another commonplace connotation of the word *doctrine* is a religious tenet or dogma—and the doctrines of American foreign policy have also had a religious or metaphysical dimension. Referring to the Monroe Doctrine, William Graham Sumner said that in order to describe it, "we must have recourse to theological language. A doctrine is an article of faith. It is something which you are bound to believe, not because you have some rational grounds for believing it true, but

9. See, for example, the views of Paul Y. Hammond, *The Cold War Years: American Foreign Policy Since 1945* (New York: Harcourt, Brace and World, 1969), 10; and Ball, *The Discipline of Power,* 200–201.

10. Alexis de Tocqueville, *Democracy in America* (New York: Random House, 1945), 102–109.

11. Andrew M. Scott and Raymond H. Dawson (eds.), *Readings in the Making of American Foreign Policy* (New York: Macmillan, 1965), 35.

because you belong to such and such a church or denomination. . . . A doctrine is an abstract principle; it is necessarily absolute in its scope and abstruse in its terms; it is a metaphysical assertion."[12]

Another student of the Monroe Doctrine said that it came to be viewed as a "sacred principle" analogous to the Ten Commandments, which "are not questioned or limited or construed, but obeyed." The diplomatic historian Thomas A. Bailey quotes an unidentified English observer concerning the Monroe Doctrine: "To the Americans, the Monroe Doctrine is like God or religion to a small child—something fearful, something to inspire awe, something, if necessary, to fight for." To the mind of the Spanish philosopher, Salvador de Madariaga, the Monroe Doctrine was "not a doctrine but a dogma . . . not one dogma but two, to wit: the dogma of the infallibility of the American President and the dogma of the immaculate conception of American foreign policy."[13]

Some of the later doctrines of American foreign policy exhibited this same religious-like or sacrosanct quality. The Open Door policy–Stimson Doctrine was regarded by President Hoover as exemplifying America's moral censure of Japan's aggressive behavior. Frank Tannenbaum concluded that it reflected the American society's "sense of justice" and the application of this idea to foreign affairs.[14] A number of commentators believe that the Truman Doctrine manifested the Manichean outlook of the American people toward external political developments, or the tendency to regard the conflict with communism as a struggle between the forces of good and evil.[15] In John Spanier's view, Truman's doctrine was a modern-day application of Lincoln's principle that a society could not exist "half slave and half free." Secretary of State John Foster Dulles conceived of the Eisenhower Doctrine as a "universal doctrine," embodying transcendent moral and ethical

12. Graebner (ed.), *Ideas and Diplomacy*, 259–60.
13. Hart, *The Monroe Doctrine*, 371; Bailey, *The Man in the Street*, 256–57; Dozer (ed.), *The Monroe Doctrine*, title page.
14. Wayne S. Cole, *An Interpretive History of American Foreign Relations* (Homewood, Ill.: Dorsey Press, 1974), 375; Robert A. Goldwin (ed.), *Readings in American Foreign Policy* (2nd ed.; New York: Oxford University Press, 1971), 675–79.
15. James Chace, *A World Elsewhere: The New American Foreign Policy* (New York: Charles Scribner's Sons, 1973), 85. Manichaeism derived from the teachings of the third-century Middle Eastern philosopher, Mani, who taught that the world was in the grip of a struggle between two great contending forces, light and darkness or good and evil.

precepts. In a somewhat different vein, the Johnson Doctrine for Southeast Asia was described by one commentator as reflecting the "missionary impulse" in American diplomacy or the desire of Americans to "transform the world" morally and ethically.[16] (Few commentators viewed the later Nixon and Carter doctrines in this light.)

Former Secretary of State Dean Acheson has said that "the moral element is inevitable and indigenous to the [foreign] policy of a democracy such as ours." For some century and a half after President Monroe set the precedent, America's diplomatic doctrines have exhibited a high religious-moral content. Considering that they were American diplomatic pronouncements, this fact was perhaps predictable and inevitable. One of the earliest American political tracts, the Mayflower Compact (1620), was a profoundly religious document. The Declaration of Independence was infused with religious and moral concepts, as was the American Constitution. "In God We Trust" was the motto of the new Republic. Tannenbaum has concluded that the concept of "the juridical equality and moral integrity of states" has been perhaps the most conspicuous theme of American diplomacy since 1787.[17]

Beginning with the Monroe Doctrine, each of America's doctrines has exhibited a third fundamental characteristic. These doctrines have involved a forceful assertion of the ideological principles espoused by the American society. Throughout the nation's diplomatic history, there have been two broad interpretations of pronouncements like the Monroe Doctrine, the Truman Doctrine, the Carter Doctrine, and the other doctrinal pronouncements included in our study. One school of thought—the realpolitik approach—has emphasized the idea that, behind the ideological verbiage clothing these doctrines, in actuality the United States was attempting to maintain the "balance of power"; to assert its "national interest" in the face of existing (or assumed) threats to it; and to apply American power abroad in an effort to preserve

16. John Spanier, "Choices We Did Not Have," in Charles Gati (ed.), *Caging the Bear: Containment and the Cold War* (Indianapolis: Bobbs-Merrill, 1974), 134; Jules Davids, *America and the World of Our Time: U.S. Diplomacy in the Twentieth Century* (New York: Random House, 1960), 522; James C. Thomson, Jr., "Historical Legacies and Bureaucratic Procedures," in Thomas G. Paterson (ed.), *Major Problems in American Foreign Policy* (2 vols.; Lexington, Mass.: D. C. Heath, 1978), II, 480.

17. Dean Acheson, *This Vast External Realm* (New York: W. W. Norton, 1973), 13; Goldwin (ed.), *Readings in American Foreign Policy*, 665.

national security. Here, we shall confine our analysis to the second interpretation: the idea that the diplomatic doctrines of the United States have exemplified ideological and political principles deeply embedded in the American ethos.

As emphasized in Chapter 1, the Monroe Doctrine was a forceful assertion of the uniqueness of American ideological principles. The leading student of the Monroe Doctrine has called attention to one of its most prominent themes—the incompatibility between the two political "value systems" of America and Europe. In Paul Seabury's words, the Truman Doctrine was "an American declaration of ideological hostilities." President Truman was convinced that his doctrine reflected "the ideals and traditions of our nation." [18] More concretely, we may identify seven specific tenets of American political ideology which have been reflected in the nation's major diplomatic doctrines.

1. The uniqueness of the New World. One of the most prominent and enduring themes of American history has been the idea "that America occupies a unique place and has a special destiny among the nations of the world." [19] In 1765, John Adams viewed the settlement of America "with reverence and wonder, as the opening of a grand scheme and design in Providence for the illumination of the ignorant, and the emancipation of the slavish part of mankind all over the earth." The poet Walt Whitman described the American society "as the custodian of the future of humanity." An experienced diplomat has said that Americans have always regarded their society as "a pristine land in a corrupt world." The uniqueness of the American society (coupled with the idea of America's "mission" to the world, which we shall discuss below) has been a recurrent motif in the national ethos for over two centuries. [20]

As much as any other factor, this conviction prompted the issuance of the Monroe Doctrine. According to Dexter Perkins, much of the adulation which the American people subsequently accorded to the

18. Dexter Perkins, *The American Approach to Foreign Policy* (Rev. ed.; New York: Atheneum, 1968), 6; Paul Seabury, *The Rise and Decline of the Cold War* (New York: Basic Books, 1967), 16; Harry S. Truman, *Memoirs: Years of Trial and Hope, 1946–1952* (Garden City, N.Y.: Doubleday, 1956), 101.

19. Edward M. Burns, *The American Idea of Mission: Concepts of National Purpose and Destiny* (New Brunswick, N.J.: Rutgers University Press, 1957), 5.

20. These and other examples illustrating the uniqueness of the American society are cited in *ibid.*, 5–32. See also Ball, *The Discipline of Power*, 25.

Monroe Doctrine stemmed from its emphasis upon "the distinction between the institutions of Europe and the institutions of America."[21] Basically the same point could be made about most of the "corollaries" of the Monroe Doctrine after 1823, and about the other doctrinal pronouncements in American foreign policy which followed during the next century and a half. One commentator has described the "Polk Corollary" to the Monroe Doctrine in 1845, for example, by saying that a leading purpose was to prevent the importation of foreign ideological concepts (balance of power, despotism, and political machinations) into the New World. According to Walter Lippmann, for countless Americans the Open Door policy toward China similarly struck "chords of memory and of [political] faith" for Americans; it communicated the nation's "indelible antipathy" toward monarchy, special privilege, monopoly, and imperialism.[22]

With the possible exception of the Nixon Doctrine (where the theme of conflict between the United States and the Soviet Union as ideological rivals was muted, if not eliminated), all of the postwar doctrines of American foreign policy have carried on this tradition. The Truman Doctrine, Seabury concluded, reflected ideological values that have been part of the American tradition since the time of Thomas Jefferson and were conspicuous in Wilsonian thought. The two Johnson doctrines presupposed that ideological values were at stake in the conflict between Soviet-supported communism and American efforts to preserve freedom in Southeast Asia and in Latin America. The Carter Doctrine (while recognizing America's strategic interest in the Persian Gulf area) similarly conceived of the threat posed to the security of the Persian Gulf region in ideological terms. This ideological dichotomy could be interpreted as merely a modern adaptation of the Monroe Doctrine's earlier distinction between the New World and the Old World.

2. Belief in peace and nonviolent relationships. "If there was one

21. Perkins, *The American Approach to Foreign Policy*, 80. See also the contention of Samuel F. Bemis that the Monroe Doctrine reflected long-standing American political ideas and principles, as exemplified in Thomas Paine's *Common Sense* and other writings in the eighteenth and early nineteenth centuries. Samuel F. Bemis, *A Diplomatic History of the United States* (Rev. ed.; New York: Henry Holt, 1942), 12.

22. Frederick Merk, *The Monroe Doctrine and American Expansionism: 1843–1849* (New York: Random House, 1966), 54–57; Goldwin (ed.), *Readings in American Foreign Policy*, 269–70.

fond hope of the Founders of the American republic," one study of the national ethos asserts, "it was to keep it a nation dedicated to the arts of peace." The leaders of the new Republic were determined "to do everything in their power to prevent the growth of a dominant military clique or a habit in the people of looking to force or conquest for a solution of their problems."[23]

Beginning with the Monroe Doctrine, through the Carter Doctrine, all of the major foreign policy pronouncements encompassed by our study have had the preservation of peace as a leading objective. The promulgators of the Monroe Doctrine believed that the peace of the Western Hemisphere would be promoted by keeping the Holy Alliance out of Latin America and by preventing threatened Russian expansionist moves on the American west coast. Secretary of State John Hay and later advocates of the Open Door policy were convinced that adherence to it by the great powers would assure peace in East Asia. In the early 1930s, President Hoover and Secretary of State Stimson viewed the acceptance of the Stimson Doctrine as an essential step toward peace in Asia, and possibly for the world. Similarly, the purpose of the containment strategy enunciated by the Truman Doctrine was to halt the drift toward a possible new global conflict between the superpowers. For Truman, and for Senator Vandenberg, the chief congressional spokesman on foreign policy questions in this period, the lessons of the 1930s—when the Allies failed to act decisively in halting the steady drift toward World War II—served as a profoundly influential factor in the issuance of the doctrine.[24]

The same generalization can be made about the postwar doctrines of American foreign policy: each of them was designed to enhance the prospects for peace and to reduce the likelihood of war. President Eisenhower believed that his doctrine would avert a great power conflict in the Middle East, and some twenty-five years later, President Carter believed the same thing about his Persian Gulf doctrine. President Johnson viewed his Southeast Asian doctrine as an essential step toward achieving peace in Vietnam; and his doctrine for Latin America was designed to prevent a cold war encounter south of the border.

23. Burns, *The American Idea of Mission*, 247.
24. Truman, *Memoirs: Years of Trial and Hope*, 101; Arthur H. Vandenberg, Jr. (ed.), *The Private Papers of Senator Vandenberg* (Boston: Houghton Mifflin, 1952), 341–42.

Richard M. Nixon regarded his doctrine as providing a new "structure for peace" in the post–Vietnam War era. The common denominator of these doctrinal pronouncements was an underlying American belief that a peaceful international system is possible and that (in keeping with the mission of the New World) America had a special obligation to exhibit leadership in its achievement.

3. Faith in self-government. The diplomatic doctrines of the United States have also reflected the American society's belief in, and preference for, the principle of self-government. The ideal was conspicuous in the Monroe Doctrine. Although he was dissuaded from doing so, President Monroe wanted to include in his policy declaration a resounding statement of American support for the effort by the Greek people during this period to acquire self-rule from Turkey. Monroe's contemporaries were well aware that his doctrine indirectly conveyed America's strong pro-Greek sentiments in that struggle. As a general philosophical principle, the Monroe Doctrine meant that Americans were willing to sacrifice their lives for the concept of self-rule.[25]

The same point can be made about the Open Door policy-Stimson Doctrine. Despite frequent criticisms that it represented little more than American "sermonizing" and posturing in the conduct of foreign affairs, the United States did in fact defend the principle of Chinese independence from Japanese hegemony. If it did so belatedly (failing to provide large-scale assistance to China until after the attack on Pearl Harbor in 1941), Japan's encroachments nonetheless steadily alienated American opinion. In time, the rulers of Japan decided that war with the United States was inevitable, and it came at Pearl Harbor.

Perhaps more than any doctrine in American diplomatic experience, the Truman Doctrine exemplified America's attachment to the ideal of national independence and self-determination. In effect, the doctrine stated that threats to the independence of Greece and Turkey would be forcibly resisted by the United States, and comparable threats to the security of other nations in the future would also be resisted. Significantly, the "new era" in American foreign policy contemplated by the Nixon Doctrine did not change America's commitment to that principle. It was again reiterated forcefully in the Carter Doctrine, after the

25. Perkins, *The American Approach to Foreign Policy*, 79; Hart, *The Monroe Doctrine*, 398.

Soviet Union had embarked upon what the doctrine called "aggression" against independent Afghanistan.

4. The power of America's "example." Americans, Kennan has said, "like to attribute a universal significance to decisions we have already found it necessary, for limited and parochial reasons, to take." This conclusion applies with special pertinence to American foreign policy doctrines. A major ideological component of them has been the conviction that the American way of life constituted a model for mankind and was destined to become universally adopted. The Monroe Doctrine, W. P. Cresson has emphasized, manifested a sincere expression of belief in the "superiority of American institutions and ideals." This same idea was reflected in President Wilson's conviction that the Monroe Doctrine was destined to become "universalized" and serve as the guiding principle of conduct for the international community.[26]

Similarly, the Open Door policy revealed the American society's commitment to such principles as equality of opportunity and laissez faire. China (along with all other countries) would benefit if such principles were adhered to in the diplomatic rivalry existing in East Asia. Seabury has observed that implicitly the Truman Doctrine indicated a belief that the principles of the American Revolution (or Lockeian precepts), rather than Communist revolutionary strategies (or Marxist ideas), should guide foreign societies seeking to achieve internal political freedom.[27]

5. The concept of the American "mission." One of the oldest ideas, and a perennial one, in the American ethos has also been implicit in the nation's foreign policy doctrines. This is the notion of the American society's "mission" to the civilized world. Although no foreign policy doctrine was named for him, President John F. Kennedy delivered a modern variation on this idea in his State of the Union Message of 1962, when he declared, "People everywhere, in spite of occasional disappointments, look to us—not to our wealth or power, but to the splendor of our ideals. For our nation is commissioned by history to be either an observer of freedom's failure or the cause of its success."[28]

26. George F. Kennan, *Memoirs (1925–1950)* (New York: Bantam, 1969), 340; W. P. Cresson, *James Monroe* (Chapel Hill, N.C.: University of North Carolina Press, 1946), 448; David Y. Thomas, *One Hundred Years of the Monroe Doctrine: 1823–1923* (New York: Macmillan, 1923), 567.

27. Seabury, *Power, Freedom, and Diplomacy*, 369.

28. John Paton Davies, Jr., *Foreign and Other Affairs* (New York: W. W. Norton, 1964), 202.

Several commentators have identified this "missionary" impulse as an evident trait of the Monroe Doctrine. Monroe's message not only was concerned with what policy-makers perceived as· immediate threats to American security; it sought also to promote the American society's felt mission to convert other countries to new political principles and modes of behavior. More than a century later, Charles E. Bohlen noted the Truman Doctrine expressed America's "feeling of duty towards the civilized world." As Norman A. Graebner has described it, President Truman's doctrine had an unmistakable "messianic" flavor: not only was the United States determined to defend its own freedom, but it felt obliged to act as the defender of "freedom everywhere" throughout the world.[29]

The Nixon Doctrine purported to offer a "new structure for peace," under American auspices. While this messianic component was considerably less prominent in the Carter Doctrine, its underlying premise was that the United States was required to maintain not only its own security, but that of Europe, Japan, and other advanced nations as well, by safeguarding the Persian Gulf area from Soviet domination.

6. The "millennial" character of American thought. The foreign policy doctrines of the United States have also exemplified the "millennial" or utopian quality of American attitudes toward political questions. From the beginning, the discovery of the New World and utopian ideas have been linked. Sir Thomas More's *Utopia*, for example, was published less than a generation after Columbus discovered America. More's conception of a utopian "commonwealth" envisioned a new political order, in which citizens enjoyed peace and security. The French philosopher Jean-Jacques Rousseau's image of the "noble savage"—uncorrupted by the evils of traditional social and political systems—was undoubtedly derived from his conception of (or vision for) society in the New World.[30] On every one-dollar bill, there is inscribed the motto, *Novus Ordo Seclorum* (proclaiming America the "new order of the ages"). That this has been an enduring theme in the American ethos is indicated by the judgments of more recent political com-

29. Claude Julien, *America's Empire* (New York: Random House, 1973), 46; Charles E. Bohlen, *The Transformation of American Foreign Policy* (New York: W. W. Norton, 1969), 95; Graebner (ed.), *Ideas and Diplomacy*, 716.

30. These and other examples of the "millennial" theme in the American ethos are cited in Louis J. Halle, *Dream and Reality: Aspects of American Foreign Policy* (New York: Harper and Row, 1959), 18–22.

mentators. During World War II, for example, Walter Lippmann observed that Americans widely believed that "when this particular enemy had been forced into unconditional surrender, they would reenter the golden age. . . . This crusade would make the whole world safe for democracy." Or, as a recent commentator said about Soviet-American relations: the American people would not have accepted the idea of détente "unless it was wrapped up as the millennium."[31]

Nearly every doctrine of American diplomacy has implicitly or explicitly exhibited this utopian quality. Particularly after it became "universalized," the Monroe Doctrine would reduce the incidence of violence and instability within the international system. The Truman Doctrine exemplified what the historian Arnold Toynbee called an "American peace"—the only alternative to continued international violence and upheaval (a "Russian peace"). Secretary of State John Foster Dulles believed that Congress' failure to approve the Eisenhower Doctrine would lead to "the inevitability of a world war," while its adoption would have the opposite result.[32] As emphasized in Chapter 7, the Nixon Doctrine not only presumably inaugurated a new era for American foreign policy; it contemplated the emergence of a new and more stable international system as well. Nixon's doctrine, said Secretary of Defense Melvin Laird, represented "a turning away from past discouragement and toward future hope."[33] The basic premise of the Carter Doctrine was that if the Communist challenge to the security of the Persian Gulf area could be successfully met, the stability of the region would largely be assured.

7. The tradition of American "unilateralism." Finally, we may identify as a common denominator of American diplomatic doctrines an idea which was conspicuous in isolationist thought down to World War II and which has been present in the American approach to foreign policy since the founding of the Republic. During the heyday of

31. Walter Lippmann, *The Public Philosophy* (Boston: Little, Brown, 1955), 21; Leslie H. Gelb, "Kissinger as Flawed Strategist, Brilliant Tactician," in Paterson (ed.), *Major Problems in American Foreign Policy*, II, 519.

32. Seabury, *The Rise and Decline of the Cold War*, 41; Townsend Hoopes, *The Devil and John Foster Dulles: The Diplomacy of the Eisenhower Era* (Boston: Little, Brown, 1973), 407. See also Dwight D. Eisenhower, *Waging Peace, 1956–1961* (Garden City, N.Y.: Doubleday, 1965), 199.

33. Robert Goralski (Moderator), *The Nixon Doctrine: A Town Hall Meeting on National Security Policy* (Washington, D.C.: American Enterprise Institute, 1972), 23.

isolationism, this was known as the concept of the "free hand," or more formally, the concept of American "unilateralism" in foreign affairs. Throughout its history, Perkins has observed, the United States has insisted upon "plowing its own furrow" diplomatically.[34]

Unilateralism was a conspicuous feature of the Monroe Doctrine. As we noted in Chapter 1, the Monroe Administration rejected the proposal that the doctrine be issued jointly with Great Britain. A Mexican diplomat said that the doctrine exemplified American "rugged individualism" vis-à-vis America's willingness to solve international problems collaboratively with other nations. In his view, the Monroe Doctrine was "a monologue, not a dialogue."[35] Prime Minister Bismarck of Germany called the Monroe Doctrine an "international impertinence": under its guise, the United States was attempting to alter international law unilaterally.[36] As illustrated by the Johnson Doctrine for Latin America—and by the Kennedy Administration's militant response to the installation of Soviet missiles in Cuba—the United States remains the sole instigator and interpreter of the Monroe Doctrine.

Unilateralism has been a characteristic of the other doctrines in American diplomatic experience. The Open Door policy in China—together with the later "nonrecognition" policy of the Hoover Administration toward Japanese aggression in China—was a unilateral policy statement by the United States. The containment policy, promulgated by the Truman Doctrine, was America's unique response to the challenge of Communist expansionism. In the Eisenhower Doctrine, Washington took pains to point out that the United States was following a separate diplomatic course in the Middle East from its European allies. The Johnson Doctrine for Southeast Asia was again a unilateral policy declaration by the United States, and the escalation of America's involvement in the Vietnam conflict was carried out often in the face of outspoken opposition by the nation's friends and allies overseas. President Nixon's new "structure for peace," in the form of the Nixon Doctrine, was formulated by the Nixon-Kissinger foreign policy team, with no discernible contribution by other countries. Perhaps the most graphic example of American unilateralism in recent his-

34. Perkins, *The American Approach to Foreign Policy*, 41.
35. See the views of Luis Quintanilla, in Goldwin (ed.), *Readings in American Foreign Policy*, 225.
36. Dozer (ed.), *The Monroe Doctrine*, 9.

tory is the Carter Doctrine. As we observed in Chapter 8, gaining the support and cooperation of other nations in its behalf proved an extremely difficult challenge for the Carter and Reagan administrations.

The Issuance of Diplomatic Doctrines

Several aspects of the circumstances surrounding the issuance of American diplomatic doctrines are also noteworthy. Almost without exception, the diplomatic doctrines of the United States illustrate W. W. Rostow's overall verdict on American foreign policy: that policymaking in the United States "consists in a series of reactions to major crises." [37] The promulgators of America's diplomatic doctrines were responding to actual or potential crises, usually involving the prospect of regional or global war. From the Monroe Doctrine in 1823 to the Carter Doctrine in 1980, the president and his chief foreign policy advisers have used the occasion of an external crisis to issue major doctrinal pronouncements in foreign relations.

In the early nineteenth century, President Monroe was concerned about the possible machinations of the Holy Alliance and of czarist Russia in the Western Hemisphere, perhaps in time posing a threat to the security and independence of the United States. The Open Door policy was issued to avert what appeared to be a possible clash among the great powers having economic and diplomatic interests in China. The Stimson Doctrine was America's "answer" to the Manchurian crisis of 1931–1932.

Similarly, after World War II, with the exception of the Nixon Doctrine, the doctrines of American foreign policy were responses to external crises. The internal political struggle within Greece—viewed by American officials as a prototype of the conflict between democracy and communism globally—precipitated the Truman Doctrine. President Eisenhower was convinced that, in the absence of his doctrine, the Middle East would soon succumb to Communist domination. The two Johnson doctrines were also crisis-induced instruments of American foreign policy. The first was issued in response to the Tonkin Gulf crisis, involving an attack upon American naval units; the second was

37. Scott and Dawson (eds.), *Readings in the Making of American Foreign Policy*, 304.

promulgated as a result of a revolution in the Dominican Republic offering new opportunities for Communist inroads in the Western Hemisphere.

The Nixon Doctrine was issued in response to a different kind of crisis. Designed to prevent "another Vietnam," it was offered as a remedy for the psychological enervation and trauma Americans experienced as a result of the Vietnam War—and, more generally, the burdens the nation had carried for many years in trying to act as "the policeman of the world." A decade later, the Carter Doctrine, however, fit the usual mold: it was issued in direct response to the Soviet invasion of Afghanistan and the ensuing Communist threat to the security of the Persian Gulf area.

Another striking feature of America's foreign policy doctrines is the fact that, to the minds of many diplomatic historians and commentators, the threat against which they were directed was exaggerated or misperceived by officials in Washington. Most historians, for example, doubt that the Holy Alliance or czarist Russia seriously planned expansionist moves in the New World during the early nineteenth century. The Japanese threat to China's integrity in the early 1930s was of course genuine enough; neither the Hoover nor Roosevelt administrations exaggerated the danger to Asian security posed by Japanese expansionism.

After World War II, a vast body of "re-examinist" literature contended that the Truman Administration had greatly exaggerated or misread the Communist threat to the independence of Greece and Turkey and to other countries facing Communist control after 1947.[38]

---

38. The list of "revisionist" interpretations of American foreign policy—which challenge the official or "orthodox" explanations of the Cold War and American moves in response to it—is almost endless. A sampling of such studies includes: D. F. Fleming, *The Cold War and Its Origins: 1917–1960* (2 vols.; Garden City, N.Y.: Doubleday, 1961); Ronald Steel, *Pax Americana* (Rev. ed.; New York: Viking Press, 1970); Stephen Ambrose, *Rise to Globalism: American Foreign Policy, 1938–1970* (Baltimore: Penguin, 1971): Simon Serfaty, *The Elusive Enemy: American Foreign Policy Since World War II* (Boston: Little, Brown, 1972); David Horowitz, *The Free World Colossus: A Critique of American Foreign Policy in the Cold War* (New York: Hill and Wang, 1971); N. D. Houghton (ed.), *Struggle Against History: U.S. Foreign Policy in an Age of Revolution* (New York: Simon and Schuster, 1968); J. William Fulbright, *The Arrogance of Power* (New York: Random House, 1966); and Richard J. Walton, *Cold War and Counter-Revolution: The Foreign Policy of John F. Kennedy* (Baltimore: Penguin, 1972).

While re-examinist commentators are by no means unified in their conclusions, some of them are persuaded that the Communist danger to Greece and Turkey was "invented" by policy-makers of the Truman Administration to serve their ulterior purposes (one of which was to impose a *Pax Americana* upon the world). A more charitable interpretation is that—ignorant as Americans were of the political background in Greece and nearly all other societies beyond their own borders—the nature of the political contest in Greece was misperceived as part of a "worldwide" Communist drive for hegemony.[39] As these revisionist interpreters view it, by erroneously identifying communism as America's global enemy, the Truman Doctrine largely ignored the "real" causes of international instability and violence—such as Afro-Asian nationalism, revolutionary movements, poverty, and demands for racial justice.

Basically the same point has been made about the doctrines of American foreign policy that were promulgated after 1947. In the Eisenhower Doctrine, for example, "international communism" was incorrectly identified as the dominant threat to the security of the Middle East. Critics asserted that the Johnson Administration misconstrued the nature of the Tonkin Gulf crisis, viewing it as a deliberately aggressive move by North Vietnam; the Johnson White House also greatly exaggerated the danger of a Communist seizure of power in the Dominican Republic. In the early 1980s, the Carter and Reagan administrations similarly erred in identifying Soviet expansionism as the principal danger to the stability and security of the Persian Gulf area.

A closely related aspect of the issuance of diplomatic doctrines by the United States has been their episodic character. Promulgated in response to real or imagined external crises, the doctrines have epitomized the American society's traditional eclectic approach to problem solving. Nearly all the doctrines examined here illustrate Louis J. Halle's overall verdict on this American diplomatic propensity: "It has seemed to us that it is our role to intervene in world affairs with spo-

---

39. For a detailed analysis of the Cold War written on the premise that policy-makers in Washington and Moscow "misperceived" each other's intentions during and after World War II, see John G. Stoessinger, *Nations in Darkness: China, Russia, and America* (New York: Random House, 1971), 95–197.

radic and violent bursts of energy and with decisive and definitive effect—to appear on the scene in the nick of time like the knight errant, rescue the lady, and ride away."[40]

A former State Department official has used the term "dogmatic pragmatism" to describe the American approach to foreign policy.[41] Contradictory as it sounds (and perhaps is), the approach has been both dogmatic-doctrinaire and pragmatic-eclectic at the same time! It has been dogmatic, in that these doctrinal statements have expressed general principles which could be invoked and reinvoked to guide American officials in their response to external problems. It has been pragmatic, in that the nation's foreign policy doctrines have not been offered as abstract intellectual or philosophical propositions, but have been issued as the result of concrete challenges requiring an American response. In effect, whether the doctrines were issued depended primarily upon the behavior of other countries.

As crisis-induced instruments of American foreign policy, the nation's diplomatic doctrines have also had another common feature. For the most part, they have been formulated *hurriedly*, under great pressure, and with minimum opportunity for consideration of many of their long-term implications. Sen. Arthur H. Vandenberg (Republican of Michigan) complained about the Truman Doctrine that it was "unfortunate when such important decisions have to be made on a crisis basis. But we confront a condition and not a theory."[42] Comparable laments were expressed (particularly by legislators) about the Eisenhower Doctrine, the two Johnson doctrines, and (to a lesser degree) the Carter Doctrine. Particularly for those doctrines involving formal congressional participation, legislators repeatedly complained that they were given insufficient time in which to consider White House requests and that in effect, the very announcement of the diplomatic doctrine in question had given them no choice except to support the president. Such complaints usually had considerable justification. The pressure of events left very little time for leisurely and reflective action and little opportunity to assess the meaning and consequences

40. Louis J. Halle, *Civilization and Foreign Policy* (New York: Harper and Row, 1955), xv–xvi.
41. Ball, *Diplomacy for a Crowded World*, 60–61.
42. Vandenberg (ed.), *The Private Papers of Senator Vandenberg*, 340.

of the doctrine in question. This reality to some extent accounts for another characteristic of American diplomatic doctrines—their ambiguity and flexibility—which we shall discuss more fully below.

Still another salient fact about the issuance of American foreign policy doctrines—seldom given the attention which its importance deserves—has been the influence of domestic forces upon the policy process. In nearly every instance, internal political and public opinion considerations have been major factors in the promulgation of particular doctrines.

As has been true in many other respects, the Monroe Doctrine served as a prototype. The Monroe Doctrine, Bailey has emphasized, was formulated within a context of "violent political contention" in the United States. Wayne S. Cole has said, "Its anti-foreign, anti-European, and anti-monarchial tenor reflected American chauvinism in the Era of Good Feelings." The Monroe Doctrine was clearly designed to strengthen the political position of President Monroe and his followers against their domestic political opponents.[43] James K. Polk's important "corollary" to the Monroe Doctrine in 1845 was also prompted in no small measure by domestic political influences. A leading purpose of the corollary was to enhance the public appeal of the Democratic party over its political rivals.[44]

The influence of commercial and trading interests was no less pronounced in the issuance of the Open Door policy. These groups demanded maximum American participation in the "China trade" and vigorously opposed attempts by foreign competitors to monopolize, or impede American access to, markets in the Orient. Nor was the McKinley Administration unmindful of the policy's domestic political implications. The Open Door policy was expected to be—and it was —immensely popular with the American people, enhancing the Republican party's foreign policy record.[45] Conversely, a generation later, the Hoover Administration was mindful of domestic political con-

---

43. Bailey, *The Man in the Street*, 257; Cole, *An Interpretive History of American Foreign Relations*, 110–11. For a more detailed examination of internal political influences upon the Monroe Doctrine, see Ernest R. May, "The Product of Domestic Politics," in Paterson (ed.), *Major Problems in American Foreign Policy*, I, 179–82.
44. Merk, *The Monroe Doctrine and American Expansionism*, 7.
45. Kennan, *American Diplomacy*, 37–41; Perkins, *The American Approach to Foreign Policy*, 52.

straints upon the American response to Japanese aggression in Manchuria—a major reason why the sanctions contemplated by the Stimson Doctrine ("nonrecognition" of Japanese territorial conquests) were relatively mild.

The postwar diplomatic doctrines of the United States were no less influenced by internal political considerations. Unquestionably, a primary goal of the Truman Doctrine was to counteract the Republican party's frequent complaint that the Roosevelt and Truman administrations had been "soft on communism." Increasingly, American opinion—led by vocal groups like Catholic voters and Polish-Americans—demanded that Washington exhibit "firmness" in responding to Soviet expansionism.[46] The Eisenhower Doctrine was designed in part to restore the diplomatic "credibility" of the Eisenhower Administration after the Suez Crisis in 1956, a massive setback for Western influence in the Middle East. It was also intended to refute the idea that the Eisenhower-Dulles approach to foreign relations had been marked by drift and incompetence, permitting the Soviet Union to enhance its influence within the Middle East.[47]

Political motivations were also present in the two Johnson doctrines. LBJ's doctrine for Southeast Asia, for example, was designed to hasten the end of the Vietnam War—a struggle that was becoming progressively more politically divisive and a liability for the Democratic party. His doctrine toward Latin America was intended to demonstrate that Washington was prepared to take decisive action against Communist inroads within the Western Hemisphere, at a time when Premier Castro of Cuba was sponsoring revolutionary movements in the region. The Nixon Doctrine sought to capitalize politically upon the American people's aversion to involvement in "another Vietnam"; and it sought to demonstrate that, under Republican management, American foreign policy could achieve objectives shared by most of the American people. A few years later, one of the purposes of the Car-

46. For more detailed commentary on this aspect of the Truman Doctrine, see Ernest R. May, *"Lessons" of the Past: The Use and the Misuse of History in American Foreign Policy* (New York: Oxford University Press, 1973), 46–47; Anatol Rapoport, *The Big Two: Soviet-American Perceptions of Foreign Policy* (New York: Pegasus, 1971), 112–13; and Graebner (ed.), *Ideas and Diplomacy*, 718.

47. Emmet John Hughes, *The Ordeal of Power: A Political Memoir of the Eisenhower Years* (New York: Atheneum, 1963), 177; Stephen E. Ambrose, "The Cold War Restrained," in Paterson (ed.), *Major Problems in American Foreign Policy*, II, 390–91.

ter Doctrine was to answer the pervasive criticism that President Carter was a weak and indecisive chief executive who was incapable of responding effectively to Soviet adventurism and to the continuing growth of Russian military power.

Finally, we may identify another common characteristic associated with the promulgation of American diplomatic doctrines. The Monroe Doctrine, Salvador de Madariaga asserted, was many things, including a "dogma of the infallibility of the American President" in the foreign policy field.[48] Even before the Monroe Doctrine, the precedent had been established, and has been followed repeatedly, that the chief executive provides leadership in responding to foreign crises. Insofar as external forces have contributed to this phenomenon, the tendency toward the "imperial presidency" has been strongly reinforced by the issuance of the diplomatic doctrines included in our study.

As we have already observed, substantively the major doctrines of American foreign policy have been directly concerned with the preservation of national security during a period of real or perceived danger abroad. Owing in no small measure to the examples afforded by the diplomatic doctrines examined here, the precedent has become firmly established and frequently invoked that the president has a unique responsibility for preserving national security and that Congress' role in that process is clearly subordinate or, more accurately perhaps, symbolic and supportive. In the late 1840s, Sen. John C. Calhoun contended, in connection with a crisis in the Yucatan, that it was the responsibility of *Congress* to interpret and apply the Monroe Doctrine in cases involving the possible use of American armed forces abroad. Eloquent as he was, Calhoun's contention did not gain widespread support on Capitol Hill or with the American people. (Typically, during this period President Polk issued his "corollary" to the Monroe Doctrine for dealing with this crisis.)

Early in the twentieth century, President Taft indicated his opposition to the "Lodge Corollary" to the Monroe Doctrine, which had been formulated in, and approved by, the Senate. Taft stated that he would not regard this congressionally instigated interpretation of the Monroe Doctrine as binding upon the White House. On the eve of World War II, without consulting Congress President Roosevelt "ex-

48. Dozer (ed.), *The Monroe Doctrine*, title page.

tended" the scope of the Monroe Doctrine to include foreign threats to the security of Canada. In 1939, FDR went further: he proclaimed that the security zone of the United States extended eastward as far as the Rhine River. In the early postwar period, under the Truman Doctrine the American security zone was extended still further to the east, to include Greece and Turkey. Even more significantly—in one of the most profound changes in the underlying concept of American security—Truman's policy declaration altered the definition of the American security zone from a geographic idea to a political-ideological one. After the promulgation of the Truman Doctrine, the geographical locale of the threat to the United States was less important than the object of the threat (*i.e.*, it was directed against efforts by "free peoples" in any region to preserve their independence from outside threats). It has been said of Truman—but the designation would also fit other postwar presidents, in their foreign policy role—that he envisioned himself "as a sort of super-protector of the free world, operating largely at his own discretion."[49]

To no inconsiderable degree, President Lyndon B. Johnson came to be viewed as epitomizing the "imperial presidency" because of his diplomatic doctrines, and the actions carried out under them, for Southeast Asia and for Latin America. Despite the Nixon Doctrine's emphasis upon "partnership" with Congress, in reality the Nixon Administration's principal diplomatic moves—such as extending the conflict in Southeast Asia to Cambodia, the management and conclusion of the Vietnam War, and the normalization of Sino-American relations—were carried out almost entirely by executive officials. While the Carter Doctrine envisioned an important role for Congress in its implementation, legislators had no significant voice in its formulation and issuance.

The major diplomatic doctrines of the United States have been issued by the chief executive; their meaning has repeatedly been interpreted by the president or his agents; and the provisions of these doctrines have in the main been applied by decisions made in the White House, sometimes with participation by Congress. Consequently,

---

49. Sidney Warren, *The President as World Leader* (New York: McGraw-Hill, 1964), 197; Richard W. Leopold, *The Growth of American Foreign Policy: A History* (New York: Alfred A. Knopf, 1962), 651; Merlo J. Pusey, *The Way We Go to War* (Boston: Houghton Mifflin, 1971), 9.

America's foreign policy doctrines have strongly reinforced the position of the president as the initiator and manager of foreign policy.

The Ambivalent Role of Doctrines

What has been the role of doctrines in American diplomatic experience? A convenient starting point for our analysis is French President Charles de Gaulle's observation that "the United States brings to great affairs elementary feelings and a complicated policy." [50] The image of a "complicated policy" is strongly reinforced by the nation's foreign policy doctrines. From the Monroe Doctrine to the Carter Doctrine, students of American foreign relations have been puzzled about the meaning of particular doctrines and perhaps the cumulative impact of them collectively for the conduct of foreign affairs. A common feature of these doctrines has been their highly ambivalent and flexible character.

In the light of the extensive evidence already presented in previous chapters, it is hardly necessary to provide detailed documentation here indicating the ambiguous and imprecise terminology of American diplomatic doctrines. The quandary identified with respect to the Monroe Doctrine at the beginning of the chapter ("I would die for the Monroe Doctrine. All I said was that I do not know what it means") could equally well apply to the other doctrines promulgated after 1823. Concerning President Monroe's pronouncement, Bailey observed that it meant "pretty much what we wanted it to mean, which at times was highly convenient." President Monroe's pronouncement might accurately have been called the "India-rubber doctrine." One indication of its flexibility is the fact that the Monroe Doctrine has been invoked approvingly throughout American diplomatic history by isolationists and interventionists alike. According to Kennan, the Open Door policy suffered from the same disability. Identified with the principle of the "territorial integrity" of China (as the policy in time came to be construed), in a country as internally divided and fragmented as China, it was always difficult to know exactly what this concept really meant. [51]

50. Lincoln P. Bloomfield, *In Search of American Foreign Policy: The Humane Use of Power* (New York: Oxford University Press, 1974), 79.
51. Bailey, *The Man in the Street*, 263; Pratt, *A History of United States Foreign Policy*, 167; Merk, *The Monroe Doctrine and American Expansionism*, 288–89; Kennan, *American Diplomacy*, 44–49.

From the Truman through the Carter administrations, this same quality pervaded the post–World War II doctrines of American diplomacy. The same basic criticism was made about the Truman Doctrine. As Jules Davids expressed it, "Many Americans wanted to know precisely what American commitments would be in the future, and how they would be fulfilled—points on which [President Truman's message to Congress on March 12, 1947] was quite ambiguous."[52] A pivotal idea in the Truman Doctrine—the concept of "free peoples," whose independence the United States was now pledged to defend—was especially susceptible to widely varying interpretations. Left-wing and liberal groups tended to assume it signified a pledge by the United States to defend democratic governments abroad (although neither Greece nor Turkey in 1947 satisfied many Western democratic criteria). Right-wing and conservative spokesmen often interpreted it as a pledge to defend capitalist or non-Marxist governments throughout the world. In practice, the term "free peoples" usually denoted *any* government facing a Soviet-sponsored threat to its security, irrespective of its ideology or political system.

What factors account for the overall ambiguity of America's principal foreign policy doctrines? Several answers to the question may be suggested. By definition, with the exception of the Nixon Doctrine, these doctrinal statements have been relatively brief and general statements of foreign policy guidelines. They were intended to apply to an immediate crisis facing the United States abroad and to more or less analogous cases in the future. Only a general and loosely worded policy statement is inherently capable of serving that purpose. The doctrines of American foreign policy have been comparable to constitutional concepts or principles—like "interstate commerce" or "due process of law." Defining the precise meaning of such concepts under a variety of circumstances during the nation's two-hundred-year history has been a difficult and ongoing challenge. Just as the American society's conception of freedom internally has changed, so too has the idea of "free peoples" contained in the Truman Doctrine, or the notion of "international communism" in the Eisenhower Doctrine.

Nearly all of America's diplomatic doctrines, it needs to be reiterated, were formulated hurriedly—in response to an actual or a perceived foreign crisis. Only rarely (and the Nixon Doctrine is the prin-

---

52. Davids, *America and the World of Our Time*, 403.

cipal example to the contrary) did time exist for a careful evaluation of the doctrine's possible connotations under differing circumstances overseas.

Other factors also of course account for the lack of clarity about the inherent meaning of the nation's diplomatic doctrines. A leading one—illustrated by most of America's post–World War II doctrines—has been an underlying lack of public and official understanding of the nature of significant developments in international politics. This has led national leaders to employ—and the news media to repeat—confusing and ambiguous terminology, like the "territorial integrity" of China (the Open Door policy), the concept of "free peoples" (the Truman Doctrine), "international communism" (the Eisenhower and Johnson doctrines), and détente (the Nixon Doctrine). The most basic reason perhaps why the doctrines of American foreign policy have been imprecise in using such language is that the public and official thinking behind them has not infrequently been confused, faulty, and in some instances simply wrong.

At the same time, it must also be noted that the vagueness and imprecision characteristic of American diplomatic doctrines has in some instances been intentional. In British diplomatic parlance, the doctrines of American foreign policy have exemplified "masterful ambiguity": they were designed to serve as highly flexible and adaptive policy instruments, affording officials in Washington maximum freedom to interpret and apply them to a wide range of diverse conditions abroad.

Paradoxical as it appears, the ambiguity of the nation's diplomatic doctrines may be accounted for by both of these explanations. Inevitably perhaps, the nation's traditional lack of interest and experience in foreign affairs has affected the content of its important diplomatic statements. It is no less true—as officials of the Truman Administration freely conceded about the Truman Doctrine—that some doctrines were deliberately left vague and imprecise, so that they could be interpreted flexibly in the light of developments overseas. In Paul Seabury's view, the main doctrines of American foreign policy have been realistically and properly ambiguous, thereby avoiding "the traps laid for too zealous, overly doctrinaire men."[53]

On a much deeper philosophical level, the ambiguity characteristic

53. Seabury, *Power, Freedom, and Diplomacy*, 376.

of most diplomatic doctrines can be explained in some measure by the pluralistic nature of the American society and the implications of this fact for the foreign policy process. The nation's diplomatic doctrines have usually been imprecise and ambivalent statements because the American people's conception of the "national interest" of the United States is normally confused and disunited, and changes over time. Given the highly diversified nature of the American society—along with a constitutional system erected upon such concepts as checks and balances and separation of powers—formal embodiments of America's "national interest" in the form of diplomatic doctrines have inescapably tended to be couched in generalities which evoke conflicting interpretations.[54]

A closely related phenomenon is the fact that, as Seabury has emphasized, the national "political consensus" which has traditionally supported policy-making by the leaders has been fundamentally different for internal and external affairs. In the latter sphere, a deep ambivalence has always been present in the people's attitude toward America's proper relationship with other countries. This is illustrated by the American belief in what Seabury calls "permissive pluralism" (according to which, for example, the Cuban people ought to be allowed to choose Castroism as a system of government if they desire) versus a concurrent belief in "doctrinal orthodoxy" (whereby Americans expect that other societies should choose "civilized, constitutional, democratic politics" in the American, or possibly Western European, mode). Moreover, even when a substantial consensus has existed among the American people on foreign policy issues, it has "seemed to change from decade to decade, as conditions in the external world also changed."[55] This transition was graphically illustrated by the shift in American public and congressional opinion during the decade of the 1970s. For a period of several years, American diplomacy was dominated by the "Vietnam War syndrome" of guilt and self-doubt. By 1980, this mood had reverted to the kind of determined opposition to communism that had produced the Truman Doctrine in the late 1940s.

54. Bohlen, *The Transformation of American Foreign Policy*, 96.
55. Seabury, *Power, Freedom, and Diplomacy*, 372, 395. As Ernest R. May has analyzed the matter, the lack of a domestic consensus on foreign policy issues is likely to become an even more acute problem in the years ahead than it was for twenty years or so after World War II. See his *"Lessons" of the Past*, 146–50.

The Contributions of Doctrines to American Diplomacy

The doctrines examined in this study have made a number of contributions to achieving the diplomatic goals of the United States. First, it needs to be reiterated that they have expressed and communicated America's commitment to the democratic ideal and its encouragement abroad. Establishing the precedent, the Monroe Doctrine was an ideological testament, militantly asserting the values of the New World in the face of possible European threats to their survival. Despite the fact that the Monroe and later doctrines may, as disciples of realpolitik contend, have contributed to creating or maintaining the balance of power, these doctrines were infused with ideological principles consonant with America's own ethos and tradition. Implicitly at least, the doctrines of the United States have conveyed the idea shared by the American people and their leaders that ideological values and principles are an important component of the nation's power and its ability to influence the behavior of other nations. Without exception, America's diplomatic doctrines have expressed that realization.

A second function of American diplomatic doctrines has been to serve as "legitimatizing" instruments for the application (or potential application) of American power overseas. That the doctrines of American foreign policy have traditionally played this role can hardly be doubted. Again, the Monroe Doctrine established the tradition. Why has this foreign policy declaration in time become known as the "Monroe Doctrine," rather than the "American Doctrine" or the "Noncolonization Doctrine" or some alternative designation? The answer, several diplomatic historians believe, is that the American people wanted to endow this fundamental statement of foreign policy with a unique sanctity and sense of veneration. They wanted to elevate the Monroe Doctrine into a de facto constitutional principle or doctrine, thereby raising it above the level of an ordinary official policy statement; and in the popular mind they often succeeded. President Monroe, Bailey has stated, "walked and talked with the Virginia giants like Washington and Jefferson, and his name gave the Doctrine the aura of venerability and immortality." The very term *Monroe Doctrine* evokes "pictures of the Founding Fathers." [56]

56. Bailey, *The Man in the Street*, 262.

In 1845, when President Polk faced a crisis in Mexican-American relations, ultimately he issued the "Polk Corollary" to the Monroe Doctrine for dealing with it. Instead, he might have issued the "Polk Doctrine" (or no doctrine at all) in this situation. But Polk deliberately chose to connect his pronouncement with President Monroe's earlier declaration. This act, according to one historian of this period, was "an excellent tactic. It created the impression that old problems were being met by the new [Polk] administration in the spirit of [the Founding Fathers]."[57]

Half a century or so later, President Theodore Roosevelt did essentially the same thing. Confronted with conditions of financial chaos in the Caribbean, which invited continuing European intervention, he issued a major policy statement known in time as the "Roosevelt Corollary" to the Monroe Doctrine. President Roosevelt might just as easily have promulgated a new diplomatic doctrine in his own name, since his was in fact a new policy by the United States which had no necessary relationship to the Monroe Doctrine. Instead, Roosevelt linked his declaration to "the time-tried Doctrine of Monroe. So the venerable Virginian was made to say things that he never said or meant."[58]

Informed students of American foreign policy are aware of a sense of continuity uniting the principal foreign policy doctrines of the United States. In this respect, the Monroe Doctrine stands apart. As we have seen, it came to be viewed by many Americans in a unique way—as embodying the wisdom of the Founding Fathers and as being equivalent to a constitutional provision. Later diplomatic doctrines sought to perpetuate this tradition and to capture some of the prestige which adhered to the Monroe Doctrine. Thus, as we noted in Chapter 2, the Open Door policy and the Stimson Doctrine were regarded by some commentators chiefly as extensions of Monroe's principles to the Asian setting. In 1947, President Truman conceived of his new doctrine in comparable terms. He believed the Truman Doctrine reflected the spirit and overall purpose of Washington's Farewell Address and of the Monroe Doctrine earlier.[59] According to one of his closest advisers, President Truman also envisioned his doctrine as a kind of be-

57. Merk, *The Monroe Doctrine and American Expansionism*, 4.
58. Bailey, *The Man in the Street*, 259.
59. Truman, *Memoirs: Years of Trial and Hope*, 102.

lated application of the Stimson Doctrine to the problem of aggressive international conduct.[60]

Maintaining continuity with the doctrines which preceded it, the Eisenhower Doctrine could legitimately be construed as an application of the Truman Doctrine's containment strategy to the Middle East. The Johnson Doctrine for Southeast Asia was an extension of the Truman Doctrine's containment principle to that region. The Johnson Doctrine for Latin America combined elements of the earlier Monroe Doctrine with ideas in the Truman Doctrine. One of the purposes of the Nixon Doctrine was to revise the Truman Doctrine, making it more relevant and effective in a world of revolutionary change. As applied to Latin America, its concept of "partnership" echoed the old notion (implicit in the Monroe Doctrine) of a community of interests between the United States and the other American republics.

Accepting the idea that the nation's diplomatic doctrines have served to legitimatize the use of American power abroad, the next question becomes: why has the American society felt the need for such legitimatizing devices in the conduct of foreign affairs? Several possible explanations come to mind. Traditionally in the American ethos, all governmental power has been suspect—none more so perhaps than the "power politics" actuating global political relationships. For early nineteenth-century philosophers like Ralph Waldo Emerson, "Every actual State is corrupt. Good men must not obey the laws too well." For Henry David Thoreau, America's achievements had been made in spite of government; its most useful contribution was to reduce its influence over citizens. Even today (while citizens are surrounded by countless governmental programs operated by a host of federal, state, and local agencies), Americans would still likely endorse the old Jeffersonian adage, "That government is best which governs least."[61]

The traditional American suspicion of government applies with particular salience to the use of military power to achieve national objectives. In the Declaration of Independence, the colonials remonstrated vocally about Great Britain's misuse of armed forces at the expense of American liberties. Financial levies (like the hated "stamp tax") were

60. See the views of Bernard Baruch on Truman's position regarding Communist expansionism, as discussed in May, *"Lessons" of the Past,* 81–82.
61. The views of Emerson, Thoreau, and many other prominent Americans on the role of government are cited in Burns, *The American Idea of Mission,* 35–41.

imposed upon the American colonies largely to defray the cost of Britain's wars, from which the colonials believed they derived no benefit. Down to the post–World War II period, Americans were suspicious of what was sometimes called a "strong" (or interventionist) foreign policy. As Monroe's declaration expressed the idea, the American society wanted neither to become actively embroiled in Europe's political quarrels, nor did it want the great powers of Europe to pursue interventionist policies in the New World. American involvement in Old World political conflicts risked ideological "corruption" of the democratic ethos; and from a realpolitik perspective, a new and weak nation could be expected to have minimum influence upon the outcome of such controversies. European intervention in the Americas could result in the reimposition of foreign rule upon the independent nations of the Western Hemisphere. Both contingencies were fraught with perils for the young Republic. There was, therefore, only one legitimate and acceptable reason for employing the nation's power abroad, and President Monroe's message in 1823 asserted it forcefully: to defend the security and independence of the governments within the New World against their enemies. That was what the Monroe Doctrine proposed to do—and in effect, with suitable variations in time and circumstances, that was what nearly every foreign policy doctrine issued by the United States after 1823 committed the nation to do.

The extension of American power abroad required a legitimatizing rationale for another reason, deeply rooted in the American tradition. Down to World War II, Americans lacked sustained experience in foreign affairs. Foreign relations constituted both a largely unknown realm and a source of possible danger for a democratic society. As late as 1886, for example, a member of Congress from Texas contended that America did not need a diplomatic corps. Diplomats were perhaps useful "when the world was ruled by monarchs, and when there were but few liberal legislative bodies in existence," but the growth in democratic political ideology meant that in time diplomats would no longer be needed merely to promote the selfish intrigues of nations![62]

For much of the nation's history, vast numbers of Americans were

62. See the views of Rep. John H. Reagan of Texas and Rep. Owen Lovejoy of Illinois on the need for an American diplomatic corps in Warren Fredrick Ilchman, *Professional Diplomacy in the United States: 1779–1939* (Chicago: University of Chicago Press, 1961), 20.

convinced that "republican institutions and diplomacy were either difficult to harmonize or completely incompatible." Even President Washington expressed his "horror of finesse and chicane [chicanery]" which were the essence of the diplomatic method. John Adams cautioned his countrymen against trying to compete successfully with the European powers in diplomatic machinations, entailing "bribes well placed" and "intrigues of pleasure with a woman." That perceptive French student of American democracy, Alexis de Tocqueville, observed in 1835 that success in foreign affairs demands "scarcely any of those qualities which are peculiar to a democracy; they require, on the contrary, the perfect use of almost all those in which it is deficient." As many Americans saw it, diplomacy was an aristocratic and amoral realm from which a democratic society could derive little positive benefit, while incurring grave risks.[63] If America entered this dangerous arena at all, it ought to do so only occasionally and for the most compelling reasons. The idea conveyed by the nation's diplomatic doctrines—that departure from the isolationist norm was justified by an appeal to the wisdom of the Founding Fathers, and as a defense of the nation's constitutional principles—provided the most compelling reason imaginable, except perhaps for an overt attack by a hostile country.

Finally, the legitimacy which the foreign policy doctrines of the nation have given the use of American power abroad was needed for another reason. As our earlier reference to the "millennial" character of the national ethos emphasized, the American society has traditionally believed that one of its missions was not only to introduce new political principles and processes at home, but to alter international political behavior patterns as well. If and when America became actively involved in global political controversies, the result ought to be exactly what the Nixon Doctrine particularly contemplated: a "new era" in global political relationships, in which the prospects for peace and stability were greatly enhanced. Implicitly or explicitly, every doctrine of American foreign policy has conveyed this idea.

Another significant contribution of American foreign policy doctrines is highlighted by Spanier's conclusion about the Truman Doc-

---

63. These and other American viewpoints toward foreign affairs during the eighteenth and nineteenth centuries are included in *ibid.*, 24–28.

trine: "Policy makers [in 1947] needed *some* conceptual foundations upon which to base policy if they were to do more than flounder around with a series of ad hoc responses to Soviet challenges in response to what was increasingly perceived in Washington to be coherent and persistent Soviet policy aimed at dominating Europe." [64]

America's dependence upon foreign policy doctrines may be at least a partial answer to the criticism—heard frequently during the heydey of the Cold War—that the United States had no clear "philosophy" of foreign affairs which provided a semblance of unity to its discrete diplomatic decisions. During certain periods, this lack has led to purely "incremental" decision-making—a prominent feature of the decision-making process throughout the Vietnam War.

By contrast, collectively the major diplomatic doctrines of the United States have served to impart a sense of continuity to the nation's foreign policy efforts. Together, over a span of some one hundred and fifty years, these doctrines have asserted and reasserted certain enduring principles identified with the United States in foreign affairs. As a number of commentators view the matter, the doctrines have expressed and clarified the "national interest" of the United States in matters intimately related to its security. Hans J. Morgenthau, for example, has said that the Monroe Doctrine expressed the national interest of the United States in the Western Hemisphere. Several commentators have made the same point about the Truman Doctrine—that it embodied and communicated America's national interest and its determination to preserve the balance of power in the face of Soviet efforts to destabilize it. Similarly, in Melvin Gurtov's view, the Eisenhower Doctrine designated the stability of the Middle East as a "vital national interest" of the United States. [65]

Admittedly, no single doctrine of American foreign policy—nor all of them collectively—can be said to constitute a comprehensive and coherent "philosophy" of foreign relations. They may, however, be viewed as a step in that direction. Certainly with regard to specific for-

64. John Spanier, "Choices We Did Not Have," 133 (italics in the original).
65. Hans J. Morgenthau, "The Mainsprings of American Foreign Policy," in Goldwin (ed.), *Readings in American Foreign Policy*, 642; Warren, *The President as World Leader*, 312; Raymond Aron, *The Imperial Republic: The United States and the World, 1945–1973* (Cambridge, Mass.: Winthrop Publishers, 1974), 24; Goldwin (ed.), *Readings in American Foreign Policy*, 46; Melvin Gurtov, *The United States Against the Third World: Antinationalism and Intervention* (New York: Praeger, 1974), 14.

eign policy issues—the threat of outside intervention in the Western Hemisphere, or the challenge of Communist expansionism, or the need for diplomatic retrenchment in the post–Vietnam War era—they were attempts to supply guiding principles governing America's relationship with the outside world.

Implicitly, the message conveyed by these doctrines has been that, while the United States may normally engage in eclectic decision-making on external questions, it does so within the bounds of certain parameters or policy constants supplied by its principal foreign policy doctrines. For example, the United States has attempted a variety of approaches to Latin America since the early 1800s—but the constant factor in its Latin American policy has been firm opposition to foreign intervention in the Western Hemisphere (as expressed in the Monroe Doctrine and the Johnson Doctrine for the Americas). Or, recent administrations in Washington have favored détente with the Soviet Union—provided Moscow did not endeavor to subordinate weaker countries (which was proscribed by the Truman Doctrine). Or, the United States was willing to respect the desire of nations in the Middle East to remain independent and diplomatically nonaligned—as long as Soviet Russia did not attempt to dominate the region (which was prohibited by the Eisenhower and Carter doctrines). The major diplomatic doctrines of the United States have expressed the constant elements in an otherwise highly pragmatic (and often unpredictable) process of foreign policy decision-making. Within the policy bounds set by these doctrines, the process of eclectic policy-making could go on.

If this interpretation is warranted—that the principal foreign policy doctrines of the United States conveyed America's enduring "national interest" in its relations with other countries—then the question logically arises: were these doctrines really essential to the foreign policy of the United States? Did President Monroe's or President Truman's or President Johnson's foreign policy declarations really contribute anything new or substantive to the American foreign policy process? To pose the question differently, in 1823 might the United States have responded equally well to the threatened machinations of the Holy Alliance or czarist Russia in the New World without the Monroe Doctrine? Or could American policy-makers in 1947 have adopted the containment strategy in the absence of a new foreign policy doctrine by President Truman?

A number of students of American foreign policy are convinced that the nation's diplomatic doctrines have largely been extraneous to the policy process, since in the main they represented little more than the formulation of diplomatic objectives that were already identified with the United States and that enjoyed widespread public support. From this perspective, the Monroe Doctrine was really superfluous; Monroe's statement in 1823 merely communicated dramatically certain ideas and diplomatic guidelines motivating American foreign policy for many years previously. Over a century later, the same observation was made about the Truman Doctrine. Tannenbaum's verdict was that there was really nothing very original or innovative about it; in reality, it was little more than "a modern version of the basic propositions of President Monroe." Acheson's judgment on the doctine was that it constituted merely "a description of what was happening anyway" during the late 1940s in America's response to the Soviet challenge. Thomas C. Schelling commented several years later in this vein about the Nixon Doctrine. He said that there was very little original or distinctive about Nixon's "new structure for peace." His doctrine should more accurately have been called the "American Doctrine," because most of its ideas had in fact been followed by the United States since the late 1940s and had "progressed through several Presidents."[66]

Interpreted in this light, the principal doctrines of American foreign policy have served mainly as instruments for maintaining the continuity and tradition present in American foreign relations. In nearly every instance, particular doctrines have forcefully reasserted diplomatic objectives already announced and pursued by policy-makers in Washington.

Yet there is also a contrary interpretation of the role of doctrines in American foreign affairs. Its leitmotif is that the issuance of a diplomatic doctrine signaled the inauguration of a new era in the nation's foreign relations. One historian has said concerning the Monroe Doctrine that it marked the close of the "founding era" in American diplomatic experience and signified the opening of a new stage, which began in the early 1820s. Walter Lippmann has said substantially the same thing about the Open Door policy. Its adoption was "the most

---

66. Dozer (ed.), *The Monroe Doctrine*, 8–9; Goldwin (ed.), *Readings in American Foreign Policy*, 665; Chace, *A World Elsewhere*, 85; Goralski (Moderator), *The Nixon Doctrine*, 57.

momentous [decision] in our foreign relations." Both President Hoover and Secretary of State Henry Stimson believed that the Stimson Doctrine, aimed at curbing Japanese aggression in China, likewise marked a new departure in American foreign policy—a verdict also shared by several commentators.[67]

The Truman Doctrine was described in similar terms. Acheson called it "a major turning point" in the history of American foreign relations. Sen. Arthur H. Vandenberg (Republican of Michigan) similarly viewed it as a momentous innovation in American foreign affairs—the most important single development since the issuance of the Monroe Doctrine. The Eisenhower Doctrine was depicted as "a significant mutation" in American foreign relations. Another commentator regarded it as signifying "a revolutionary change" in the direction of American diplomacy. More than any recent foreign policy doctrine, however, it was the Nixon Doctrine which was both advertised by the administration and regarded by many informed Americans as inaugurating a "new era" in foreign affairs. As Secretary of Defense Melvin Laird viewed it, by adopting the Nixon Doctrine Americans "have broken with the principles of the past"; traditional diplomatic concepts (like American "unilateralism") had now been superseded by new principles (like the concept of "partnership" with other countries).[68]

One explanation of the paradoxical role of doctrines in American foreign affairs—as elements both of continuity and of change in the nation's diplomatic behavior—is the idea that Americans evidently value both qualities. Forceful invocations of the spirit and insight of the Founding Fathers, as exemplified by the Monroe Doctrine and later doctrinal pronouncements, are ritualistic occurrences in the American society. For political reasons, if no other, every incumbent chief executive would like to have his policies viewed as merely an "ex-

67. Robert H. Ferrell, *American Diplomacy: A History* (New York: W. W. Norton, 1959), 28; excerpt from Lippmann's *U.S. War Aims* (1944), in Goldwin (ed.), *Readings in American Foreign Policy*, 264; Robert H. Ferrell, *American Diplomacy in the Great Depression: Hoover-Stimson Foreign Policy, 1929–1933* (New York: W. W. Norton, 1970), 163–69; Robert G. Wesson, *Foreign Policy for a New Age* (Boston: Houghton Mifflin, 1977), 361.

68. Dean Acheson, *Present at the Creation: My Years in the State Department* (New York: W. W. Norton, 1969), 220; Vandenberg (ed.), *The Private Papers of Senator Vandenberg*, 341; Chace, *A World Elsewhere*, 13; Richard Goold-Adams, *John Foster Dulles: A Reappraisal* (New York: Appleton-Century-Crofts, 1962), 239; Goralski (Moderator), *The Nixon Doctrine*, 7.

tension" of the thinking of the founders to contemporary problems. At the same time, he also wishes to create a record of accomplishment while in office and to demonstrate that his administration has brought "new ideas" to Washington in approaching internal and external problems.

The paradox we have identified exists also with regard to the Constitution of the United States—viewed by many Americans as embodying "eternal principles" of democratic government. Yet the Constitution has endured primarily because it has been adapted to changing conditions—more so even by usage, convention, and judicial interpretation, than by formal constitutional amendment. The same principle applies to the nation's diplomatic doctrines: they too assert long-standing principles of America's external policy that must be modified in the light of new conditions abroad.

The contradiction we have identified may derive from two other factors. First, whether America's foreign policy doctrines are evidence of change or of continuity in the nation's external relations may hinge largely upon the perspective of the individual making the assessment. Public officials and informed students of the nation's diplomatic record, for example, may be more cognizant of the dimension of continuity. They may be familiar with the content and implications of the Monroe Doctrine or the Open Door policy, and they may detect numerous points of similarity between them and later foreign policy doctrines. A majority of Americans, however, neither knows nor cares deeply about ideas implicit in the earlier foreign policy declarations of President Monroe and his successors. They are more concerned about the implications of an immediate external crisis, to which they expect national leaders to respond effectively. As illustrated by the rising public demand after World War II that the Truman Administration stiffen its posture in relations with Russia—or that the Carter Administration protect national security in the face of Soviet expansionism—periodically citizens demand changes in existing policies, especially when they perceive that national security is endangered.

Second, the hiatus between the themes of continuity and change in American diplomatic doctrines may be accounted for by reference to certain qualities of the national ethos. Earlier, the millennial or New World character of American thought was emphasized. Millions of Americans believed after both World Wars I and II that, if the vast power of the United States is to be used abroad, then the result ought to be a new era in the conduct of international politics. The belief that America's foreign policy doctrines should inaugurate a new stage in the political relationships among nations is an enduring or constant element in the domestic context of foreign policy decision-making.

The principal foreign policy doctrines of the United States have also possessed another common quality: they have been essentially defensive policy declarations, making the extension of American power abroad contingent upon the behavior of other countries. Perhaps this is merely another way of saying that the doctrines have expressed what has been the preferred foreign policy orientation of the American society historically—isolationism. Quite possibly it remains so, in modified form, even today. Whether the United States was compelled to employ its power outside its own borders, according to the terms of these doctrines, would be a decision largely made in foreign capitals. The keynote of America's foreign policy doctrines has been the request or demand that other countries refrain from undertaking a course of action deemed inimical to American, and possibly regional and global, security.

In the popular mind, the Monroe Doctrine was a stern warning to the Holy Alliance and czarist Russia not to engage in expansionism within the New World. The Open Door policy-Stimson Doctrine sought to prevent foreign powers from despoiling China. Beginning with the Truman Doctrine, every postwar diplomatic doctrine (except President Nixon's) was directed specifically against some form of Communist (usually Soviet) aggression or interventionism in the affairs of weaker countries. In nearly all cases, if foreign countries heeded America's warning, then the power of the United States would *not* have to be used overseas. During the long isolationist era—and perhaps even during most of the post–World War II period—the *non-use* of American power was the dominant desire of the American people and their leaders. (As earlier chapters have shown, for almost all doctrines analyzed here, a considerable period of time elapsed before an incumbent administration finally decided to issue a particular doctrine—and usually, an even longer period of time elapsed before the doctrine was enforced.)

From the perspective of diplomatic effectiveness, the defensive nature of American foreign policy doctrines has both a positive and negative side. To anticipate the answer to a question we shall examine in detail later—the question of whether the United States has been a hegemonial power—the weight of the evidence indicates that the nation has *not* attempted to impose political hegemony over weaker countries. A warning to the Holy Alliance not to engage in a new colonization campaign in the Western Hemisphere did not mean that the United States sought to dominate Latin America politically. Issuance of the Truman Doctrine did not signify that Washington intended to convert Greece, Turkey, and other vulnerable societies into "satellites" in the postwar era. Eventually, American power was withdrawn from Southeast Asia. Whatever it may have meant specifically, the Carter Doctrine did not mean that the United States sought to impose its own ideology or system of government upon Persian Gulf states.

Moreover, the defensive nature of American foreign policy doctrines is consonant with the society's own values and ethos. As former Secretary of State Acheson has expressed it, there is "an initiative which the United States and her allies cannot seize—the initiative in aggression." The American society must by its very nature "be defenders, not offenders" in its relations with other countries.[69]

The nation's diplomatic doctrines have also enhanced the element of predictability in American diplomacy—a not unimportant gain for a nation normally prone to *ad hoc* and pragmatic responses to external crises. However "ineffectual" the Monroe Doctrine and the Open Door policy-Stimson Doctrine may have been for many years because of America's military weakness, these policy declarations nonetheless alerted the great powers of the day to the realization that if they embarked upon an expansionist course, the United States could be expected to resist such behavior. Neither policy-makers in Washington nor those in other countries were perhaps certain of the precise mode of the American response. But after the United States emerged from World War II as a superpower, its announced intention to resist behavior by other countries threatening its security and diplomatic interests was coupled with both the possession of vast power and the determination to employ it.[70]

69. Acheson, *This Vast External Realm*, 35.
70. Acheson has said, "Our government should give to foreigners as well as to our own people as clear an idea as possible of its intentions. To do so should inspire confidence and increase [international] stability." *Ibid.*, 128.

As emphasized in Chapter 3, several commentators believe, for example, that this was one of the most significant and durable contributions of the Truman Doctrine: it induced greater rationality and restraint in Soviet behavior, thereby preparing the way for the next stage in Soviet-American relations—détente—which was to follow. Insofar as international peace and stability are generally enhanced by making the behavior of powerful states more predictable to other countries (especially to possible adversaries), the major doctrines of American foreign policy have contributed to that result.

It is equally true, however, that the defensive nature of America's diplomatic pronouncements has led to the criticism that the foreign policy of the United States is essentially negative and reactive. In too many cases, this criticism holds, Washington has "left the initiative" to other countries, and the United States (like certain lower forms of animal life) has merely "reacted" to external stimuli. Expressed differently, the main doctrines of American foreign policy have forcefully communicated what the United States was *against* in foreign affairs. Conversely, as a rule they provided little guidance to other countries concerning the positive goals of American foreign policy.

The defensive or negative quality of American foreign policy doctrines has reinforced another complaint: that Washington was aligned with and committed to the maintenance of the status quo abroad. This defect was often viewed as especially serious since the nation's recent diplomatic doctrines were nearly always directed against Communist adventurism at the expense of other countries. As many critics assessed them, the doctrines promulgated since World War II were essentially antirevolutionary instruments; as such, they allowed Marxist groups to spearhead revolutionary change and to become the unchallenged agents of "modernization" in backward societies. A typical criticism in this vein is Gurtov's assessment of the Eisenhower Doctrine and the Johnson Doctrine for Latin America. In his view, the former was a counterrevolutionary policy statement by the United States, directed against radical and revolutionary movements in the Middle East. Similarly, Johnson's doctrine for Latin America sought to avert the process of revolutionary change in that region.[71]

This assessment of postwar American foreign policy may not be

71. Gurtov, *The United States Against the Third World*, 7, 15.

(and was not) always justified. It was an American-sponsored idea—President Wilson's concept of "self-determination"—that profoundly altered the nature of the postwar political system. With strong American encouragement, Great Britain, France, and other European countries dismantled their colonial systems after World War II, thereby bringing into existence some one hundred independent nations. It is a fact, however, that the doctrines of American foreign relations have usually emphasized what the United States opposed in international relations, rather than what it advocated or was prepared to do positively to preserve global peace and security.

The diplomatic doctrines of the United States have made another positive contribution to the foreign policy process. In this and earlier chapters, attention has been devoted to the essentially apathetic and uninformed character of public opinion relating to foreign affairs. As one study of the public opinion context of foreign policy decision-making has expressed it: "The great majority—the 'mass public'—is almost always most interested in personal lives and careers, secondarily in friends and community, third in state and national domestic issues, and last in foreign policy issues." Even during those eras (such as World War II) when external concerns impinge most directly upon the lives of citizens, the intensity of public interest in domestic problems is still considerably higher than for external problems. With regard to foreign policy issues, the "attentive public" in the United States normally comprises no more than 15 percent of the adult population. To cite another index of this phenomenon: the national press in the United States regularly devotes no more than 10 percent of its news columns to coverage of foreign affairs.[72]

According to some informed students of American diplomacy, even the "interventionist" episodes in the nation's experience have had the overriding objective of removing a foreign threat so that Americans could once again devote themselves to their favorite pursuits—domestic affairs. Antithetical as it might appear, isolationist and interventionist behavior in foreign affairs thus had a common underlying goal.[73]

72. Ralph B. Levering, *The Public and American Foreign Policy: 1918–1978* (New York: William Morrow, 1978), 29–30, 32.
73. For a detailed discussion of the similarity between isolationism and interventionism, see Max Lerner, *America as a Civilization* (New York: Simon and Schuster,

Except during periods of external crises, the ordinary American has little sustained interest in or understanding of foreign affairs. As crisis-induced instruments of American policy, the nation's diplomatic doctrines from time to time focus citizen interest upon this vital realm and remind the people that resources must be allocated for the protection of the nation's external interests, no less than its domestic pursuits.

Given the context of public opinion within which foreign policy decision-making occurs, the diplomatic doctrines of the United States have performed several functions. For example, they have "personalized" often complex external questions in a manner which is consonant with the American approach to public issues generally. President Monroe's edict became known as the Monroe Doctrine (rather than the "American Doctrine" or the "New World Doctrine"); the containment strategy was widely referred to as the Truman Doctrine. Before the Watergate episode at least, President Nixon's efforts to effect retrenchment in American foreign policy were designated the Nixon Doctrine. As Bailey observed about the Monroe Doctrine, this tendency to personalize often remote and complicated foreign policy issues "gives the public something tangible on which to pin a rather abstruse principle; it helps polarize the idea of 'Hands Off' around a personality; and it provides a convenient catch phrase, which the public so often needs to sustain interest." [74]

The personalization of American diplomatic doctrines is characteristic of the internal behavior of the American electorate (which often prefers to "vote for the man and not the party"). Identifying a particular foreign policy strategy as the Monroe Doctrine or the Truman Doctrine provides an easily remembered label for an often complex foreign policy principle. Periodic invocation of these doctrines gains the attention of the people and allows national leaders to capitalize at critical junctures upon the well-known tendency of public opinion to "rally around" the chief executive whenever the nation confronts an external crisis.

This process of personalizing diplomatic strategies is of course not

---

1957), 881–907. From a different perspective, George Ball has also observed that the "universalism" in American foreign policy has in reality been "the expression of isolationism in different terms." Ball, *The Discipline of Power*, 293–94.

74. Bailey, *The Man in the Street*, 262.

without certain disadvantages. As illustrated by the history of the two Johnson doctrines and the Nixon Doctrine, when their author has fallen significantly in public credibility and esteem, the foreign policy doctrine associated with him suffers the same fate. The process may also contribute to the American people's tendency to substitute slogans and catchwords for serious thought and difficult choices in foreign affairs. Militant verbal opposition to "international communism" (as expressed in the Eisenhower Doctrine), for example, may mistakenly be viewed by the American people as equivalent to effective action reducing the appeal of communism for societies in the Middle East. Or the Nixon Doctrine's reiteration of the theme of partnership may erroneously be regarded by Americans as a sufficient concession to the viewpoints of the nation's allies on major global issues. Admittedly, throughout American history the language of the nation's diplomatic doctrines has sometimes degenerated into national shibboleths and incantations, as though their mere repetition would somehow drive off hostile forces threatening the United States. For many Americans, such shibboleths have often become substitutes for serious thought and action with regard to external problems—but toward foreign policy issues, little evidence exists that a majority of citizens was prepared to engage in that process anyhow.

A Revolutionary War flag carried the inscription: DON'T TREAD ON ME. To a greater or lesser degree, the doctrines of American foreign policy have reflected that spirit. A notable feature has been their militancy in conveying American viewpoints toward the outside world. In the early 1820s John Quincy Adams urged the Monroe Administration to issue "a state paper which would, if it did nothing else, thrill American pride." The American people, Bailey has said, found the Monroe Doctrine to be "intoxicating to the national spirit," because the young Republic "hurled defiance into the teeth of a despotic Europe." At the end of the century, the Open Door policy was no less uplifting to national morale. According to Kennan, Americans were elated about the policy, viewing it as a "major achievement." The American people's "imagination was fired, its admiration won" by the policy.[75] Similarly,

75. Perkins, *A History of the Monroe Doctrine*, 42; Thomas A. Bailey, *A Diplomatic History of the American People* (8th ed.; New York: Appleton-Century-Crofts, 1968), 185; Kennan, *American Diplomacy*, 40.

the Truman Doctrine elicited widespread public enthusiasm. After several years of following a conciliatory approach (critics often said "appeasement" tactics) in their approach to Soviet Russia, national leaders had finally "stood up" to the Stalinist dictatorship and had "drawn a line" across which the Kremlin was prohibited from advancing. In the mid-1960s, the Johnson Doctrine for Southeast Asia exemplified the same frame of mind. For President Johnson, North Vietnam's attack against American ships in international waters was comparable to the Mexican assault against the Alamo. Consequently, the Johnson Doctrine for Southeast Asia had a kind of "Remember the Alamo!" flavor about it: national honor was at stake, and the American response to the Communist threat must be decisive and heroic.

Most of the diplomatic doctrines of the United States have unquestionably served as ego-bolstering and psychologically gratifying devices for the American people and their leaders. As a rule, their issuance has elated public opinion and provided a tonic for national morale. But along with this effect, the doctrines have achieved two other, more notable, purposes. They have directed public attention to an important (on occasion, critical) foreign issue. For a society which is as normally indifferent toward foreign policy questions as the United States, this is not always an easy accomplishment. And they have served notice to foreign governments that continuance in their behavior is likely to elicit a forceful American response. Diplomatic doctrines in the spirit of "Remember the Alamo!" are cues to other countries that their conduct is a provocation which the United States cannot ignore.

Yet the most important contributions of American foreign policy doctrines in terms of their impact upon public opinion lie in two other respects. First, the doctrines have served dramatically to mobilize public support for a course of action deemed essential in foreign affairs. The circumstances surrounding the issuance of these doctrines have nearly always constituted "high drama" for the American society. Not untypically, the president has promulgated his doctrine before a joint session of Congress or (if the nation faced an urgent crisis) in a nationwide radio-television message. Short of a declaration of war or national emergency, it is difficult to imagine a more dramatic setting— and the purpose is usually accomplished. Within a short period of time, the American people have heard about the diplomatic issue involved, and they have nearly always expressed their overwhelming support for the course of action proposed by the White House.

The nation's leaders have not of course been unmindful of this function of diplomatic doctrines. In some instances, it has been one of the primary reasons why a doctrine was promulgated. In the case of the Truman Doctrine, for example, the need to awaken and "shock" American opinion was viewed by executive and legislative policy-makers alike as a precondition for adoption of programs like the Greek-Turkish Aid Program and the Marshall Plan, which the Truman Administration regarded as essential in carrying out the containment strategy. As John L. Gaddis concluded, the Truman Doctrine was perhaps "aimed more toward the American public than toward the world." The doctrine was a successful form of "shock therapy" which the chief executive administered to the American people.[76]

Second, the major diplomatic doctrines of the United States—particularly those issued since World War II—have played a pivotal role in promoting national unity on key foreign policy issues. The creation and maintenance of a national consensus on foreign policy issues has a dual dimension. Internally, such a consensus gives policy-makers a firm base of public support for the foreign policy proposals they advocate. In the phrase current during the 1940s and 1950s, it provides a "bipartisan" foundation for American diplomatic efforts; substantial majorities in both major political parties—and officials on both ends of Pennsylvania Avenue—support the policy in question. The evident intention has been to follow the maxim invoked by the Wilson Administration during World War I: "Politics stops at the water's edge." Normally for a period of several months after the issuance of a foreign policy doctrine, if internal political controversies over foreign policy questions did not altogether disappear, they were at least muted and sublimated.[77]

Externally, the role of doctrines in generating a high degree of national unity on foreign policy issues is no less important. When the

76. Acheson, *Present at the Creation*, 219, 225; John L. Gaddis, *The United States and the Origins of the Cold War* (New York: Columbia University Press, 1972), 351.
77. See Cecil V. Crabb, Jr., *Bipartisan Foreign Policy: Myth or Reality?* (New York: Harper and Row, 1957).

Truman Administration, for example, adopted the containment strategy, it did so with confidence that its approach to the Soviet Union enjoyed overwhelming public endorsement. Insofar as its policy-making process allows an objective evaluation of the outside world, thereafter the Kremlin could hardly mistake the determination of the American people and their leaders to resist Communist expansionism. Moscow could not (as Hanoi apparently did during the Vietnam War) count on internal divisiveness to undermine the policies of the incumbent American administration.

To a lesser degree perhaps, the same point could be made about all of the other postwar foreign policy doctrines of the United States. Modern restatements of the Monroe Doctrine (like the Johnson Doctrine for Latin America) have evoked an almost "automatic" and overwhelming public endorsement of steps taken to resist communism in the Americas. Even the Johnson Doctrine for Southeast Asia—promulgated during the Vietnam War, in one of the most internally divisive eras of American history—for a period of several months enjoyed massive public and congressional support.

Admittedly, the role of foreign policy doctrines in heightening national unity on external issues has sometimes proved a short-range and ephemeral phenomenon. Indeed, some doctrines—particularly those (like the Eisenhower Doctrine and the Johnson Doctrine for Southeast Asia) calling for supportive congressional resolutions—have in the end themselves generated considerable *disunity* in the foreign policy field. A vocal group of legislators expressed opposition both to the language embodied in these resolutions and to the process by which they were formulated. In some cases, members of the House and Senate felt they were coerced, deceived, or otherwise pressured into approving these White House–sponsored resolutions uncritically.

Two observations can be made about the "Middle East Resolution" and about the "Tonkin Gulf Resolution." The first is that there has been no comparable development in American foreign policy since Congress passed the "Tonkin Gulf Resolution" in 1964. The second observation, which can be made with a fairly high degree of certainty, is that if Congress is called upon in the future to support foreign policy doctrines by passage of similar resolutions, both their provisions and the process by which they are adopted are likely to be very different from these earlier cases.

Doctrines as Diplomatic Liabilities

If the diplomatic doctrines of the United States have contributed positively to American foreign relations, there are of course a number of entries on the liability side of the ledger. Since 1823, the American propensity for formulating doctrinal statements in foreign affairs has been criticized at home and abroad. Five such criticisms deserve fuller analysis.

First, for over a century and a half critics of American diplomatic practice have been disturbed by the unilateral nature of these doctrines, particularly as it relates to the evolution of international law. As our discussion in this and earlier chapters has shown, factually the criticism is warranted: in nearly every case, the diplomatic doctrines of the United States have been unilateral undertakings. Throughout American diplomatic history, informed commentators have lamented the tendency of policy-makers in Washington to promulgate foreign policy doctrines unilaterally—and afterwards (as Secretary of State John Hay did in the case of the Open Door policy) to assert that the doctrine enunciated was universally recognized as a principle of international law.

The unilateral character of America's diplomatic doctrines has had a number of adverse consequences for the nation's foreign relations. It has established and maintained a precedent which has often embarrassed the United States. During the 1930s, for example, America was not prepared to honor Japan's claim to its own "Monroe Doctrine" in Asia, nor, in the more recent period, has Washington accepted the Soviet Union's right to issue its own "Brezhnev Doctrine" for Eastern Europe.

This practice has also opened the United States to the charge of "hypocrisy" in its approach to international law. On the one hand, America has traditionally been at the forefront of nations calling for the observance and strengthening of international law. On the other hand, the United States has (for the most part, successfully) resisted efforts to subject its own foreign policy doctrines to the limitations of existing international law—sometimes by asserting that they were international law!

The unilateral nature of these doctrines has also impaired efforts by the United States to promote a greater sense of regional and global community. The Monroe Doctrine assumed the existence of a sense of community among the nations of the New World. Yet the very issuance of the Monroe Doctrine, along with the numerous "corollaries" which were appended to it over the years, was viewed by the Latin Americans as a serious impediment to the development of closer community ties within the hemisphere. In the recent period, a keynote of the Nixon Doctrine was the concept of "partnership" among the United States and its friends and allies. Yet repeatedly, the Nixon Doctrine was criticized because of the fact that in practice, the kind of partnership contemplated by it was allied acceptance and support of American diplomatic moves.

Second, the diplomatic doctrines of the United States have often been criticized because they introduced rigidity and inflexibility into the conduct of foreign affairs. Summarizing the advice of the nineteenth-century French Foreign Minister Talleyrand, one critic of the Stimson Doctrine observed that in diplomacy, "the best principle was to have none." An experienced American diplomatic official has concurred in Talleyrand's judgment. George Ball is convinced that "To be effective, [foreign] policy should not be announced in pompous declarations—or 'doctrines' . . . it should evolve from give-and-take of conferring, working and acting together [with other countries]." [78]

In response to this criticism, several things can be said about the impact of doctrines upon the conduct of American foreign relations. Perhaps an even more frequent and pervasive complaint about them has been the opposite contention: that the doctrines have been imprecise and highly elastic statements of external policy—meaning in effect anything policy-makers in Washington wanted them to mean at any given time. Moreover, there is very little convincing evidence that the alleged "rigidity" of American foreign policy doctrines has in fact caused the United States to engage in behavior it could not have taken in the absence of the doctrine. To mention merely one prominent example, the Eisenhower Doctrine's identification of "international communism" as the paramount danger to the security of the Middle East during the late 1950s expressed this idea because (correctly or incorrectly) American officials, supported by vast numbers of citizens, be-

78. Ferrell, *American Diplomacy in the Great Depression*, 166–67; Ball, *Diplomacy for a Crowded World*, 305; Graebner (ed.), *Ideas and Diplomacy*, 259–61.

lieved it to be so. Yet in practice, as was explained at length in Chapter 4, the diplomatic behavior of the United States under the Eisenhower Doctrine was in fact highly selective and pragmatic. Issuance of the doctrine did *not* compel the administration to embark upon an anti-Communist "crusade" in the Middle East. As for the criticism generally, it would be difficult to document the assertion that the supposed rigidity of American diplomatic doctrines has in any significant way prevented the United States from approaching external problems flexibly and with due regard for the circumstances of particular cases. Indeed, a pervasive criticism of American postwar foreign policy is that it lacked "consistency" or that it was guided by *no* discernible principle.

A third widely expressed complaint about America's propensity to rely on diplomatic doctrines is epitomized by William Graham Sumner's denunciation of the Monroe Doctrine in 1903. Just think, Sumner contended, "what an abomination in statecraft an abstract doctrine must be. Any politician or editor can . . . put a new extension on it. The people acquiesce in the doctrine and applaud it because editors repeat it because they think it is popular. . . . It may mean anything or nothing, at any moment. . . . If you allow a political catchword to go on and grow, you will awaken some day to find it standing over you, the arbiter of your destiny." [79]

More succinctly, Salvador de Madariaga said that perhaps the most outstanding trait of the Monroe Doctrine was its "admirable elasticity"; it permitted the United States to take virtually any position it desired toward political questions in Latin America! George F. Kennan found the same fault with the Open Door policy. It lacked "any adequate and practical generic meaning." With this fundamental defect, the policy produced "bewilderment, suspicion, and concern in the minds of foreigners." [80]

Complaints were expressed about the fact that the Truman Doctrine was flawed for the same reason: it was too "open-ended" and imprecise in several crucial respects. For example, the doctrine failed to distinguish clearly between those regions that were vital to American security and those that were not. In addition, as Kennan later con-

79. Graebner (ed.), *Ideas and Diplomacy*, 259–61.
80. *Ibid.*, 530–34; Kennan, *American Diplomacy*, 48–49.

tended, the Truman Doctrine did not differentiate between the "military" and the "political" containment of communism.[81]

Similar complaints were expressed about the diplomatic doctrines promulgated after 1947. As was pointed out in detail in Chapter 8, many commentators believed this was a serious weakness of the Carter Doctrine: the exact threat against which it was directed was never very clearly specified, and the steps taken to implement it were, therefore, perhaps of marginal value in preserving the security of the Persian Gulf area.

As the evidence presented in earlier chapters indicates, collectively the doctrines of American foreign policy *have* comprised elastic, and sometimes vague and confusing, diplomatic guidelines for the United States. Does this fact mean that America's fondness for such doctrinal pronouncements has been an obstacle to diplomatic success? It would be difficult to prove such a contention. In our earlier analogy, the Constitution of the United States is also a relatively brief document, and it contains comparably flexible (not to say sometimes, confusing) language. As with constitutional provisions, America's foreign policy doctrines have been susceptible of new interpretations, as significant changes occur throughout the international system and as the United States is confronted with novel problems abroad. The Truman Doctrine, for example, committed the United States to apply the containment strategy against expansive communism (known for many years thereafter as "international communism"). If the concept of containment was not invoked as frequently in the 1980s as in the 1950s, this did not alter the reality that the United States continued to oppose Soviet hegemonial behavior. At the same time, after 1947 there was unquestionably an evolution in the official and public understanding of communism within the United States; in time, Americans accepted the fact that not all varieties of Marxism abroad threatened the security interests of the United States; and they learned to differentiate more intelligently among the many species of communism existing in the modern world.

81. See the criticisms of the Truman Doctrine expressed in Chace, *A World Elsewhere*, 12–13; and Charles Yost, *The Conduct and Misconduct of Foreign Affairs: Reflections on U.S. Foreign Policy Since World War II* (New York: Random House, 1972), 64. The most thorough, even today perhaps still most cogent, critical analysis of the Truman Doctrine was provided by Walter Lippmann, *The Cold War: A Study in U.S. Foreign Policy* (New York: Harper and Row, 1947).

If a choice must be made—diplomatic rigidity produced by adherence to a precisely and narrowly worded policy statement versus diplomatic flexibility permitted by a more general and perhaps inherently ambiguous policy declaration—then on balance the latter seems preferable to the former. Ideological and doctrinal rigidity is, after all, one of the indictments which Americans have long made against communism and other totalitarian movements. If the former course were followed—if the guiding principles of American foreign policy were set forth in an almost infinite number of precisely and narrowly worded policy statements addressed to specific issues—the results could well be merely a different form of confusion and bewilderment about the content of American foreign policy. Over the course of time, the sheer volume of such statements—not to speak of the problem of how one is compatible with another—would itself be a serious impediment to successful diplomacy.

A fourth recurrent criticism of American diplomatic doctrines has been that they exemplified a long-standing defect in the nation's approach to foreign affairs: a tendency to believe that the mere issuance of a forthright policy statement was tantamount to achieving beneficial results abroad. This group of critics believes that the foreign policy doctrines of the United States exemplify what Bohlen has called a tendency toward "naïve sentimentality" in American foreign relations; or what Pratt has termed a penchant for "moralizing" by the United States; or what Bailey has described (in reference to the Stimson Doctrine) as reliance upon resounding declarations as "a cut-rate substitute for force" in responding to external threats.[82] Speaking of the Nixon Doctrine another commentator described it as "doctrinal verbiage"; he found little that was new or constructive in it. President Nixon's keen interest in proclaiming a foreign policy doctrine bearing his name in reality served to divert national leaders from the task of directly addressing serious and difficult external problems.[83]

In essence, this criticism of diplomatic doctrines involves a twofold charge: that they have largely been irrelevant to the conduct of Ameri

---

82. Bohlen, *The Transformation of American Foreign Policy*, 97; Pratt, *A History of United States Foreign Policy*, 728; Bailey, *A Diplomatic History of the American People*, 697.

83. See the views of Thomas C. Schelling on the Nixon Doctrine, as contained in Goralski (Moderator), *The Nixon Doctrine*, 47.

can foreign policy; and that they have been for the most part exercises in self-delusion, whereby Americans thought that words—rather than deeds—could affect external political developments. Throughout their history, the American people and their leaders have relied heavily upon the written and spoken word to influence the behavior of other nations. In many cases—and the Declaration of Independence, President Wilson's famous "Fourteen Points" during World War I, and President Franklin D. Roosevelt's enunciation of the "Four Freedoms" during World War II have been prominent examples—such statements unquestionably *have* had a potent impact at home and abroad. An experienced diplomatic official has commented that the distinction between word and deed in diplomacy is "quite misleading. In international affairs words are deeds." If, for example, an American president advocated that Country X should be placed under the rule of Country Y, "those mere words of his would upset international relations just as thoroughly as if they had been marching armies."[84] Traditionally, Americans have evinced great faith in the efficacy of such policy declarations—and in many instances, they thought that their mere issuance was sufficient to accomplish the desired goal. A basic premise of such behavior perhaps has been the conviction that other nations were prepared (in the words of the Declaration of Independence) to exhibit "a decent respect for the opinions of mankind." In other cases, Americans may simply have not understood the difference between the effects of a ringing policy declaration and decisive action in achieving external objectives.

Every major foreign policy doctrine promulgated by the United States beginning in 1823 can perhaps be described as an exercise in such American "moralizing" and "sermonizing" in its relations with other countries. Undeniably, the doctrines have reflected the American society's own ethical and ideological values, and in most instances perhaps, their implicit premise was that these values were (or at least should be) universally accepted throughout the international community. Moreover, as foreign spokesmen often complained, many times in the past the United States has been more willing to contribute a rhetorical and militant diplomatic statement to the world than it has been to accept responsibility for the solution of vexatious problems disturbing global peace and security.

84. Halle, *Dream and Reality*, 155.

Even today, no more than a small minority of Americans is aware that for almost a century after its issuance, the success of the Monroe Doctrine depended upon two crucial conditions: Great Britain's readiness to provide the sea power required to enforce its provisions, and the recurrence of intra-European quarrels and rivalries, preventing the European powers from encroaching against the New World. Over a century later, much as they applauded his firmness in "standing up" to the Russians, relatively few Americans understood the long-term costs and implications accompanying the issuance of the Truman Doctrine. The same thing could be said about the Carter Doctrine in 1980: Americans applauded President Carter's expressed determination to defend the Persian Gulf area from Communist control, but they evinced little comprehension of the likely consequences of doing so. (To cite but one specific example: Americans wanted their leaders to preserve access to Persian Gulf oil, while they concurrently wanted overall governmental spending reduced, taxes cut, and the principle of volunteer service in the armed forces to be retained.)

A final criticism of American diplomatic doctrines to be considered here is one that is associated particularly with spokesmen for the "New Left" and "revisionist" commentators on the American diplomatic record. Stated succinctly, this is the charge that the nation's diplomatic doctrines have nearly always proposed and attempted to legitimatize interventionist behavior by the United States abroad. Such indictments have been made about all the doctrines of American foreign policy since 1823. As Perkins formulated their reaction, Latin Americans regarded the Monroe Doctrine as an expression of American "hegemony, of supercillious arrogance, or interference" in the affairs of other nations within the hemisphere. As a Mexican diplomat said, if that was not its original purpose, in time the Monroe Doctrine became "perverted" into an instrument for American interventionism in the Western Hemisphere. Substantially the same indictment was brought against the Open Door policy and the Stimson Doctrine. According to William Appleman Williams' interpretation, their real purpose was to guarantee America's economic dominance in Asia—and perhaps in time globally.[85]

The postwar foreign policy doctrines of the United States have not

85. Perkins, *A History of the Monroe Doctrine*, 367. Williams is one of the leading "revisionist" interpreters of American foreign policy. His thesis is basically that the

escaped this criticism. The actual goal of the Truman Doctrine, some commentators are persuaded, was the subordination of weaker countries politically (and perhaps economically) by the United States. The doctrine exemplified America's determination to oppose revolutionary movements abroad and to impose a political system upon other countries in keeping with the American conception of democracy.[86] Similarly, the Eisenhower Doctrine, it has been charged, designated the United States as "the policeman of the Middle East." Or as another student of recent American foreign policy described it, the doctrine was an assertion of "unprecedented imperial power" by the United States. Secretary of State John Foster Dulles advocated a kind of global Eisenhower Doctrine, under which the United States would be permitted to use its power anywhere it liked throughout the world. Similarly, the Johnson Doctrine for Southeast Asia has been depicted as reflecting a "fascination with power" by officialdom in Washington and a determination to employ it to the fullest in behalf of American diplomatic objectives. Critics believed that President Johnson's doctrine for Latin America was cast in the same mold: it sought merely to rationalize the economic and political dominance of the region by the United States. Walter Lippmann's judgment on the doctrine was that it epitomized the "policeman of the world" mentality which had too long actuated American foreign policy.[87]

The Nixon Doctrine—whose announced goal was a retrenchment in America's overseas commitments—was subjected to fewer criticisms in this vein. Some commentators, nevertheless, regarded it as essentially hegemonial, since it did not really endeavor to curtail the use of American power abroad, so much as to make its application more effective. George Ball, for example, viewed the Nixon Doctrine as

United States has pursued hegemonial policies abroad largely because of internal economic pressures. See, for example, his *The Tragedy of American Diplomacy* (Cleveland: World Publishing Co., 1959).

86. Richard J. Barnet, *Intervention and Revolution: America's Confrontation with Insurgent Movements Around the World* (New York: World Publishing Co., 1968), 9–10. The thesis of this study is that postwar American foreign policy has sought to suppress revolutionary movements abroad.

87. Julien, *America's Empire*, 249; Hoopes, *The Devil and John Foster Dulles*, 408, 487; Thomson, "Historical Legacies and Bureaucratic Procedures," 478; Gurtov, *The United States Against the Third World*, 83–84; Goldwin (ed.), *Readings in American Foreign Policy*, 245.

nothing more than "muddy rhetoric"; it envisioned the United States "as the center of the cosmos with other nations in orbit around it." Another study concluded that under the doctrine, the United States would still function as "world policeman," with other countries "recruited to be cops on the beat." [88] The Carter Doctrine was also widely denounced as an ill-concealed American attempt to gain control over the Persian Gulf oil fields and to impose its political hegemony upon countries within the region.

The contention that America's diplomatic doctrines have in effect been nothing more than instruments for rationalizing the extension of American power abroad is not easy to answer satisfactorily in limited space. For some devotees of this approach (who purport to know the "real" and hegemonial motives of American policy-makers) no contrary evidence is likely to be convincing. In many cases, the accusation reflects profound disappointment with the results achieved by America's adoption of an internationalist foreign policy since World War II; in some cases also, implicit in the criticism is a feeling of deep "alienation" toward the nation's political leadership (sometimes described by such pejorative terms as the "foreign policy elite" or the "National Security Managers" whose machinations are presumably at variance with the wishes of the American people). And in some instances, those expressing this viewpoint overtly espouse Marxist or crypto-Marxist ideological values by which they judge the conduct of American foreign relations.

Moreover, not untypically this criticism glosses over a number of fundamental distinctions lying at the heart of the American diplomatic process. A key one is the difference among such terms as American hegemony over, and intervention in, the affairs of other countries, versus peace-keeping activities by the United States, assistance to other nations, and influence over societies beyond America's borders. That most of the doctrines of American foreign policy have ultimately resulted in the extension of the power of the United States abroad is undeniable.

Yet certain conclusions often drawn by revisionist commentators from this fact do not necessarily follow. This phenomenon does not

---

88. Ball, *Diplomacy for a Crowded World*, 9; Virginia Brodine and Mark Selden (eds.), *Open Secret: The Kissinger-Nixon Doctrine in Asia* (New York: Harper and Row, 1972), 39.

prove: (1) that the doctrine's formulators deliberately planned and intended such a result; (2) that the doctrines reflected the inherently hegemonial impulses of the nation's political leaders, and perhaps even of the American society itself; (3) that American power was usually utilized to the detriment of foreign societies, injuring their welfare and subordinating them politically; (4) that the United States used its vast power in violation of international law; or (5) that fundamentally, there is "no difference" between the behavior of the United States and the Soviet Union as the dominant powers in the international system after World War II.

In analyzing the relationship between the use of American power abroad and the nation's diplomatic doctrines, it is helpful to recall the maxim of the nineteenth-century Austrian Prince Metternich. Metternich said that for a powerful state, there was really no such thing as a foreign policy of "nonintervention" (or the classic American position of "isolationism"). There were only various forms of interventionism. His point was that, in a literal sense, a great power affects the political destiny of other countries irrespective of whether it overtly "intervenes" in their affairs or withholds its power (thereby pretending that it is following a policy of nonintervention).

The diplomatic experience of Europe during the 1930s—and of America's response to it—provides innumerable examples illustrating Metternich's axiom. During the Spanish Civil War, for example, the Allied powers consciously adopted a policy of "nonintervention" (while the Axis powers overtly aided pro-Franco forces in this struggle). This Allied decision well nigh guaranteed the demise of republican government in Spain and the imposition of Franco's authoritarian regime upon the country (which lasted from 1939 until 1975). Similarly, as Israel and its supporters have pointed out many times since World War II, the United States and other Western nations followed a noninterventionist policy toward Hitler's barbarous attempt to exterminate the Jewish population of Europe. The result was the Holocaust, in which millions of Jewish people perished because of official American indifference toward their fate. This episode in American diplomacy colors Israeli-American relations—and affects the Arab-Israeli controversy—to the present day. America's avowed policy of "nonintervention" led to a result that few officials or informed citizens could defend, either in the light of the American society's professed values or by reference to the diplomatic interests of the United States. Under the Truman Doctrine, the United States undeniably intervened in the political affairs of Western Europe, to prevent a Communist victory in the Greek civil war; after that, to bring about the economic reconstruction of Western Europe; and still later, to strengthen the defenses of the region, as symbolized by the North Atlantic Treaty Organization (NATO). Hypothetically, in the absence of American intervention, the results in Western Europe would almost certainly have been very different from the progress achieved since World War II. Conceivably, Marxist political organizations would have gained control of one or more European governments, the region would have lapsed into economic (most likely followed by political) chaos, and the United States might have found itself once again facing an ominous military threat to the security of Western Europe.

These examples call attention to two pivotal aspects of the problem of employing American power abroad (and these seldom receive detailed attention from revisionist interpreters). For the United States and all other nations, the *purposes* for which its power is used abroad are a crucial consideration. And the *circumstances* under which its power is applied overseas are no less fundamental, in assessing its diplomatic behavior. Without entering into a detailed examination of these two significant dimensions of the problem—a task that could entail a history of post–World War II American foreign relations—a few brief observations can be made about them.

Initially, a point made in our earlier discussion needs to be reiterated: nearly all the doctrines of American foreign policy were defensive in nature; the extension of American power abroad was made contingent upon the behavior of other countries. Moreover, the evolution of the international system—especially since World War II—refutes the notion that the United States has used its foreign policy doctrines to impose a *Pax Americana* upon the world. To the contrary, the international system is more "pluralistic," less susceptible to overt control by the United States (or the Soviet Union), and more characterized by independent behavior by its members, than at any time in modern history. The pervasive complaint about American foreign policy—reaching its apex perhaps under the Carter Administration—was that American power had seriously "declined" abroad, and that the United States was progressively unable to make its power effective outside its own borders. In a word, instead of a *Pax Americana* or *Pax Sovietica*, the international system was becoming increasingly anarchistic and resistant to control by *any* governmental authority.

Even in the case of the two postwar foreign policy doctrines most frequently cited as exemplifying American interventionism—the Johnson doctrines for Southeast Asia and for Latin America—revisionist criticisms of them are difficult to sustain on the basis of the evidence. In time, American power was withdrawn from Southeast Asia, as antiwar groups demanded. (The outcome was perhaps a striking example of Metternich's rule: a politically repressive system was subsequently imposed by North Vietnam, not only on South Vietnam but upon Laos and Cambodia as well.) Within a brief period of time, the United States withdrew its forces from the Dominican Republic. In the years that followed, Washington encountered a widespread complaint throughout Latin America that it was "indifferent" to its needs and well-being. That no American hegemony was imposed upon Latin America under the second Johnson Doctrine was proved by the fact that, by the 1980s, the power and influence of the United States within the Inter-American System was at the lowest level in recent memory.

In summary, the principal doctrines of American foreign policy neither contemplated global hegemony by the United States, nor was that their ultimate result. If anything, by the end of the 1970s, most Americans were convinced that the United States had become "overcommitted" abroad, and that the power of the United States would be enhanced by reducing some of the obligations America had assumed during the years after World War II.

The Future of Diplomatic Doctrines

By the early 1980s, the news media inside and outside the United States were alluding widely to what were being described as the "Haig Doctrine" and the "Reagan Doctrine" that served as the foundation of the Republican administration's foreign policy. Thus far, neither the White House nor the State Department had officially promulgated such doctrines; but this fact did not prevent news reporters and commentators from alluding to them, particularly in describing American foreign policy toward the volatile Middle East. In connection with a proposed sale of AWAKs aircraft to Saudi Arabia, for example, President Ronald Reagan "extended" the Carter Doctrine to include an

American guarantee of that country's security—an act that was interpreted by some commentators as tantamount to the issuance of a new Reagan Doctrine in American diplomacy. This was an interesting development for several reasons, not the least of which was that it showed how deeply the habit of relying upon doctrinal pronouncements in the foreign policy field had become entrenched in the American ethos.[89]

As had occurred many times in the past, a number of informed students of American foreign policy deplored the idea that a new doctrine would become the centerpiece of the nation's diplomacy. Former Under Secretary of State George Ball, for example, castigated the Reagan Administration's "noisy posturing" in the foreign policy field. Even before it had officially been issued, he lamented the possibility that a new Haig or Reagan doctrine for the Middle East would likely be forthcoming.[90]

These developments call attention to the question with which this chapter concludes: what is the future of doctrines in the diplomatic experience of the United States? A useful starting point for our inquiry is to examine briefly the current status of the foreign policy doctrines included in this study.

The Monroe Doctrine embraced a twofold principle: the United States would not normally become embroiled in the political controversies and conflicts of the Old World, while the European powers were enjoined from intervening politically in the New World. The former principle has been totally abandoned—or more accurately perhaps, it was superseded by the Truman Doctrine. Since World War II, the United States has become inextricably involved in political developments on the European continent, and there is no prospect that this process will be reversed in the future. As for the latter principle, the Monroe Doctrine's prohibition against external threats to hemispheric security has been retained and reaffirmed innumerable times since 1823—in legal instruments like the UN Charter; in the resolutions of

---

89. Dispatch by William A. Rusher, Baton Rouge *Morning Advocate*, July 4, 1981; dispatch by Bernard Gwertzman, New York *Times*, October 13, 1981; *U.S. News and World Report*, August 10, 1981, p. 36.

90. See the views of former Under Secretary of State George Ball, in the Baton Rouge *Morning Advocate*, July 17, 1981; and the discussion of the Reagan Administration's foreign policy in *Newsweek*, April 6, 1981, pp. 32, 37.

the Organization of American States; in assertions by the State Department that the Monroe Doctrine was not obsolete; in unilateral actions by the United States, as in America's firm opposition to the installation of Soviet missiles in Cuba in 1962; and in new policy declarations, like the Johnson Doctrine for Latin America.

While it is almost never cited officially today, the Monroe Doctrine remains a fundamental policy guideline of the United States. Yet two constraints inhibit overt reliance upon it: Latin America's historically negative reaction to "Monroeism"; and the inability of the United States, under the rubric of the doctrine, to prevent various forms of subtle and indirect foreign intervention in the hemisphere, such as massive Soviet financial support of Cuba, growing ties between Latin American states and the Communist world, and external Communist support for Latin American revolutionary movements. Policy-makers in Washington are fully aware that public reliance upon the Monroe Doctrine in responding to such challenges would likely impede American diplomatic efforts. Yet with regard to an overt external threat to hemispheric security, the Monroe Doctrine continues to guide the foreign policy of the United States.

The Open Door policy and Stimson Doctrine were of course rendered obsolete by the victory of communism on the Chinese mainland in the late 1940s. Yet the basic idea embodied in the Open Door policy continues to serve as a strand in American foreign policy. In the contemporary context, the principle may be restated to assert that no foreign power should establish a dominant position in black Africa, the Middle East, or other regions. By whatever term the process is described—an alien *imperium*, the creation of an exclusive foreign "sphere of influence," or the conversion of weaker societies into "satellites" of a powerful state—the subordination of a weaker nation by a stronger one will continue to encounter American opposition. Implicitly, this old precept of the Open Door policy was the heart of the Truman Doctrine. Its most recent expression—precipitated by Soviet efforts to subjugate Afghanistan—was the Carter Doctrine, pledging the United States to maintain the security of the Persian Gulf area.

Few public references are heard today to the Truman Doctrine. But again, the idea which was its essence—that Communist expansionism must be "contained" by the United States and its allies—continues to guide American foreign policy even during the new era of détente. According to some interpretations of détente, America's reliance upon the containment strategy contributed to the gradual relaxation of Soviet-American tensions, and continued détente presupposes the nation's future willingness to resist Soviet expansionist tendencies. As Kennan, the architect of containment, anticipated, some degree of "mellowing" has occurred in the behavior of the Soviet state at home and abroad, owing in some measure to America's commitment to the containment strategy. Today, the lessened risk of a nuclear clash between the superpowers may be a direct result of the Truman Doctrine. At any rate, no evidence exists that the United States is any more prepared to accept overt Soviet expansionism today than it was in the late 1940s. In that limited sense (if not clearly in the sense of producing a viable American response to various forms of indirect Communist interventionism), the Truman Doctrine has become a permanent feature of American foreign policy.

The Eisenhower Doctrine for the Middle East is clearly moribund (except as the containment principle also protects that region from overt Communist aggression). No chief executive has invoked the doctrine since the Eisenhower-Dulles era. More so today than in the late 1950s, the doctrine appears irrelevant to the underlying causes of political instability and insecurity in the Middle East.

The Johnson Doctrine for Southeast Asia was rendered obsolete by the liquidation of America's military presence in the region under the Nixon Administration. The Johnson Doctrine for Latin America was perhaps merely a special case of the Monroe Doctrine. It has not been directly invoked since 1965. Yet, as the Cuban Missile Crisis of 1962 demonstrated, the United States remains implacably opposed to foreign military intervention in the Western Hemisphere. Internal Marxist political intrigue in Latin America, Communist support for insurrectionary movements, the continued presence of a Marxist regime in Cuba—these are problems for which the Johnson Doctrine for Latin America provided no answers. It may be predicted, however, that in the light of the veneration traditionally accorded the Monroe Doctrine by the American people, if the United States again faced the prospect of the communization of a Latin American state, two things would likely happen. A general policy statement (analogous to the second Johnson Doctrine) would be issued by the president expressing opposition to this development. And the United States would act—if necessary, unilaterally—to prevent the emergence of "another Cuba" in the hemisphere. In substance then, if not in name, the Johnson Doctrine for Latin America may also have found a permanent place in American foreign policy.

The Nixon Doctrine was of course massively discredited by its author's political demise. After President Nixon's resignation, his diplomatic doctrine was almost never mentioned publicly again. Much of the Nixon Doctrine consisted of rhetoric which perhaps merited the historical obscurity it received. Yet there were also some enduring elements in President Nixon's doctrine. Its core—the idea that the United States must not become "overextended" abroad, and that it must apply its power with greater discrimination and effectiveness overseas—guided the diplomacy of the Ford and Carter administrations. To a lesser degree perhaps, the principle was accepted by the Reagan Administration. This "lesson of the Vietnam War," it may not be amiss to predict, is likely to exert a potent influence upon the American approach to foreign relations for decades to come. Moreover, the Nixon Doctrine also recognized (even if the actual diplomatic practices of the Nixon-Kissinger team often did not) that limits had to be placed upon America's traditional unilateralism in the foreign policy field. If for no other reason, more meaningful and systematic consultation with the nation's friends abroad in the policy-making stage has become a precondition for successful diplomacy. As the experience of the Vietnam conflict amply demonstrated, the United States is unlikely to achieve constructive results abroad when it acts largely alone.

As Chapter 8 indicated, the most recent addition to the list of major diplomatic pronouncements by the United States was the Carter Doctrine, expressing America's stake in the continued security of the Persian Gulf area. Implicitly (even if they seldom referred to it by name), officials of the Reagan Administration accepted the Carter Doctrine and based their diplomacy in the Middle East upon it. Even more than the Carter Administration, the Reagan White House was determined to acquire the military power requisite for its enforcement. The Carter Doctrine thus remains in force. How relevant and useful it will prove as an instrument of American diplomacy in the Middle East remains a highly controversial and conjectural issue.

According to some interpretations, doctrines have outlived their usefulness in the American diplomatic tradition. As we have seen, some commentators regard them as liabilities in efforts by the United States to achieve its foreign policy objectives. They are often cited as prime examples of empty diplomatic rhetoric, of sloganizing, and of the American tendency to reduce complex diplomatic issues to simplistic formulae and shibboleths. Moreover, most of the doctrines analyzed here are identified with the concept of the "imperial presidency"—another concept which, after the Vietnam War and Watergate experiences, Americans oppose. (Not uncharacteristically, citizens reject the idea of the "imperial presidency," even while, as under the Carter Administration, they demand that the chief executive exercise "leadership" and act "decisively" in foreign affairs!) Nor are advocates of an expanded congressional influence in the foreign policy process usually favorable to the idea of new diplomatic doctrines. By and large, they have been identified with dynamic executive influence in (if not domination of) foreign policy decision-making. Down to the period of the Carter Doctrine, many Americans were prone to believe that doctrines had become obsolete for another reason: every post–World War II doctrine (possibly excepting the Nixon Doctrine) was directly related to the Cold War, which during the 1970s many Americans believed had ended. Soviet aggressiveness in Afghanistan—followed by Moscow's threat to intervene militarily in Poland—changed the minds of many citizens and officials on this issue.

Yet for a number of cogent reasons, it seems premature to publish an obituary for a practice as deeply ingrained in American diplomatic experience as the periodic issuance of foreign policy doctrines. Doctrinal pronouncements have become an established, recognized, and in many respects, unique feature of American diplomatic practice. While other countries may occasionally issue comparable diplomatic statements, in no other nation have such doctrines played the central role they have acquired in the American diplomatic tradition. America's reliance upon them for more than a century and a half is presumptive evidence of their diplomatic utility, and it strongly suggests that the practice will not be abandoned lightly.

A number of substantive reasons combine to support the belief that America's reliance upon major doctrinal statements in foreign affairs will continue. Certain behavior patterns characteristic of the American society have encouraged reliance upon this technique in the past, and these same qualities may well do so again in the future. One, which we have already identified, is the essentially pragmatic and eclectic nature of the American response to problems at home and abroad. Historically, in the formulation of national policy the tendency of Americans has been to address themselves to, and formulate responses for, immediate and urgent challenges in internal and external affairs. In foreign relations, what is sometimes called "crisis response" or "crisis management" is a long-standing trait of American behavior. The doctrines of American diplomacy have been—and will likely continue to be—outstanding examples of this propensity. Little evidence could be cited to demonstrate that Americans are any more prepared today than in the past to exhibit a sustained and informed interest in foreign policy questions. Instead, they are likely to "discover" a problem in the external realm only after it reaches crisis proportions. On such occasions, the president may direct public attention to the problem by the dramatic issuance of a foreign policy doctrine responsive to it. We may also confidently predict that there will be no shortage of such crises overseas facing the United States in the years ahead.

The other characteristic of American society encouraging this practice (for a citizenry that normally displays little interest in foreign policy questions) is the tendency to "personalize" national policy issues— more so even in foreign, than in domestic, affairs. Traditionally, the American people have "looked to the president" for guidance and decisive leadership in dealing with problems abroad. (Significantly, despite the Vietnam War experience and the desire of Congress to become a more influential force in the foreign policy process, few citizens expect such insight and leadership to come from Capitol Hill.) As much as any other single factor, its failure to provide the expected direction and leadership in foreign affairs ultimately undermined public confidence in the Carter Administration and was responsible for the election of Ronald Reagan to the White House in 1980.

The American people thus expect that the president will take the lead diplomatically and will protect the security interests of the United States abroad. Once he has decided to do so—and has formulated a diplomatic principle or strategy incorporating his policy—several inducements exist for the White House to issue a new diplomatic doctrine. By doing so, the president will immediately gain the attention of the news media at home and abroad; his viewpoints will quickly be disseminated to millions of people in the United States and overseas; he will convey the impression to foreign countries of a high degree of executive and legislative unity in behalf of the policy; he will be able to count upon the support of the American people to endorse his policy statement; and he will impress upon other countries the seriousness with which the United States government views the issue toward which the doctrine is addressed.

Aside from their utility as diplomatic instruments, certain extraneous (but still influential) considerations reinforce the expectation that new diplomatic doctrines will be forthcoming. Several doctrines of American foreign policy have received that designation from the news media; reporters find it convenient and useful to label an important foreign policy statement President X's diplomatic doctrine. Commentators on American foreign policy also fall into the same habit: over and over again, they refer to the containment strategy as the Truman Doctrine (even though some commentators, like Kennan, believe that in fact they were not identical). Although he was the most patent example of the inclination, other presidents also likely feel the same kind of "pride of authorship" exhibited by Richard M. Nixon in his doctrinal statement. (President Hoover, it will be recalled from Chapter 2, desired that the Stimson Doctrine be called the Hoover Doctrine.) To a greater or lesser degree, all chief executives are concerned about their "place in history"; all want to leave behind a successful diplomatic record; and none is perhaps inherently opposed to the idea that his efforts in foreign affairs will be enshrined in the form of an important diplomatic doctrine bearing his name. As we have seen (and the Carter Doctrine is a particularly apt example), in many cases domestic political considerations may motivate the president to issue a new diplomatic doctrine.

Our analysis has emphasized the idea that the main doctrines of American foreign policy are closely associated with the growth of presidential power in the foreign policy field. It is no accident that (except for the Stimson Doctrine) all the doctrines examined in our study bore the names of the incumbent president. As Elmer Plischke has observed about the role of doctrines in the American diplomatic tradition, "it is worthy of note that no foreign policies or actions of similar historicity are associated with Congress, with either of its chambers, or with any of its individual members." His conclusion is that "enduring, long-range, and significant United States foreign policy . . . tends to be presidential policy." [91]

Other informed students of American foreign relations share this judgment. Thus, a recent study—calling attention to the growing interdependence between internal and external policy issues—anticipates that the president will become even more the "chief decision maker" in foreign affairs in the future than in the past, since the number of issues requiring presidential decisions "is growing." Any proposed scheme for governmental reorganization in the foreign policy field must therefore rest upon the premise that "only the President can articulate the nation's purposes, propose policies and actions appropriate to advance those purposes, and induce the machinery of government to formulate and to execute them. A system as diffuse, plural, and complex as ours requires presidential energy to make it work." [92]

Since 1823, diplomatic doctrines have been an influential technique of presidential leadership in the foreign policy field. Current public apprehensions about the "imperial presidency" and efforts by Congress to reassert its prerogatives in foreign affairs aside, the White House is likely to remain the locus of effective decision-making in foreign relations for one transcendent reason: there is no feasible alternative to it. As in the past, particularly when they are confronted with external crises, incumbent presidents are likely to find the issuance of a diplomatic doctrine a potent instrument of management in the foreign policy field.

More often than not, the doctrines of American foreign policy have been imprecise, ambiguous, and mystifying diplomatic pronouncements. At the time of their issuance and afterwards, these doctrines have been equated with, and have evoked, political rhetoric and emotionalism. For doctrines which have survived any length of time, their meaning and implications have changed in the light of circumstances. Some of the doctrines examined here have generated as much disunity as unity in foreign affairs. These and other defects in the foreign policy doctrines of the United States may be identified.

Yet we may anticipate new diplomatic doctrines in the future for the

91. Elmer Plischke, "Summit Diplomacy: Its Uses and Limitations," *Virginia Quarterly Review*, XLVIII (Summer, 1972), 325–26.

92. Graham Allison and Peter Szanton, *Remaking Foreign Policy: The Organizational Connection* (New York: Basic Books, 1976), 60–62.

same reason Napoleon once gave to justify the preparation of strategic plans by his generals: having a strategic plan was better than having none at all! All experienced students of warfare know that such plans are almost never adhered to literally under combat conditions. When the battle is joined, preexisting plans are usually found to suffer from many imperfections. Yet as Napoleon saw it, a set of strategic principles was still better than having no plan. Diplomatically, for a society as normally indifferent to foreign affairs—and as prone to engage in *ad hoc* decision-making—as the American, Napoleon's maxim seems uniquely pertinent. Imperfect as it may be, a diplomatic strategy or principle of some kind seems preferable to its complete absence. The challenge for the future lies not so much in eliminating American diplomatic doctrines, as in seeing to it that they embody sound diplomatic principles, based upon an informed and correct assessment of external events.

Index